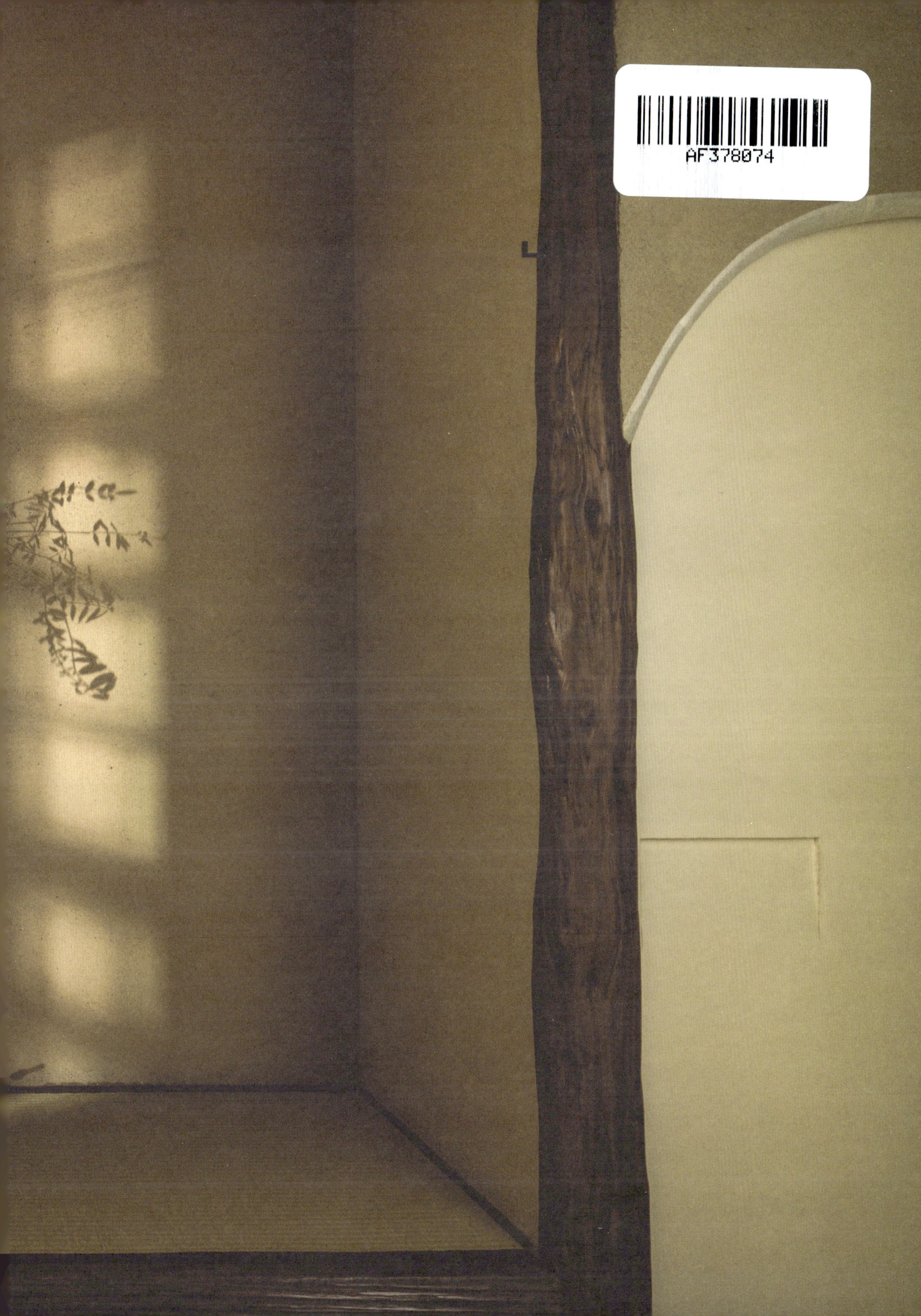
AF378074

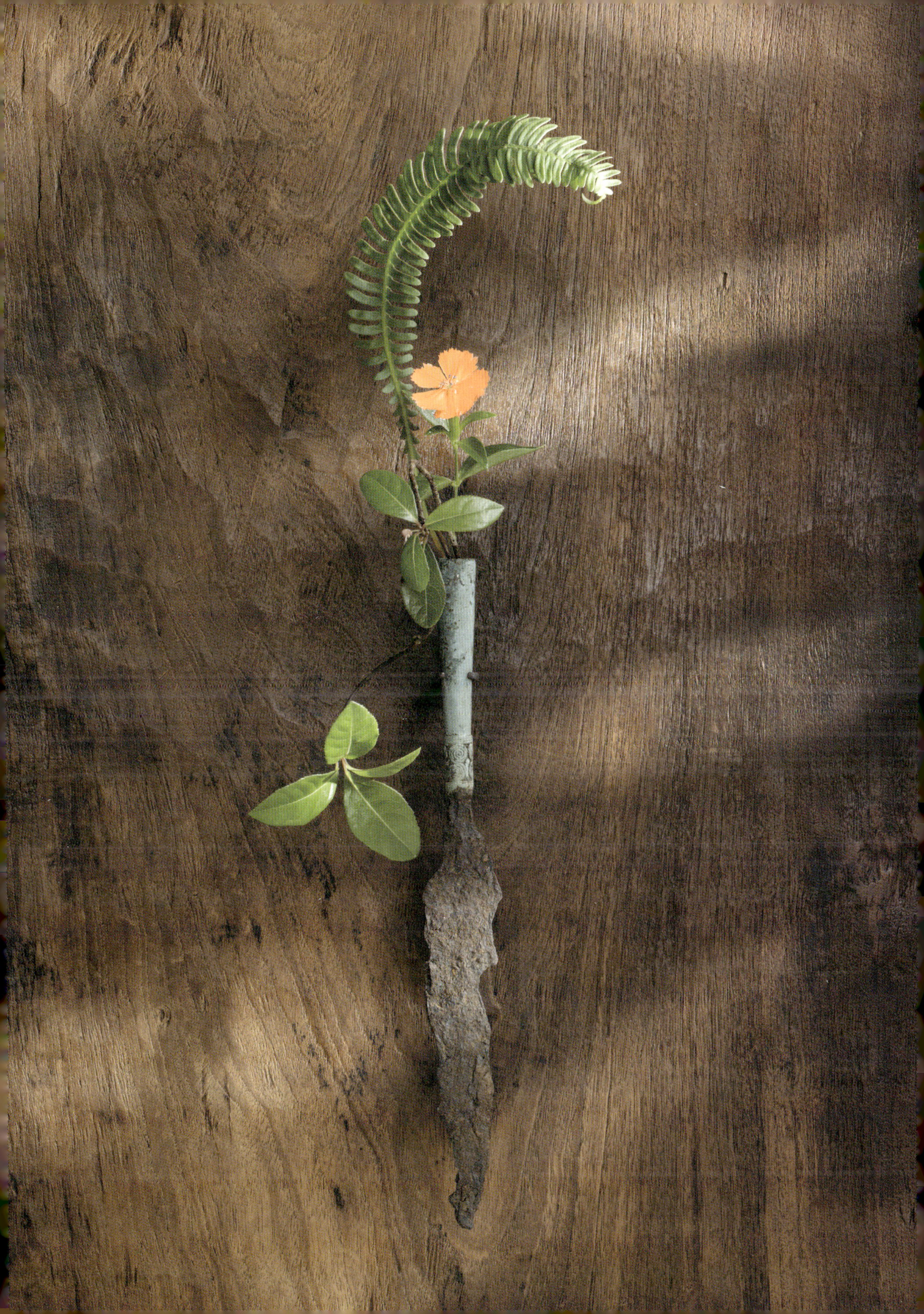

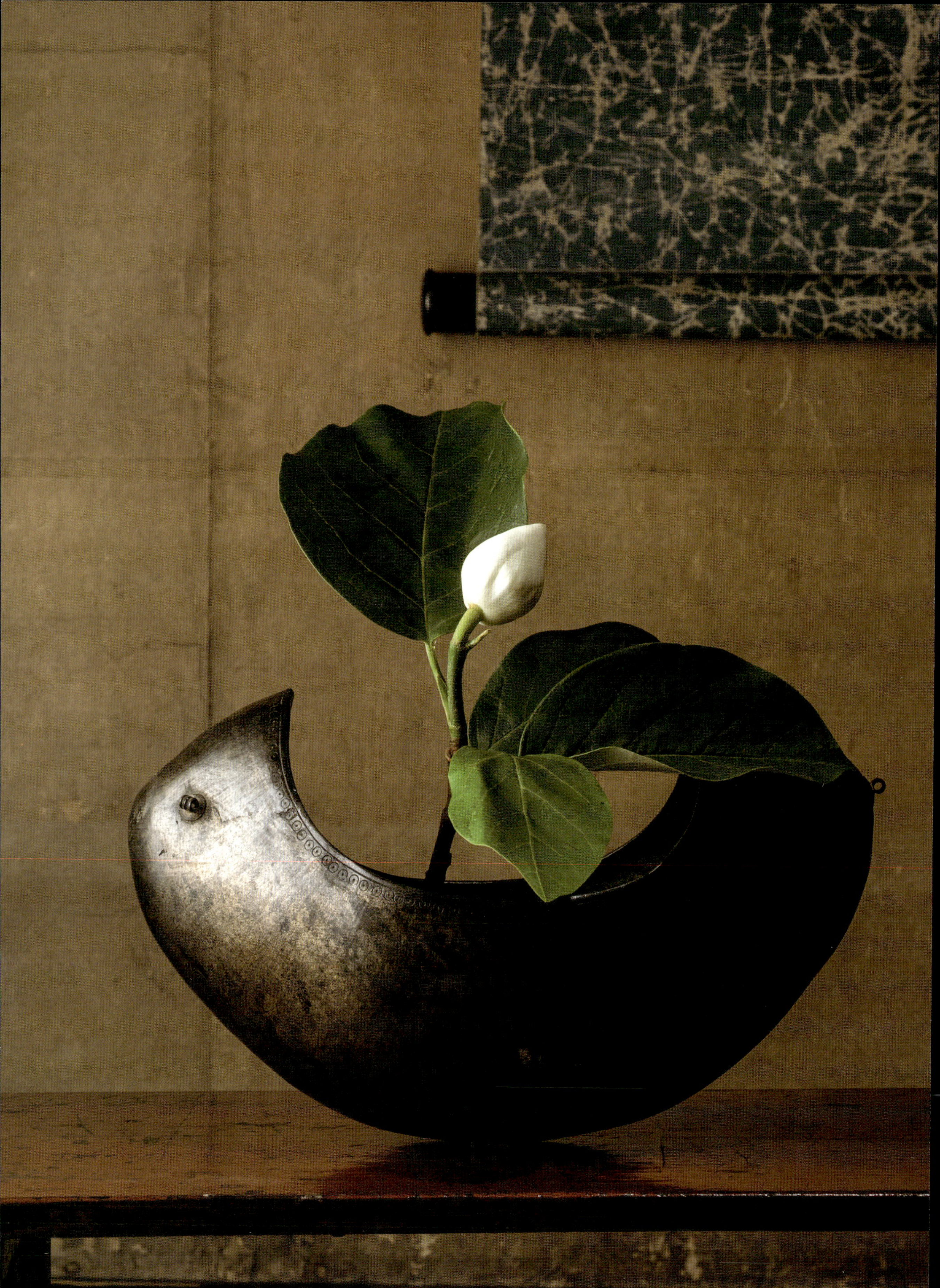

JAPANESE IKEBANA

A Year *of* Seasonal Flower Arrangements *for the* Tea Ceremony

HIROSHI TODA *and* ATSUSHI KOBAYASHI

TUTTLE Publishing

Tokyo | Rutland, Vermont | Singapore

Contents

Introduction: Why We Wrote This Book 8

JANUARY

A Tea Gathering to Mark a New Beginning

Camellia 'Seiobo' 11

    Record of the Gathering 12

    Flowers and Utensils for January 14

    Centering Flower Materials in a Container 14

    The Direction and Flow of Branches 19

    Freedom Beyond the Rules, by Atsushi Kobayashi 22

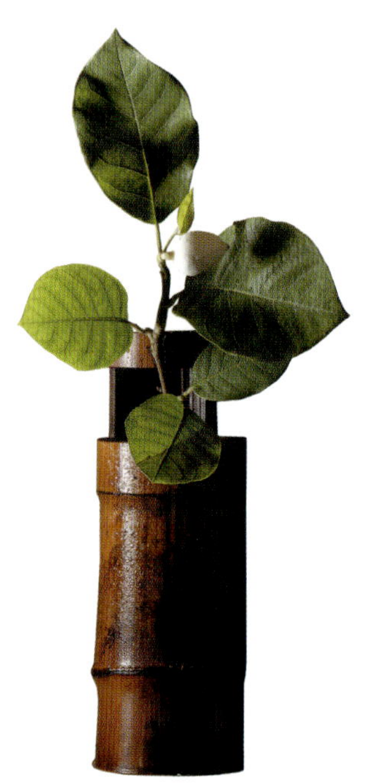

FEBRUARY

A Miraculous Encounter

Yunnan Magnolia 24

    Flowers and Utensils for February 26

    Make Flowers a Daily Habit, by Atsushi Kobayashi 30

    Reflections on the Ceramic Artist Jikinyu Raku 34

MARCH

Buds Holding the Breath of Life

White Camellia 36

    Flowers and Utensils for March 38

    Visualizing the Final Form Before Cutting 38

    How the Same Flowers and Container Change with the Space 41

    Using the Branches Themselves as a Flower Holder 44

    Choosing the Vessel, Sensing the Space, by Atsushi Kobayashi 45

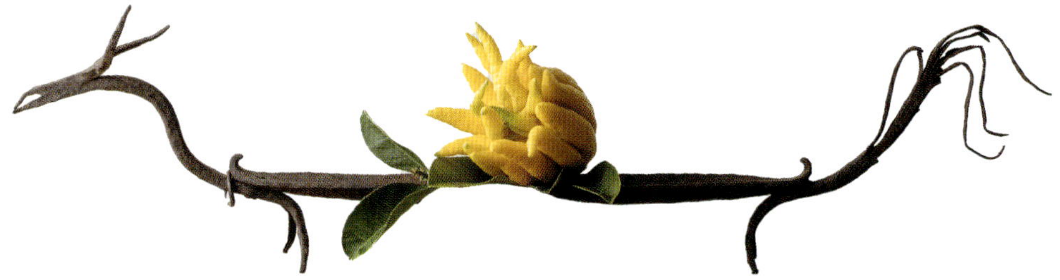

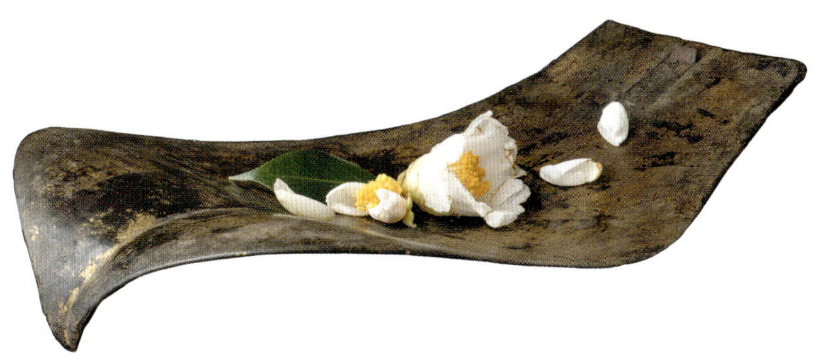

APRIL

As the Winter Hearth Season Ends

Wisteria **48**

Upright Placement of a Thick Branch 48

Flowers and Utensils for April 50

Choosing a Single Flower for One's Own Tea,
  by Atsushi Kobayashi 55

Large Branches in a Wide-Mouthed Jar 55

Stones as a Flower Holder in a Shallow Vessel 56

MAY

The Enshu Memorial Tea Gathering

Japanese Cobra Lily **58**

Record of the Gathering 62

Three Historical Figures 64

Flowers and Utensils for May 66

The Hanacho Flower Shop, by Atsushi Kobayashi 69

JUNE

Reflecting on a Phantom Flower

Woodland Peony **70**

Upright Branches in a Wide-Mouthed Container 71

Flowers and Utensils for June 72

When the Mountains Breathe Anew, by Atsushi Kobayashi 75

A Rare Seasonal Encounter—Bamboo Shoots as Containers 79

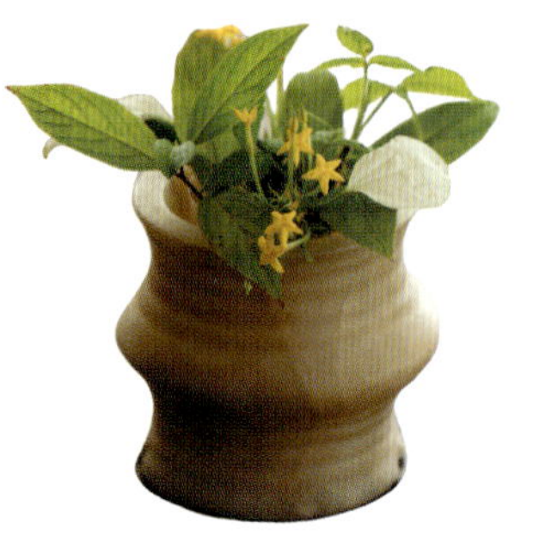

JULY

A Mountain Retreat in Izu

White Lotus 82

Flowers and Utensils for July 86

Using Flower Stems as a Support Structure 88

Flowers and the Passage of Time, by Atsushi Kobayashi 91

Surrounded by Primitive Art: Takashi Inaba's Mountain Life 92

AUGUST

Arranged with the Heart's Intuition

Midsummer Greenery 94

Dialogue: Awakened by Flowers—A Life Transformed 98

SEPTEMBER

A Tea Gathering with Wildflowers under the Autumn Moon

Pertya Rigidula 106

Record of the Gathering 108

Flowers and Utensils for September 110

Autumn Grasses in Rikyu's Gourd Basket 111

Playing with Flowers in a Thatched-Roof Farmhouse,
  by Atsushi Kobayashi 113

A Holder for Spreading Grasses 113

OCTOBER

The Final Glow of the Season

Japanese Anemone 120

Bending Slender Branches to Create
  a Natural Flower Holder 121

Flowers and Utensils for October 122

All of Life Is Reflected in Tea, by Atsushi Kobayashi 126

Unobtrusive Seasonal Flowers in Everyday Spaces 128

Everyday Vessels as Flower Containers 130

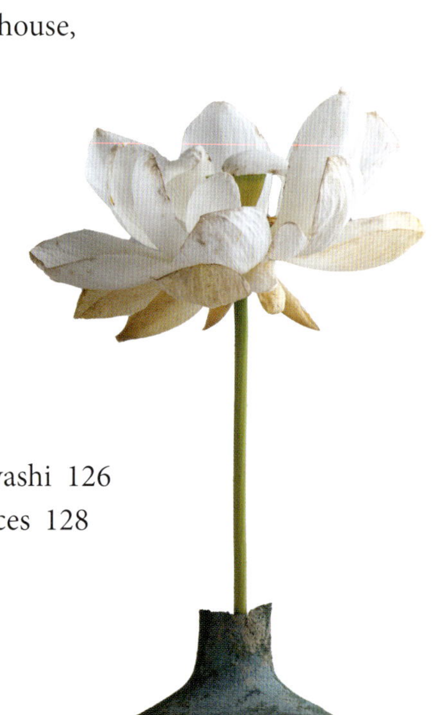

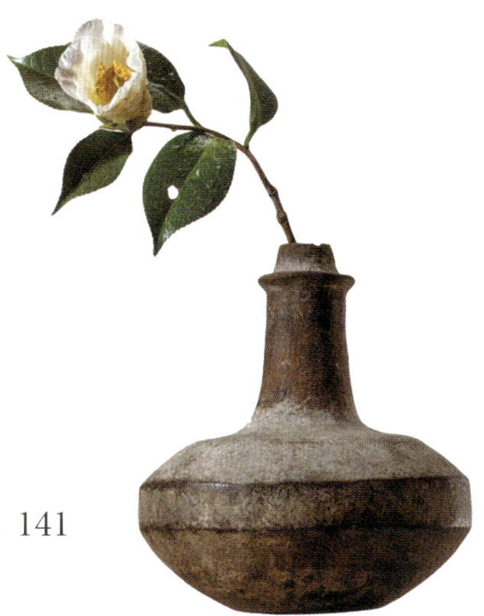

NOVEMBER

A Memorial Tea Gathering

Narcissus **132**

Record of the Gathering 134

Flowers and Utensils for November 136

Winter-Blooming Chrysanthemums 140

Arranging Two Types of Branches in a Small Vase 141

DECEMBER

With Prayers for the Year to Come

Buddha's Hand **144**

Flowers and Utensils for December 146

Sensing Power Through Objects, by Atsushi Kobayashi 148

Bringing Out the Most Beautiful Line in the Flower 150

Let Flowers Be as They Are in the Field 150

About Taizo Kuroda 154

Afterword, by Atsushi Kobayashi 158

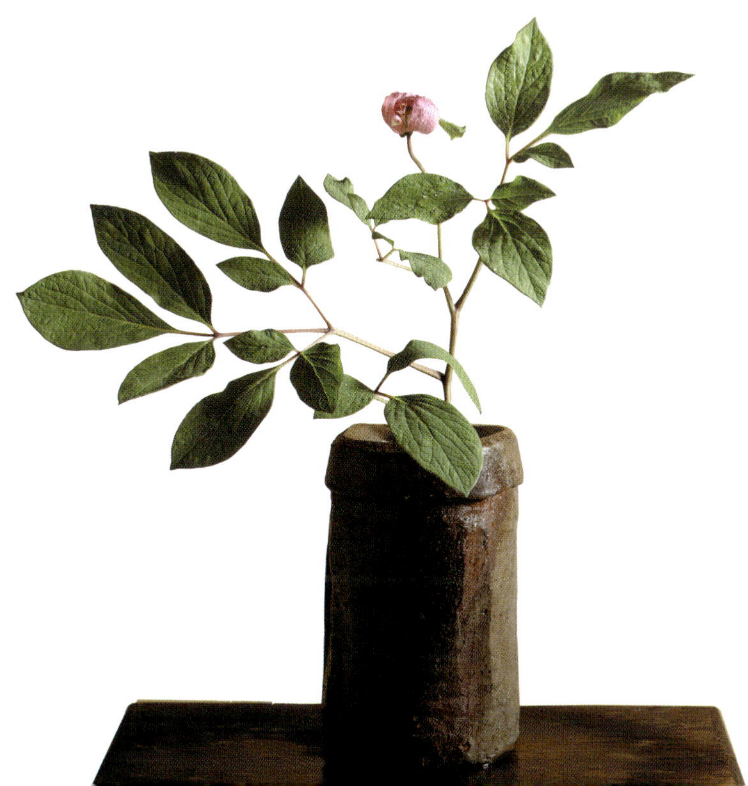

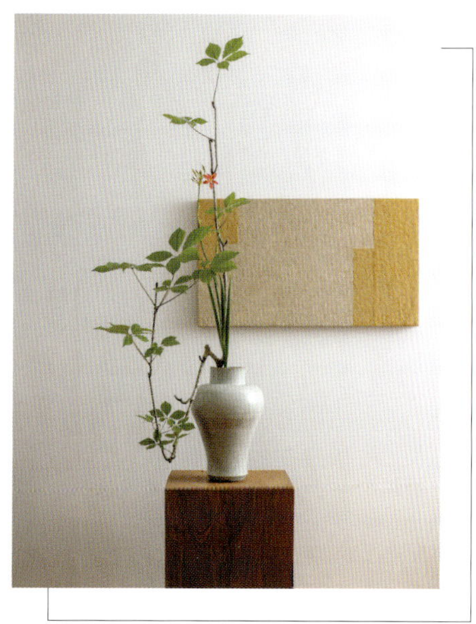

Why We Wrote This Book

Tanimatsuya Toda Shoten is a family business in Osaka that has been dealing in tea utensils for generations. Our history stretches back more than three hundred years to the Edo period (1603–1868), when we served feudal lords like Fumai Matsudaira, and later, well-established families of industrialists and tea enthusiasts. I learned the trade from my father, handling famous utensils recorded in old catalogs. At the same time, I began introducing pieces that felt right for today's tea ceremony practice, including primitive art and works by contemporary artists. Although I was born into an antiques business, my parents gave me a lot of freedom. Thanks to them, I studied abroad in the United States, and when I came back to Japan, I didn't apprentice with an antique dealer but instead trained at Yayoi Gallery in Tokyo, a respected gallery of modern art. Even though I grew up surrounded by the tea world and its four centuries of tradition, my father never once pressured me to take over. Looking back, I'm grateful I was able to spend my youth unburdened by that expectation.

Still, I eventually chose to succeed my father. Now, as I prepare to pass the business on to my own son after so many years, I was invited to take on this project to share my perspective on today's tea culture with future generations, with a focus on the flowers used in tea ceremony. Over the course of a year, I arranged flowers in both old and new vessels to present in this book. Alongside antique pieces that are treasured in the world of tea, I've used a wide range of containers to hold seasonal flowers in all their variety.

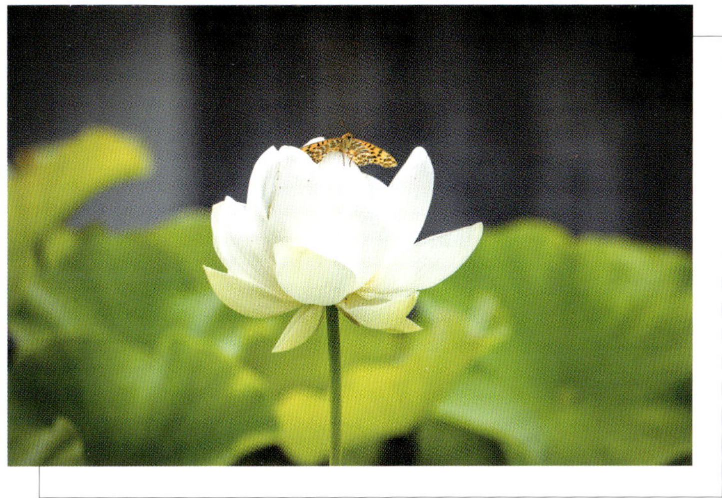

Tea flowers, as the name suggests, are simply the flowers placed in the tea room. They're the only element among the carefully chosen space and utensils that is alive. To me, the world of tea is all about the beauty you sense in each moment—something you feel directly, through all five senses. And among all the elements in a tea gathering, the flowers have a very special place. In this book I'll share more about that as the seasons unfold. Although the tea ceremony is an extraordinary, almost otherworldly experience, in the end it also asks you what kind of life you lead every day. The flowers that create a moment of wonder in the tea room and the flowers you enjoy in daily life might seem different, but really, they're two sides of the same coin. That's why, in this book, I wanted to show not only flowers for the tea room, but also ways to enjoy them in everyday spaces.

I've had many quiet moments of happiness—finding a beautiful vessel, placing just the right flower in it, and thinking simply, "How lovely." What I hope to offer in this book isn't a formal lecture about tea, but a glimpse of those small moments that bring joy. If this can encourage people who are just beginning to explore tea, or those who feel uncertain on the path, I'll be very glad. Maybe it's something I'm able to do because of where I am in my life now. I'm not someone who talks at great length, but there are things I want to share. Through this book, I hope I can guide you, even a little, toward the beauty at the heart of tea.

— **Hiroshi Toda**

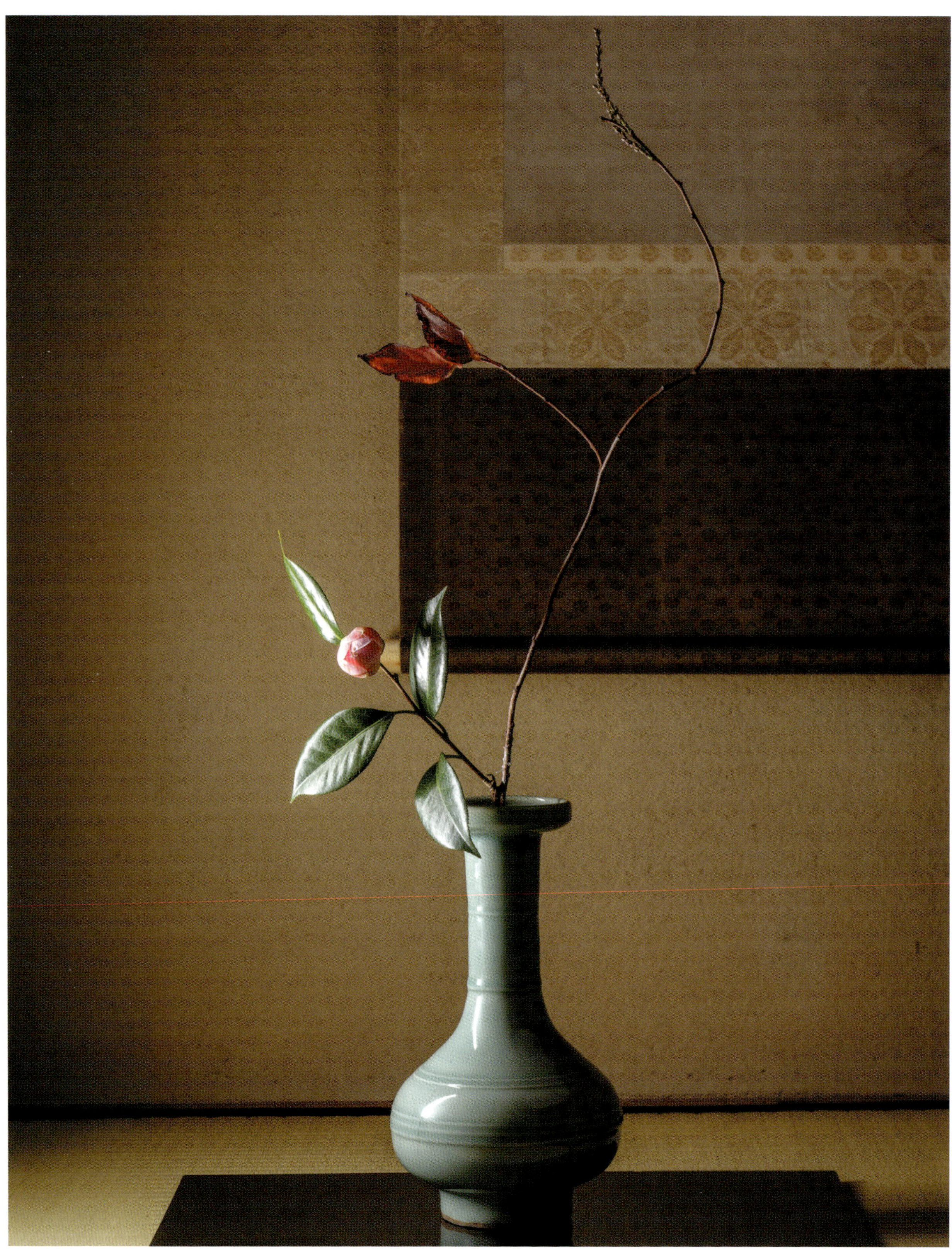

Camellia 'Seiobo,' with an early spiketail branch. Longquan celadon *shimo kabura* (turnip-shaped) flower container, shichikan type, China, Ming dynasty.

A red camellia, well suited to a celebratory occasion. The spiketail branch rises upward, overlapping with the camellia as if they were one, creating a sense of spaciousness. The celadon *shimo kabura* (turnip-shaped) flower container has seven lines around the body like bamboo joints, and so is also known as the "bamboo-shoot flower container."

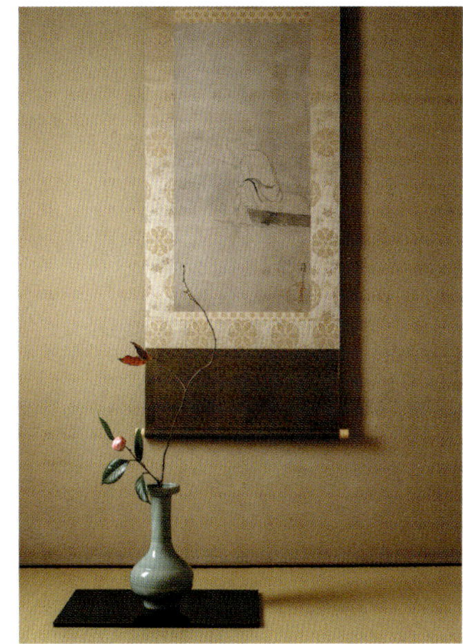

The hanging scroll in the alcove is *Funako Osho* (The boat and the young monk) by Edo-period artist Tawaraya Sotatsu. It depicts the Zen master Tokusho, who, having attained enlightenment, withdrew from the world and went into seclusion, sitting in a boat with his fishing line cast as he waits for the person who will inherit his teachings. Hiroshi says, "At first glance, it looks rather plain, but it's an exceptionally well-executed work that appeals to connoisseurs."

A Tea Gathering to Mark a New Beginning

Camellia 'Seiobo'

In June 2022, I handed over the position of president of Tanimatsuya Toda Shoten to my eldest son. Thanks to everyone's support, the shop has now reached its fourteenth generation and will continue on into the future. At this milestone, my father and I shared tea together. We didn't prepare any particularly formal utensils. In tea families such as the schools of the grand masters, there are established sets of utensils to be used for succession ceremonies, but our business has always been guided by intuition, so we tend to choose whatever feels right at the time.

The scroll in the alcove was *Funako Osho* (The boat and the young monk) by Tawaraya Sotatsu, depicting a monk leisurely fishing while waiting for his successor to arrive. A favorite quote of my father, Shonosuke, is: "In this world, we inherit neither rank nor name." Life is not about seeking titles or chasing after honor. The painting reflects that detachment and acceptance. It was actually my son Takashi who found it and brought it home.

The tea scoop we used was made by Genso. When I was young, after I finished my apprenticeship in Tokyo and returned home, my father prepared tea for me using this very scoop. It bears a

poem: "In the falling snow, the sparrow seeks out the warm darkness." I can still see my father's face, happy to see his fledgling return home. For this occasion too, I knew I wanted to use that scoop.

The fresh-water container was a late Ming red-painted flat jar with a scalloped rim. Originally, such basins were used by Chinese emperors to wash their faces, but here it was reimagined as a water container. It's a rare piece featuring a *sangi* counting-rod design within the pattern. Since the Toda family crest is a circle enclosing the sangi, it felt especially fitting. The tea bowl was a piece of katade ware, with a soft reddish tint, named "Sakurato." The Hirase family, from whom the bowl came, is a distinguished Osaka family closely connected to the Todas.

In the celadon *kabura* (turnip-shaped) flower container placed to match the hanging scroll, we arranged a camellia 'Seiobo.' The flowers were handled by Atsushi Kobayashi, who, for over twenty years, has prepared flowers for our tea rooms at Toda Shoten. He's someone I trust deeply for his artistic sensibility and his skill with flowers. Every arrangement in this book is by him. I've asked him to share his own thoughts on the flowers as well.

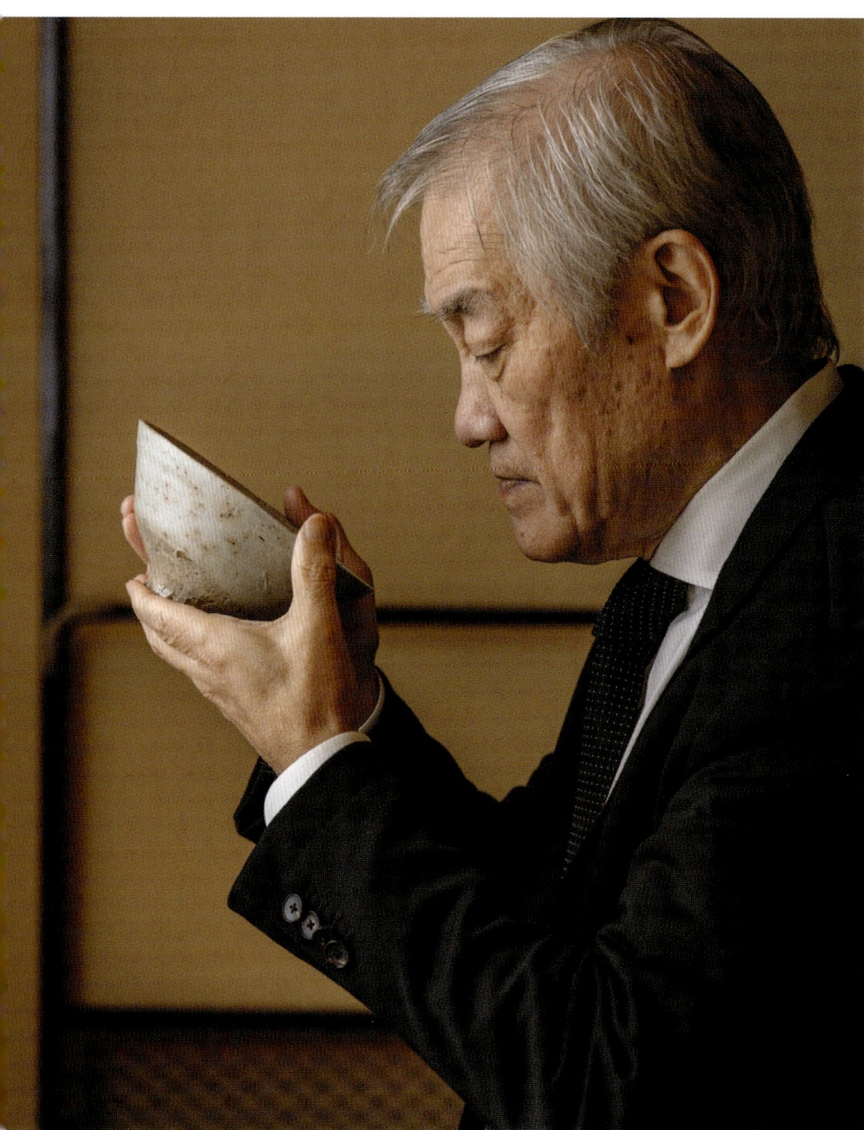

Hiroshi Toda savoring thin tea in the katade ware bowl named "Sakurato." This celebrated bowl, which can also be used for thick tea, takes its name from the image of a wicket gate woven from cherry branches. Our establishment, Tanimatsuya Toda Shoten, is an art dealer in Funaba Fushimimachi, Osaka, that has handled tea utensils for generations. With a history of more than three hundred years, the shop once served feudal lords such as Fumai Matsudaira and, in modern times, prominent families of industrialists and tea connoisseurs. Hiroshi is the thirteenth head of the Toda family. While handling tea utensils recorded in famous catalogs, he also introduced pieces suited to contemporary tea practice, such as primitive art and works by modern artists. He spent three years studying in the United States, and later apprenticed at Yayoi Gallery in Tokyo, which focuses on modern and contemporary art. He joined Tanimatsuya Toda Shoten in 1976 and eventually became president. Recently, he handed over the leadership to his eldest son, Takashi, and assumed the role of chairman. "My father, Shonosuke, was well-known in the world of antiques as a discerning expert, and thanks to his business sense, Toda Shoten has continued for this long. Takashi too — though I'm his father and maybe biased — has excellent intuition. I see myself as the link between grandfather and grandson, and now that I've finally reached the point of stepping back. I hope he will do things his own way, without feeling bound by anything," Hiroshi says.

RECORD OF THE GATHERING

Alcove: Scroll by Tawaraya Sotatsu, *Funako Osho* (The boat and the young monk)
Flower container: Celadon *shimo kabura* (turnip-shaped) vase
Flowers: Camellia 'Seiobo'; early spiketail
Kettle: Ashiya-style with plum and bamboo pattern
Hearth frame: With Kodaiji-style *maki-e* gold lacquer
Furosaki screen: Seven treasures openwork, Enshu-style
Long board: True black lacquer finish, by Seiami
Fresh-water container: Late Ming red-painted flat jar with scalloped rim

Tea caddy: Sumiyoshi-style *maki-e* lacquer decoration, by Yamamoto Harumasa
Tea bowl: Katade ware, named "Sakurato," from the Hirase family collection
Tea scoop: Made by Genso, with matching bamboo container, from the Konoike family collection
Scoop inscription: "In the falling snow, the sparrow seeks out shelter"
Waste water bowl: Namban ware
Lid rest: Seven treasures pattern and flared-wing form.

Takashi Toda prepares tea for his father, Hiroshi. On June 1, 2022, he became president of Tanimatsuya Toda Shoten, succeeding as the fourteenth generation of the family. Influenced by American abstract expressionism of the twentieth century, he is interested not only in traditional tea utensils but also in conceptual art. He sees elements in these artistic approaches that connect to the aesthetics of Japan's Momoyama culture four hundred years ago. For instance, he suggests that Oribe ware tea bowls are a form of abstract expression themselves. He sees one of his future roles as adding new interpretations and meanings to classical tea utensils — overwriting them, so to speak. "Are the things that have always been strictly emphasized truly good? Should we accept them just because they're established conventions or have always been that way? Living in the present, I believe I have to question those things — and I want to share that awareness with this generation."

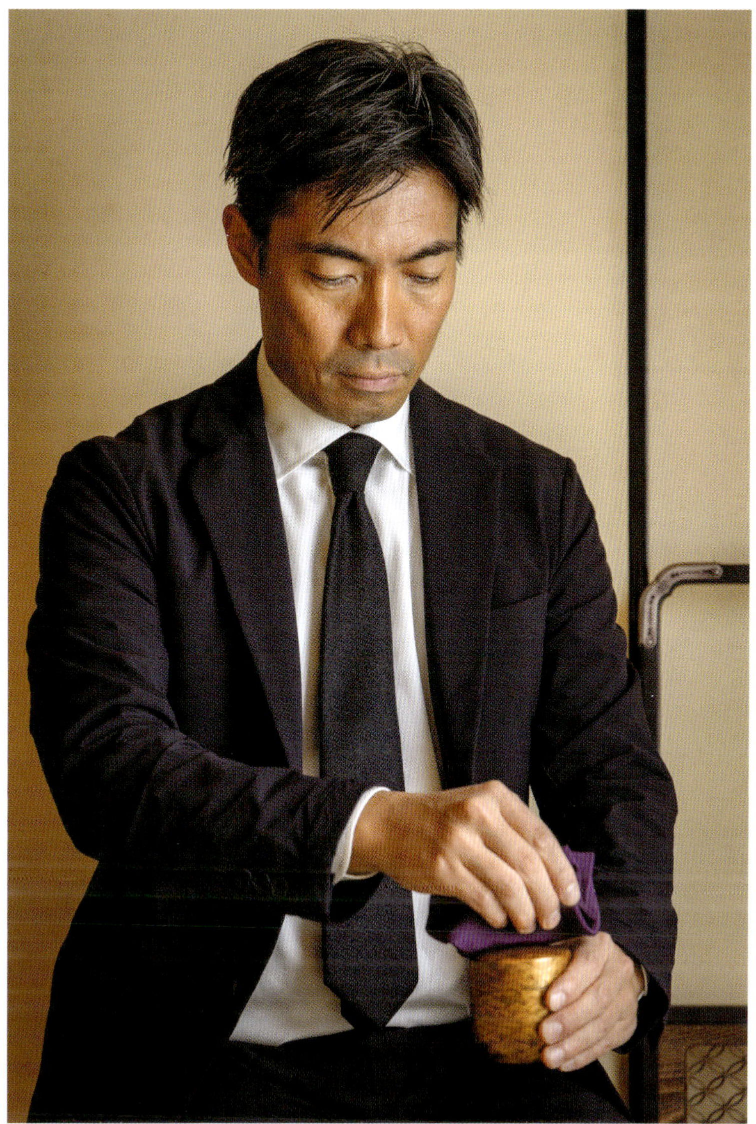

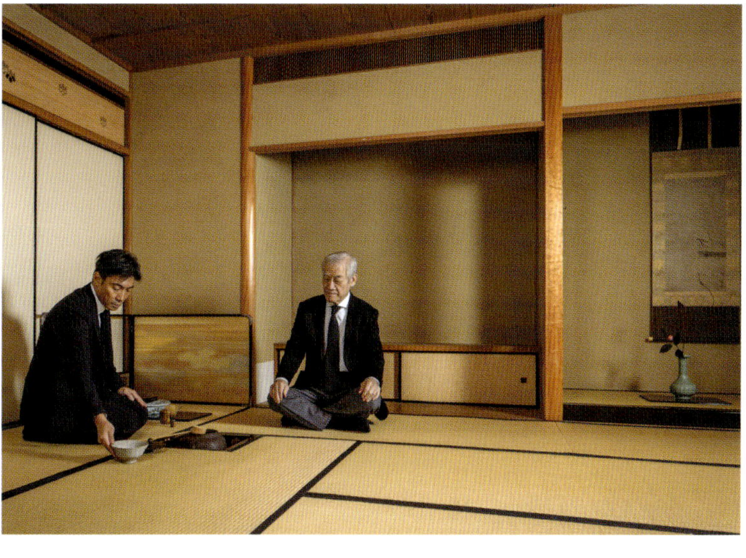

Flowers and Utensils for January

The Host's Expression

When it comes to *chabana* tea flowers, there is somehow a sense of formality—fixed ideas, standard ways of arranging them. I feel both a sort of agreement and disagreement with that. Because of my family's work, I have often been involved with tea gatherings and tea ceremonies, and over the years I have seen all kinds of tea flowers. Of course, it is important to respect the traditional forms that have been passed down through the ages—but that alone is not the most important thing. If a person's inner self and individuality do not come through in the flowers they arrange, then the arrangement isn't very interesting.

 In particular, one person who had his own stance—in other words, his own approach to tea flowers—and whom I greatly admired, was the previous head of the Enshu school, whose name was Kobori Sokei. He has already passed away, but when I first saw the flowers arranged by the late head, I genuinely thought, "Ah, this person truly loves flowers."

This sort of thing is not something you understand intellectually—it's something you feel. Kobori Sokei and I both happened to have vacation homes in Tateshina in Nagano Prefecture: his was higher up, and ours was lower down. One day, I happened to meet as he was returning from a walk. The sight of him carrying wildflowers in his hand left such a pleasant impression. He genuinely enjoyed flowers in his daily life. I could sense his connection with the flowers—how he communicated with them. It is an image I will never forget.

When I was preparing this book, the editorial department asked me, "What are your thoughts about flowers in the tea room?" The words that came to mind at that moment were these: "Once you snip a flower and bring it into the room, its life is already limited. Precisely because of that, you should go all out to use it to the fullest—to bring out its life force completely. Arrogantly, we humans impose our intentions and decide the flower's fate, so afterwards we must commit to using up that severed life to the very end."

Centering Flower Materials in a Container

There are several ways to place flowers in the center of a container, but here I will introduce a method that does not rely on support sticks or other aids, using only the branches of the materials themselves. It is important that the first material you insert is a branch, in this case red plum (see page 15). The other materials are arranged in relation to the plum branch. Bend the red plum branch so that the tip is pressed against the upper right side of the container, as shown in the photo on the right. The bent section should rest along the lower left inside of the container. At this point, adjust it so that the part rising above the water comes to the center of the container. By securing the same branch at two points, you achieve both stability and a bit of "play," making it easier to insert the other materials.

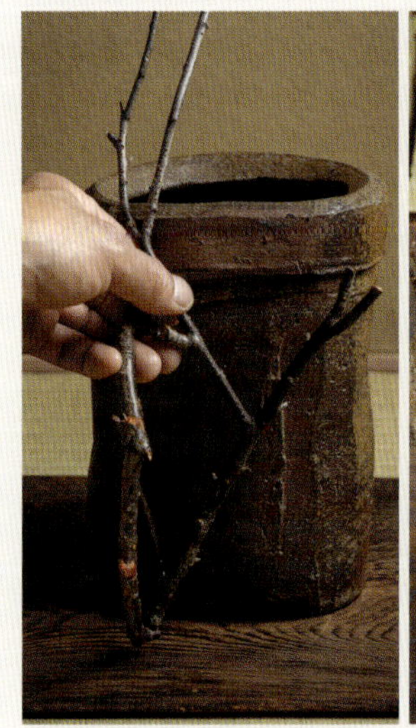
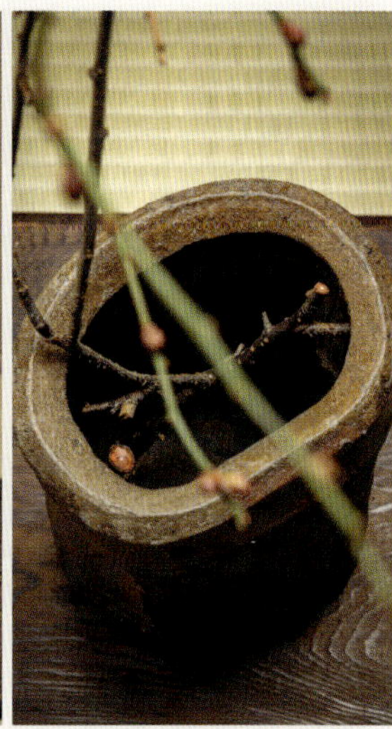

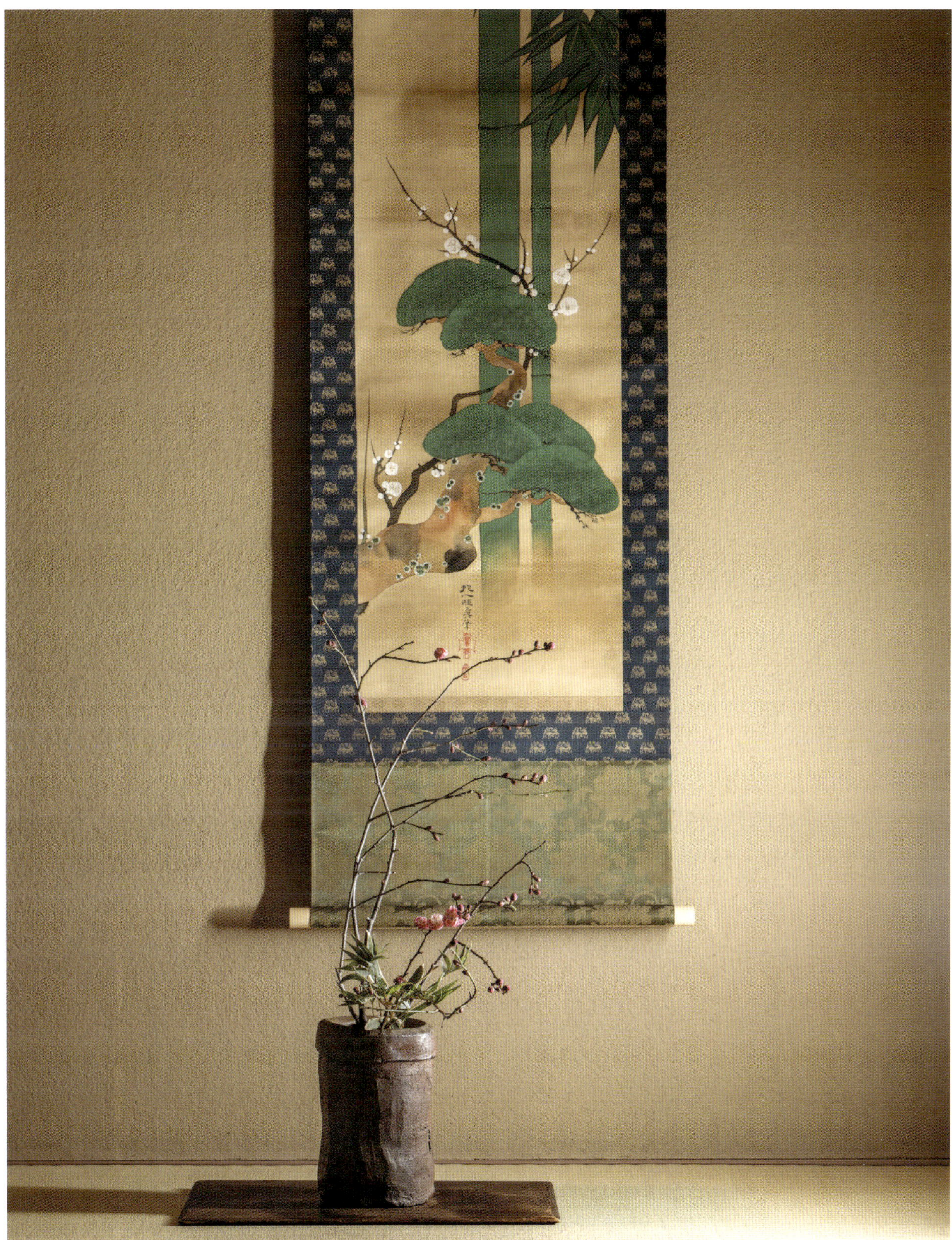

Red plum blossom, Kuma bamboo grass, phoenix bamboo. Bizen ware flower container "Takagamine," Momoyama period.

The alcove prepared for the New Year. An inspired arrangement pairing red plum blossom with the white plum blossom in the hanging scroll. The Bizen ware flower container enhances the red plum and the painting behind it. By adding bamboo and Kuma bamboo grass, the display takes on a festive New Year's atmosphere.

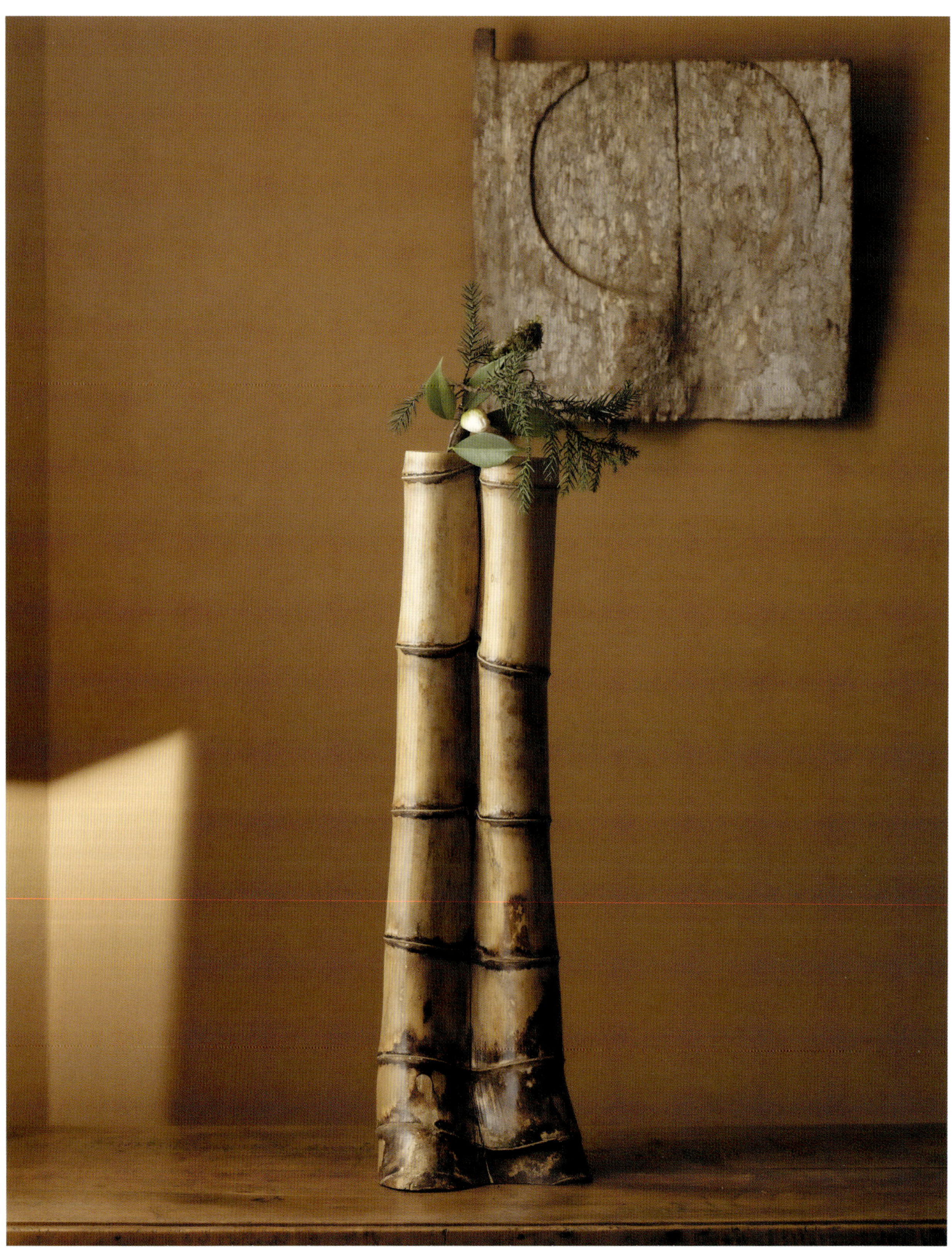

White camellia, cedar branch. Bamboo flower container by Jikinyu Raku.

A bamboo flower container about 35 inches (90 cm) tall, gives this arrangement a strong presence. The flowers are arranged compactly to balance the visual weight of the container. Hanging on the wall is a wooden grave door from the Toraja people of Indonesia, with a primitive character.

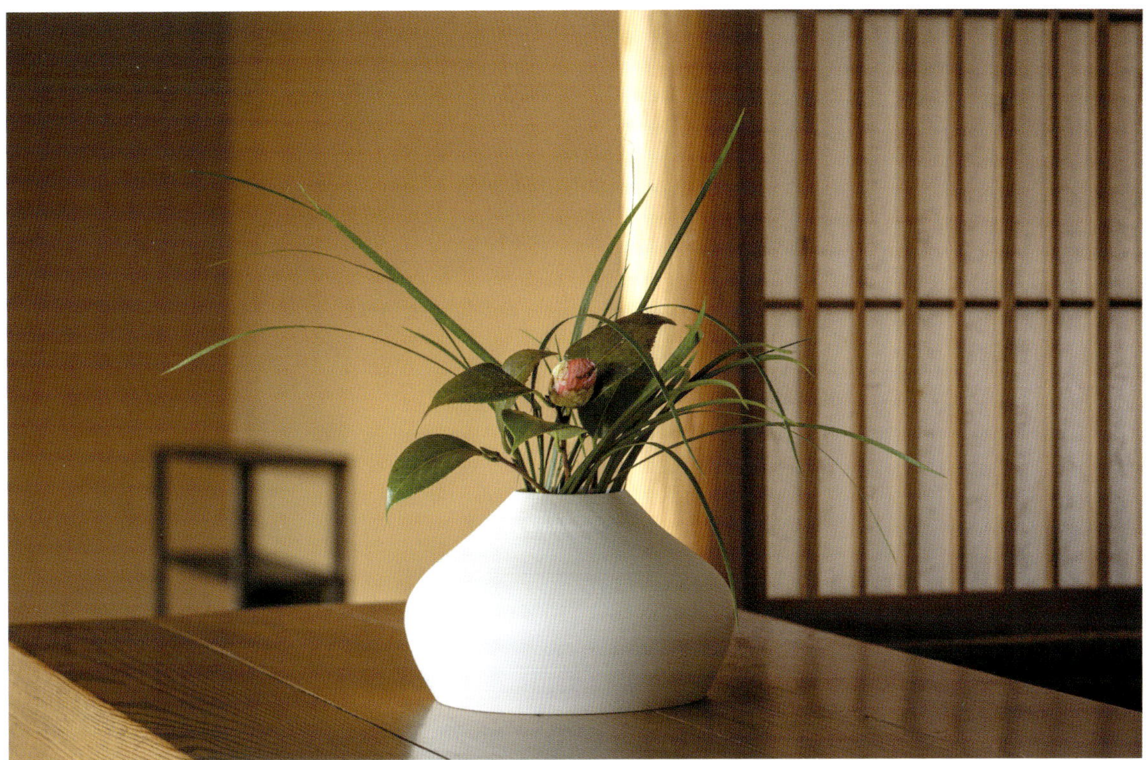

Benimyorenji camellia and Japanese sweet flag. Small white porcelain flower container by Taizo Kuroda (see page 154).

Japanese sweet flag is often used at night-time tea gatherings. It is said to absorb the oily soot from the wicks of the lamps used in the gathering and purify the air in the room. Here, it is arranged with a camellia in a small white porcelain flower container as a decoration for an everyday living space.

Those words just quoted were said by a friend of mine, someone I consider a true master of flowers and of beauty, and I think it also applies to flowers in the tea ceremony. I believe it is worth having that degree of resolve. A tea flower exists to welcome the guest through its vitality. When a guest enters the tea room, the flower is what delivers the first impact. The shape of the flower that jumps into the eyes the moment you step into the room, its breath, its life—this is what the host is trying to convey. The guest receives this and is moved. That emotion takes form as words, and in response the host replies. A game of catch with words begins.

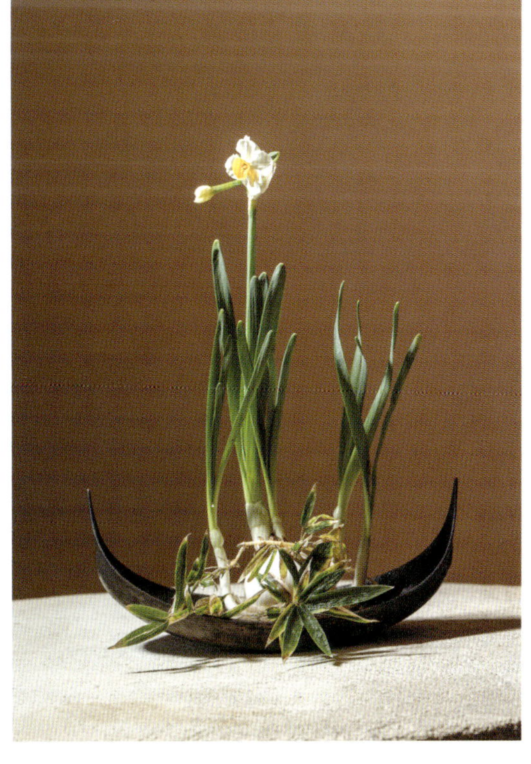

Narcissus, bamboo grass. Sand-cast bronze vessel from Indonesia, used as a boat-shaped flower container.

Centered on a narcissus with its roots left in their natural state, with bamboo grass around the base. In tea ceremony, Indonesian boat-shaped ritual vessels have long been reimagined as flower containers by attaching chains to them and using them as hanging flower holders. This one has no chains and remains in its original state.

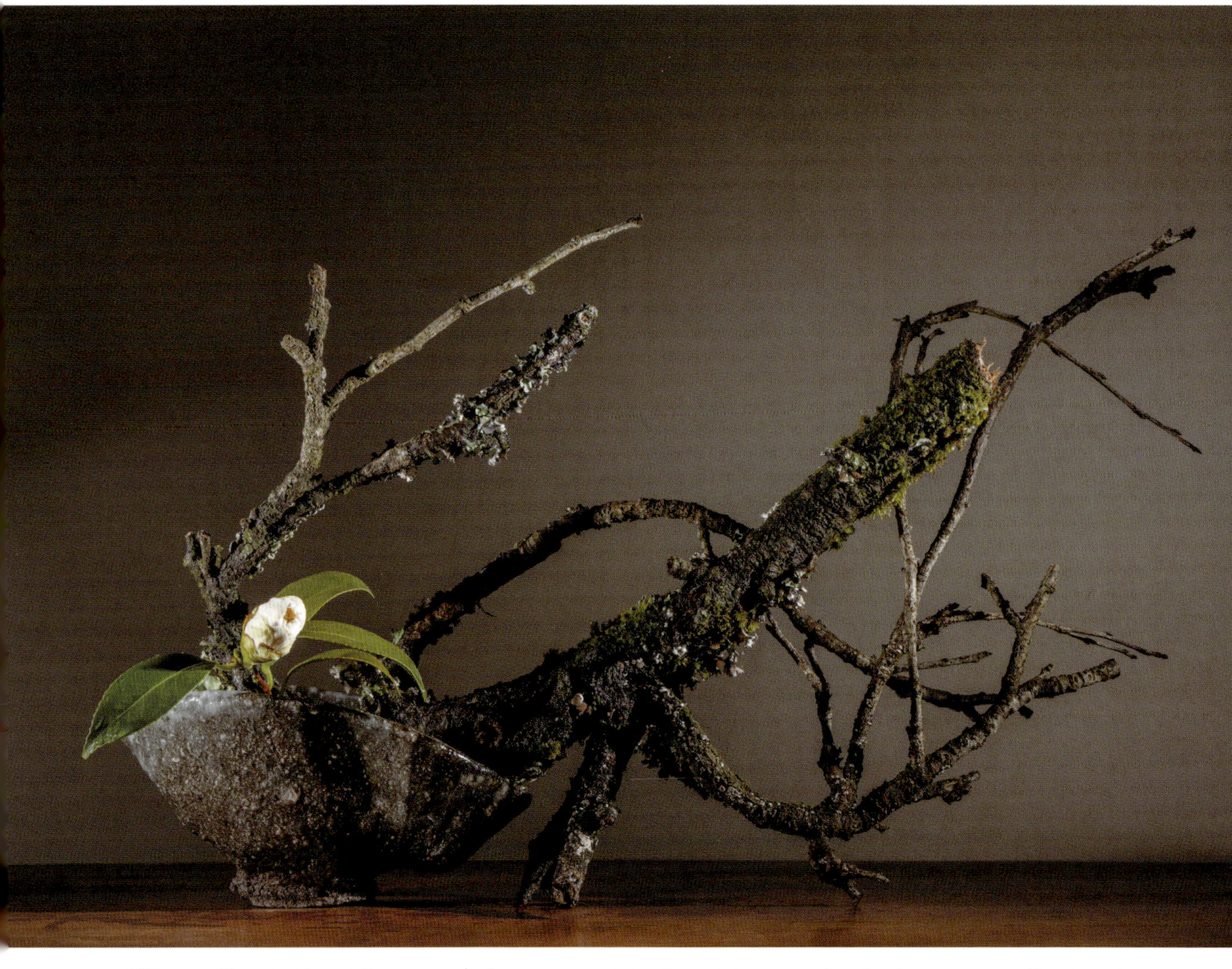

White camellia and withered cherry branch in a flower container crafted from clay from the grounds of Yakushiji Temple, by Jikinyu Raku (see page 34).

A moss-covered dead branch is arranged so that it seems to overflow from the container, balanced by a single white camellia. The line of the branch flowing to the right is anchored by the small container, made with earth from an ancient temple, resulting in a powerful work brimming with energy.

For example, there is a well-known anecdote about Sen no Rikyu—the sixteenth-century tea master who is considered the most important influence on tea ceremony— and daimyo Toyotomi Hideyoshi. Hideyoshi heard the morning glories in Rikyu's garden were in full bloom, and he asked Rikyu to host a tea ceremony so he could admire them. When Hideyoshi arrived, he found the garden devoid of flowers—only cut stems remained. Curious and displeased, he entered the tea room. There, in the alcove, he saw a single perfect morning glory, silently expressed and beautifully displayed. This may not be a true story, but I think it is quite interesting as a story that conveys Rikyu's ideas about flowers and about beauty. It feels very Japanese, and very Zen. In tea hospitality, it is not only the flowers but also the implements in the alcove and used for preparation that are chosen as the most fitting things one can think of for that moment. Both flowers and utensils are completely used to their utmost. The host applies every skill to welcome the guest and to send a message. Among them, the flower is the only living thing in the tea room. As my friend said, the host tries to use that life to the fullest.

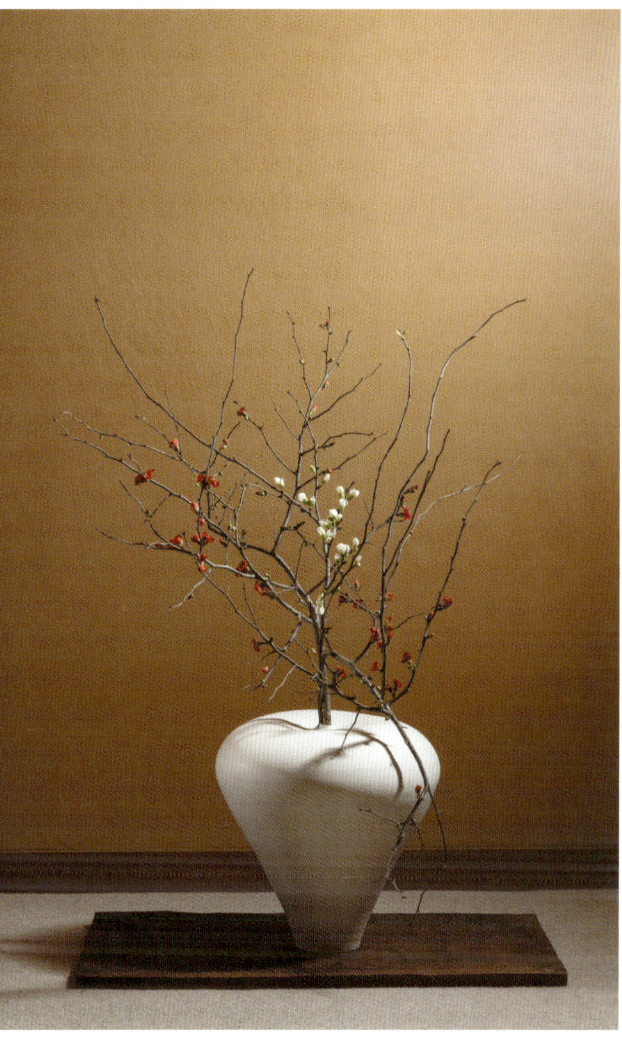

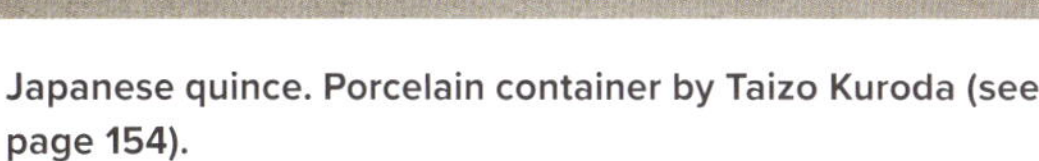

Japanese quince. Porcelain container by Taizo Kuroda (see page 154).

Red and white flowering quince are arranged to express auspiciousness. Branches have a back and a front, but it is not always necessary to place the front facing forward. The impression changes depending on which direction you orient the branch within the space. In this case, the front has been turned slightly to the right.

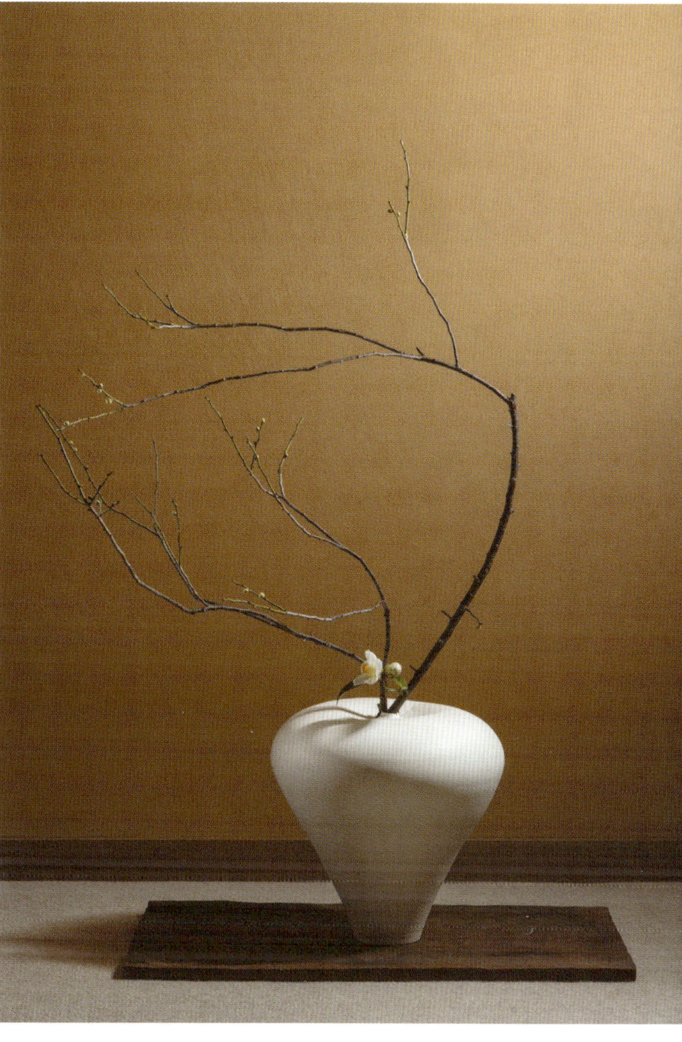

White camellia, plum branch. Porcelain container by Taizo Kuroda (see page 154).

A slender plum branch, bearing just a few buds, extends gracefully and dominates the space. The white camellia placed near the mouth of the container serves as the core that brings the whole composition together. Using only the most carefully chosen flowers, this arrangement expresses early spring. It is an example that shows how presence comes not from the quantity of materials but from their thoughtful selection.

The Direction and Flow of Branches

When working with branches as floral materials, even a slight change in their orientation can completely transform the impression. Before placing them in the container, look at the branches from various angles and form a clear image of the finished arrangement, to make the subsequent work much easier. In the camellia on page 18, the overall flow was unified extending the dead wood to the right, matching the vessel's downward slope to the right. In the plum branch arrangement, above right, since the material consists almost entirely of slender branches, considering which branches to keep allows the overall line to emerge. The original material had many more branches, but by cutting them away to the minimum, the envisioned line stands out clearly.

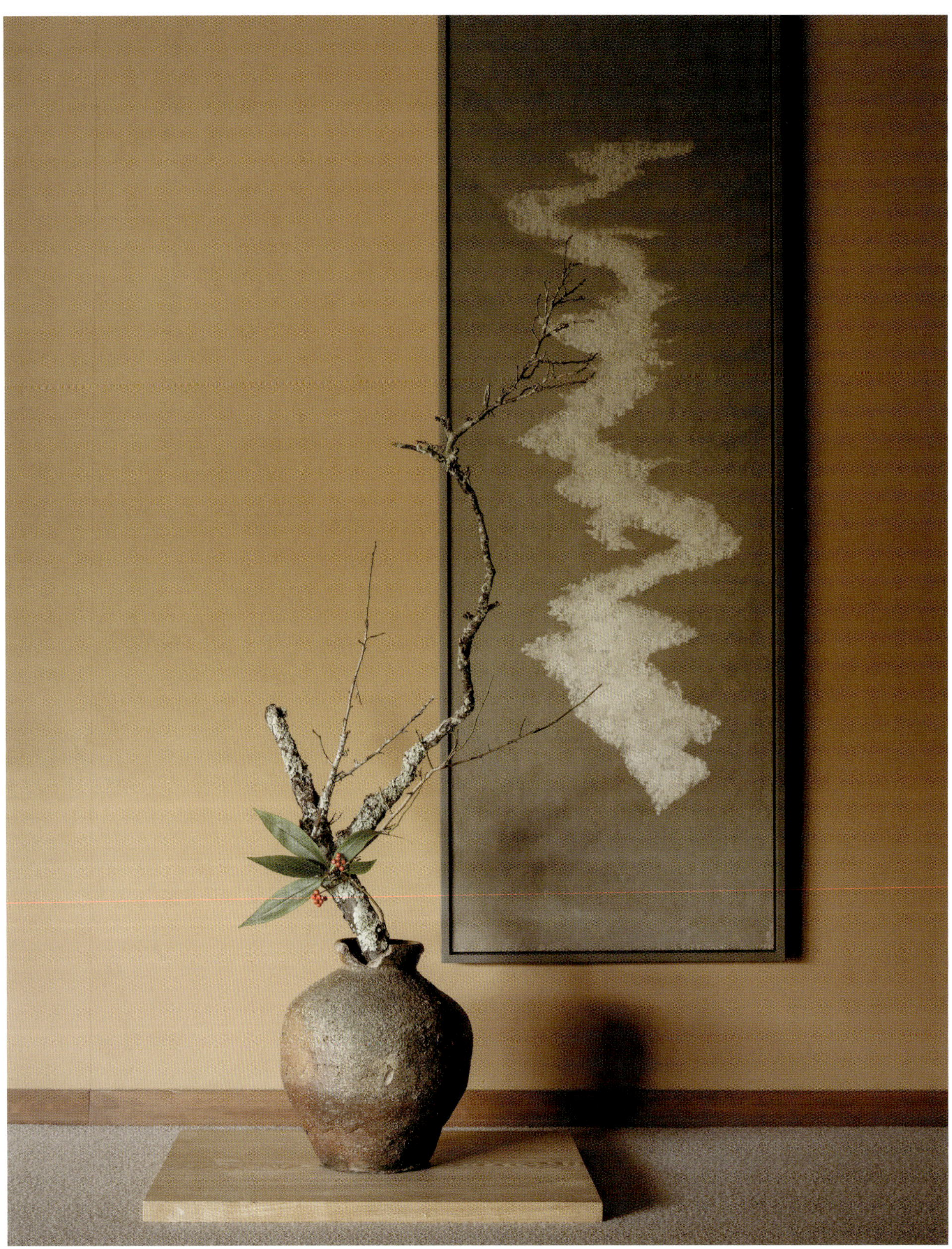

Plum branch, Chinese wild orange. Large Shigaraki ware flower container, Muromachi period.

A large, thick plum branch in a Shigaraki ware flower container that has aged over centuries. Evergreen Chinese wild orange, which bears red fruit in winter, creates an auspicious feeling. Although this is not a traditional Japanese room, the painting on the wall, *Komyo* (Radiance), by Takayoshi Sakabe, helps evoke the impression of a *tokonoma* alcove.

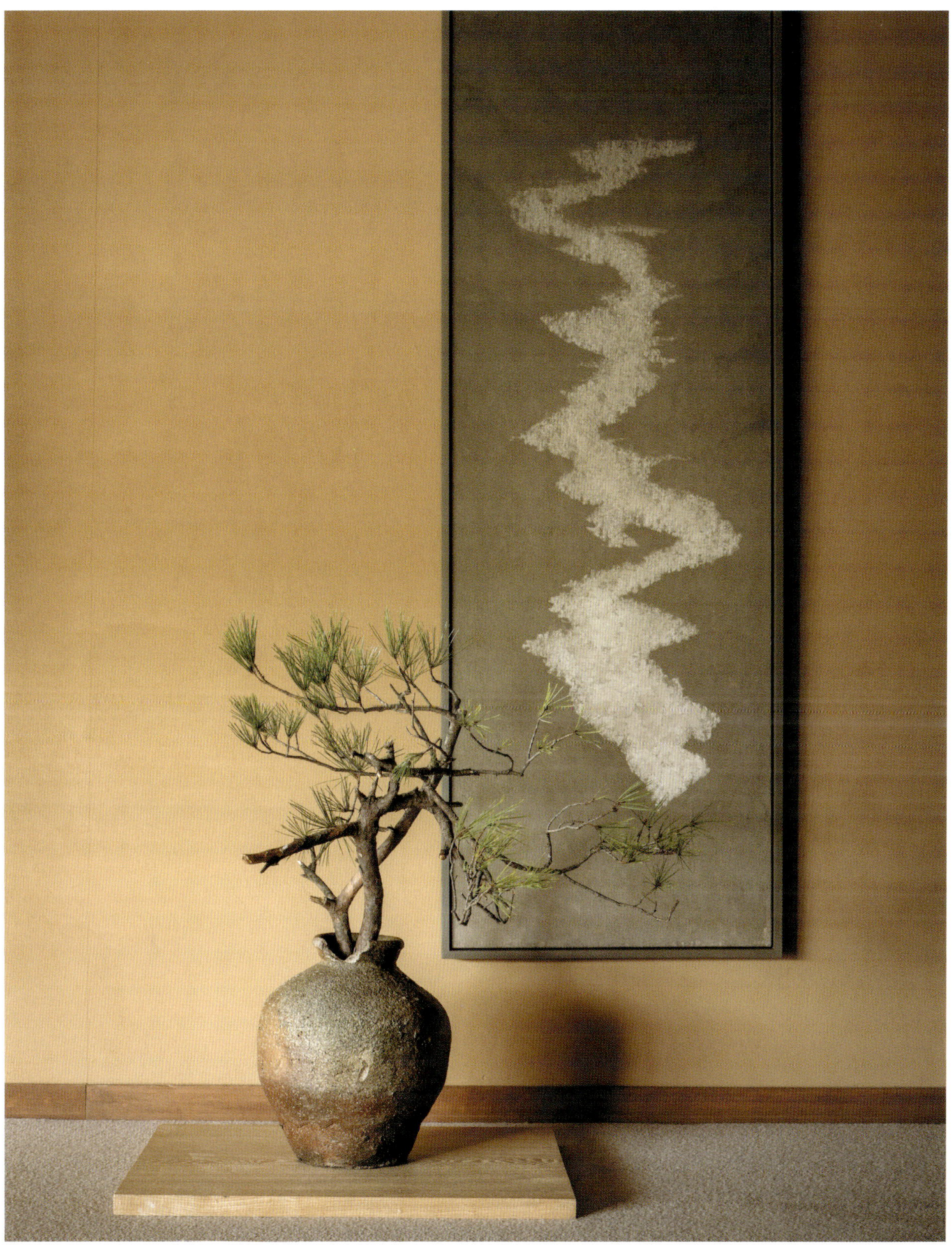

Pine branch. Large Shigaraki ware flower container, Muromachi period.

An example using the elements as on the facing page, with just the floral material changed, using only pine. The earthy quality of the Shigaraki clay of the vessel, the cracks around the mouth, the texture of the surface, and the kiln marks on the body all harmonize beautifully with the thick pine branch. A distinguished arrangement to welcome the New Year.

Freedom Beyond the Rules

— Atsushi Kobayashi

I am always conscious of how the hanging scroll in the alcove and the flower vessel suit each other. For example, if I hang a painting by Sotatsu (page 11), a celadon or Japanese-style ceramic flower vessel goes well with it. Using an old bronze vessel would feel out of place. I usually use old bronze with a calligraphic ink inscription. There is also compatibility between the vessel and the flowers. In the hearth season, camellias are indispensable and go well with many kinds of flower containers, but when arranged alone, they can lack interest, so I almost always add a branch of another tree. In the brazier season, I often use a basket container, but I only put wildflowers in it, never tree branches.

There are also rules about where to place the flower vessel in relation to the hanging scroll, and how to combine the vessel with the wooden board that it stands on. Flowers in the tea room are not simply arranged however one likes—there are many principles to consider. There are books that list concrete examples, and one also learns by observing flowers in tea gatherings. But if you become so preoccupied with the rules that you lose sight of why we place flowers in the tea room at all, then it is meaningless. Rules are not just to be followed—they serve as a standard. By being aware of them and their significance, your own unique way of arranging flowers can grow.

For a tea ceremony early in the New Year, I hung a painting of pine, bamboo and plum in the alcove and placed a branch of red plum blossom in front of it (page 15). In the tea room, when a hanging scroll depicting flowers is displayed, it is common not to arrange real flowers, and instead to place only the empty flower vessel before the painting, to avoid overlapping motifs and designs. When I first saw this method, I was very impressed. According to this rule, since a painting of pine, bamboo and plum by Sakai Hoitsu was hanging in the alcove, no flowers should have been arranged. But when I found a beautifully shaped branch of red plum blossom, I decided to place it before the painting, as if it were responding to the white plum blossom in the artwork. I did wonder whether it was really acceptable to do such a thing, but I had been inspired by the art. Until then, I had always believed one must not put real flowers with a painting of flowers, so I felt happy to break through that constraint.

In this book, I have the opportunity to arrange flowers in many settings, with a focus on tea flowers. Tea flowers are, quite literally, "flowers placed in the tea room," but to understand tea flowers, you must engage with flowers in daily life. The experiences one has outside the tea room eventually come to life in that person's practice of tea.

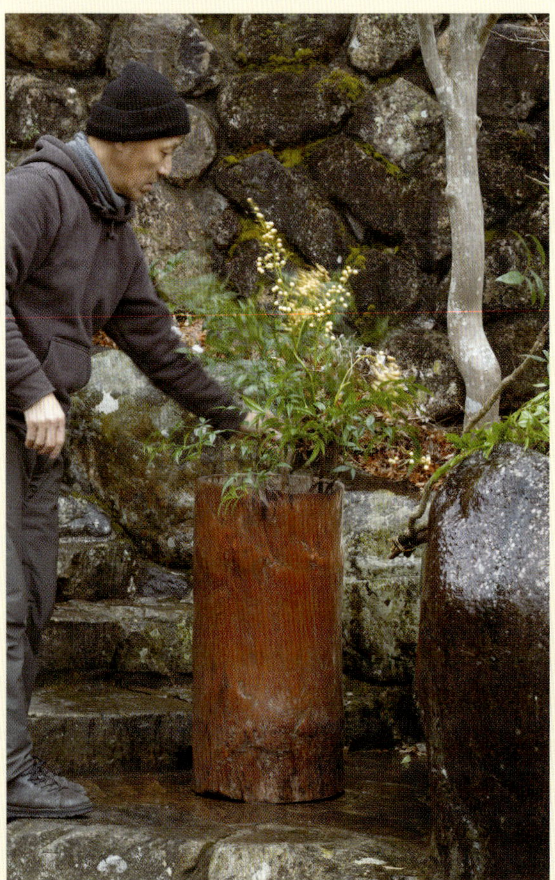

Atsushi Kobayashi places a large wooden container at the entryway. He inserts several nandina branches bearing red and white berries, adjusting the balance as he goes. "You can't just leave the branches exactly as they are," he advises. "Think of hairdressers. When someone comes in with very thick hair, it has to be thinned to look natural. The hairdresser has to bold and remove a lot. To keep it from looking messy and to achieve a clean, natural look, I imagine the hairdresser looks closely at each strand and cuts with great care. They're not just thinning things out haphazardly."

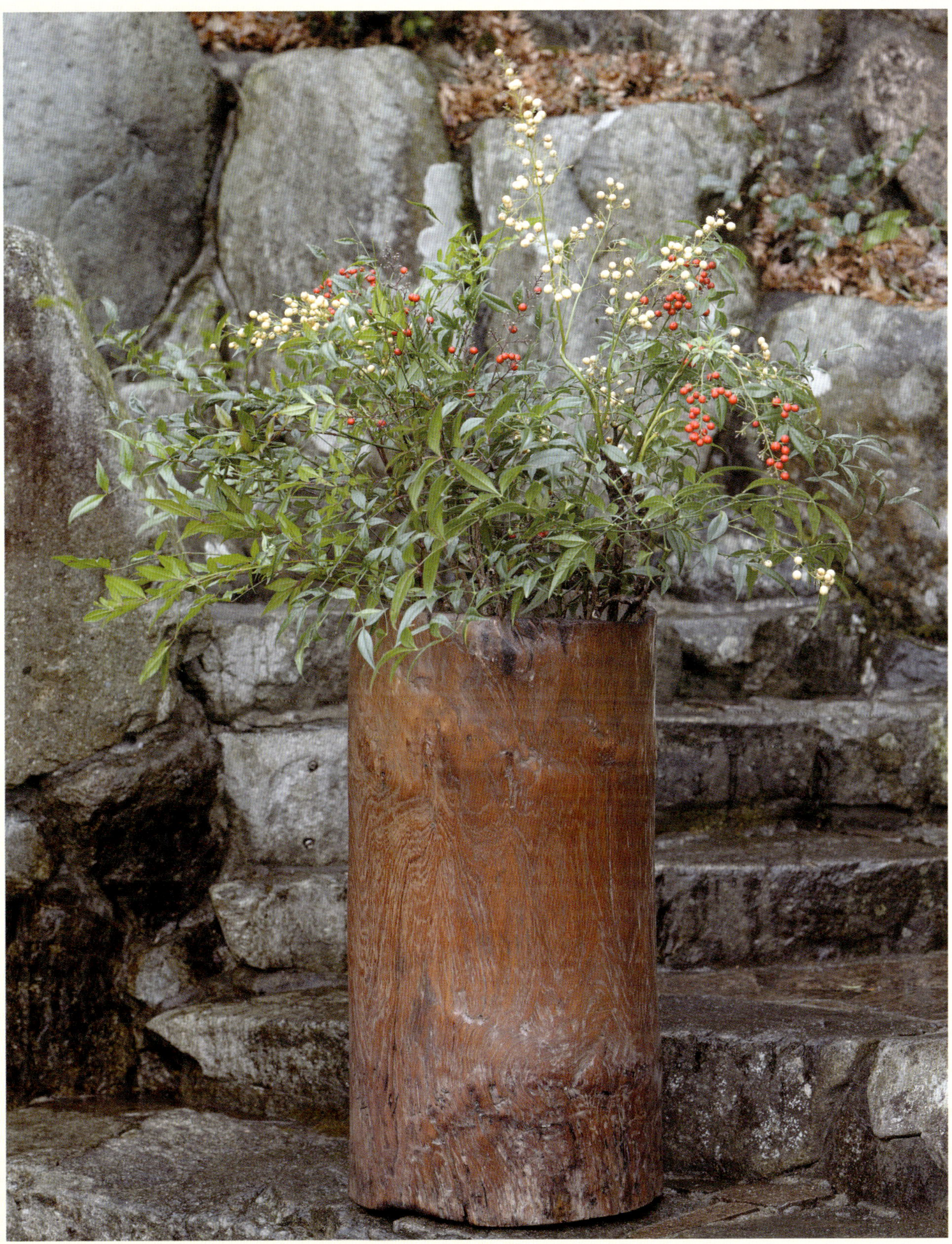

Red nandina, white nandina. Wooden container, Java, Indonesia.

Red and white nandina are arranged in a balanced way, with branches and leaves finished in a soft, full form as a welcoming display. "The way plants appear growing naturally and the way they look in a container are completely different. Making them look natural doesn't mean just putting them in as they are," says Kobayashi.

A Miraculous Encounter

Yunnan Magnolia

When I was asked to photograph tea flowers throughout the year, there was one flower I knew I wanted to use—the Yunnan magnolia.

I first encountered it about ten years ago, when we used it as the tea flower for the Daishi-kai tea gathering held every year at the end of March at the Nezu Museum in Tokyo. March is a difficult season: camellias have just finished blooming, and early summer flowers like magnolia sieboldii, which are often used, have yet to appear. It is a time when it's hard to find a single flower that could hold its own for display at a tea ceremony, and Atsushi Kobayashi was struggling to source something suitable.

He consulted the owner of Hanacho, the florist in Tokyo's Aoyama district we always rely on, and the owner offered a branch from a Yunnan magnolia he had been cultivating in his own garden. Neither Kobayashi nor I had ever seen the flower before. When we placed it in the alcove, we both thought, "What a beautiful flower—I'd love to have a tree of my own." I began searching, but even after looking online, it was nowhere to be found.

A few years later, I was asked to serve tea at the Daibi Chakai tea gathering held by the Osaka Art Club. Once again, we asked Hanacho to ship Yunnan magnolia from Tokyo. While I was arranging the flowers, an old friend of mine, Takashi Inaba, happened to stop by. He said, "So this is the Yunnan magnolia you've been talking about—what a beautiful flower." Apparently, we had been talking about it so much that he'd been curious to see it himself. I'll speak more about Inaba later, but he is someone with an incredible eye for arranging flowers. Even he had never seen this one before.

After returning to his home in Izu, he visited a local nursery—and, remarkably, found five or six Yunnan magnolia plants there. He immediately called to say, "I found it!" and bought them all, sharing some with me. Since then, the Yunnan magnolia has bloomed beautifully every year in my garden. However, that nursery hasn't carried them since. It seems the plants had arrived by some fluke, and even the nursery staff didn't know exactly what they were.

It truly was a miraculous encounter.

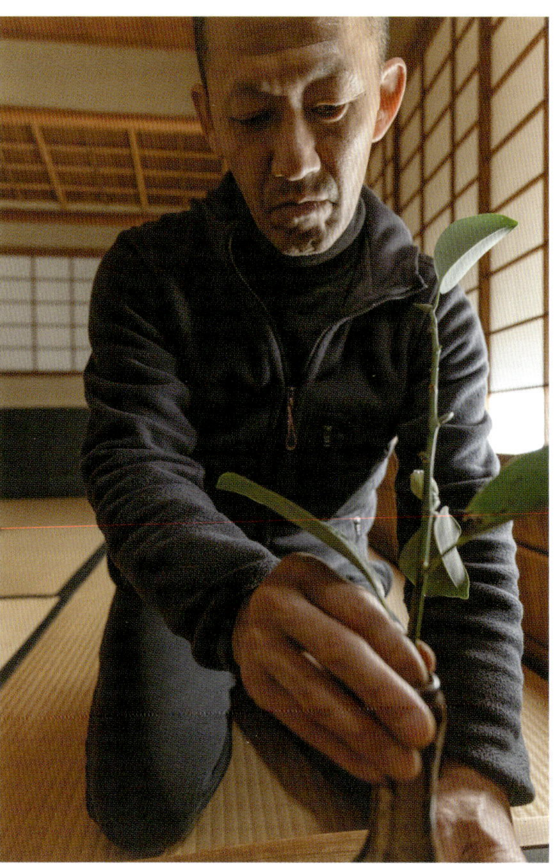

When arranging flowers, you choose the ideal section from a large branch and trim away the rest. Behind the flowers placed in the flower container are the branches, leaves and blossoms that were cut away. Aware of this, the owner of Hanacho kindly cut a thick branch all the way from the base of the tree so that the best parts could be selected. "Before he made the cut, he put his hands together in prayer toward the tree," Kobayashi recalls.

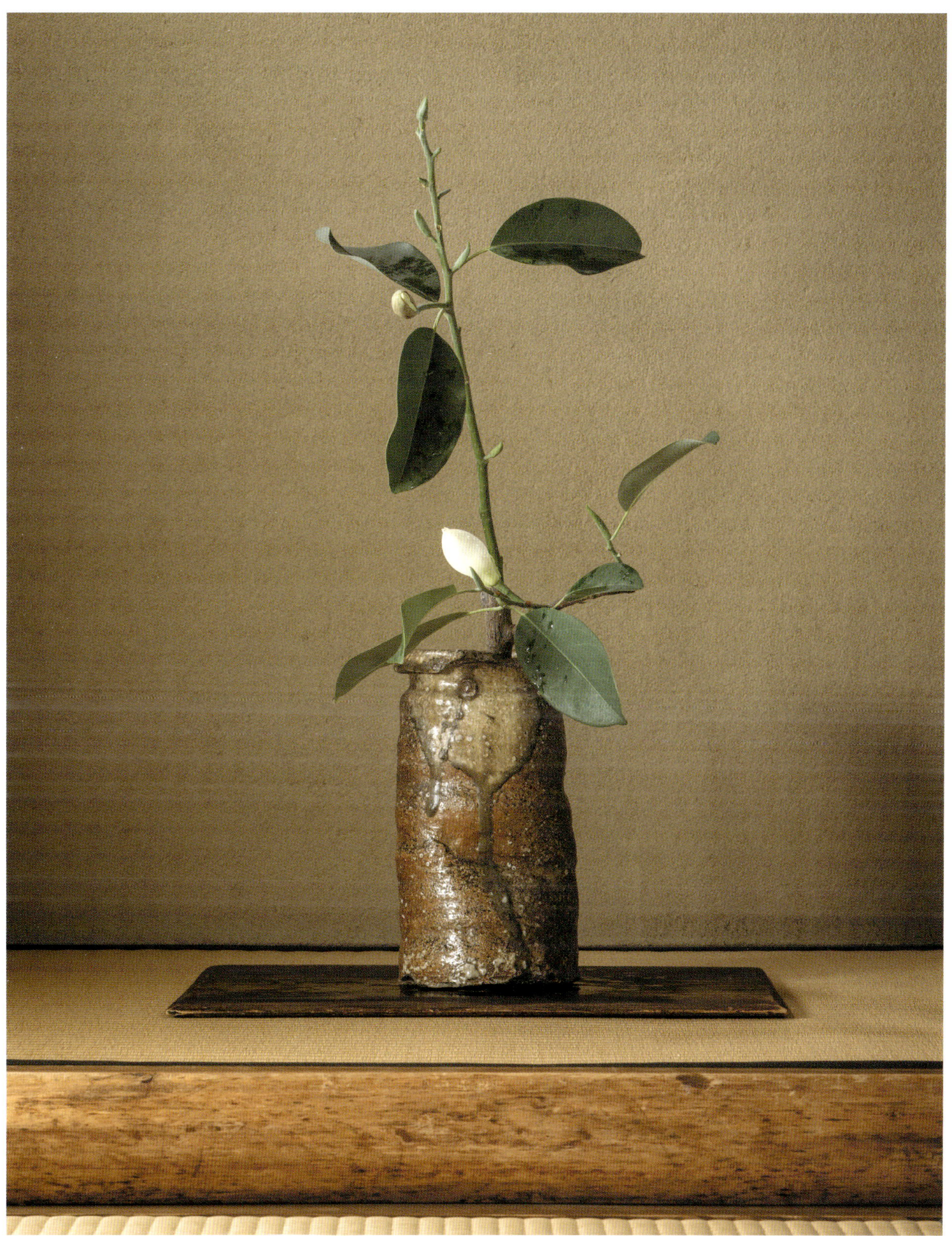

Yunnan magnolia. Shigaraki ware flower container, Momoyama period.

The Yunnan magnolia, which captivated Toda and his companions, is evergreen, and its leafy branches make it especially well-suited for use as a tea flower. "The shape of the white buds is beautiful too, don't you think? It has a delicate, unassuming appearance, yet this flower alone carries more than enough presence," says Hiroshi.

Flowers and Utensils for February

Tea Through All Five Senses

The flower containers featured in this book range widely—from antique bronze, bamboo, and pottery from the Six Ancient Kilns to contemporary white porcelain by modern artists and old earthenware from Indonesia. Some, like the bamboo ones, were originally created to be used as flower vessels, while others were later repurposed as such over time. They come from a variety of origins, but what they have in common is they possess a certain intrinsic power as objects. This is true of all tea utensils.

People sometimes ask how one should engage with or judge utensils. In the end, I believe the most important thing is sensitivity—a good intuitive sense. The world of tea is, after all, one that revolves around feeling. Ultimately, it comes down to a person's natural sensibility, and this has long been said to be the case. That said, this sensibility may lie dormant, waiting to be awakened. You could even say that the Way of Tea exists for that very purpose.

What matters is the ability to sense and feel something in the moment. Knowing about something from books or the Internet is not the same as experiencing it directly. I may place too much emphasis on intuition, but that's the nature of art and aesthetics. I hope people will learn to value their first impressions. Rather than being trapped by information, I want them to develop the kind of sensitivity that makes them stop and simply say, "Oh, wow."

Even now, I still struggle with this myself. But I believe it's important to value your initial reaction—whether you like something or not, and how it makes you feel. Of course, a basic level of knowledge is necessary, but knowledge alone is not enough. Sometimes, knowledge can interfere with your ability to truly feel.

For example, at tea gatherings, there are often people who start by reading the *kaiki*—the record of the proceedings of a gathering, the utensils used and the food served. But if they feel they've "understood" the gathering simply by reading it, then they've missed the point. I'm not saying the kaiki shouldn't be read, but personally, I prefer to look at it afterward—either during the ride home or once I've returned. And then I might realize, "Ah, that

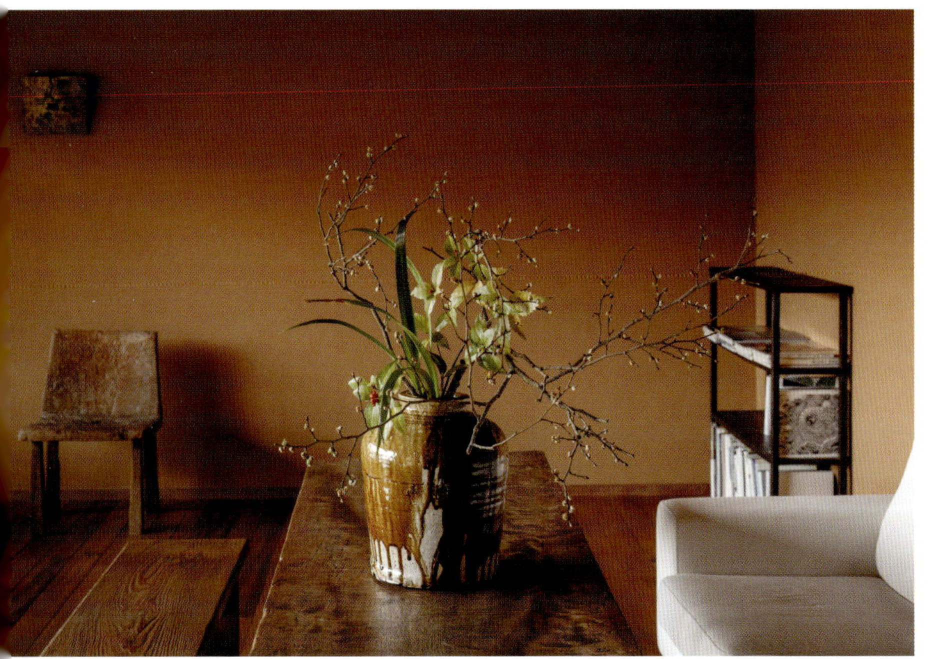

Coralberry, blackberry lily, and edgeworthia. Oribe-style flower container by Ryoji Koie.

An arrangement with two types of branches with blackberry lily leaves. The key is to balance the overlapping branches and leaves so they appear natural from top to bottom and side to side. While tea flowers are typically arranged to be viewed from a single direction, the look of an everyday flower arrangement needs to be considered from multiple angles.

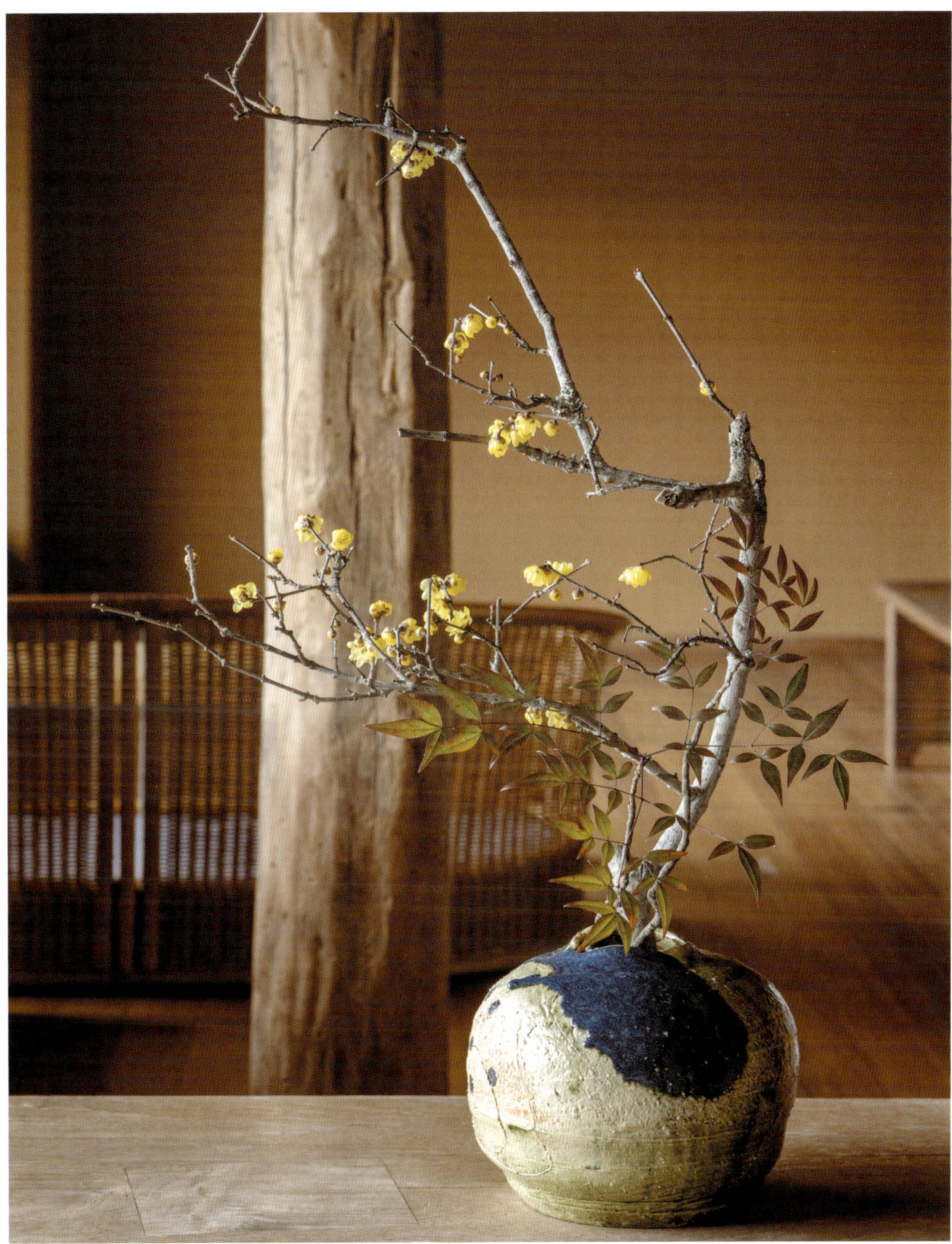

Wintersweet and nandina leaves.
Oribe-style flower container by Ryoji Koie.

Not especially large, this flower container has a stable form that allows the secure placement of tall branches. The vivid blue glaze makes a striking impression, yet it's surprisingly versatile and accommodates a wide range of floral materials. Its charm also lies in the fact that it can be displayed on its own, even without flowers.

utensil was recorded in the *Enshu Kuracho* [Record of Utensils compiled by seventeenth-century tea master Kobori Enshu]. I missed that."

It's fine to confirm the provenance of a piece afterward, but what really matters is whether it moved you at first sight. That's the real test—and also the true pleasure—of tea. Of course, there are many ways to understand tea utensils. In that sense, I suppose my son Takashi, as well as Atsushi Kobayashi, and indeed everyone at the Toda Shop may be quite intuitive. This is a way of thinking I inherited from my father, who was known as an exceptional connoisseur. I think we place great value on the intuitive judgments he passed down to us.

When it comes to utensils, it's primarily about seeing and sensing. But in the world of tea, it's not just about sight—we value all five senses. Because, in the end, tea is about what you feel.

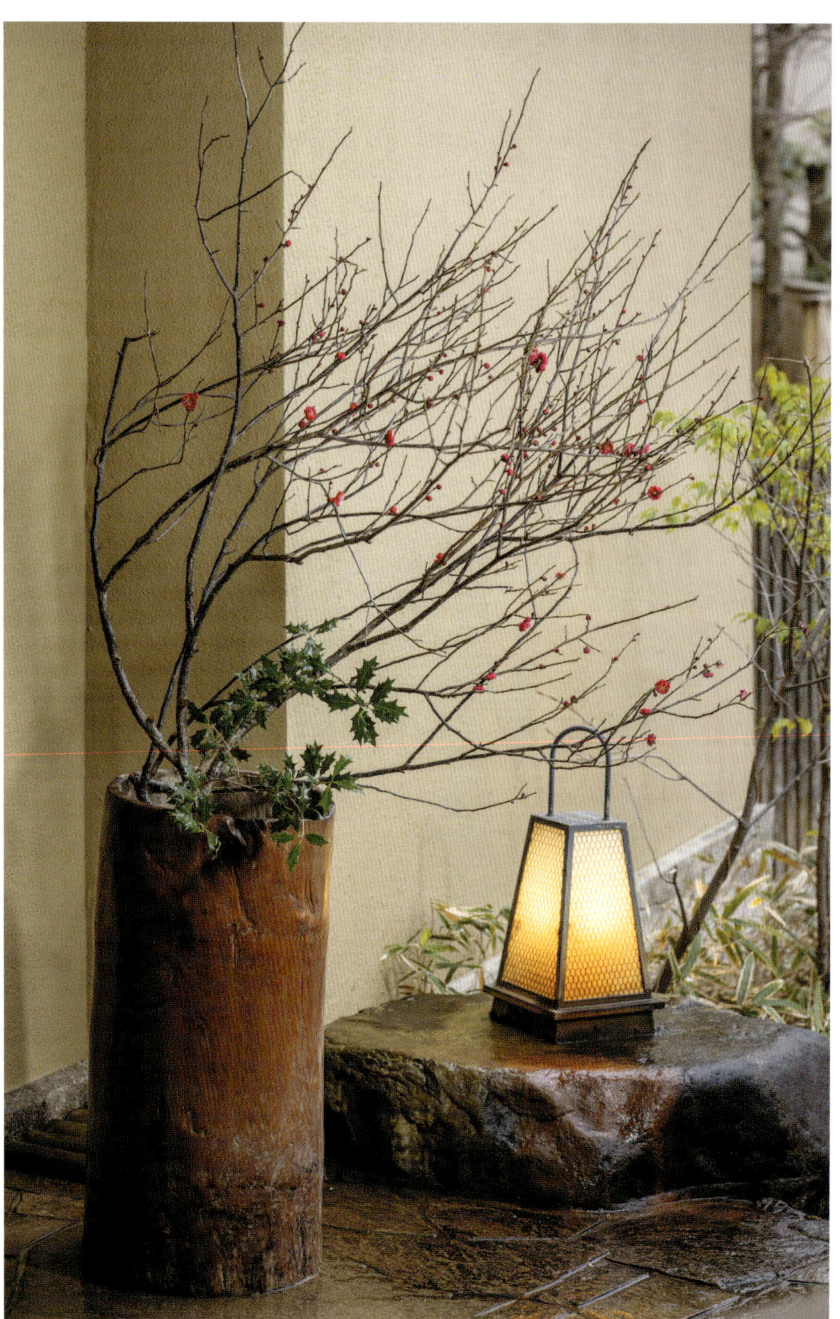

Red plum blossom and holly. Wooden container, Java, Indonesia.

The flowing, graceful lines of the branches of red plum blossom are allowed to shine, with holly at the base to anchor the arrangement and follow the branches' movement. Traditionally, holly was hung at an entryway to mark the start of spring and here it is arranged in a wooden vessel, a welcoming entryway arrangement from late January through the start of spring.

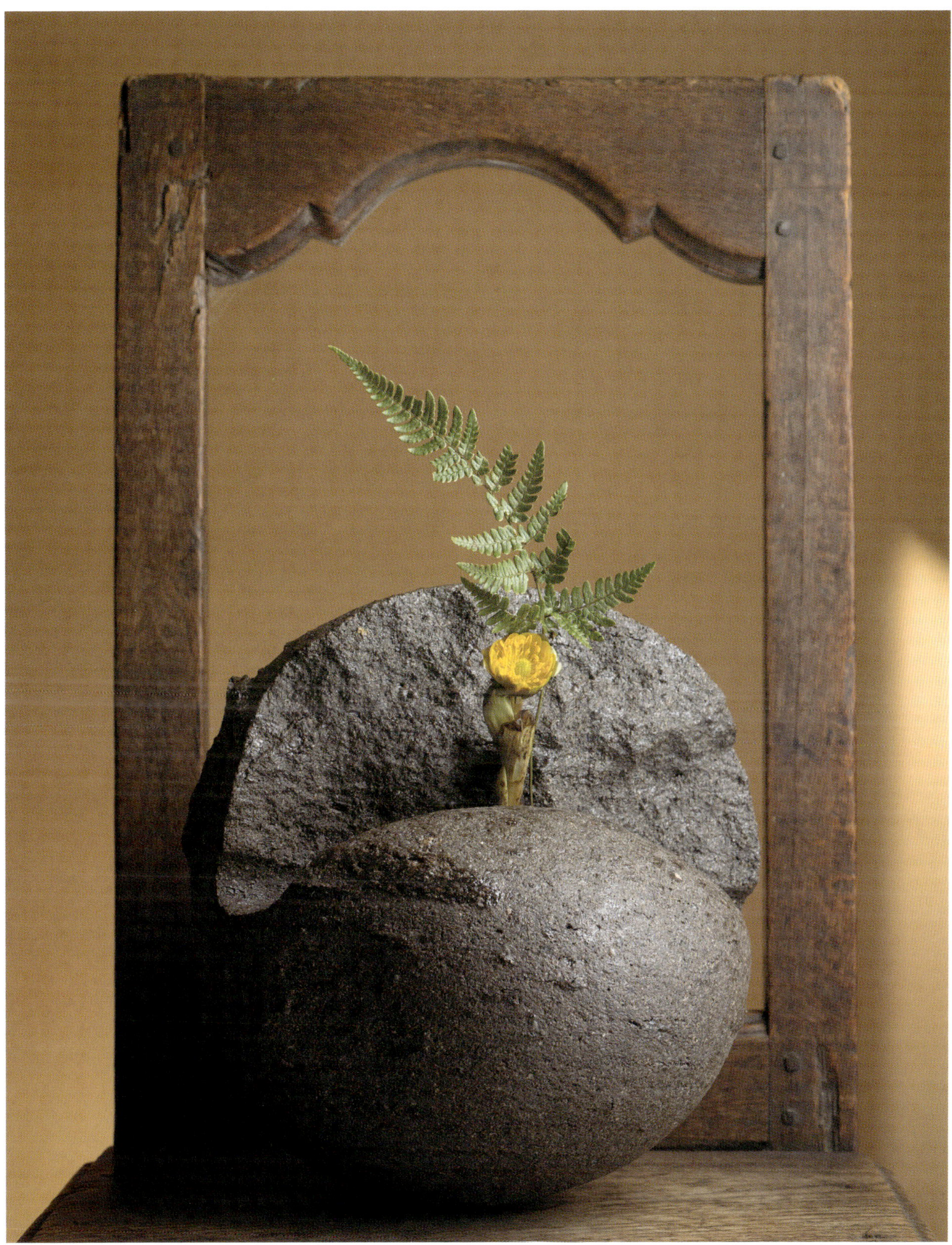

Adonis and fern. Stone sculpture *Rinne* (Samsara) by Masaomi Raku.

An example of using a stone sculpture as a flower vessel. The rooted adonis flower and fern seem to grow directly from the piece itself. An antique chair, once used in a French church, is the flower stand, its backrest framing the space like a picture frame.

Make Flowers a Daily Habit
— Atsushi Kobayashi

Perhaps the most direct path to improving one's skill with tea flowers is to regularly engage with flowers outside the tea room setting. One way to do this is to find a flower container you like and place flowers in it every day. A medium-sized vessel is a good choice. Generally, ceramic or earthenware vessels are the easiest to work with. Even within ceramics, porcelain has a harder, cooler texture that makes it a little more difficult to find flowers that suit it. Materials other than pottery—such as sand-cast bronze, or woven materials—tend to further narrow your floral options. So if you're going to have just one flower container for daily use, I recommend starting with an earthenware vessel.

Take for example the containers by Ryoji Koie on pages 26 and 27. At first glance, their glaze may seem quite lively, but they work well with branches and are equally easy to use with grasses and other flowers. I think these types of container suit nearly any kind of floral material. They have mouths that narrow gently, making it easy to hold the flowers in place. You can also change the orientation of the container to give the arrangement a different look. This type of container this is excellent for practice. If it is too large, it limits the types of flowers you can use and where you can display them, but something of this size can be enjoyed in many settings.

On the other hand, while small containers may seem manageable, single-stem vessels are actually not ideal for practice. They're designed to look good with just one flower, which makes them too easy. A container of moderate size allows you to work with several types of flowers and practice anchoring and balancing them. I think the containers by Koie really come alive in a subdued space. Even without flowers, containers like this have a strong presence as an object, so I keep them out where I can see them rather than putting them away.

If your home has a more Western style, a white porcelain piece, such as the Taizo Kuroda one shown on page 17, might be a good option. Try finding a vessel that suits your own space.

Of course, if you can get your hands on old pottery, even better. I especially recommend smaller ceramic vessels with chipped rims. Somehow, chipped rims make flowers easier to arrange—I can't explain why, but it's true. Japanese people tend to appreciate the beauty of imperfection, and such pieces also tend to be more affordable. Old earthenware flower containers have a certain depth—a groundedness that connects them to the earth—and they're wonderful for arranging flowers.

For instance, I placed the Yunnan magnolia in an old Shigaraki ware vessel (see page 25), and it just felt right. The vessel isn't chipped, but it does have a repaired crack. The visual texture of the repair and the earthy quality unique to Shigaraki ware are both beautiful. What suits a flower may come down to intuition, but in the case of the Yunnan magnolia, I felt that an old Shigaraki or Iga ware piece was best.

Let me share one more story—about the bamboo container from the Raku Museum (page 32). This was given to us by the Raku family in Kyoto, who are close to Hiroshi Toda. The sheen on the bamboo shows signs of regular use, though it isn't actually very old. Until recently, it was used at the Raku Museum.

Each year at the start of the new year, the museum places a freshly cut bamboo container at its entrance, and for the entire year they continue to arrange seasonal flowers in it. I've heard that they change the water daily, wipe the bamboo with a cloth each time they arrange flowers, and polish it with the natural oils of their hands. At year's end, they replace it with a new piece, and one of the used containers was kindly given to us.

Even a new container, if used with care over time, can become a flower vessel full of character. The deep relationship between person and vessel, built through time spent together, manifests visibly in its form.

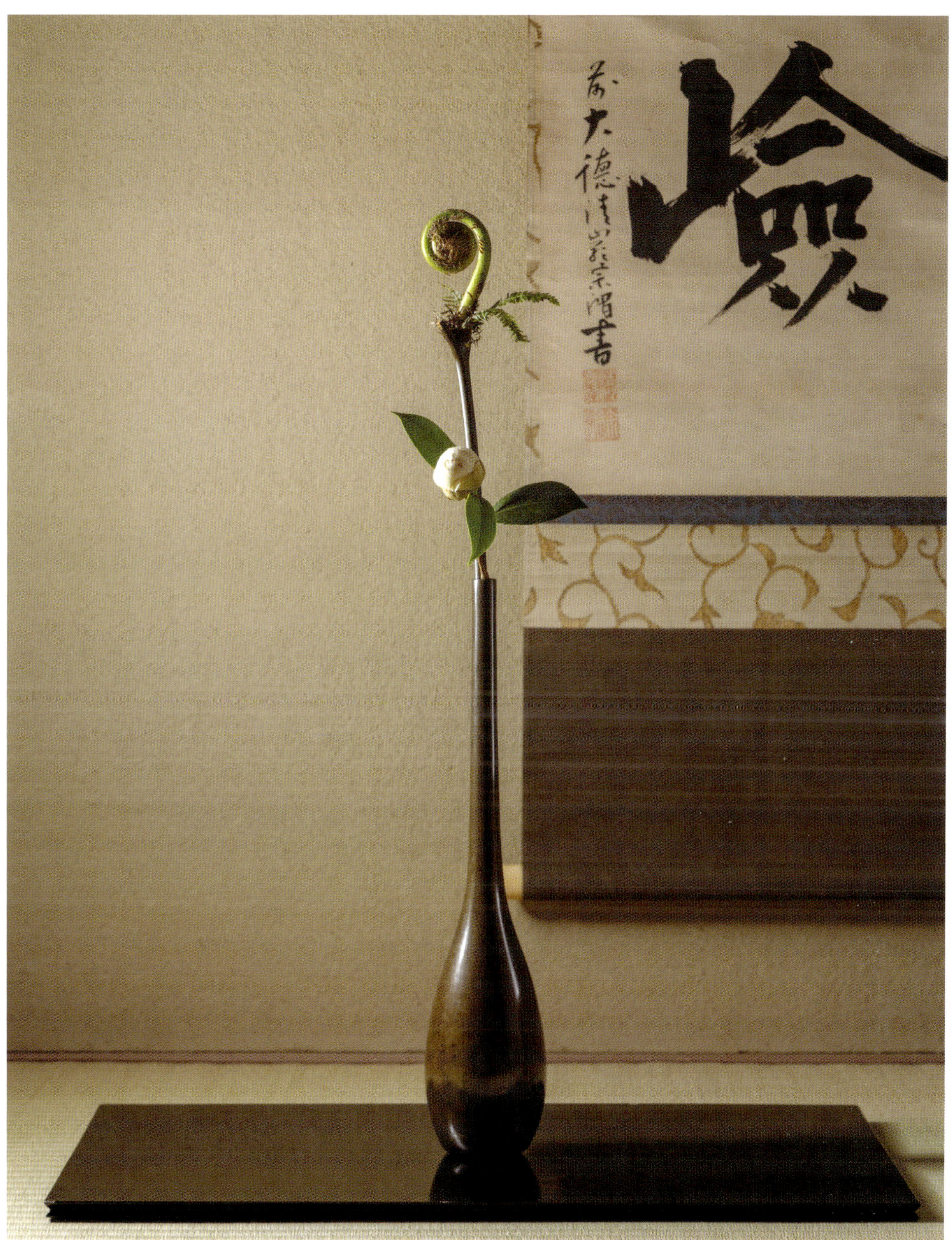

White camellia and young fronds of urajiro fern in a sand-cast bronze container with a peach-shaped base, China, Southern Song or Yuan dynasty.

A classical *karamono* (Chinese-style) flower container arranged with camellia, in an alcove with a calligraphy piece by Zen monk Seigan Soi (a contemporary of Sen Sotan, grandson of Sen no Rikyu). While camellias are often paired with woody materials, here they are accompanied by charming young fronds of urajiro fern.

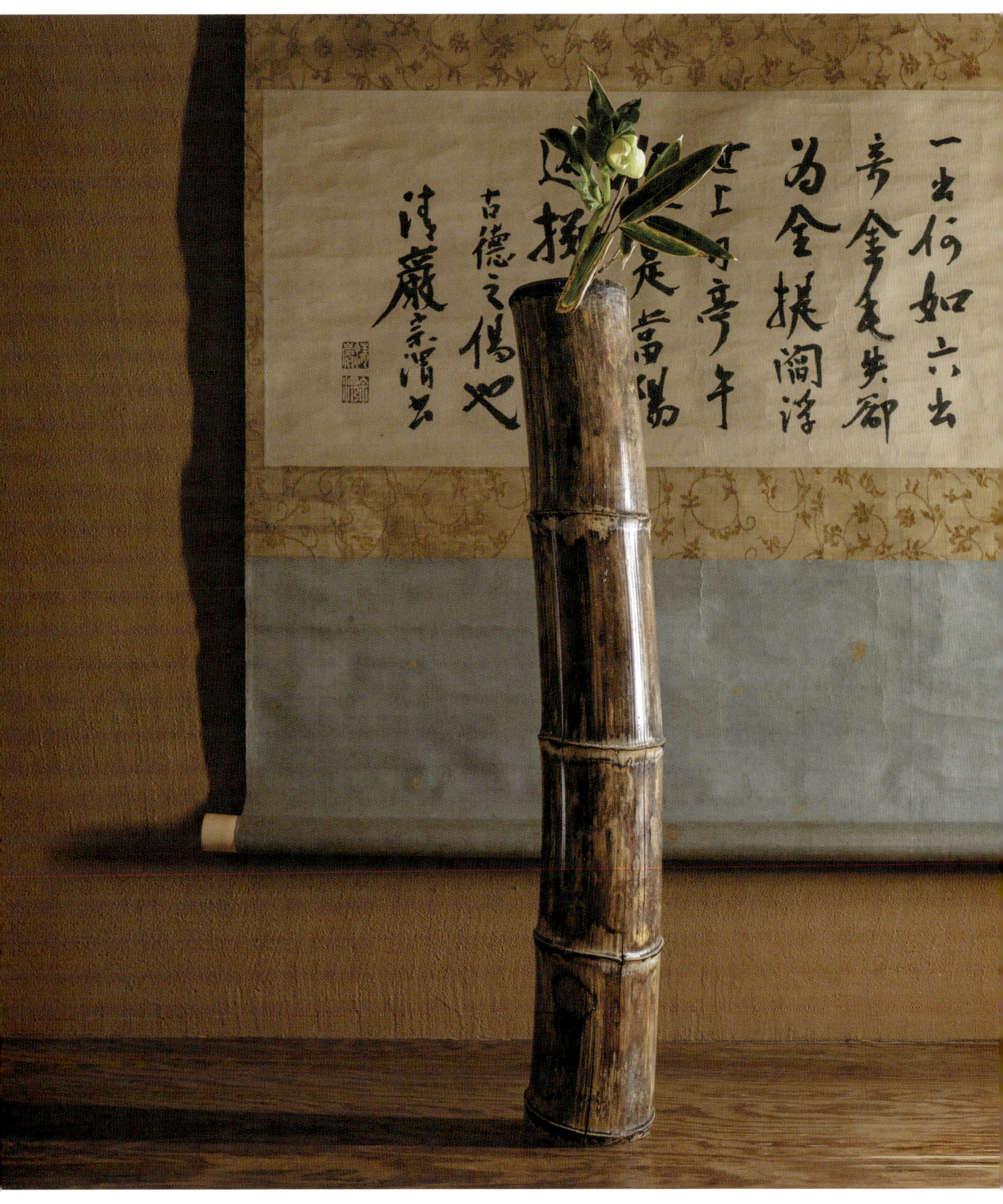

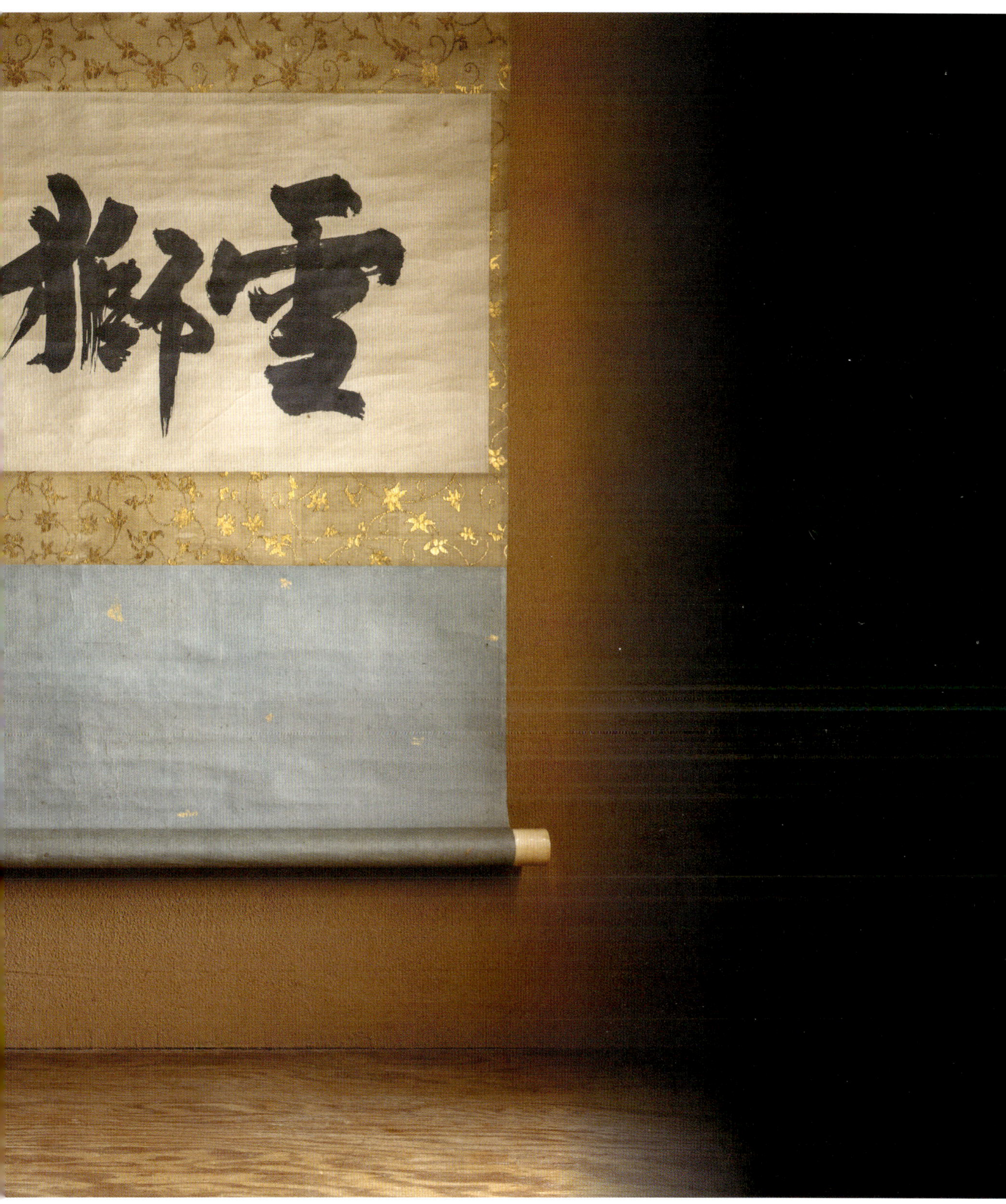

**Hellebore and Kuma bamboo grass.
Bamboo flower container by Jikinyu Raku.**

This alcove-style space has limited height. The calligraphic hanging scroll is *Yuki Jishi* (Snow lion) by Seigan Soi. In a formal alcove, a horizontal scroll and flower container would never be arranged in this positional relationship, but here, the balance between the calligraphy and the flowers was considered carefully. A tall bamboo flower container, about 31 inches (80 cm) high, was used to suit the proportions of the space.

Reflections on the Ceramic Artist Jikinyu Raku

Both the Raku and Toda families have long been involved in the world of tea, so I imagine there has always been some kind of connection between our two households. However, my personal relationship with Jikinyu Raku—fifteenth-generation head of the Raku family—began when he came to Tanimatsuya Toda Shoten to borrow tea utensils for his solo exhibition *Tenmon* at the Kikuchi Kanjitsu Memorial Tomo Museum in Tokyo in 1990. He had come to see my father, but that was the first time I spoke with him in depth. I remember how happy I was to discover that a ceramic artist with such presence and originality existed.

Afterward, I visited the Raku house to deliver the utensils, and over time we began to see each other more frequently. By chance, we happen to be the same age. Although our roles have been different, both of us are engaged in work that involves confronting beauty, and when we first got to know each other, we made an intuitive connection. I think he, too, felt he had never met someone quite like me within the world of tea, and that made our conversations enjoyable for him as well.

I was especially impressed to learn that he had studied sculpture at Tokyo University of the Arts. Being trained as a sculptor, his skill in sketching and figure drawing is truly outstanding. He has a remarkable sense of intuition, but it's balanced by a strong analytical side as well. He places great value on words, often giving his powerful works titles inspired by classical Chinese literature and philosophy. These inscriptions deepen and expand the world his ceramics evoke—and he seems to genuinely enjoy that process.

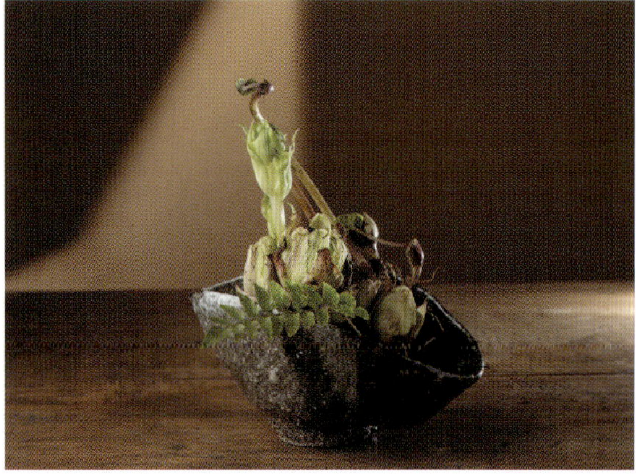

 Butterbur buds and fern. Flower vessel made with clay from Yakushiji Temple, by Jikinyu Raku.

A vessel made from clay taken from the grounds of Yakushiji Temple in Nara, repurposed here as a flower container. Created through the same process as Raku tea bowls, it is small, but it radiates a strong presence. This early spring arrangement features freshly sprouting butterbur buds and fern.

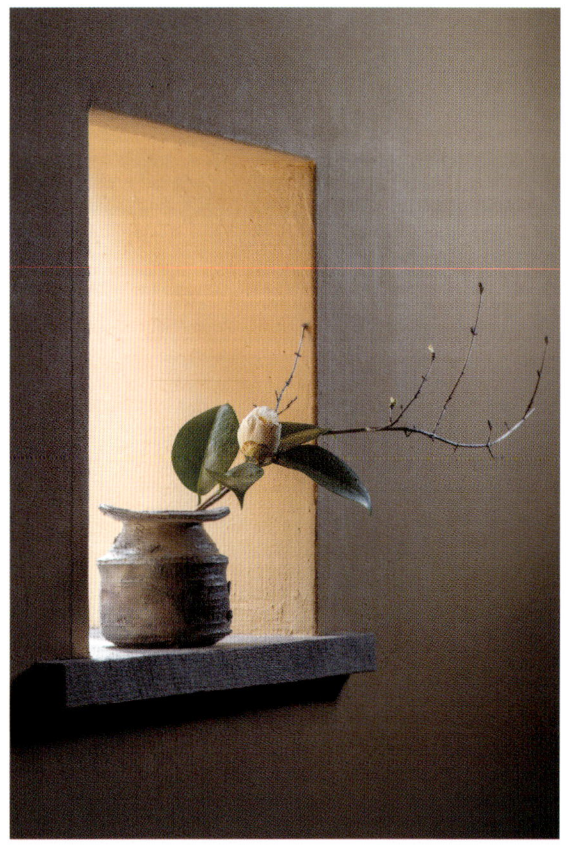

 Kamo-honnami camellia and *uguisu-kagura* (Lonicera gracilipes), a spring-blooming honeysuckle native to Japan. Flower vessel by Jikinyu Raku.

A work from Jikinyu Raku's younger years. This small vessel was crafted with a distinctive flat-rimmed opening, giving a unique character. The Kamo-honnami camellia has relatively large buds and leaves compared to other camellias.

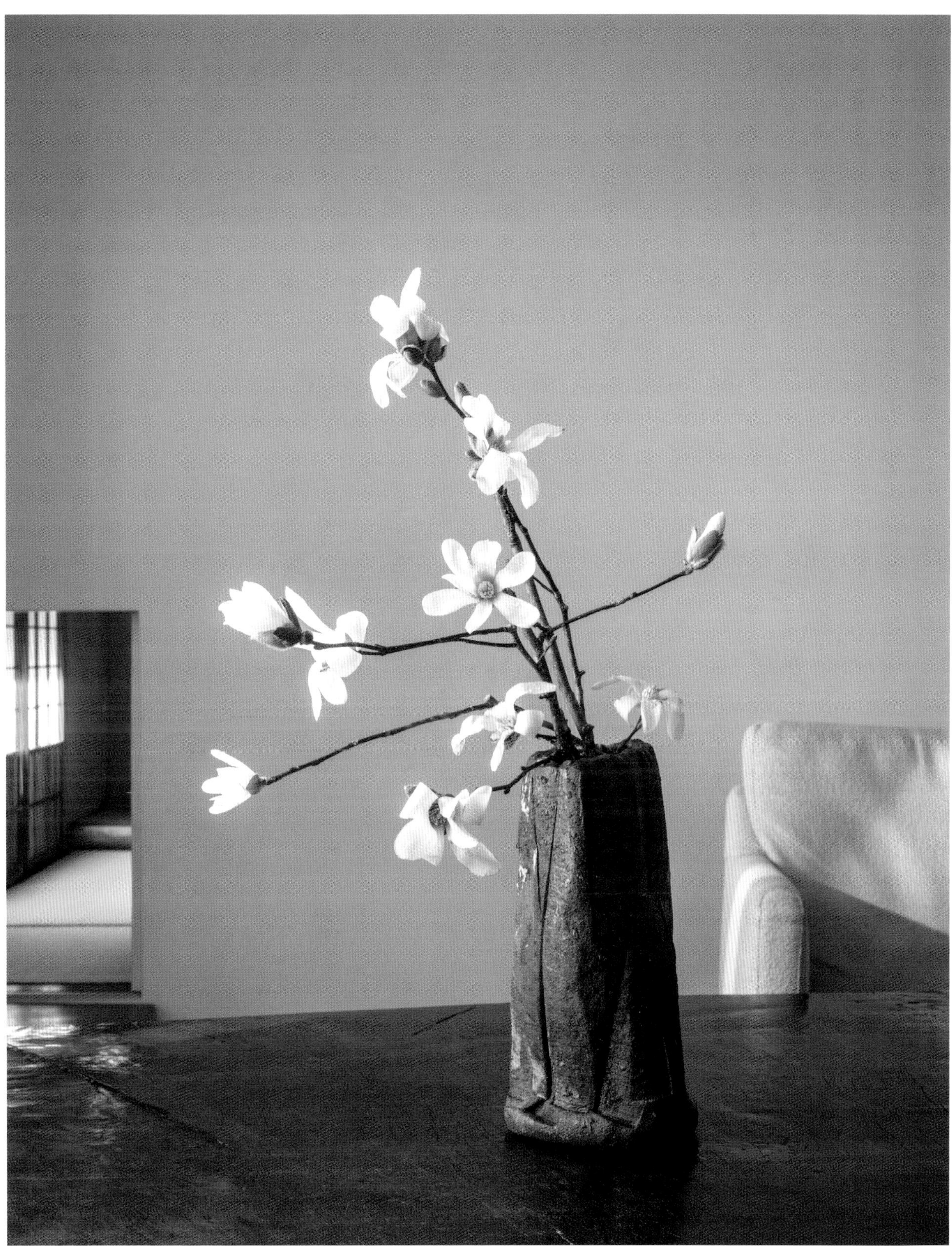

Magnolia kobus. Flower vessel by Jikinyu Raku, made with clay from Loubignac, France.

One of the works created over several years at the studio of French ceramic artist Andoche Praudel, in the south of France. This style is often referred to as "French Raku." It represents Jikinyu Raku's free and expressive approach — honoring the traditions of the Raku family while continually exploring avant-garde forms.

Buds Holding the Breath of Life

White Camellia

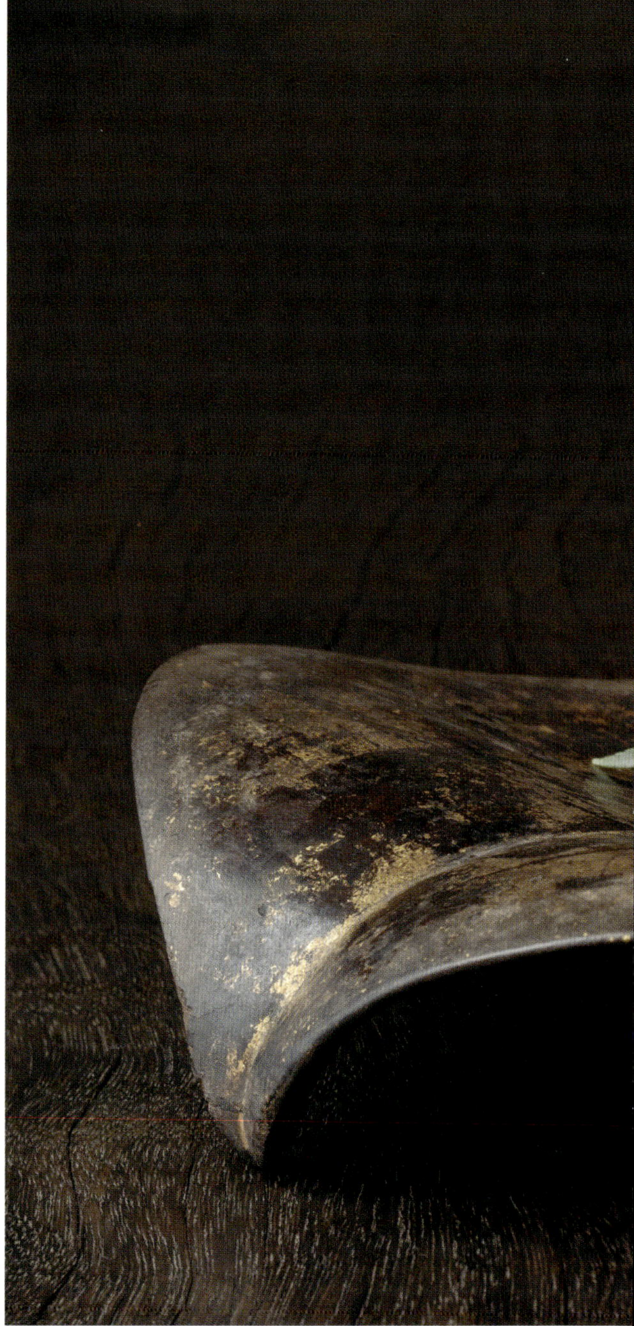

This month, I've used a lotus petal that was once part of a Buddhist sculpture from the Asuka period (538–710) as a flower container. Some flower containers used in the tea room—bamboo vases, for example—were originally made to hold flowers, but others, like this lotus petal, are objects that have been reimagined as vessels for flowers. When bringing items into the tea room for purposes other than they were originally intended for, I think the guiding principle is whether they are "objects you never tire of looking at." A tea-flower container is not just for holding flowers—it must also have a compelling presence of its own.

This doesn't apply only to flower containers, but to all tea utensils. That's because the Way of Tea is, by nature, about building a singular world, shaped by the practitioner's own aesthetic sensibility.

This lotus petal is, in a sense, the ultimate example of reimagining an object. It was originally part of an artwork—and more than that, it was actually part of a sacred Buddhist statue. It has a divine presence, and when you look at it, it naturally makes you bow your head and say, "How beautiful." Even without any flowers, this fragment of a statue radiates powerful presence. And yet, to use it as a flower container—that's what truly sends a shiver down the spine.

There are many ways of reimagining objects, and usually a flower vessel is expected to hold water. But this lotus petal cannot even do that. In that sense, it brings us back to the Japanese concept of *mitate*—the act of imaginative reinterpretation. And yet, it doesn't feel forced or artificial. I hoped the flower would be arranged in a way that wasn't overdone, and Kobayashi quietly placed a single white camellia on it. The slightly weathered look of that simple, single-layered flower matched perfectly. It was beautiful.

The camellia is one of the most iconic flowers for the hearth season in the tea room. Its small, tightly closed buds form in the crisp, taut air of winter, and from that quiet form we can sense the vastness of nature and the stirring of life. In the tea room, the tea flower is the only living thing. And here, atop this ancient lotus petal, that life is shining.

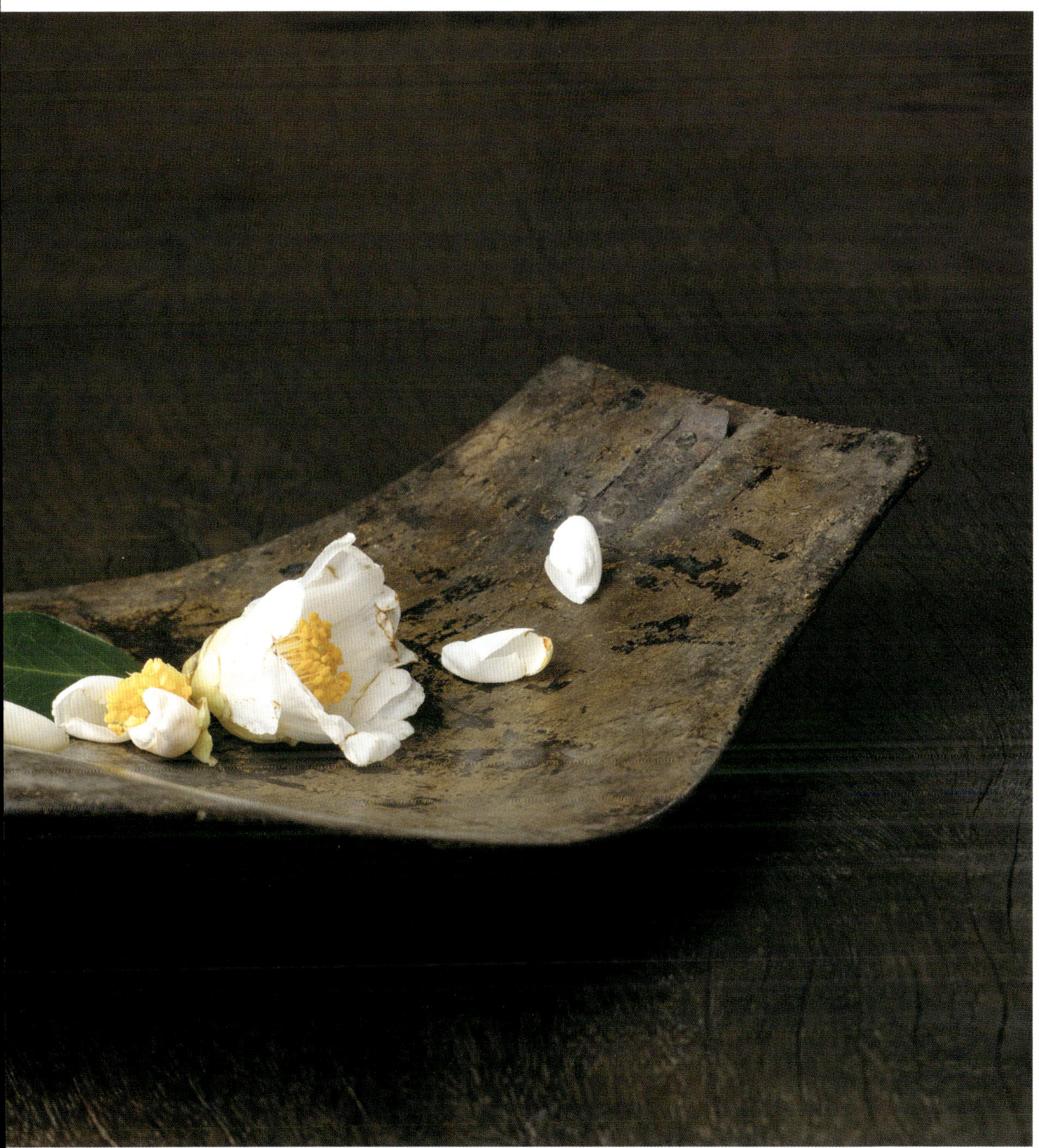

As this shows, flower containers do not have to be vessels originally made for that purpose. Some were reinterpreted as flower containers long ago; others have only recently been repurposed. Across time, people have always carried a flexible spirit. Something may not have been a flower container—but once someone placed a flower in it, or set it down in just the right place, it became beautiful. There's no logic behind it.

White camellia. Dry-lacquer lotus petal, reclaimed wood from Horyuji Temple, Asuka period.

A white camellia with petals damaged as if scorched — withered, yet still in bloom. Its fleeting form echoes the aged lotus petal on which it is displayed. The large lotus petal, once part of a grand Buddhist statue, retains traces of gold in one area, hinting at its former magnificence. "It's beauty is fragile," says Hiroshi.

Flowers and Utensils for March

Cutting Away, Cutting Away

Where do we draw the line between flowers enjoyed in daily life and those arranged for the tea room? Tea flowers may be guided by certain principles or conventions when arranged, but if we allow ourselves to be overly bound by those rules, the practice becomes lifeless. "Leaves must be an odd number"; "Only one flower should be used"; "Flowers must be in bud, not in bloom"—if we begin to approach tea flowers with these rigid preconceptions, the arrangements grow increasingly formal, the focus shifts entirely to outward form, and they lose their vitality.

This is no different from how the tea tradition itself can wither when formalism is prioritized over spirit. If there's no sense of depth or boldness within the larger system of tea—in its utensils, and in its spaces—then I fear the tradition will struggle to move forward. It's not healthy for tea to be made dull by the very conventions meant to support it.

And if we look at tea flowers not through the lens of formality, but through spirit, we sometimes fall into another trap—assuming that the tea room flower must be wholly separate from the everyday. But that kind of thinking is equally limiting. What's more compelling is when you can sense a person's intention to take hold of everyday life and formality—and then gently step beyond these boundaries. If you're only arranging flowers so no one will criticize you, never straying from convention, then what is the point of practicing tea at all?

I often think of Sen no Rikyu and the resolve he must have had when tea was still without fixed form, without prototype. He gave everything to create something new. Because of Rikyu, we all came to know what beauty beyond the everyday truly is. The idea that camellias in the tea room must only be in bud is nonsense. What matters more is the heart that can perceive beauty, that has the sensitivity to feel impermanence. If you wish to express something fading, something fleeting, then why shouldn't the flower be in full bloom?

When it comes to flower containers, too, it's not necessary to restrict yourself to those that have been made specifically for tea. What's more important is to choose a vessel you find beautiful. If it

Visualizing the Final Form Before Cutting

Before making any cuts, stand in front of the container and visualize the completed arrangement. This process, which is known as *hanazumori*, helps you determine which branches to keep and which to remove. For climbing or trailing materials like chocolate vine, gently coil the stems by hand as you assess which sections have the best shape and flow.

The key to deciding what to leave is asking yourself, "Which line do I want to emphasize?" As you imagine the balance between the branches, the container, and any accompanying materials, it becomes easier to see what's needed. If you start cutting without a clear sense of direction, it's easy to lose control of the composition. At this stage, it's important to picture the overall form you want to achieve.

Consider what kind of lines will bring the flowers to life in relation to the container. Running through that simulation in advance will make the next steps go much more smoothly.

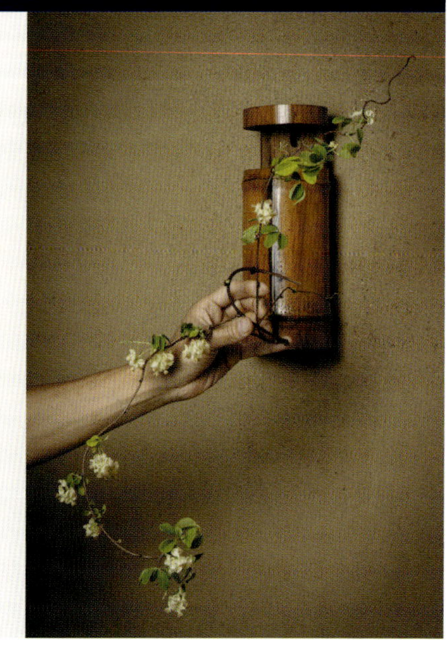

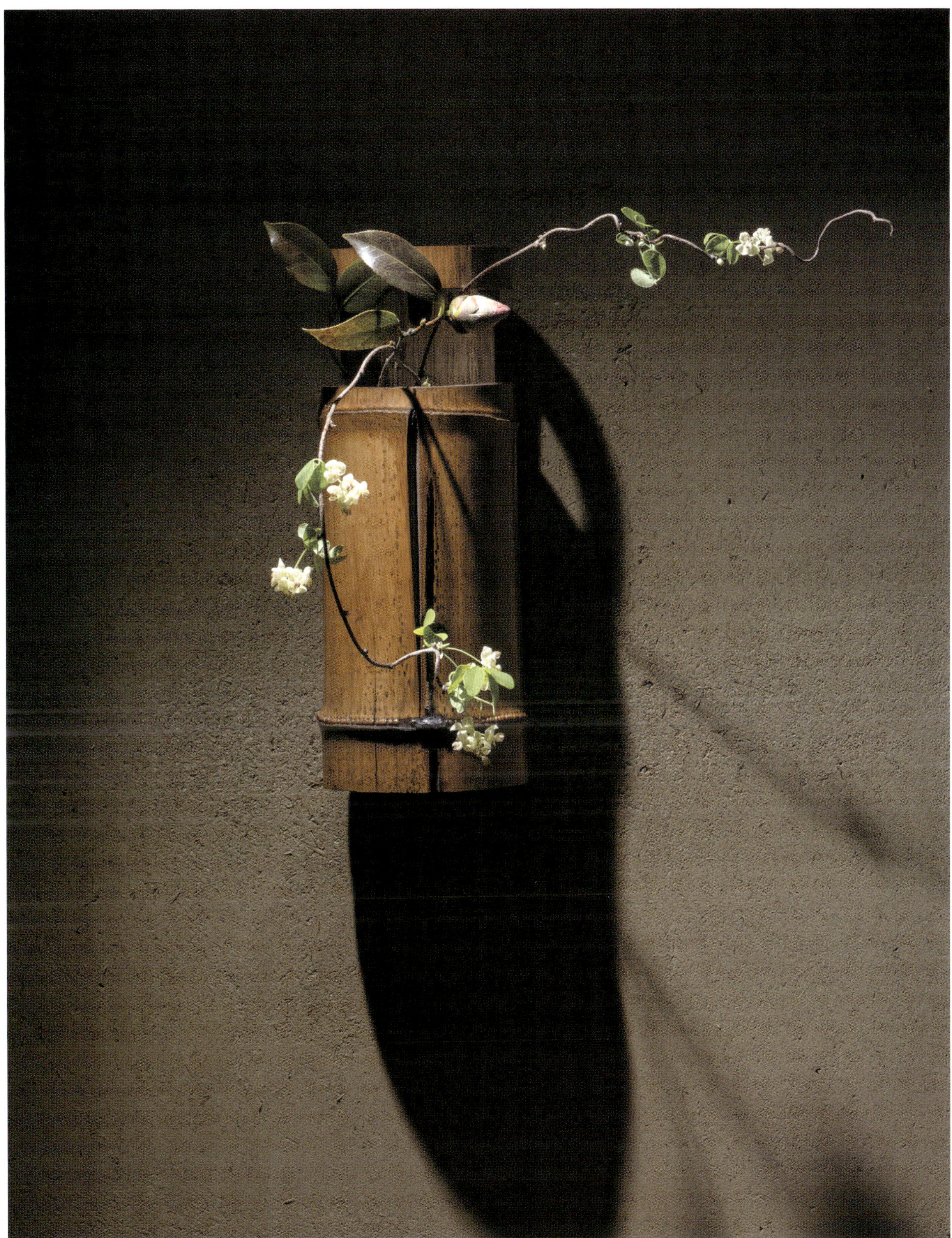

Camellia and chocolate vine. Single-node bamboo flower container, attributed to Katagiri Sekishu.

Place the chocolate vine in the container, step back, and observe the overall shape. Then identify branches to highlight and gradually remove any unnecessary flowers or leaves. The angle and direction of the camellia are also important. This single-node bamboo vase is a bold presence, attributed to daimyo Katagiri Sekishu, 17th-century tea practitioner.

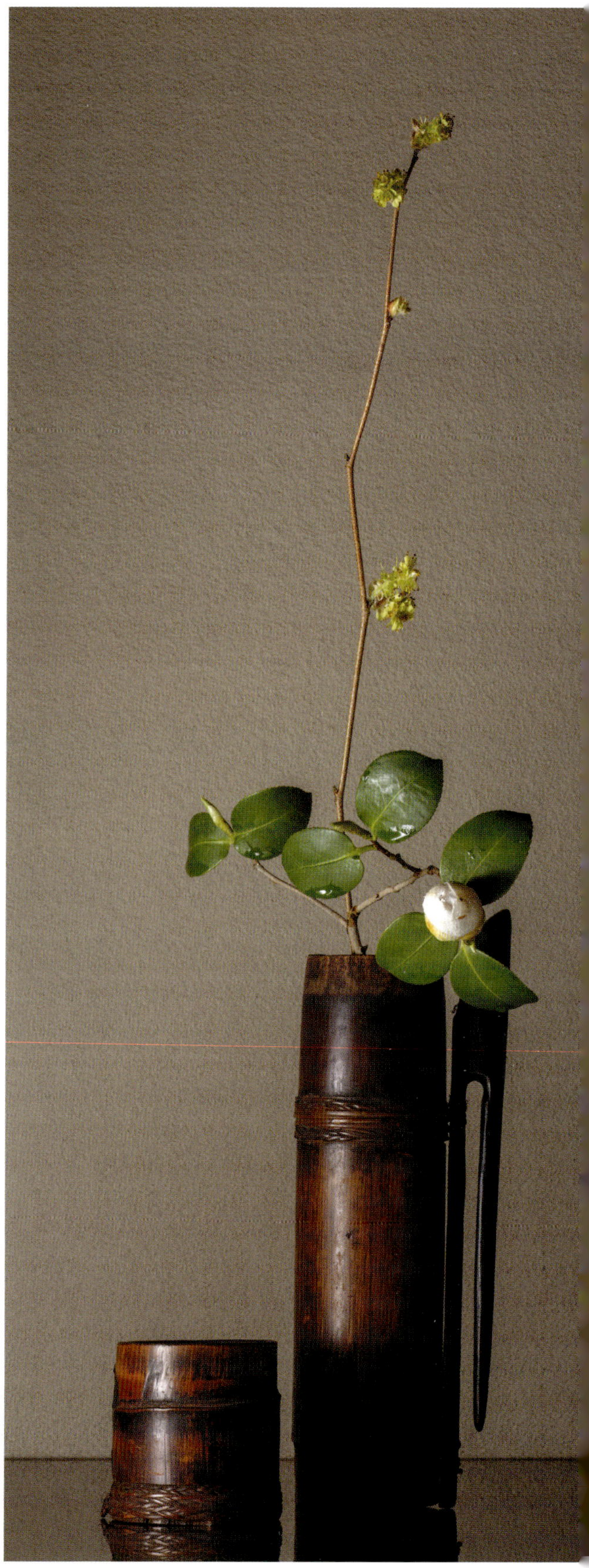

White camellia, spike winter hazel. Bamboo blow-pipe-case flower container, Borneo, Indonesia.

An example of two arrangements created with different spaces in mind. The arrangement on this page was designed for an everyday living space, while the one on page 41 was made with a small tea room in mind — paring down the materials to their absolute essence. It features the last remaining white camellia from the garden.

strikes you as beautiful, it doesn't matter whether it was originally a flower container or not. In the end, the Way of Tea is about the pursuit of beauty.

So what actually matters when arranging flowers in the tea room? I believe it comes down to the concept of subtraction. Not simply things like how many leaves to use or whether the flower is in bud—those are surface-level concerns. What's important is learning how to discern what to leave behind. Cutting away, cutting away, until something essential remains. This is not limited to tea; it's a view of the world deeply rooted in Zen.

When you're applying this to tea flowers, and when you've taken away enough, what's left might only be a bud or a handful of leaves. If you can't start from a state of subtraction, then try beginning with everything, and take away from there. Easier said than done, of course. Even removing a single leaf gives me pause, because you can't predict the outcome. But Atsushi Kobayashi's flowers show no waste. He was born with a natural talent for floral arrangements, and that instinct has been sharpened through experience in a wide range of situations. Watching him work, I'm amazed at how decisively and efficiently he snips away branches and leaves. And yet, the final arrangement—what ends up in the flower container—is always beautiful. When he looks at the materials, he already sees the final form in his mind, and cuts toward that vision. It's impressive to watch.

In this chapter for March, I've included an example where the same bamboo flower container is used to hold two different camellia arrangements— one for a domestic space (this page), and one for a tea room (facing page). When I look at the flowers on their own, I think either could hold up as an arrangement for a tea room. But in the version

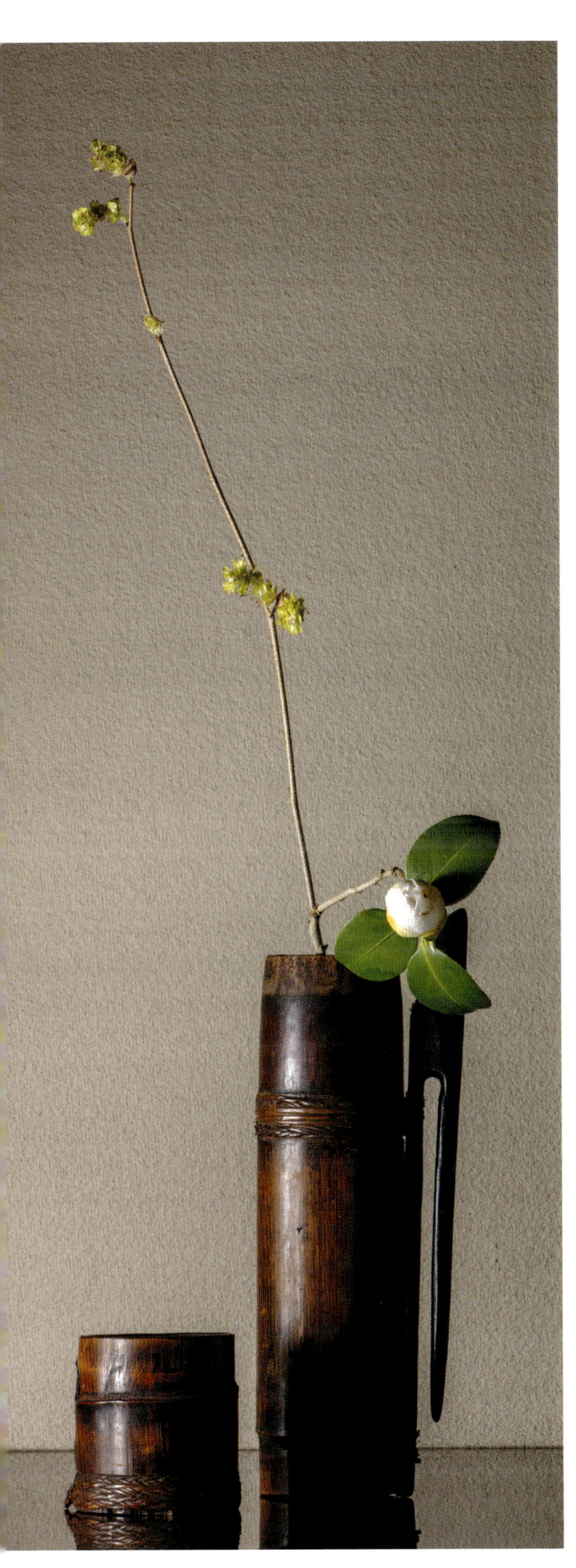

How the Same Flowers and Container Can Change with the Space

Using the same floral materials and the same container, what changes when the surrounding space changes? In a small tea room, where the space is tight and every element must balance with the utensils, the floral materials are reduced to their bare essentials to achieve a more impactful expression. When too many elements are included, the arrangement loses its sense of tension. Just like a hanging scroll, a tea flower must carry a refined intensity. In contrast, flowers placed in everyday living spaces are not about creating a momentary impact, but about whether they can be present for a long time without becoming tiring to look at. That's one of the major differences between tea flowers and those meant for daily life. Even when working with the same materials, being conscious of the space where the flowers will be placed reveals entirely new perspectives.

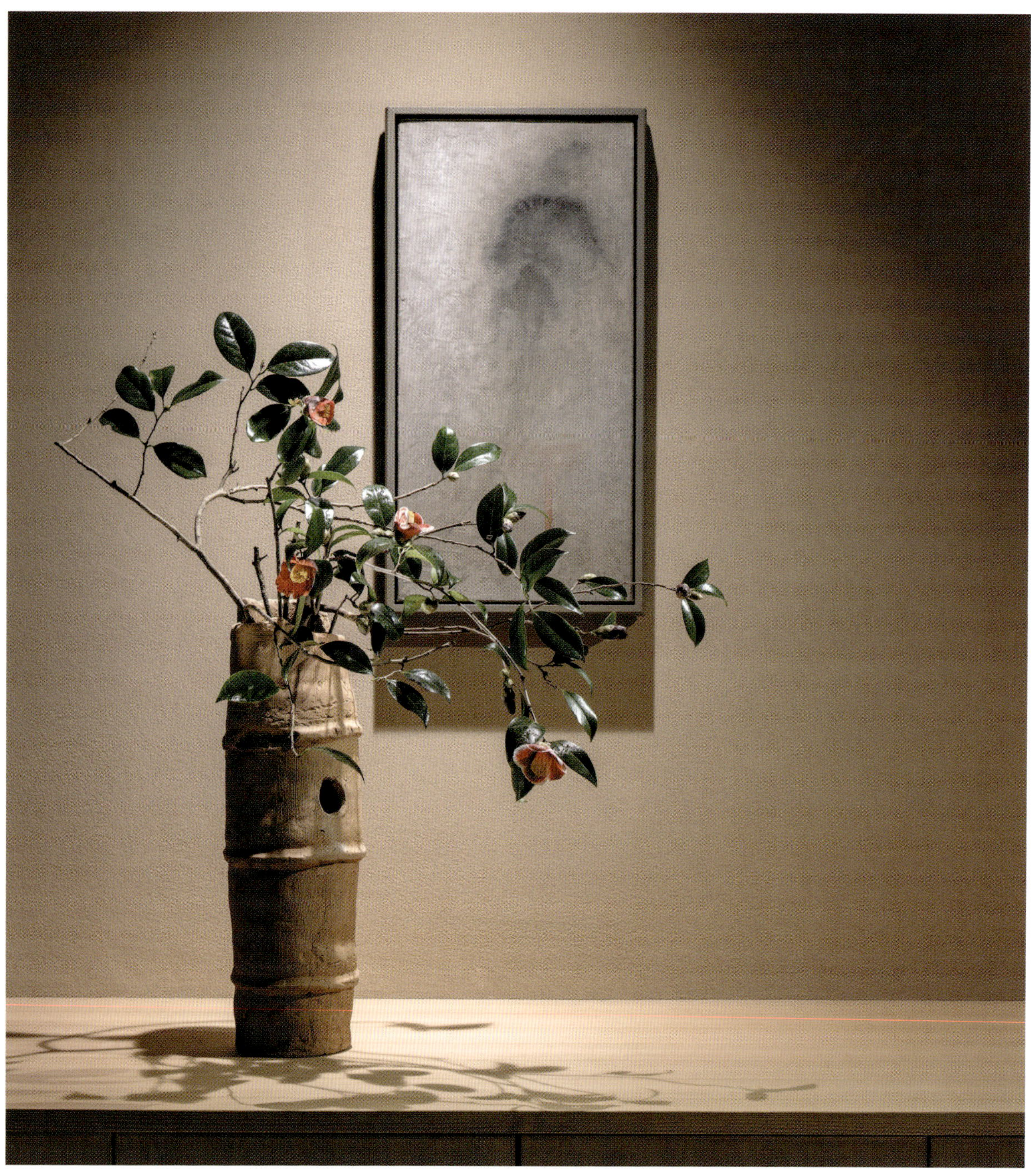

that Kobayashi intended for the tea room, I can feel a fierce determination—like he's pushing right to the edge. Of course, even within the category of "tea room," the size of the space or the choice of utensils will affect the flower's form, so you really have to be in the actual space to make a final judgment.

In fact, in most cases, people would probably stop at the earlier version on page 40. Even that one has been thoroughly refined.

Wild camellia, Tamanoura camellia and black camellia. Yayoi-period earthenware.

An arrangement of camellias for an everyday living space. Three varieties are used: deep red wild camellia, Tamanoura camellia with white-edged petals, and a dark-toned black camellia, all placed in a cylindrical Yayoi-period vessel. On the wall hangs the painting *Hisomu* (Hidden) by Takayoshi Sakabe.

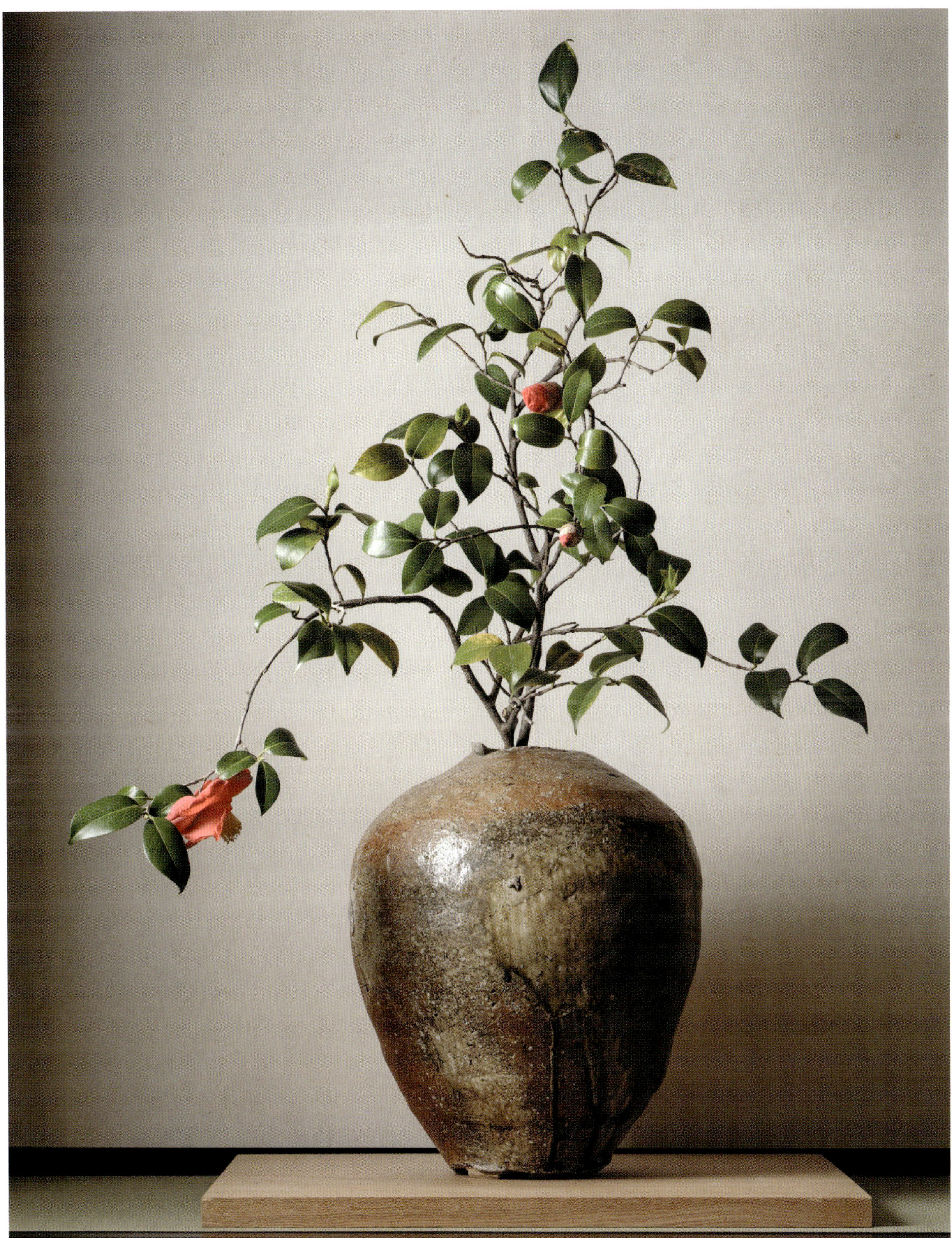

Akashigata camellia. Large Shigaraki ware flower container, Muromachi period.

On a single camellia branch, one bud, one half-open blossom, and one spent flower have been left. Originally, it was a large branch with three to four times as many leaves as the final arrangement. Each branch and leaf were carefully trimmed so the flowers would stand out.

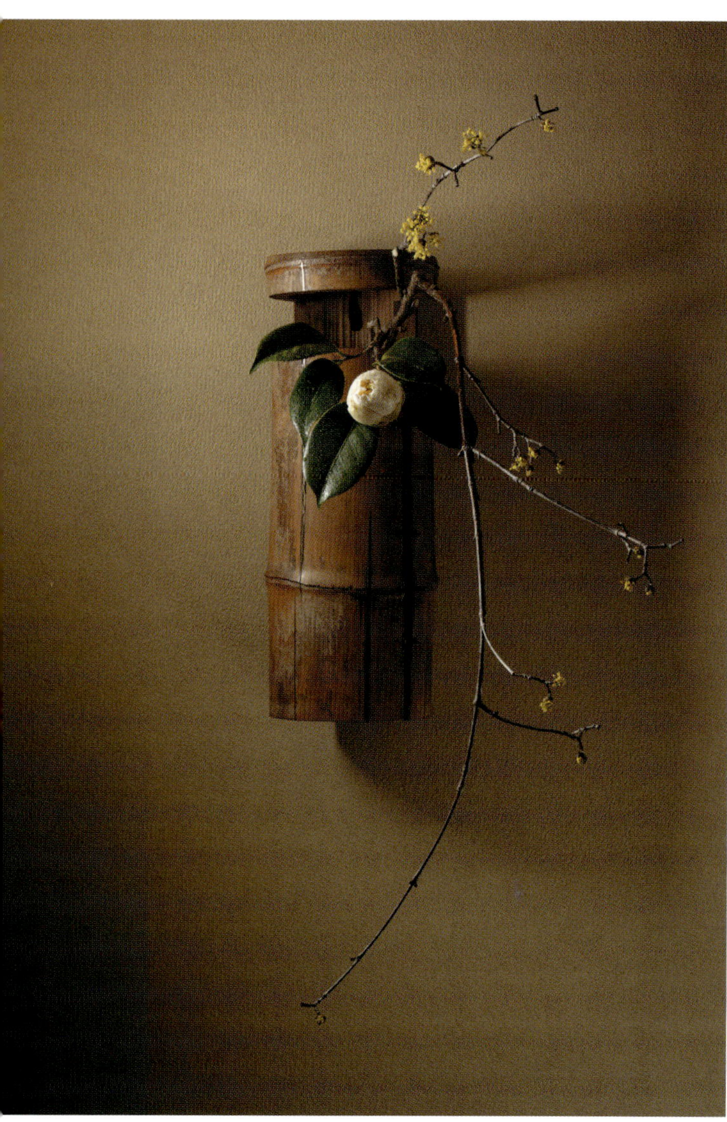

A camellia arrangement for the tea room. A single camellia bud is paired with Japanese cornel branches in a bamboo container attributed to Kanamori Sowa. Though composed of only minimal elements, the flowing line of the cornel gives the piece a strong presence. The gently opening white bud of the Kamo-honnami camellia also makes a striking impression.

A bold and expansive arrangement featuring three distinct types of branches, set in a powerful vessel over three feet (one meter) wide. The arrangement is centered around the thick, dominant branch of edgeworthia, which is paired with early spiketail and witch hazel to evoke the feeling of stepping into the mountains at the beginning of spring.

Using the Branches Themselves as a Flower Holder

In cases like the arrangement on the facing page, where the container has a wide, shallow opening, the bases of the branches remain visible to the viewer. For that reason, artificial flower holders are best avoided. However, when using tall, substantial branches in a shallow vessel, the stems must be securely fixed, otherwise they'll fall over. To solve this, I cross two pieces of branch into an X shape and anchor that X shape below the rim of the vessel to act as a flower holder. Alongside these crossed branches, smaller twigs are also left in place to help hold the stems being added. By combining the crossed branches with the individual branches of the floral materials themselves to balance the forces, I achieve a more stable arrangement.

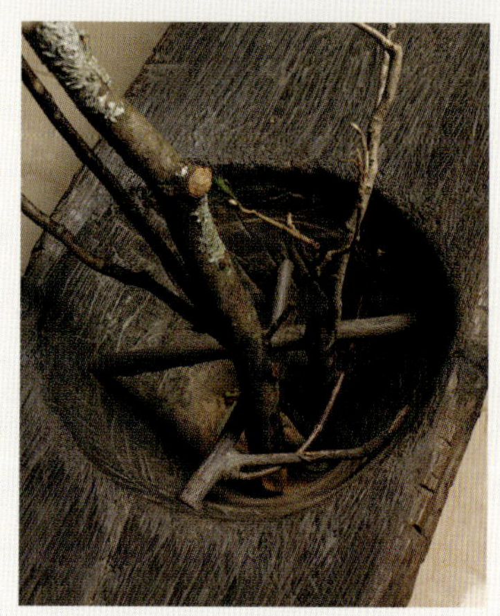

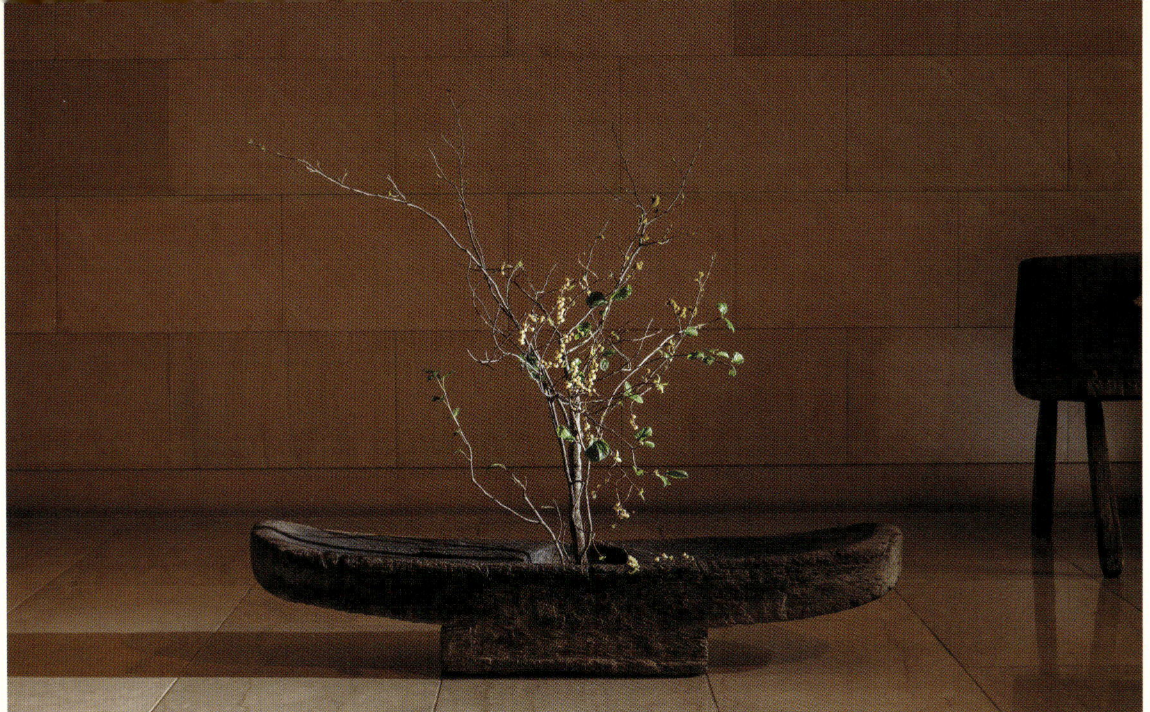

Choosing the Vessel, Sensing the Space

— Atsushi Kobayashi

Flower containers have many different origins. The lotus petal container on pages 36–37 was once part of a Buddhist statue—a sacred object of worship. I believe that objects with such sanctity are meant to be brought out only for special occasions, not for everyday use. When it comes to ceramics, earthenware feels familiar and well-suited to daily life, but something like Chinese celadon holds a more special status. Tea utensils are items that have been handed down and cherished for generations, and in their essence, they carry that weight. To have in my hands something once used by tea masters of the past and to use it in a tea gathering is no ordinary act. It must be treated with genuine reverence— and I want to bring that same feeling into how I arrange flowers.

On the other hand, for everyday flowers, I often use old vessels from Indonesia. An earthen jar, a wooden container, a basket—each has its own charm. Their primitive, organic forms create a natural connection to the materials, whether branches or wildflowers. Many of these vessels were originally part of everyday life, which is likely why they feel so approachable.

As for the plant materials I use overall, they are almost entirely Japanese—wildflowers and plants you might find in the hills and fields of Japan, rather than what are commonly considered Western flowers. There's something about the fleeting beauty of Japanese flora that pairs well with Indonesian objects.

For example, I arranged a flower in an old Indonesian bamboo blowpipe case to be placed in a living space (page 40). From there, by paring the arrangement down to its minimum elements, it can easily be adapted to a tea setting as well (page 41). Even if something was originally made for daily use, if it's old, it carries the presence of time and history. Placing flowers in such a vessel brings added depth. In a simple earthen vessel, I placed a single white camellia (page 47). The old piece quietly received the energy of the just-blooming flower, and I think the result had a gentle lightness overall.

In this way, even if a container wasn't originally intended to hold flowers, it's deeply enjoyable to seek out the right vessel with your own eyes. That lotus petal I mentioned earlier wasn't made to hold flowers either, but by thinking about what role it once played, or what kind of space it was placed in, you naturally start to imagine the kind of setting in which it might now be appropriately reinterpreted. The ideal is a relationship where both the flower and the vessel bring out the best in each other.

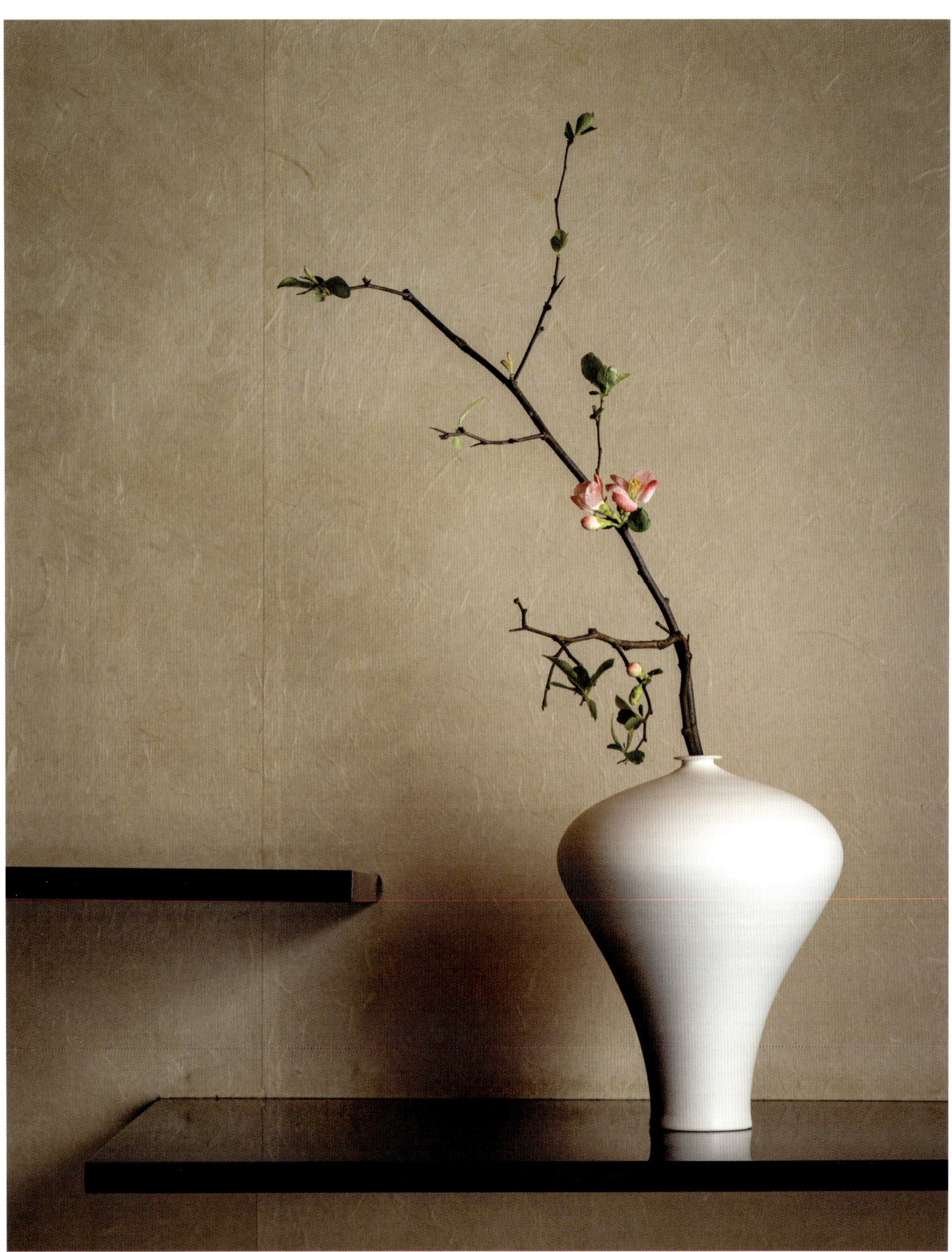

Japanese quince. White porcelain flower container by Taizo Kuroda (see page 154).

One quince branch is placed in a white porcelain flower container, on a tiered shelf in the tea room. The vessel's rounded, tapering form counterbalance the stark strength of the branch, allowing flower and vessel to enhance each other's beauty. The small opening naturally functions as a flower holder, offering both support and stability for the arrangement.

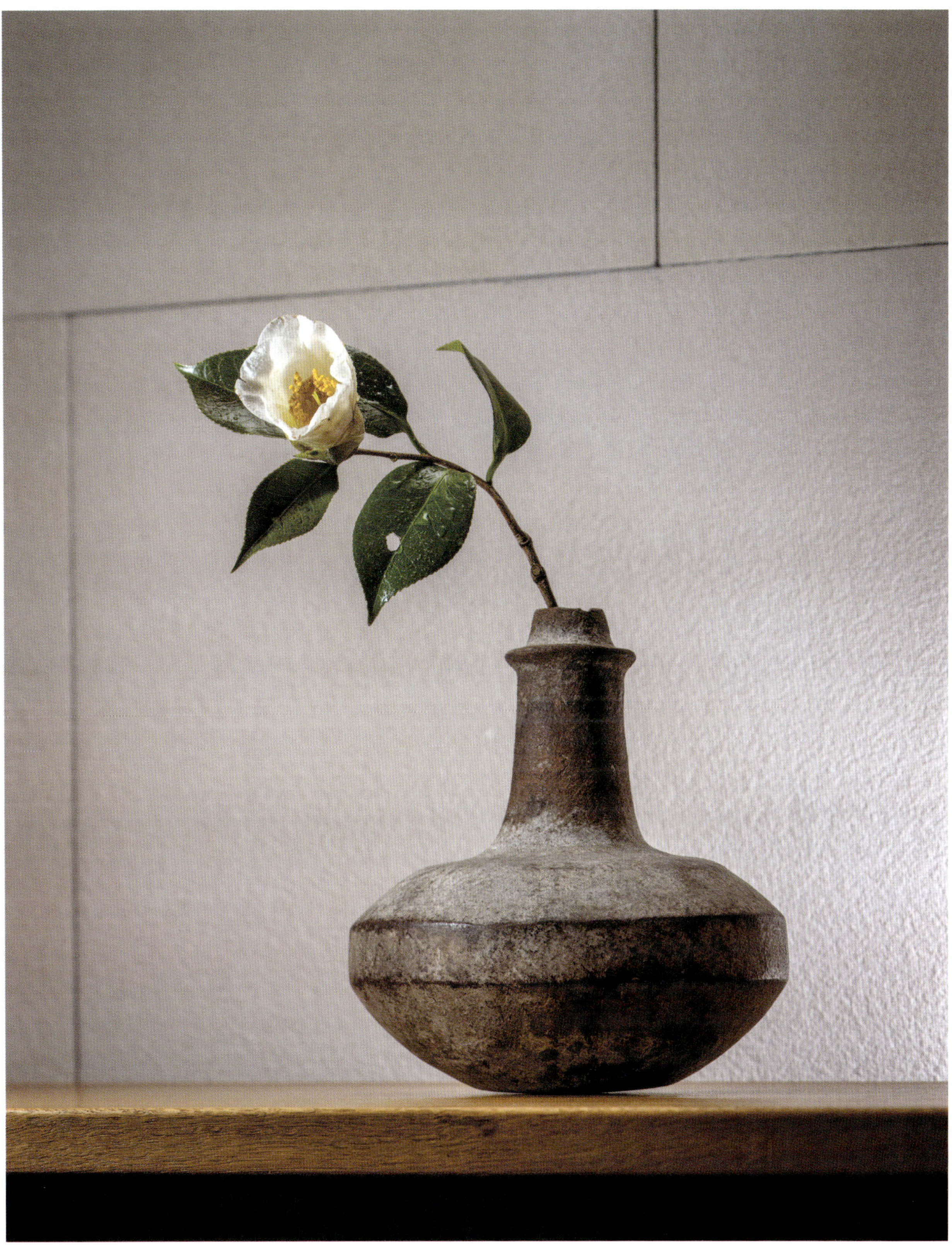

Kaga Hassaku camellia. Earthenware vessel, Borneo, Indonesia.

Which vessel best suits this camellia? And what kind of flower would suit this vessel?
By regularly looking over the containers you have on hand and running through such simulations in your mind, when the moment comes and the flower you want to use is before you, you can place it without hesitation.

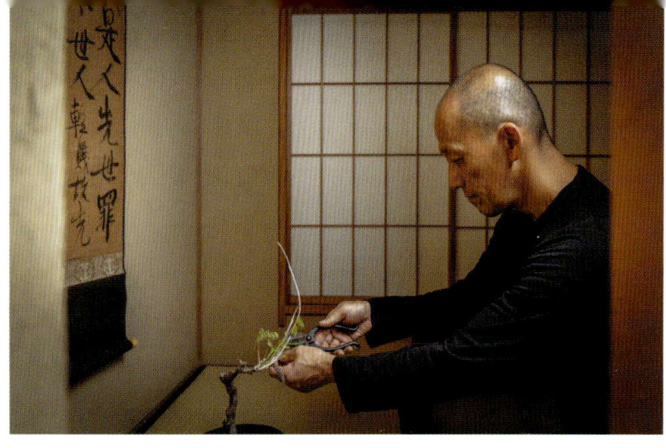

A wisteria branch with an intriguing natural form in an antique bronze *usubata* flower container. To bring out the energy and movement held within the flower just before it blooms, all unnecessary branches and leaves are pared away to the bare minimum.

As the Winter Hearth Season Ends

Wisteria

In the Way of Tea, the year traditionally has two main seasons: the *ro* sunken-hearth season, and the *furo* portable-brazier season. The furo was once used year-round, but since Sen no Rikyu formalized the use of the ro, it has come to represent the heart of *wabicha*—an approach to tea ceremony that places importance on the spiritual aesthetic. April is the final month of the ro season—a transitional moment just before the shift to furo. I've always liked this time of year. There's something unique about tea gatherings held on the cusp of change.

April is the start of the fiscal and school year in Japan—a season of endings and beginnings. For this occasion, I chose a powerful three-line calligraphy artwork by Ikkyu Sojun for the hanging scroll and paired it with an antique bronze container with a dragon motif around its body. It's not unusual to choose the hanging scroll first, followed by the container, and lastly the flower. I chose *fukuro* wisteria buds (the Japanese name refers to the bag-like shape of the buds) to match the character of the utensils. It's rare to see wisteria used during the ro season, but this particular branch had an elegant, commanding form.

The setting was imagined for an *usucha* thin-tea gathering in a large room, though the weight and presence of the utensils gave it the quiet gravity of a *koicha* thick-tea gathering. The result was a deeply satisfying expression of the season—one that quietly honors the closing days of the ro hearth season.

Upright Placement of a Thick Branch

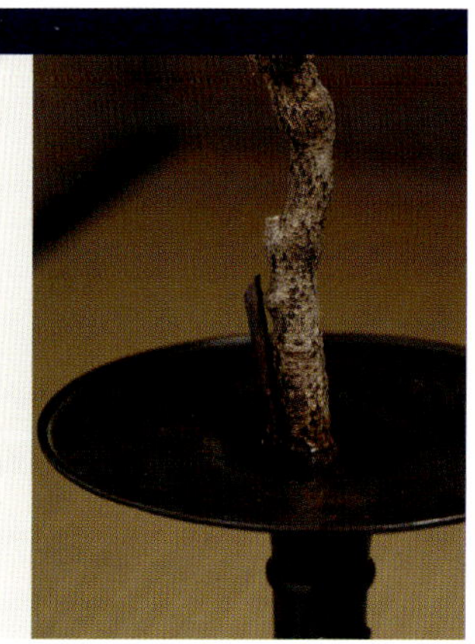

When using a flower container such as an antique bronze *usubata*, where the base of the flower is fully visible, one key point is how cleanly you can present the area where the branch meets the water. To arrange a thick, striking wisteria branch upright on its own, one technique is to place a support branch behind it. A single wisteria stem tends to tip forward on its own, but by fitting another branch snugly behind it like a wedge, it stabilizes the arrangement and prevents wobbling. With this kind of vessel, the support branch will inevitably be visible, so the challenge lies in placing it in a way that feels natural and unobtrusive. That subtlety is part of the skill that goes into an arrangement like this.

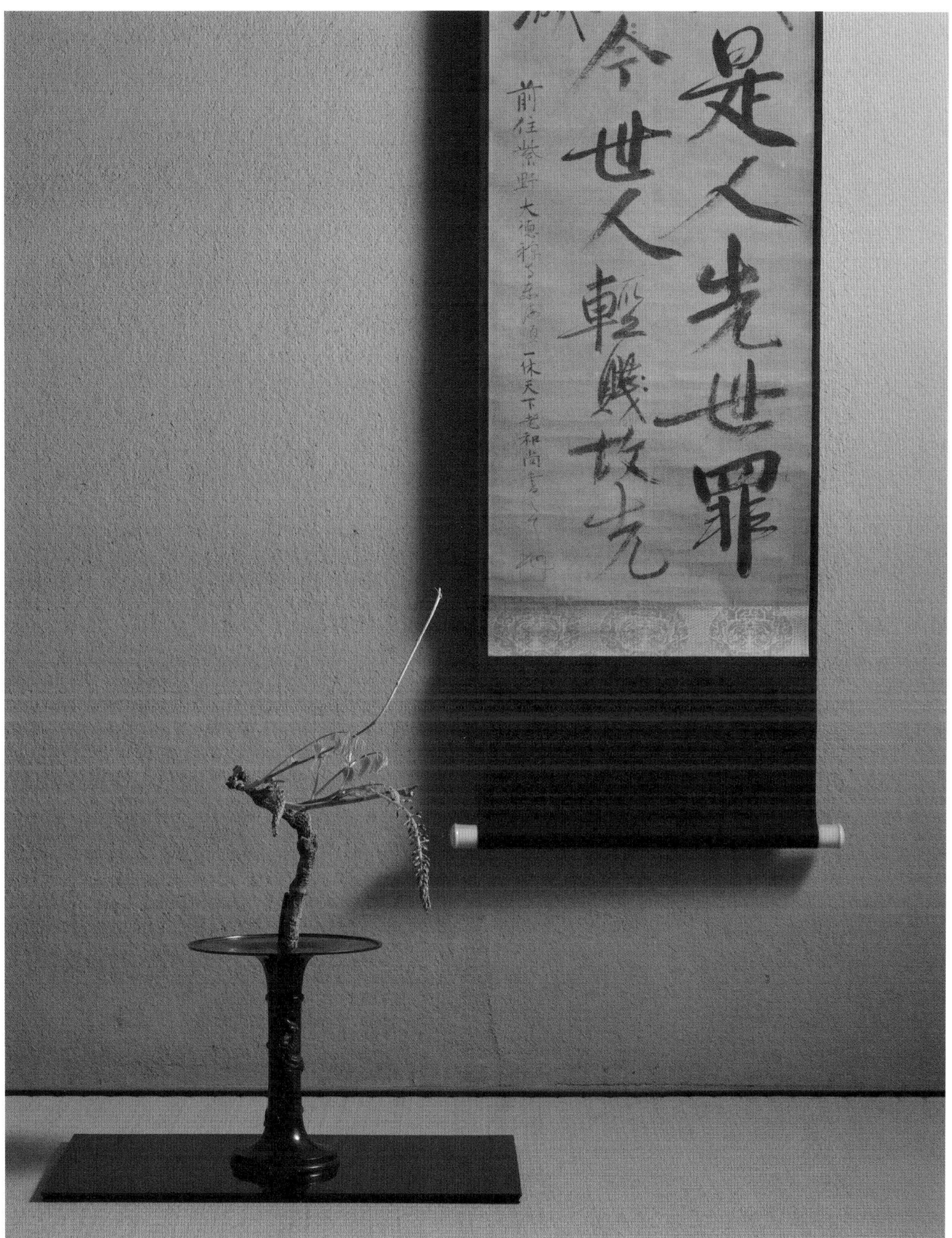

Wisteria. Bronze *usubata* flower container with coiled dragon design, China, Ming dynasty.

In the alcove of a large tea room, an antique bronze container is placed beneath a calligraphy piece by Ikkyu Sojun. It holds a single wisteria stem with firm, unopened buds. No other materials are used, highlighting the striking wisteria. Unopened *fukuro* wisteria is especially valued as a flower for the end of the *ro* winter hearth season.

Flowers and Utensils for April

The Bamboo Flower Container

While in March we saw the example of the bronze lotus petal, where the beauty of the object itself inspired its use as a flower container, there are also flower containers that were created specifically for use in the tea room. The most representative of these is the bamboo container. Said to have been devised by Sen no Rikyu, it seems to perfectly capture the essence of his approach to tea. Later, tea masters such as Furuta Oribe, Kobori Enshu and Katagiri Sekishu each came to treat the bamboo flower container as suitable for the tea setting.

I believe bamboo flower containers have continued to be used in tea not out of a sense of formality or tradition, but because tea practitioners in each era have understood Rikyu's intention and sought to carry that spirit forward. Personally, I love them without needing any explanation.

Take for example the double-cut (two-node) bamboo flower container on the facing page, which is attributed to seventeenth century tea master Kobori Enshu. Just looking at it, I am filled with wonder. First, there's the strength of its presence as an object in itself. The inscription on its storage box reads: "This flower container is by Soho (Kobori Enshu); it is listed in the *Enshu Kuracho*." The *Enshu Kuracho* was Enshu's own record of utensils he selected and held dear. If a piece was entered into that record, it meant he particularly favored it and kept it close at hand—it belonged to his personal aesthetic lineage.

There is a crack along the body of the container, which has been repaired with metal staples. In everyday life, a crack would be seen as a flaw, but in the world of tea, flaws such as these can be transformed into a kind of value. The tea aesthetic embraces what is broken, chipped or incomplete—absorbing those imperfections and allowing them to become part of one's expression. I think that's what makes flower arranging so compelling: the way those elements interact with the flower itself

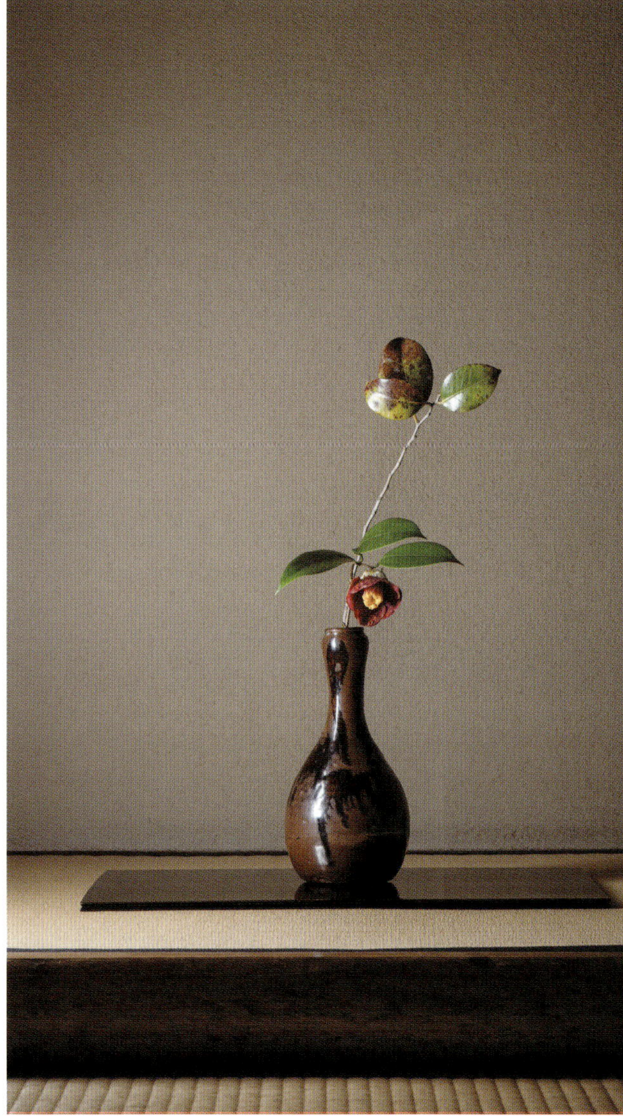

Eiraku camellia, and leaves from a different camellia variety. Seto ware wide-rimmed container, with the seal of Sen no Rikyu, Momoyama period.

The Eiraku camellia is a deep blackish color with a single layer of petals. Camellias are often arranged with a branch of woody material, but here, the visual interest of the leaves is used instead, with leaves from a different camellia variety added.

and transform the whole. I'm especially drawn to the way the addition of flowers can change the impression of a bamboo container. The combination of bamboo and flower communicates something beyond either alone. What it conveys to the viewer—or what the viewer perceives in it—is deeply moving and endlessly fascinating.

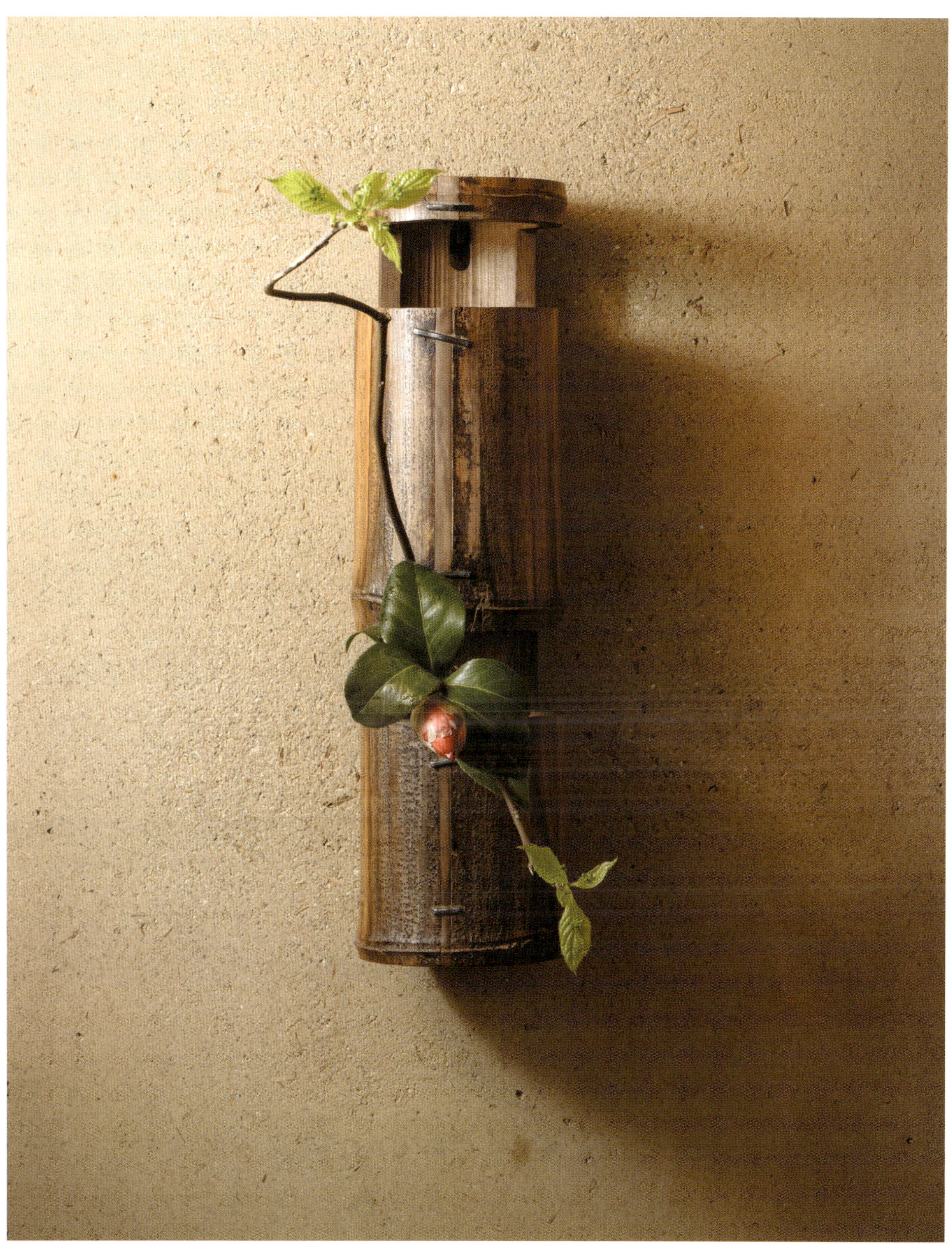

Iwamine-shibori camellia in a *hana-ikada* flower raft arrangement. Double-cut bamboo flower container, with the seal of Kobori Enshu.

This double-node weathered bamboo container bears the seal of 17th-century tea master Kobori Enshu, and is recorded in the *Enshu Kuracho* (Enshu's record of utensils). A metal staple repairs a split, suggesting the container has been treated with great care. The storage box bears an inscription by Sozui, 4th-generation head of the Enshu school.

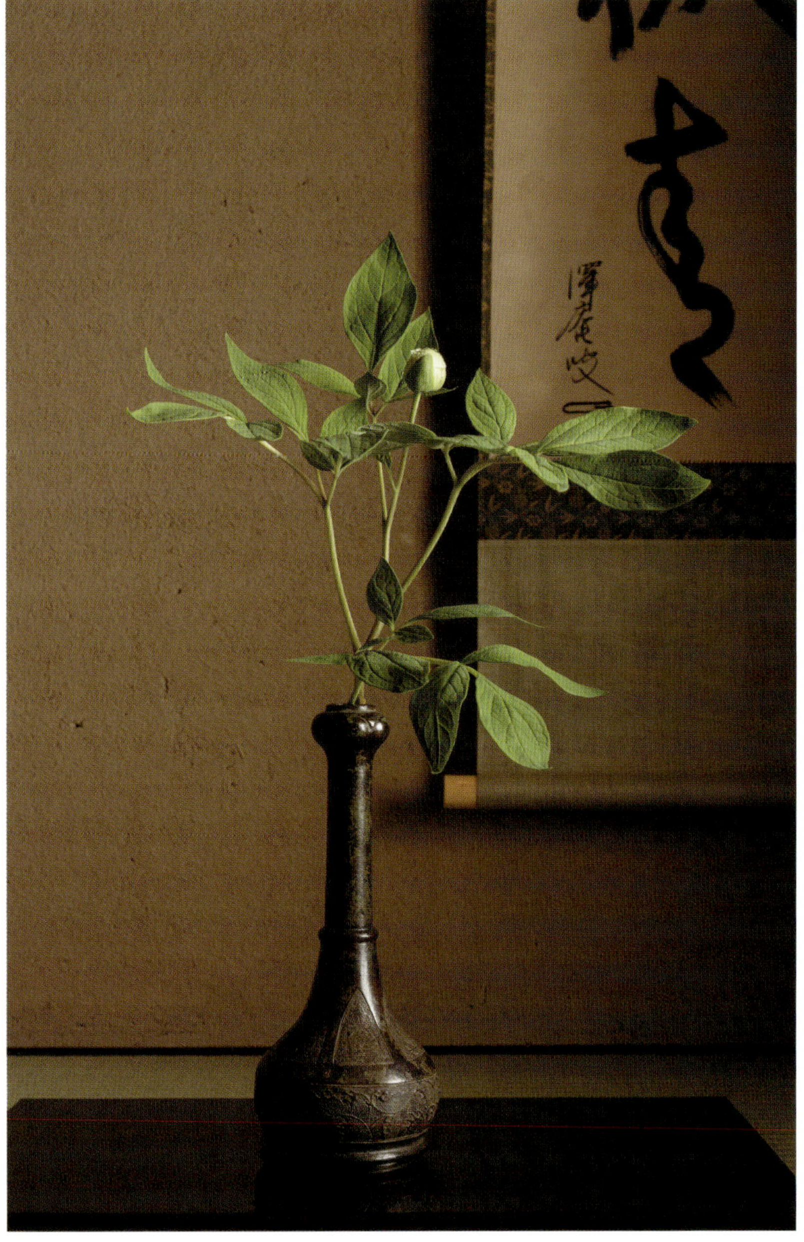

Of course, bamboo isn't the only kind of container used in the tea room. Old pottery from
Japan's Six Ancient Kilns or ceramics from China
are also common. Japanese and Korean ceramics
often have irregularities or asymmetries that reflect
a beauty in imperfection, while Chinese ceramics
are prized for their flawless, pristine completeness.
These are two opposing values. Which is favored
in the world of tea? The answer is—both. The host
chooses what they find beautiful, or what suits
the message they wish to convey at that moment.

You could call it an intentional blend of the best of
both approaches. That openness is one of the great
strengths of the tea tradition.

Here, I've chosen to include pieces from Seto
(page 50) and Tokoname (page 55) as examples of
containers from Japanese domestic kilns. As examples of Chinese ceramics, I've used a Longquan
celadon vessel (facing page), and a Cizhou ware
meiping-style container traditionally used to display plum branches (page 54).

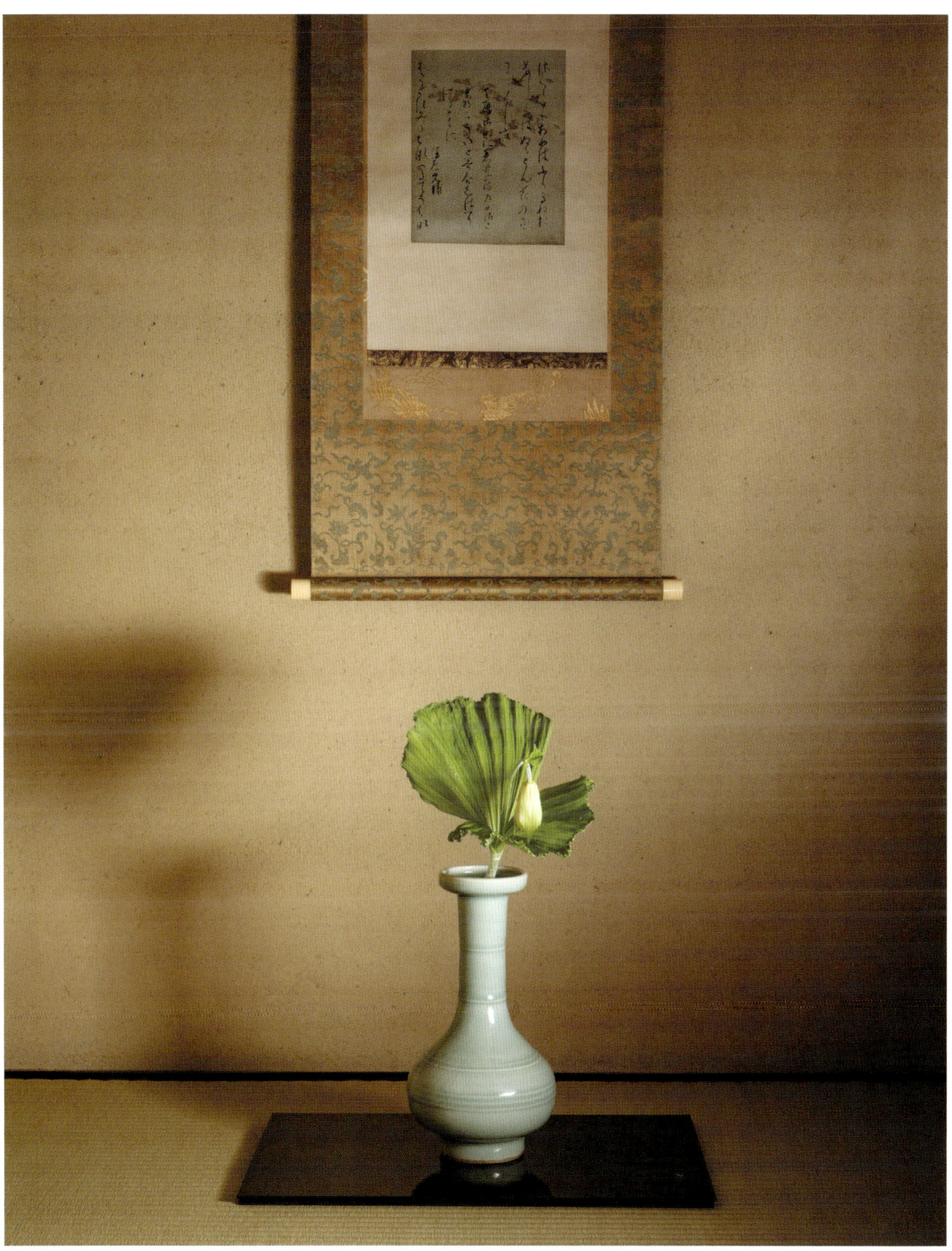

Lady's Slipper Orchid. Longquan celadon *shimo kabura* (turnip-shaped) flower container, shichikan type, China, Ming dynasty.

The scroll has a fragment of a Heian-era calligraphy version of the poem *Sakuragari* (Cherry Blossom Viewing) from the collection *Shui Wakashu-sho*, in the hand of Fujiwara no Korefusa. In a celadon flower container a lady's slipper orchid — recalling the Heian-era warrior Kumagai Naozane — harmonizes beautifully with the refined atmosphere of times past.

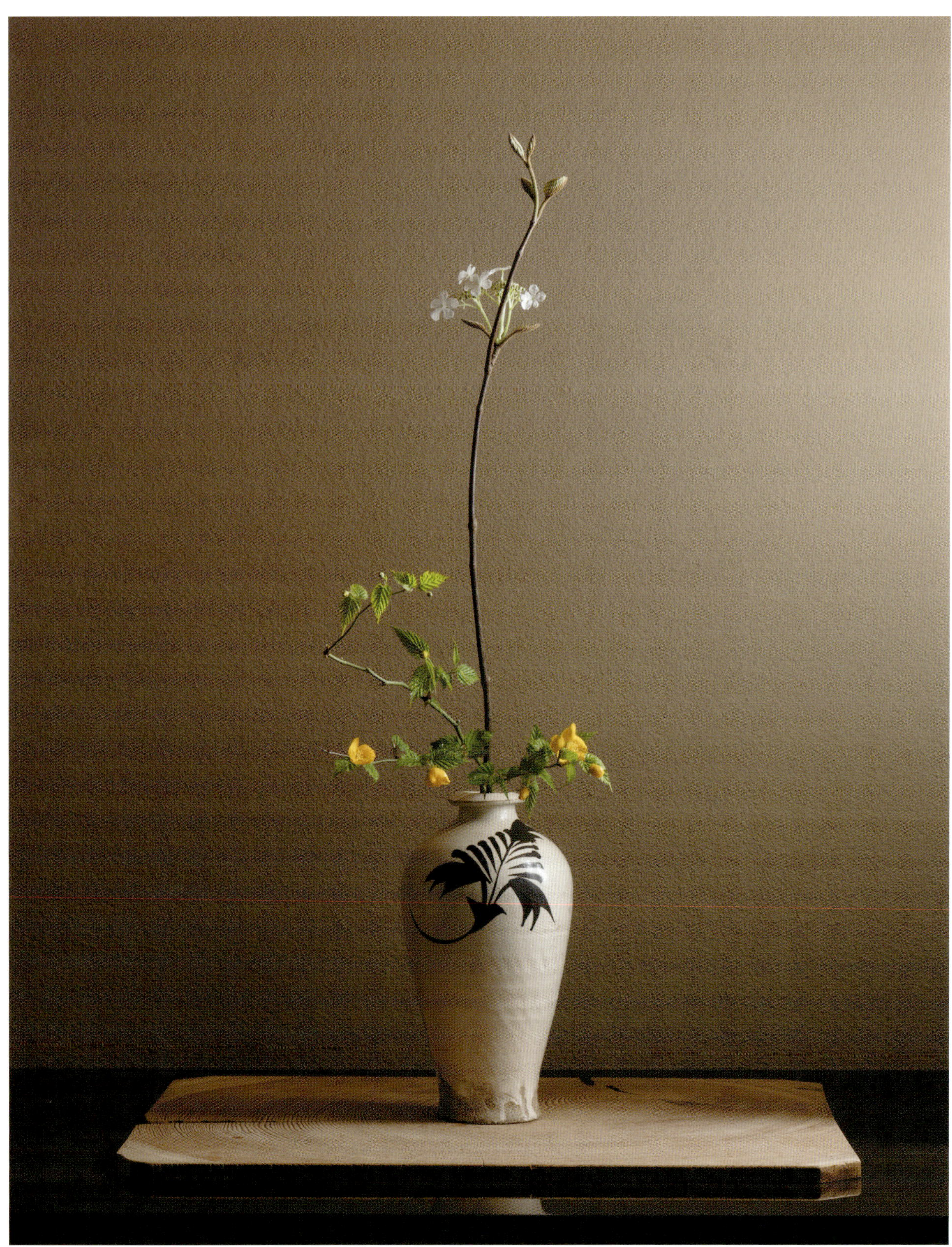

Japanese kerria, and daylily. Cizhou ware meiping, the classic high-shouldered vase form with arabesque design, China, Ming dynasty.

To bring out the distinct lines of each branch, only the essential flowers and leaves are kept. The contrast between the white and yellow blossoms is also striking. This flower container uses a technique where designs are brushed in iron-rich pigment over a white clay coating.

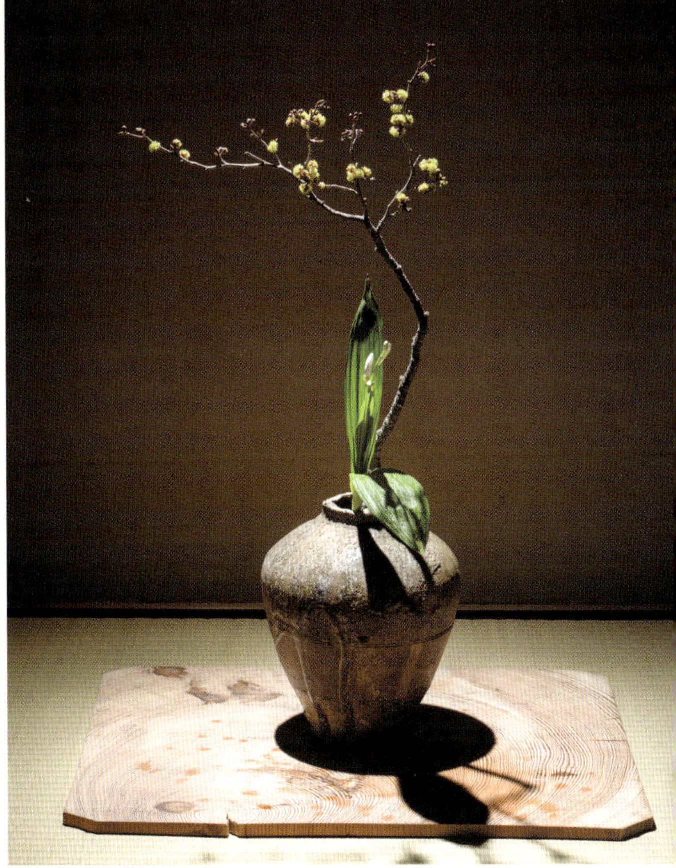

Shiran orchid, shiramoji branch. Tokoname ware triple-ridge flower container, Kamakura period.

In this superb old vessel from Tokoname, one of the Six Ancient Kilns — its uncontrived, simple form a mark of excellence — one piece of branch material and one piece of leafy material are arranged. The natural branching of the shiramoji is highlighted, with a white shiran orchid added for balance. The Tokoname kiln produced vessels of this type called *misuji-tsubo*, that have three raised lines encircling them. "Unglazed, naturally fired, yet beautiful," says Hiroshi.

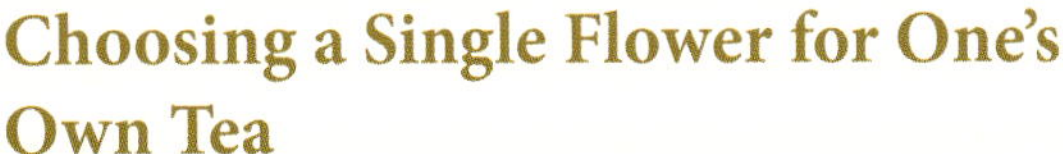

Choosing a Single Flower for One's Own Tea

— Atsushi Kobayashi

Up through March, camellias are the primary flowers used in the tea room. But once April arrives, other flowers begin to appear—such as delicate woodland peonies or the bold and distinctive lady's slipper orchid. When using flowers like these, adding anything else often detracts from their presence. A single stem is enough for an expression of the season.

Camellias are mainly used in the tea room from October through March. Even in April, we still include some late-season camellias in tea ceremony flower arrangements, but since they're used for over half the year, it's often the accompanying branch material that reflects the seasonal shift.

For those just beginning to study the arrangement of flowers used in tea, I recommend starting by arranging only one type. While one or two varieties are usually typical in a tea room, dealing with just a single flower and a single flower container will force you to think about their balance—building the discipline that you need to truly engage with flowers. If you can't work with one flower, working with two or three flowers is even more difficult. It all begins with selecting that one flower. And in fact, once you've chosen the right one, then the outcome is almost decided.

Large Branches in a Wide-Mouthed Jar

An effective way of arranging branches in a wide-mouthed vessel is to use the lower part of the branch — which is normally trimmed away — as structural support. You can bend the tip of the branch into an L-shape to act as a natural holder inside the vessel. The bent section braces against the inner wall of the vessel, and a small wedge can be added at the point where the branch tries to spring back, helping stabilize it. For added security, try tying a heavier branch or even a stone to the end of the branch inside the vessel. Ideally, the branch should stand upright in the center of the mouth of the vessel — avoid having it leaning against the rim or slanting to one side. To achieve this, it's essential that the branch is firmly fixed in place.

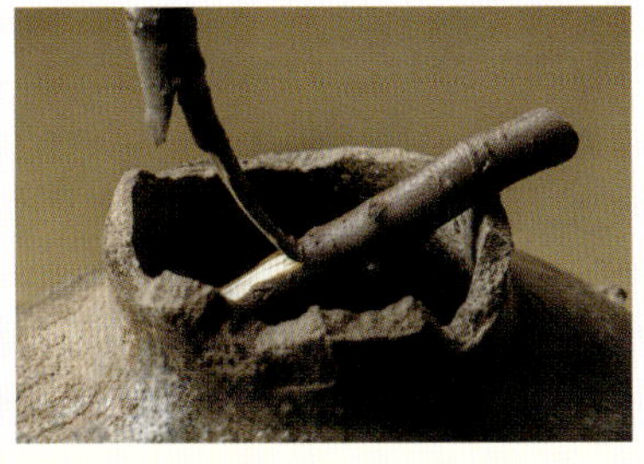

Try walking into the countryside and searching with your own eyes for just one branch you feel is right. This is extremely difficult. At first, you won't know what to choose. You won't be able to decide unless you can imagine what space it will be used in, and what kind of vessel it will go into. Take the wisteria I arranged in an antique bronze flower container (page 49)—its form was beautiful, but the branches were thick and mature, and cutting them felt almost wasteful. I even wished I could return them to the earth after using them.

Still, in the tea room, we commit to the flower for the sake of a single moment. When I considered what flower to pair with Ikkyu's calligraphy and the antique bronze flower container shown earlier in this chapter, the answer was clearly this wisteria. It happened to be sent by a florist, but such beautiful branches are incredibly rare. The first task is to see if the flower can stand on its own, then consider its balance with the vessel. Woodland peonies and lady's slipper orchid too, are best treated this way— with a single flower.

And here's something I believe to be essential: do you truly think the flower you're choosing is beautiful? Even a child knows what's beautiful. Everyone has that innate sense, so just trust your own eyes and choose the part of the plant that moves you. Don't choose based on rarity or novelty— choose the one branch you genuinely want to bring to life.

As for what makes a flower arrangement beautiful, if I had to put it into words, I'd say that the two most important elements are "color" and "line." Color is the natural beauty of the plant itself. Line is something the person arranging the flower discovers within that plant. In that sense, flower arrangement resembles calligraphy: the precision of the lines, the balance, the use of space. Everything that humans create with aesthetic awareness contains beautiful lines. You can't just stick things in and expect it to work. The trick is to select flowers whose colors you find beautiful, and then bring out the lines hidden in the plant. That's the key to arranging flowers.

Stones as a Flower Holder in a Shallow Vessel

A key point when arranging flowers is how to make the area around the base — the waterline — look clean and elegant. Ideally, the stems should appear to emerge from a single point, without spreading out too widely. To achieve this, it's crucial to secure the flowers firmly, and the method of support must suit the shape of the vessel. In the case of a large, shallow Jomon-style pottery bowl (see facing page), the inside of the vessel inevitably remains visible. To maintain a natural look even when the flower holder is exposed, several stones with a texture similar to the pottery are placed inside to anchor the stems. This way, the materials blend harmoniously and do not distract from the overall arrangement.

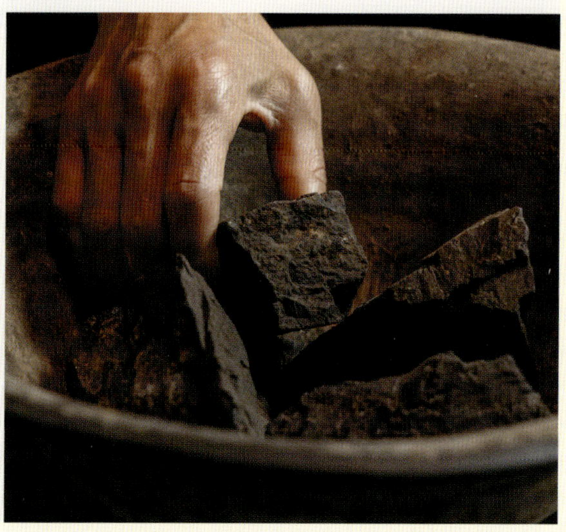

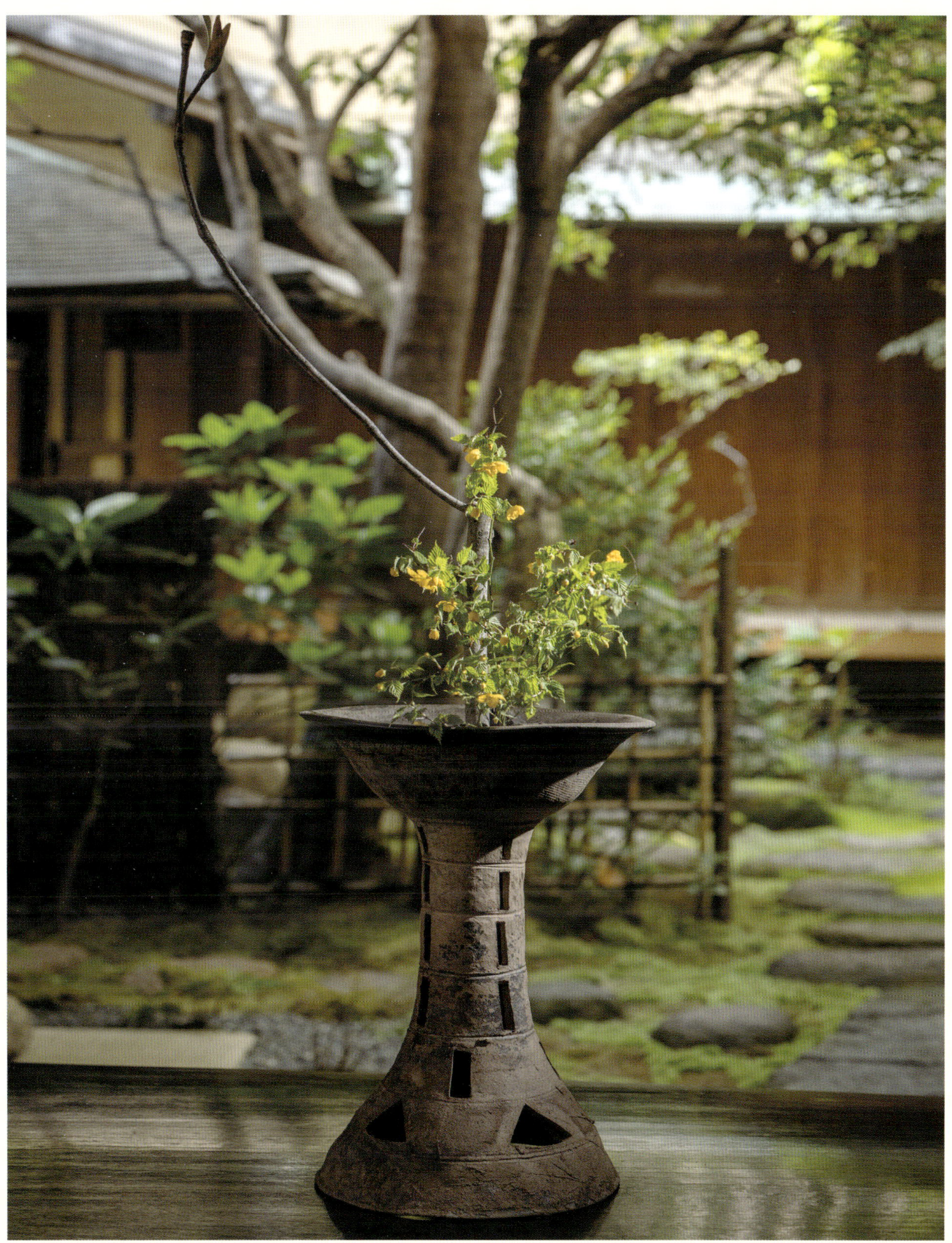

Japanese kerria, Japanese bigleaf magnolia. Jomon-period earthenware.

The magnolia branch is placed upright in the center, with the yellow kerria encircling it. The striking Jomon-period earthenware, likely once a ritual vessel, contrasts unexpectedly with the delicate, gentle flowers. The green garden backdrop softens the weight of the large composition, giving it an unexpected feeling of lightness and spaciousness.

The Enshu Memorial Tea Gathering

Japanese Cobra Lily

The Enshu Memorial Tea Ceremony is held at this time of year, often at Koho-an, a subtemple of Daitokuji Temple. Located in Murasakino, Kyoto, Koho-an is the family temple of tea master Kobori Enshu (1579–1647). The ceremony includes a memorial service for Enshu, who was both a daimyo and a man of culture, followed by a commemorative tea gathering hosted by the head family of the Enshu school. In May 2022, the *usucha* thin-tea gathering was conducted by Tanimatsuya Shoten.

Koho-an also has deep ties to the Toda family. For that reason, in our own tea room, we prepared a *koicha* thick-tea alcove arrangement in memory of Enshu. We displayed the painting and inscription *Nunobukuro-zu* (Cloth bag), which is recorded in the Unshu Kuracho (the record of utensils of daimyo Fumai Matsudaira), and placed a Heian-period sutra container with a Musashi-style stirrup inside. Sutra containers were originally metal vessels used to store Buddhist scriptures and bury them in the ground—a kind of time capsule to preserve the Buddha's teachings for future generations. Because of their spiritual significance, they are treated with deliberate gravity and are used in koicha tea gatherings.

With this bronze sutra container used as a flower vessel comes a brief note written by my

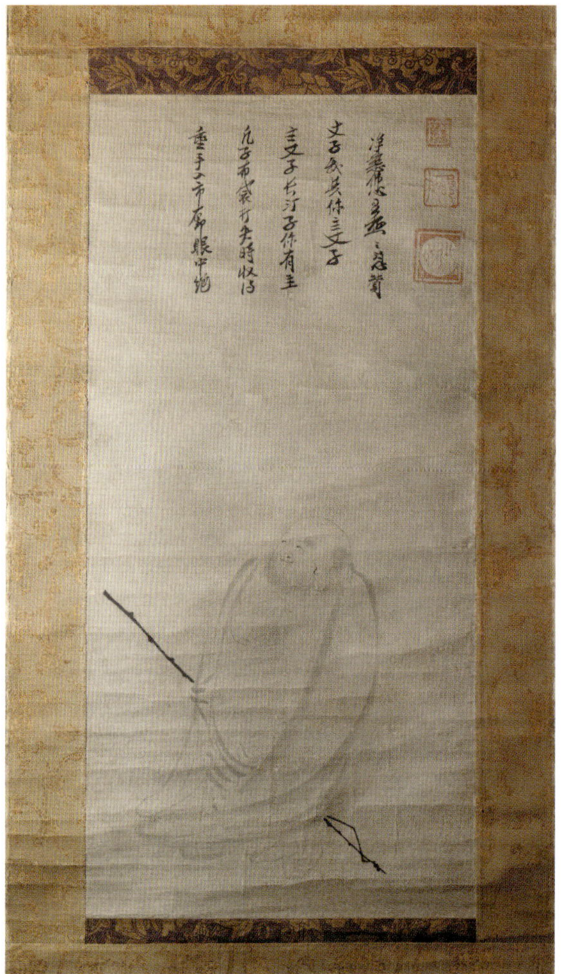

ABOVE "Cloth Bag" by Hu Zhifu, a thirteenth-century Chinese artist. Although the details of his life remain uncertain, many works attributed to him have been handed down, including the National Treasure "Landscape in Summer." The inscription was written by Wuji Zhihui, a Chinese monk active in the thirteenth to fourteenth centuries. This work bears an attribution slip from Japan's Muromachi period (1336–1573) identifying the artist as Hu Zhifu. It also has a noted provenance, having been owned by Kobori Enshu and Fumai Matsudaira. It is listed in the *Unshu Kuracho* Record of Utensils.

RIGHT The bronze sutra container from the Heian period has, over time, suffered damage at its base. A wooden stand (see facing page) was made to fit the missing portion, providing support so that the container remains upright. The way the base and stand fit together so precisely — almost imperceptibly — speaks to how carefully this piece has been preserved and passed down.

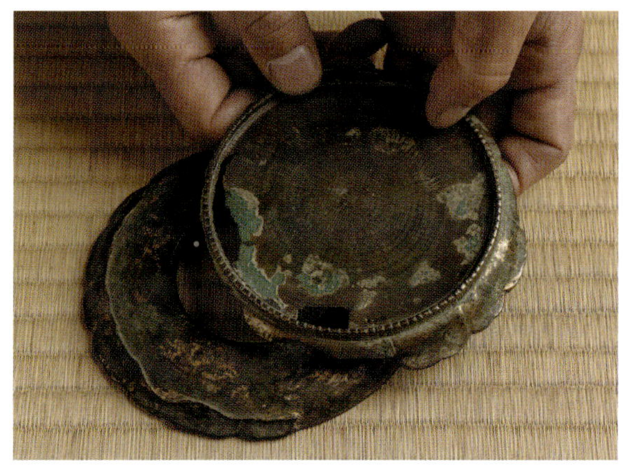

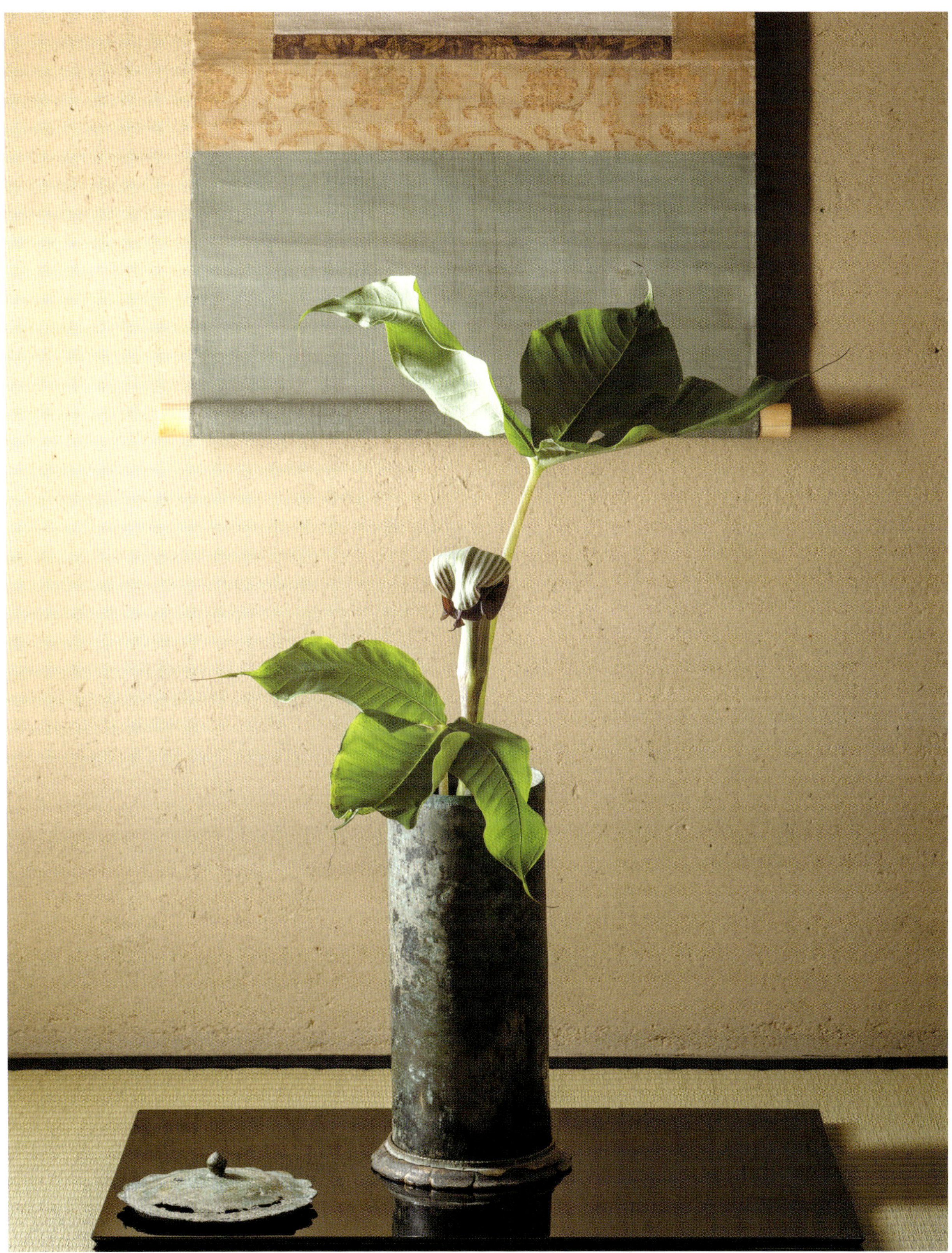

Japanese cobra lily. Gilt bronze sutra container, Heian period, formerly owned by Masuda Don'o.

The sutra container is a Heian-period masterpiece, passed down through the Dan family and later owned by tea connoisseur Masuda Don'o (1848–1938). It is well preserved, with its original lid still intact. "Sutra containers tend to be used in the *furo* brazier season," says Hiroshi, "but they are dignified enough to be used in the *ro* hearth season without any issue."

father, Shonosuke: "Bronze sutra container flower vase, Heian period. This flower vessel, formerly passed down through the Dan family, was used at Kigyu-an during the Koetsu Gathering in 1978." The sutra container, originally owned by the family of Dan Takuma (1858–1932) director general of Mitsui, was later acquired by Masuda Don'o, and its subsequent provenance is clearly documented, marking it out as an item of distinguished lineage. It is also notable for still having its original lid, a rarity, and is among the best-known sutra containers. Sutra containers are often used in memorial tea gatherings and frequently hold lotus flowers. That said, lotus is not a requirement—other flowers may certainly be used. Here, the flower chosen is Japanese cobra lily (*Musashi abumi*), a wild plant that is distinguished by a sheath-like bract which protects the flower, and is said to resemble the flame-shaped halo that is often seen behind Buddhist statues. The flower arrangement possesses a dignity that harmonizes well with both the painting in the alcove and the sutra container.

A Special Arrangement

At the Enshu Memorial at Koho-an, in the tea room *Bosen,* the alcove was adorned with the hanging scroll *Ryuryoku Kako* (Green willows, red flowers) by Suigan Somin, and a magnolia seiboldii was arranged in a sand-cast bronze *tsuribune* boat-shaped flower container, designed for hanging, whose storage box bears an inscription by Enshu. Upon seeing the shape of this tsuribune container, I felt it looked more beautiful when set down rather than suspended. That may not be true for all tsuribune, but this one has a unique form that makes it more interesting when set down. Just as I was wishing for a suitable stand, I happened upon a negoro lacquer stand from the Masuda family collection. It felt perfectly right—when I placed the flower container on top of the stand, the combination was a flawless match.

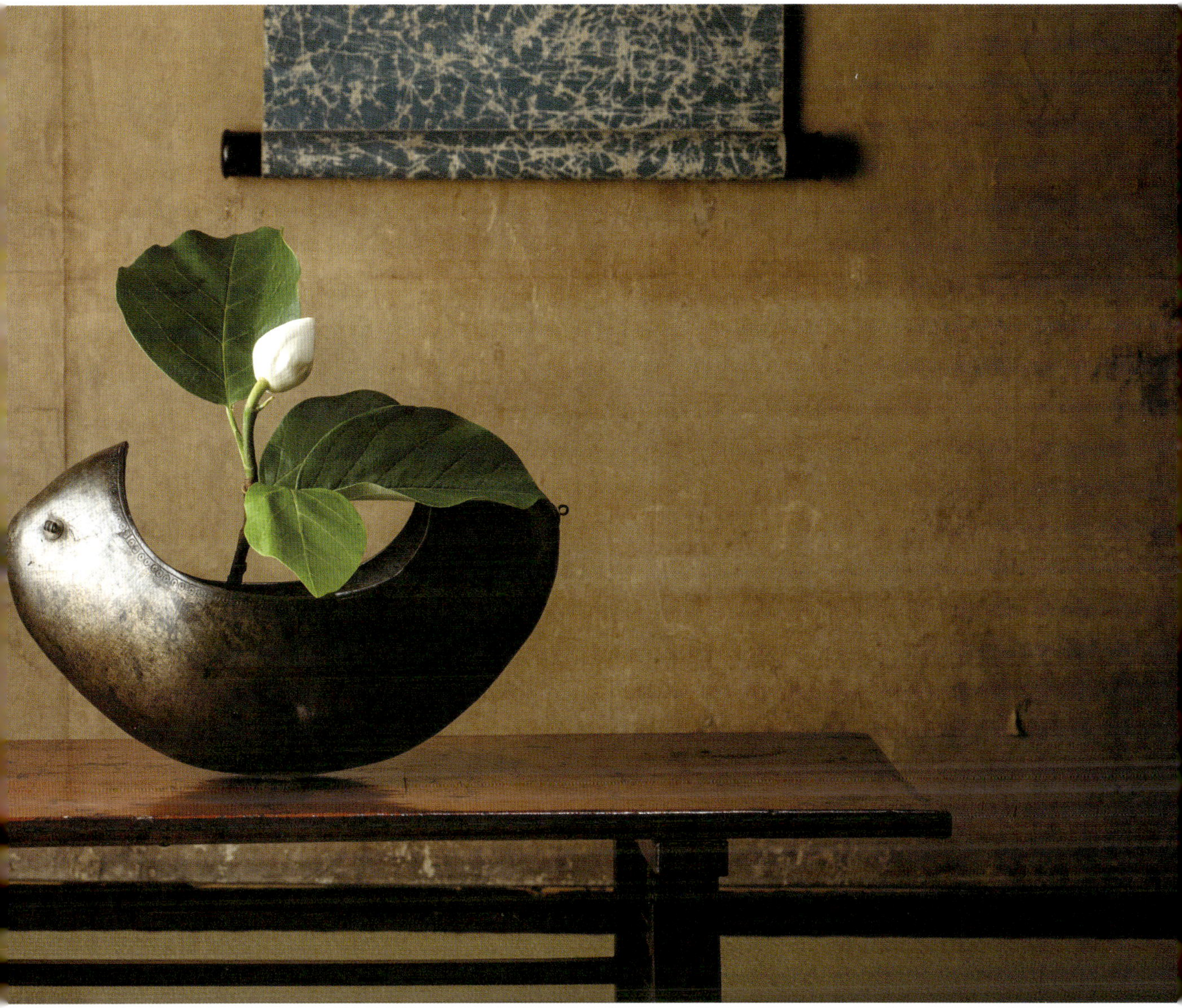

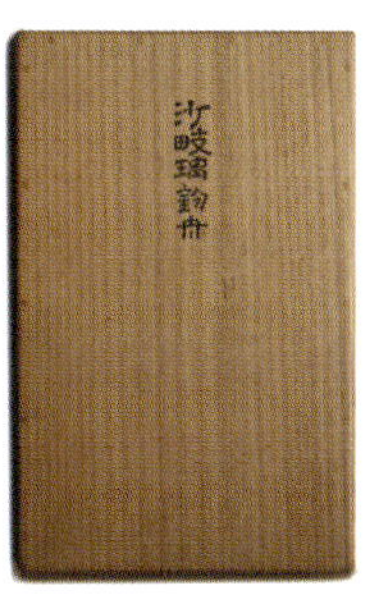

The Bosen tea room is said to have been designed by Kobori Enshu. A seventeenth-century daimyo tea master, Enshu was also the shogunate's commissioner of works, responsible for architecture and garden design. He created this tea room next to the main hall of Koho-an. Essentially a large *shoin-zukuri*–style chamber, it incorporates elements of the rustic *soan* style—like the central threshold that functions as a *nijiriguchi* crawl-in entranceway. The result is a distinctive and carefully composed space. The alcove calligraphy is *Ryuryoku Kako* (Green Willows, Red Flowers) by Suigan Somin, and the bronze flower container is associated with Enshu. Suigan Somin was a seventeenth-century Rinzai Zen monk and 195th abbot of Daitokuji Temple.

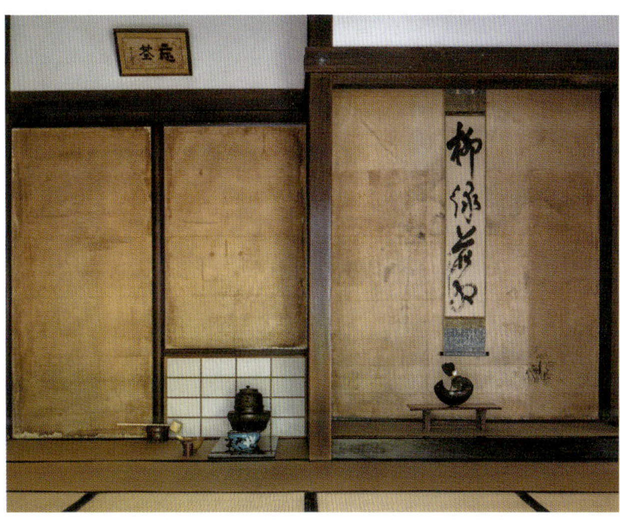

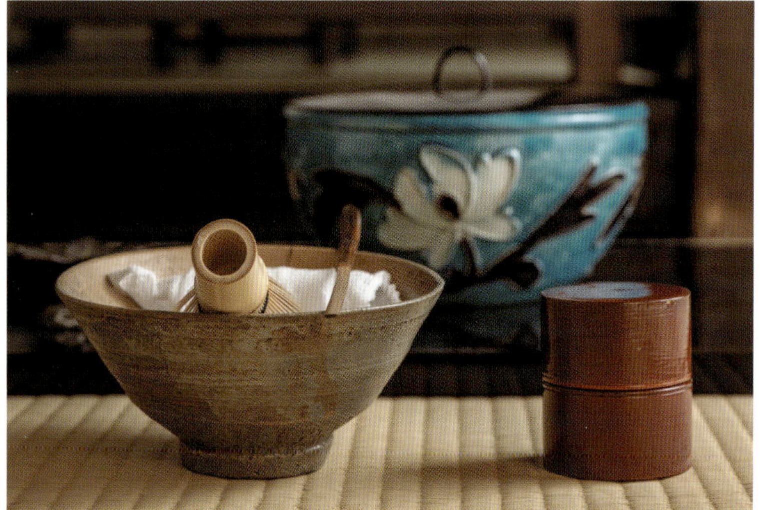

A board on the floor would have worked as well, but at that moment, I wanted the piece to float in the space. With a different hanging scroll, a board placed on the floor might offer better balance.

In the area for serving *usucha* thin tea, we used a red-lacquered cylindrical tea caddy with a box inscription by Enshu's third son, Gonjuro Hosetsu, along with a cylindrical tea bowl) named "Haruyama," bearing a box inscription by the second-generation Enshu school master, Daizen Sokei. The tea scoop, named "Itsuun," was by the eighth-generation master, Wao Sochu; its outer box bears inscriptions by Roko Hirase and Rogin Toda. I'll speak more about Roko Hirase later, but he was from an old Osaka household with deep ties to Koho-an, like the Toda family. For the *mizusashi* fresh-water container, we chose a brilliant blue Fahua ware enameled jar with a rich lotus design, creating a contrasting yet harmonious pairing of two masterful utensils.

RECORD OF THE GATHERING

Alcove: Scroll *Ryuryoku Kako* (Green willows, red flowers") by Suigan Somin

Flower container: Sand-cast bronze boat-shaped container, box inscription by Enshu, Maeda family collection

Flower: Magnolia sieboldii

Flower stand: Negoro lacquer flat stand, Masuda family collection

Incense container: Lacquered black *daruma* with reed design

Kettle: Ashiya-style with plum and bamboo pattern; Fujita family collection

Furo brazier: Korean sand-cast bronze, Fujita family collection

Long board: True black lacquer finish, by Seiami

Fresh-water container: Fahua ware, lotus design

Tea caddy: Chinese red-lacquer cylindrical tea caddy, box by Gonjuro Hosetsu

Tea bowl: Classic Totoya-style, named "Haruyama," box inscription by Daizen Sokei. *Secondary* bowl: Satsuma ware, formerly owned by Hakusui-an

Tea scoop: by Wao Sochu, with matching tube and box; outer box inscribed by Roko Hirase and Rogin Toda

Waste water bowl: Seto ware, *shibugamite* style

Lid rest: Seven treasures pattern

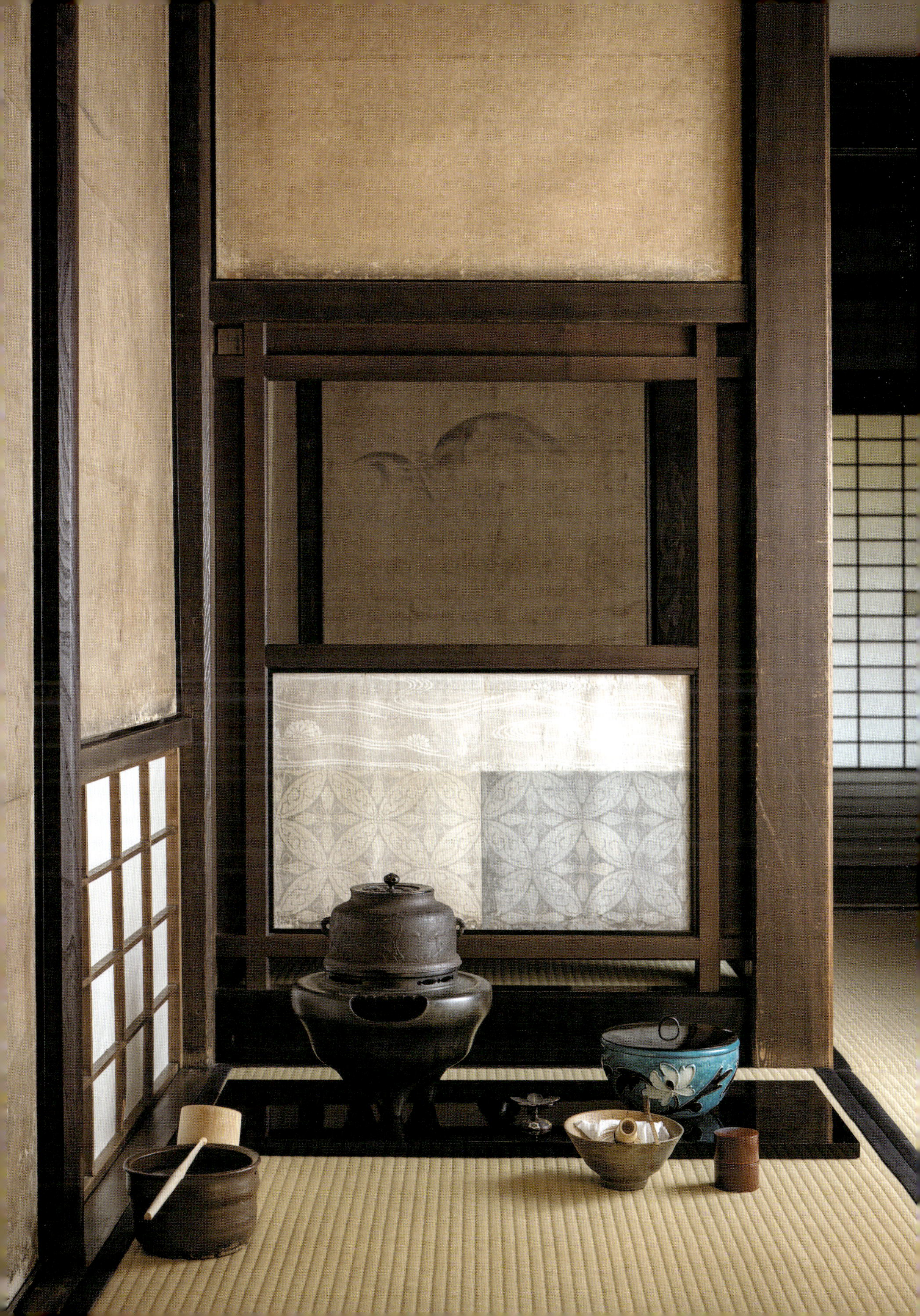

Three Historical Figures

Koho-an was the retirement hermitage where Kobori Enshu spent his final years. It was destroyed by fire at the end of the eighteenth century, but later rebuilt thanks to the devotion of the daimyo Fumai Matsudaira, who deeply revered Enshu. Because of this connection, Koho-an also became Fumai's family temple. It is thus a temple linked to two major tea masters from the early and late Edo period (1603–1868). The Toda family also shares a long-standing relationship with Koho-an, and we have had the honor of hosting the Enshu Memorial Tea Gathering on several occasions.

At the far end of the Koho-an grounds there is a special corner where three stone memorial monuments stand side by side: the central one commemorating Fumai Matsudaira; on either side are monuments commemorating Roko Hirase and Rogin Toda. The presence of the two latter monuments in such privileged proximity to Fumai's is a testament to the key roles that were played by these two men. Roko Hirase was a merchant banker in Osaka's Semba district who was active from the mid-to late-nineteenth century, and he was also known as a leading cultural figure of the Osaka region. Living in the same period was Rogin Toda, who was the eighth head of our family, and who revitalized its fortunes.

With the fall of the Tokugawa shogunate in 1868, after more than 260 years, many former daimyo lords and tea families were forced to part with heirloom utensils in order to survive. During this turbulent time, Rogin, known as a connoisseur of tea ware, used his refined eye and courage to acquire these distinguished utensils and pass them on to appropriate custodians for the future. He worked alongside Roko, who was also a fellow practitioner of tea, and together they supported Koho-an. For this reason, both were given the exceptional honor of having a memorial monument erected beside that of Fumai Matsudaira. Rogin delivered many fine utensils to the Hirase family, and during the sale of the Hirase collection, he even served as the official appraiser. The name "Rogin" was a literary name that was bestowed upon him by Roko.

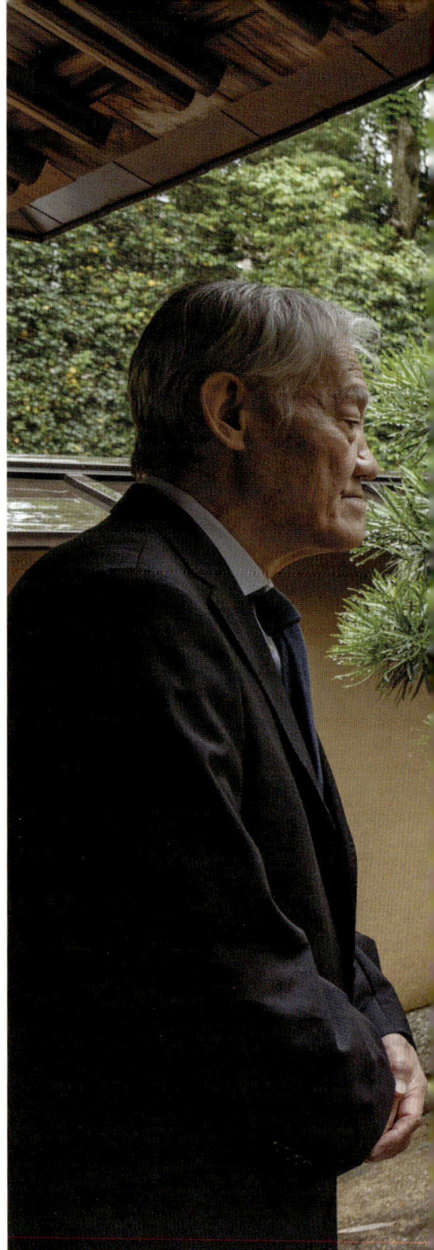

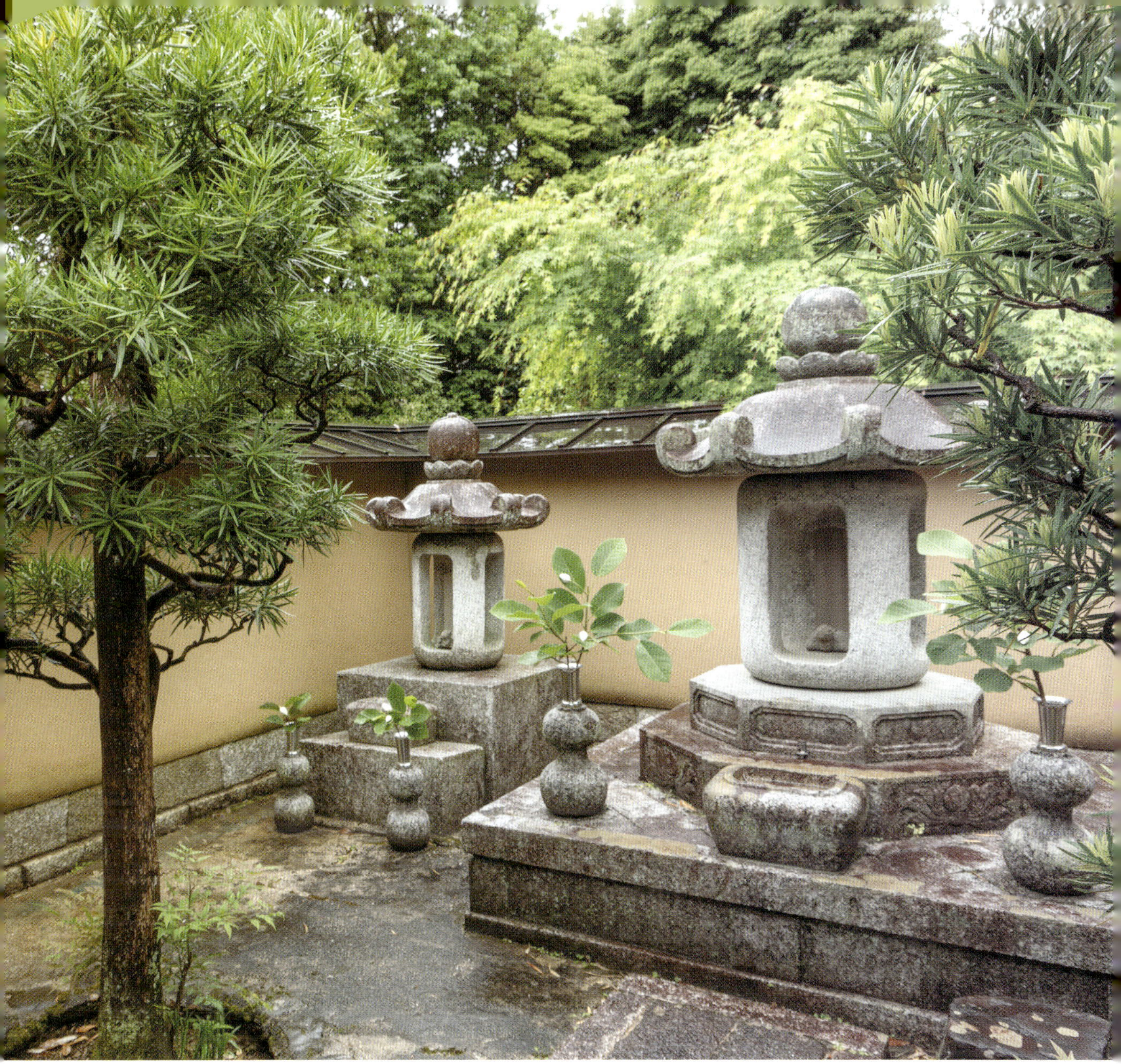

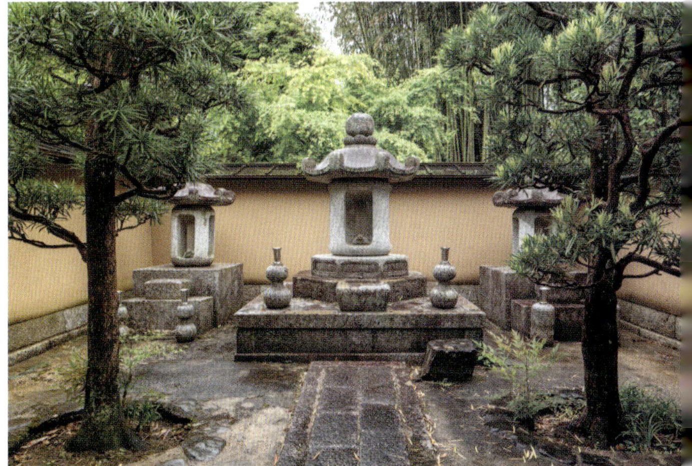

Before hosting the Enshu Memorial Tea Gathering, Hiroshi Toda visits the memorial monuments of Fumai Matsudaira, Roko Hirase and Rogin Toda. The large central monument is in memory of Fumai Matsudaira; to its left is Rogin's monument, and to the right, Roko's. On this visit, Toda-san brought branches of magnolia sieboldii from his garden to place at the monuments. A branch from the same tree was also placed in the alcove of the Bosen tea room. "I've been coming here since I was in kindergarten, brought by my father. The former abbot and my father were close through their shared appreciation of tea utensils."

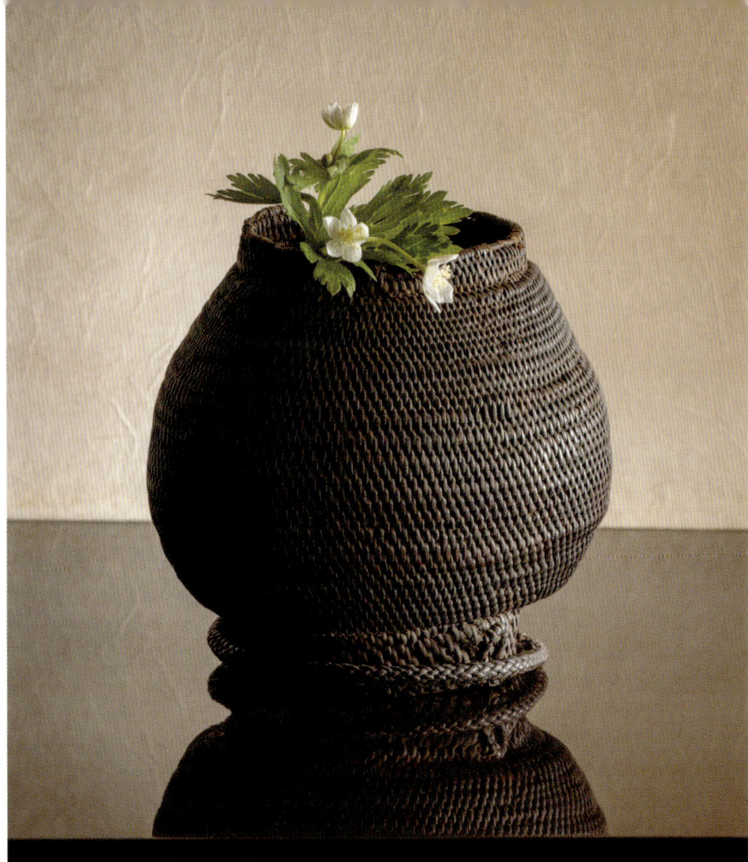

Windflowers in Toraja basket, Sulawesi, Indonesia.

Wild windflowers blooming in the forests around Lake Akan in Hokkaido, were picked by Ainu indigenous people and, through a series of human connections, happened to make their way to the Toda shop. These kinds of fascinating encounters — in this case between Ainu mountain flora and a traditional Indonesian craft object — can sometimes happen in the world of ikebana.

Flowers and Utensils for May

Beyond Fashion or Fad

The sand-cast bronze boat-shaped flower container used at the Enshu Memorial Tea Gathering (see page 61) is the one and only container of this kind that I absolutely had to acquire. In the past, these boat-shaped flower containers were reasonably popular and held in good regard, but in recent years their appeal has sharply declined. In the world of tea utensils, things like this happen—sometimes because certain pieces end up being evaluated unfairly; sometimes for no obvious reasons. I've always felt strong resistance to fashions or fads. Even if it means being a little stubborn, I make a point of actively seeking out and purchasing pieces I believe deserve proper appreciation—things I truly find beautiful.

Rather than going along with trends that come and go, I'd say it comes down to a kind of spirit or commitment—a readiness to engage seriously with objects like these. After all, the art world is about confronting beauty. If we reduce everything to mere business, our profession becomes something very base. I'm not trying to sound pretentious, but if you're involved in this world, I believe you must never lose your sense of aesthetic value. When I encounter something that embodies true aesthetic sensibility, I feel it's my duty to pursue it regardless of the market value that has been assigned to it. Then it's my role to convey its appeal, and to help others acquire and appreciate it. That's what I see as my true vocation.

That said, I'll admit—I'd really rather keep this boat-shaped flower container in my own collection. These were originally ritual vessels from Indonesia, used on altars during tooth-blackening ceremonies on islands like Sumatra. It was Japanese tea practitioners who attached chains and repurposed them as hanging flower containers—probably someone in the circle around Rikyu. "Let's hang it in front of the scroll," they must have thought. The person who first came up with that idea—what an imagination!

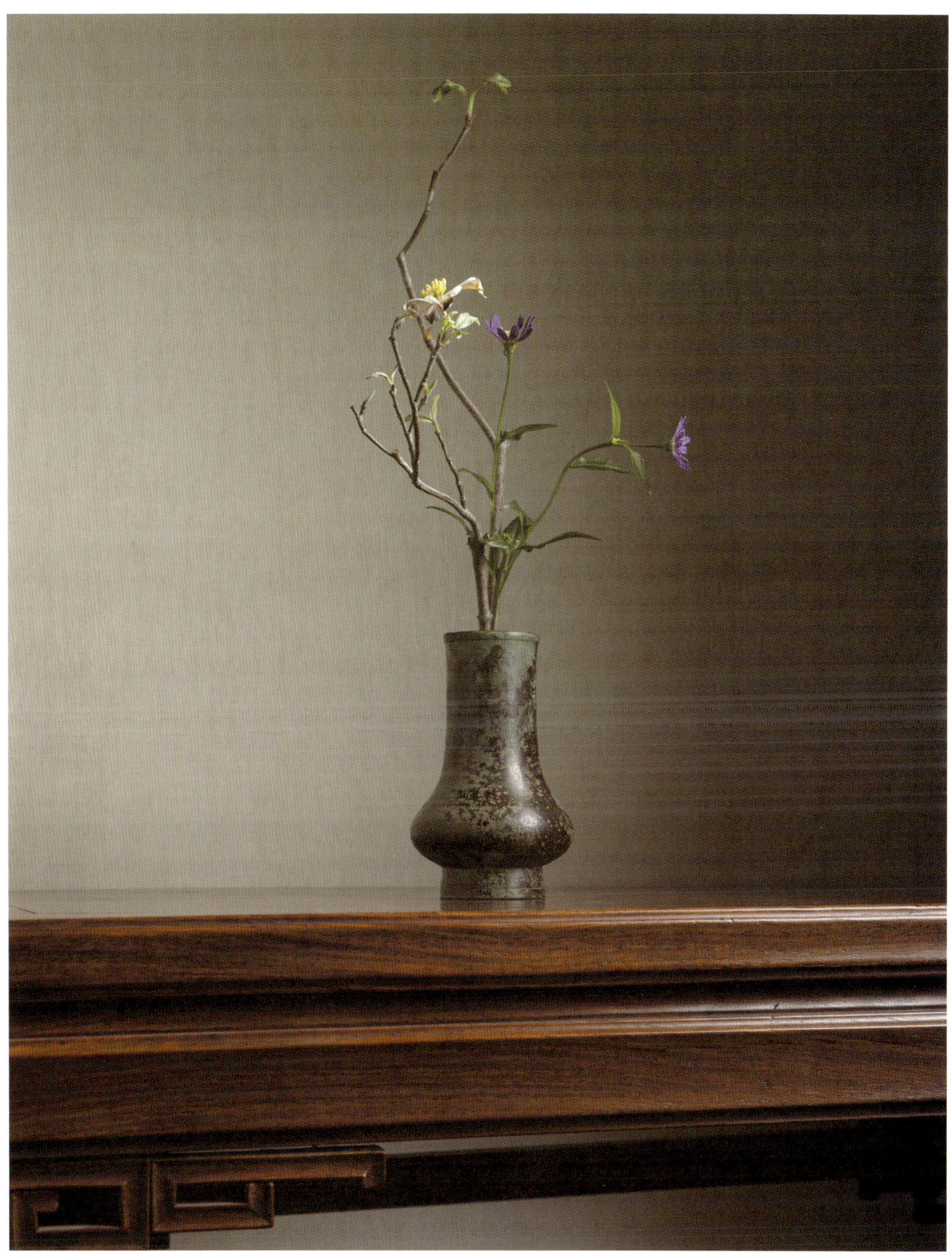

Japanese aster and dogwood. Bronze
kabura (turnip-shaped) flower container,
China, Ming dynasty.

In a small antique bronze flower container, arrange one woody stem and one flowering stem. Simply remove any unnecessary leaves to clean up the base, and gather the stems together at the center of the container. With just this adjustment, even the same materials can give a completely different overall impression.

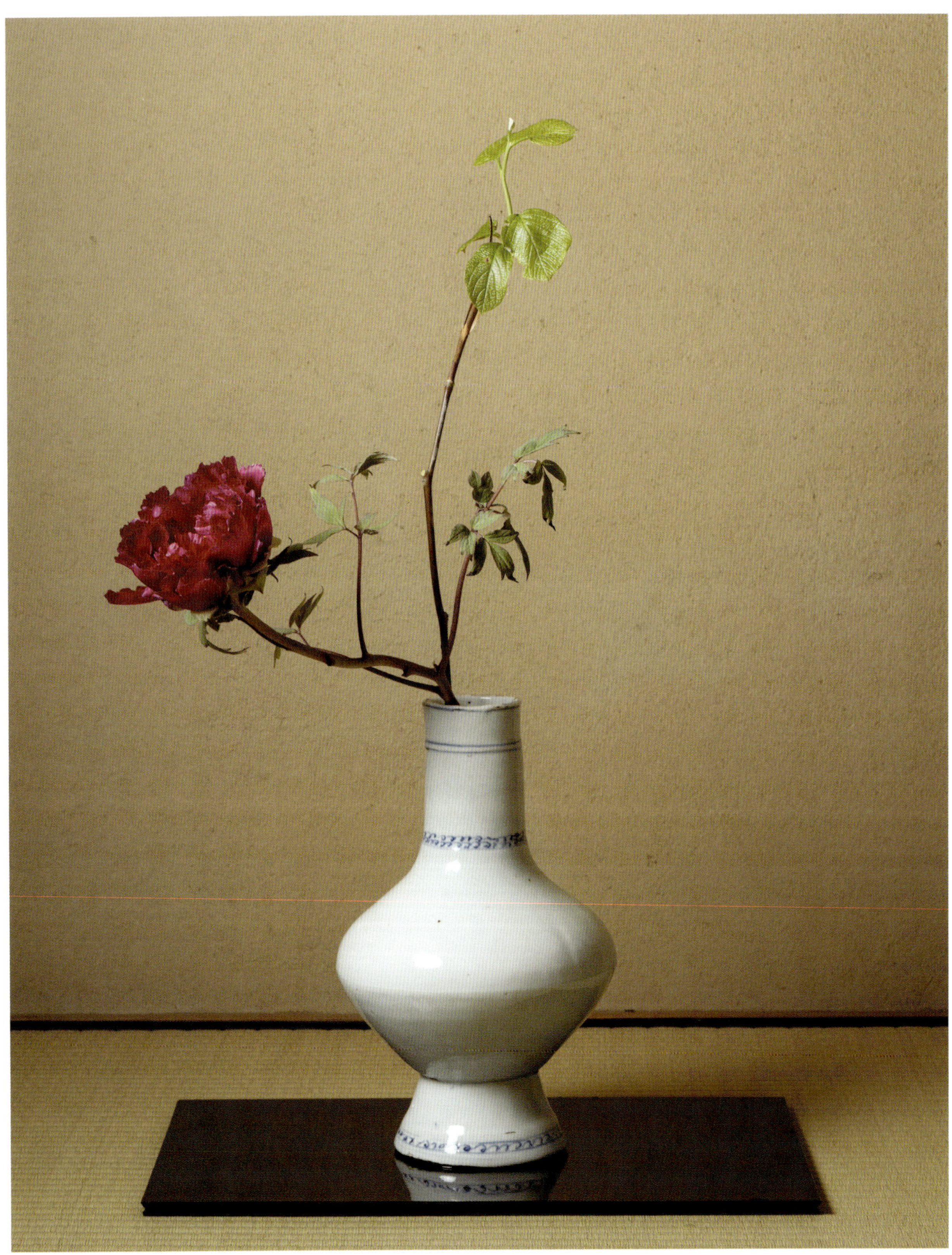

Peony and Japanese snowbell.
Jingdezhen ware blue-and-white porcelain
naka kabura **(turnip-middle) flower con-**
tainer, China, Ming dynasty.

A deep red peony. In January, peonies in bud — called *kan-botan* (winter peonies) — are preferred, but in this season, fully opened blooms are used to reflect the passage of time. Regarded as the "king of a hundred flowers," peonies pair really well with Chinese ceramics like celadon and antique blue-and-white porcelain, according to Atsushi Kobayashi.

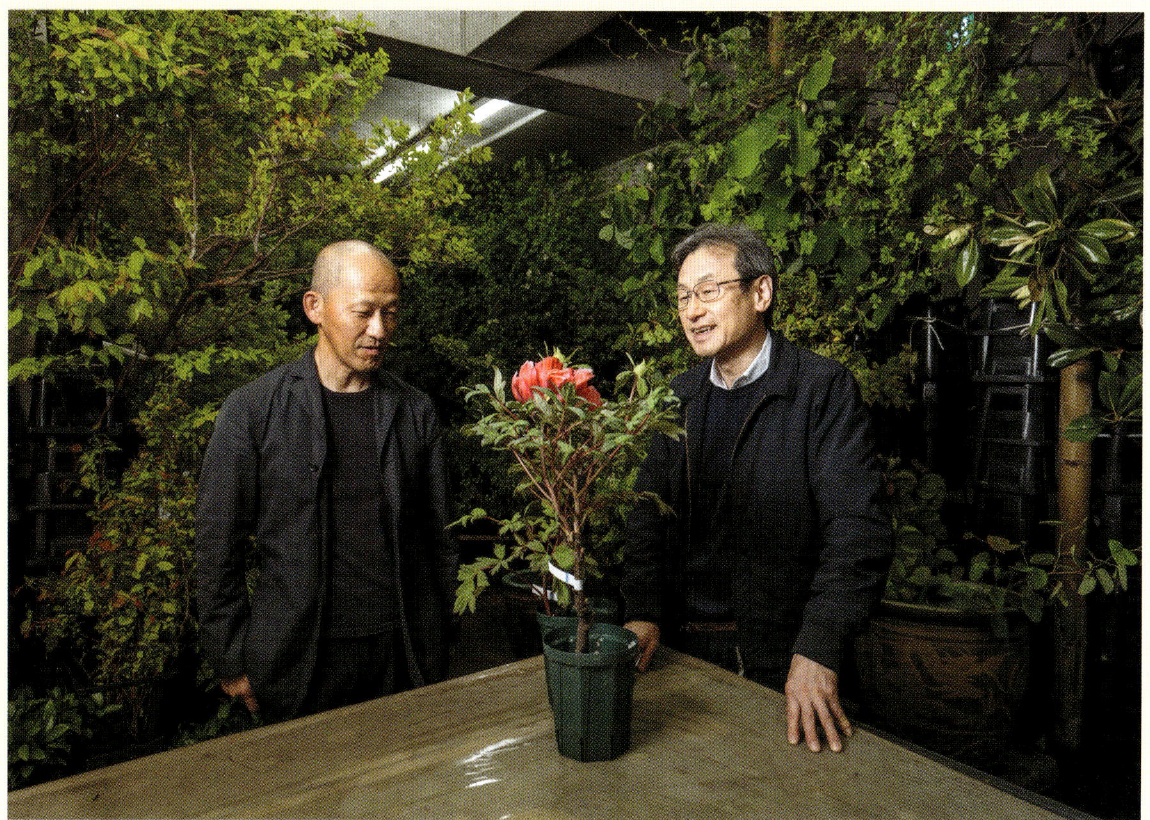

At the Hanacho flower shop in Aoyama, Tokyo, Atsushi Kobayashi (left) consults with the owner, Kikuto Nomura (right), about floral materials. It has been more than twenty-five years since he began sourcing flowers here for tea gatherings. When he explains the context of each occasion, the right flowers seem to appear effortlessly.

The Hanacho Flower Shop

— Atsushi Kobayashi

May is the season when flowers emerge in abundance, bridging spring and early summer. Many trees bloom at this time of year, and a wide range of plants come into view—from bold, striking flowers to delicate, charming ones.

Most of the flowers featured in this book were arranged with the help of Hanacho, a florist in Tokyo's Aoyama district. They've been my go-to shop for many years whenever I prepare for a tea gathering in Tokyo. Hanacho serves many clients involved in the tea world, as well as practitioners of ikebana. The proprietor, Kikuto Nomura, naturally understands these contexts. He always begins by asking how the flowers will be used, and then, sensing the needs of the occasion, swiftly brings out several suitable selections. That's something only someone who has deep familiarity with tea

flowers could do—and I suspect he knows ikebana equally well.

Some customers may walk in with specific requests—"I'd like some magnolia sieboldii, please"—but when you do that, you're not really seeing everything the shop has to offer. It might feel like you're choosing for yourself, but in truth, you may be missing the opportunity to encounter the best possible flowers. Hanacho keeps flowers not only inside the shop but also on the rooftop, and sometimes you'll find blooms you didn't even know were for sale. There's a kind of serendipity in discovering an unexpected flower or having a new idea sparked by what the staff brings out.

Choosing the right flower for a tea gathering is crucial—in fact, once I've found the right floral materials, the work is nearly done. Even among the same type of flower, each individual blossom has its own form. That's why, for me, Hanacho is an incredibly dependable and invaluable shop.

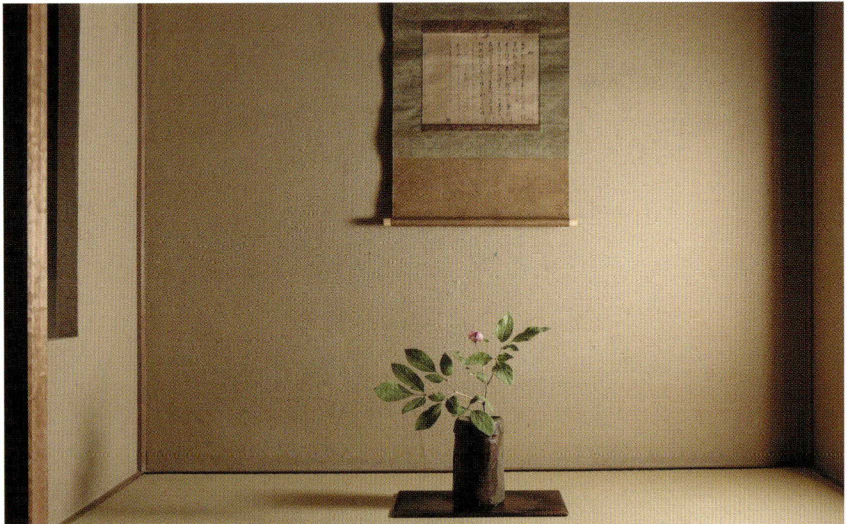

An *usucha* thin-tea setting in a large tea room. The hanging scroll shows a fragment of classical waka poetry from the Heian period (794–1185), in calligraphy by Fujiwara no Yukinari. This fragment is one of the most famous surviving sections of the *Kokin Wakashu* poetry collection. The poetry here is on the theme of rain, evoking scenes of fine, threadlike showers or misty rain mingled with the beauty of blossoms and fresh greenery. This calligraphy fragment comes from the Matsudaira family collection.

Reflecting on a Phantom Flower

Woodland Peony

We were lucky to receive a rare woodland peony. Those familiar with woodland peonies might imagine a white flower, but this is a different variety—an endangered species. It wasn't taken from the wild; it was grown and sent to me by the Tokyo florist Hanacho, who I often work with. Even though it was cultivated, it's the kind of flower you'd normally only find deep in the mountains. To receive its quiet vitality, I chose a Bizen ware flower container from the Momoyama period (1573–1600) called "Takagamine."

This Bizen ware piece was made with a sticky clay known as *tado*, or rice-field soil, and has a subdued, earthy quality. Bizen ware has a wide range of styles, with well-known varieties like *botamochi* or *hidasuki*, which show striking firing patterns and patches of color. This flower container seems modest at first glance, but its strong vertical spatula marks and sturdy mouth give it character. Its thick walls relative to its size add weight and strength—an understated piece favored by connoisseurs. It's one of my personal favorites. When I placed it in the alcove and arranged the woodland peony inside, the result was a wonderfully crisp and refreshing display. The box for this piece is labeled *hosoi mizusashi* suggesting it was once used as a fresh-water container for an autumn *nakadoki* tea gathering when the brazier is placed in the center of the tatami. But traces of a filled-in ring attachment on the body suggest it was originally made as a flower vessel. That duality of purpose is part of what makes tea utensils so interesting.

The hanging scroll, its calligraphy written in the hand of Fujiwara no Yukinari, is an excerpt from a Heian-era poetry anthology themed around "rain."

This was an *usucha* thin-tea gathering, but the combination of utensils could just as well serve a *koicha* thick-tea gathering. Using utensils for thin tea normally reserved for thick tea—intentionally placing them in a humbler setting—is one of the true pleasures of the tea ceremony, and a form of hospitality to the guest. It's a quiet kind of boastfulness, gently restrained. It's not simply about using things out of context—there's an art to knowing how to adapt their role with balance and sensitivity.

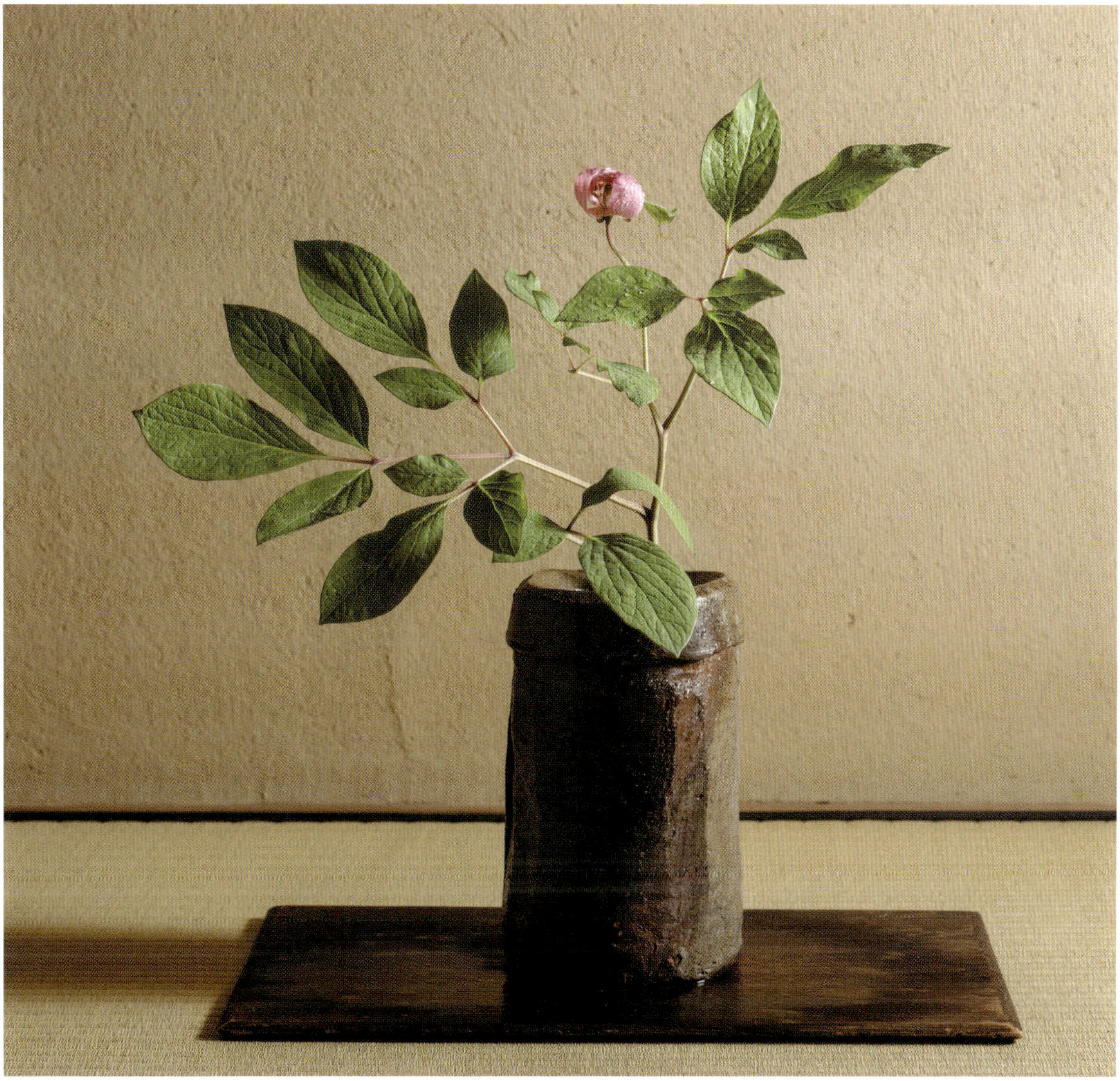

Woodland peony. Bizen ware flower container "Takagamine." Momoyama period.

A Bizen ware flower container formerly owned by the Konoe family, named "Takagamine," given by Fumimaro Konoe. Made with the distinctive clay said to come from rice fields, it has the earthy character typical of Bizen ware. The powerful spatula marks along the body are striking. With a presence like the earth itself, it cradles the delicate peony with quiet strength.

Upright Branches in a Wide-Mouthed Container

This method keeps the stems from leaning against the rim and allows them to rise straight from the center. The lower part of the flower stem is bent into an L-shape and inserted into the container as is. The tip of the bent stem is pressed against the inner right side. A separate branch is laid horizontally inside the container to serve as a brace. By pressing the flower stem against this brace, it can be held firmly in place. With the combined tension between the L-shaped stem and the brace, the flower stands straight up from the center without leaning toward the rim.

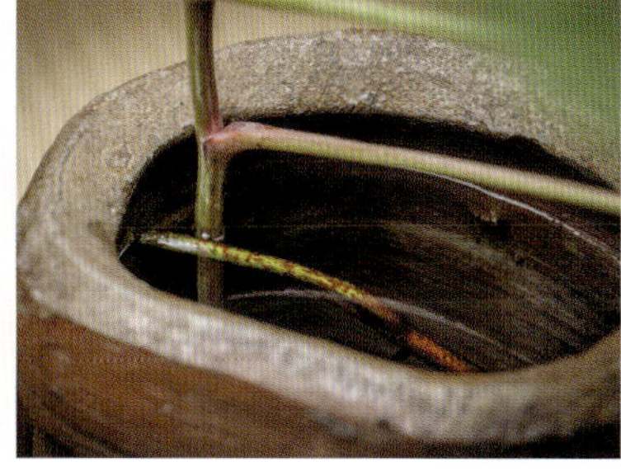

Flowers and Utensils for June

An Oda Urakusai Vase

As I've mentioned, the first thing that catches the eye on entering a tea room is the flower container and the flowers. You could say that they set the tone for the entire tea gathering—that's how important they are. Among the many types of flower containers, the one that most readily comes to mind is the bamboo one. I believe the presence of the bamboo flower container holds great significance. I've yet to see anything that truly surpasses the bamboo vessels conceived by Sen no Rikyu. Even after the years that have passed since Rikyu, no tea practitioner has outdone his style, showing how profoundly Rikyu's sensibility continues to shape the world of tea.

So, what is embodied in a bamboo flower container? I believe what Rikyu sought was, ultimately, a kind of primitivism. Not something overly crafted, but elemental. A vessel that draws out the beauty of the flowers, just as they are and the beauty in the heart that arranges them. That, I believe, is the true meaning of the bamboo flower container.

Here, I arranged a magnolia sieboldii blossom in a single-node bamboo container by samurai tea master Oda Urakusai. This particular container is

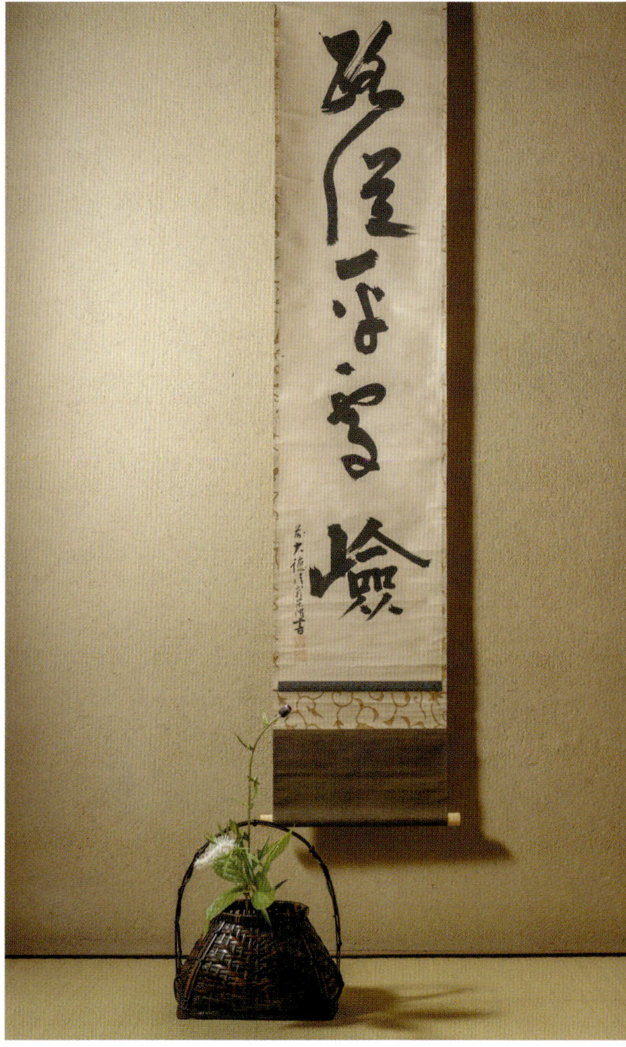

Cloranthus, Bowman's root and wild thistle. Sozen-style basket flower container.

"The road from level ground turns steep" is written on the scroll in the hand of Seigan Soi. It is paired with three kinds of wildflowers arranged in a Sozen basket, a handled basket favored by Edo-period tea master Hisada Sozen.

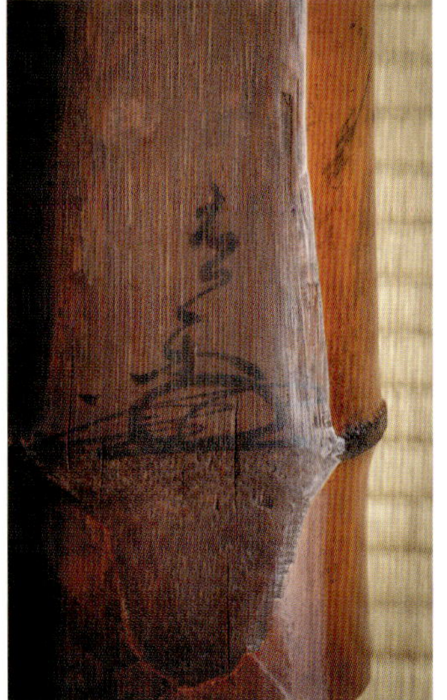

The reverse side of the flower container on page 73 bears Oda Urakusai's signature in ink. Flower containers by Urakusai are exceedingly rare. That an item with such an inscription has survived shows how deeply people involved in tea through the ages have cherished their utensils and carefully passed them down.

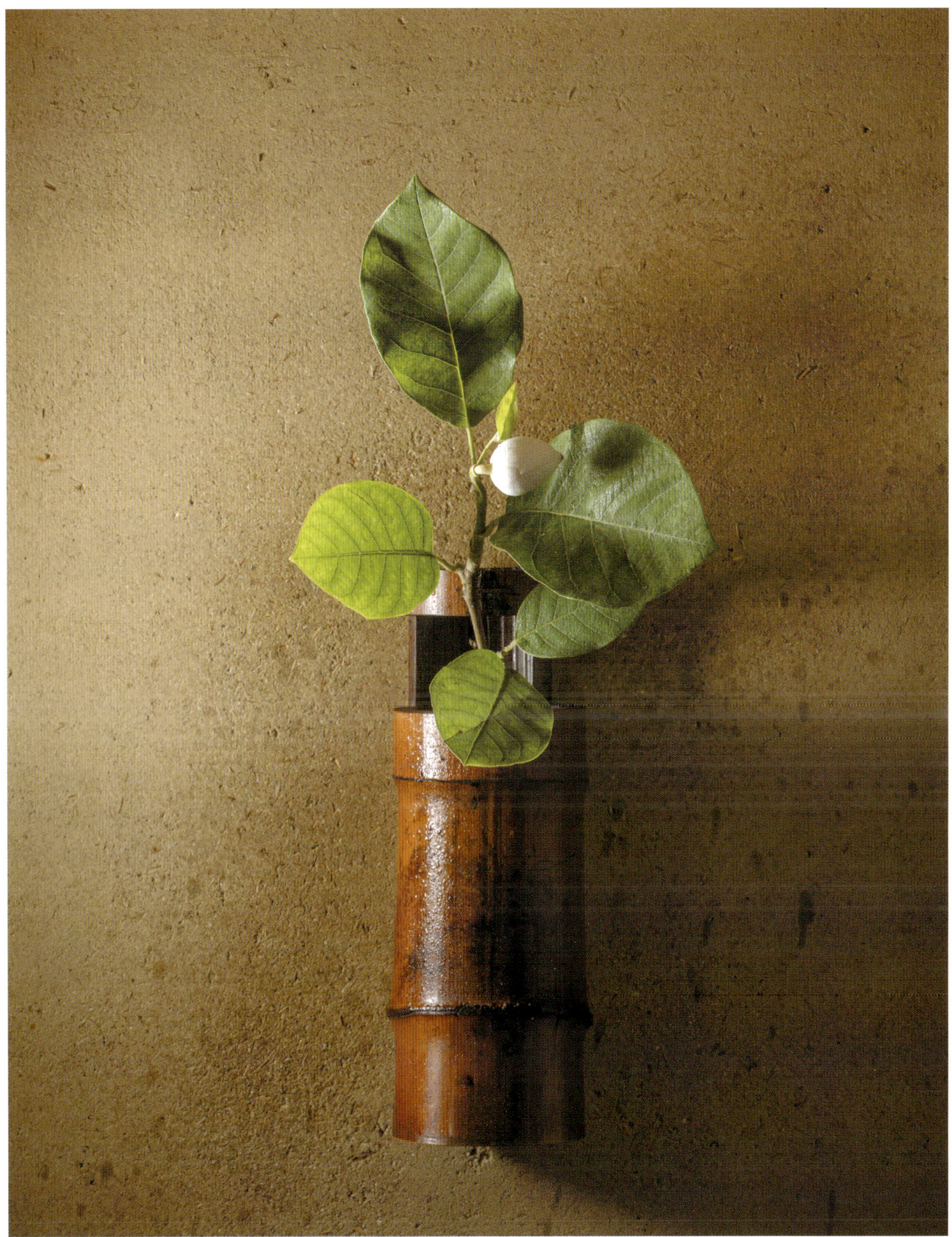

Magnolia sieboldii. Single-node bamboo flower container with inscription by Oda Urakusai. Passed down through the Honganji temple collection.

In a small tea room, the white magnolia bud is arranged in a bamboo flower container by Oda Urakusai. At this time of year, the magnolia sieboldii is a favored tea flower. This branch is modest in size, but the balance between blossom and leaves is just right. "Just one stem, placed simply, is enough to make it work beautifully," says Atsushi Kobayashi.

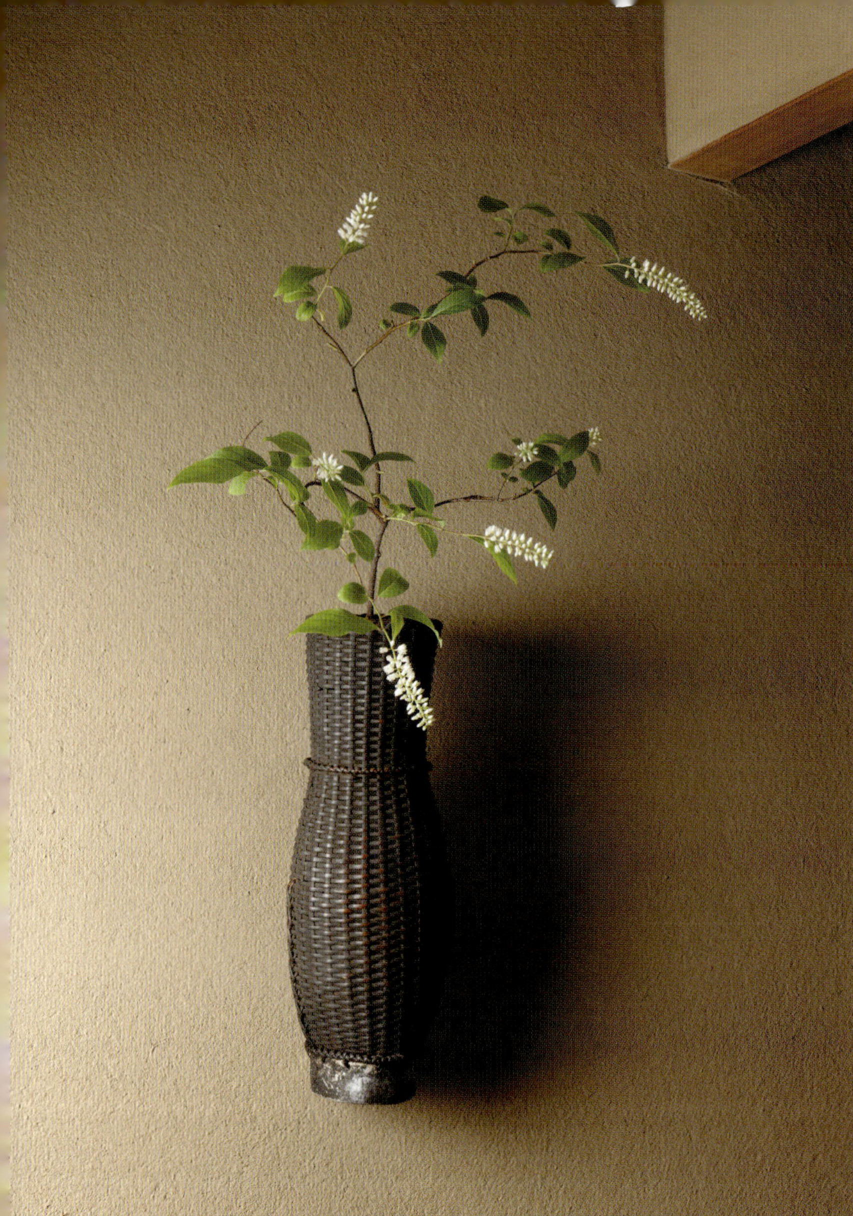

extremely rare, bearing its creator's florid signature brushed in ink. Because flower containers often get wet, the signature is usually written in gold or lacquer. But writing in gold or lacquer can be traced or copied by someone else, so its authenticity is less certain. Ink, however, can only be written by the person themself; it cannot be imitated. The clearly preserved ink signature on this flower container therefore carries strong credibility. Of course, its form is remarkable even before one considers that. Hung in the alcove of a small tea room, it has a beautiful presence—and when a flower is placed in it, the effect is beyond words.

Oda Urakusai was one of Sen no Rikyu's Seven Disciples. He was a relative of daimyo Oda Nobunaga and a samurai during the Warring States period (1467–1600), but he managed to survive through turbulent times. After Nobunaga's death, he lived on when Hideyoshi and then Ieyasu came to power. That speaks to his political strategy and cunning, but I think his deep involvement in the world of tea played a major role as well.

Though Rikyu began the tradition of the bamboo flower container, the forms they take vary depending on who favored them. When I first saw this piece by Urakusai, my immediate reaction was, "Ah, this is wonderful!" I'm deeply grateful it has been so well preserved and passed down.

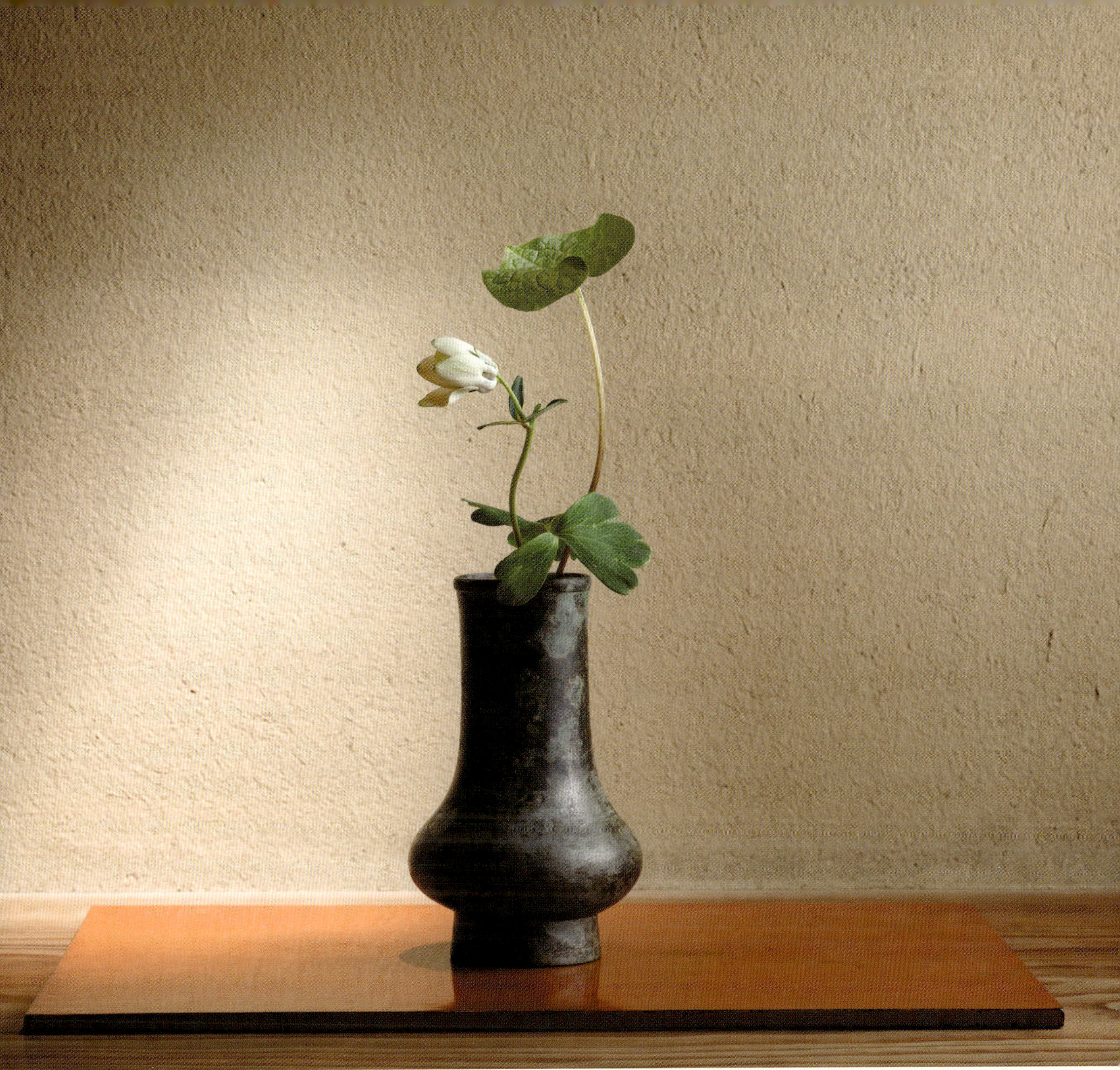

When the Mountains Breathe Anew

— Atsushi Kobayashi

In May and June in Japan, the variety of flowers begins to increase. Among them, woodland peonies and magnolia sieboldii are often chosen for the tea room. These flowers have such a strong presence that they can stand on their own without the need for additional materials—they are complete as tea flowers. Still, each requires a different approach when working with them. The woodland peony, though delicate and graceful at first glance, is actually quite difficult to handle. The branches can't be bent, which limits how you can arrange them. In addition to this, the weight of the leaves causes them to lean, and the flower heads are hard to keep stable. Even getting the stem to stand straight is a challenge.

The way the leaves grow is interesting, so I trim and shape the branches with care, thinking about how best to highlight that feature. Since even a single stem carries presence, matching it with a flower container that holds its own can be tricky. This time, I used a solid Bizen ware vessel that dates from the sixteenth-century Momoyama period, and I feel the balance was well achieved (see pages 70–71). The magnolia sieboldii has a charm that

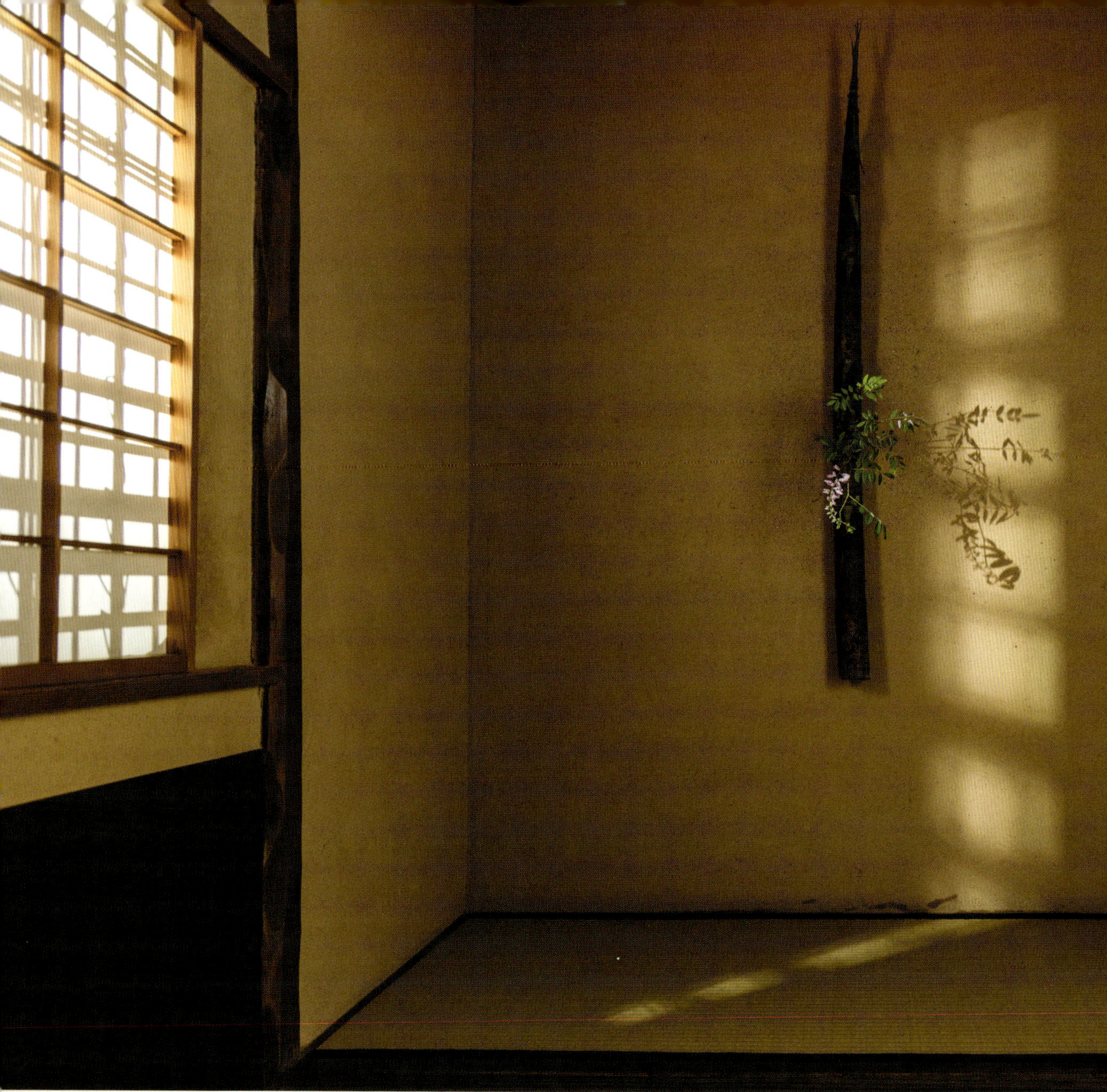

combines strength and delicacy. It comes in many forms, making it fun to choose the right branch. Even a small one can be arranged beautifully (see page 73), and since the tree itself grows over three feet (one meter) tall, long branches can be enjoyed outside the tea room too (see page 81). It's a wonderfully versatile and appealing flower material.

The Tokyo florist Hanacho delivers flowers to me on a regular basis, and included with one particular delivery there were several long bamboo shoots. Hanacho knows my flower style and preferences well, but this time I felt the regular delivery also reflected their own tastes and playful spirit. It felt like a subtle challenge—to see how I might bring these flowers to life. Even when flowers I wouldn't normally use arrive, I still want to make something of them, so I spend several days arranging them in different vessels and spaces. With flowers for the tea gathering, I only need to arrange one for the day, so I can concentrate entirely on that. But being given multiple types of flower and arranging each one is quite demanding. Still, I want to give every flower its moment. I never imagined I'd receive bamboo shoots, but thinking about what

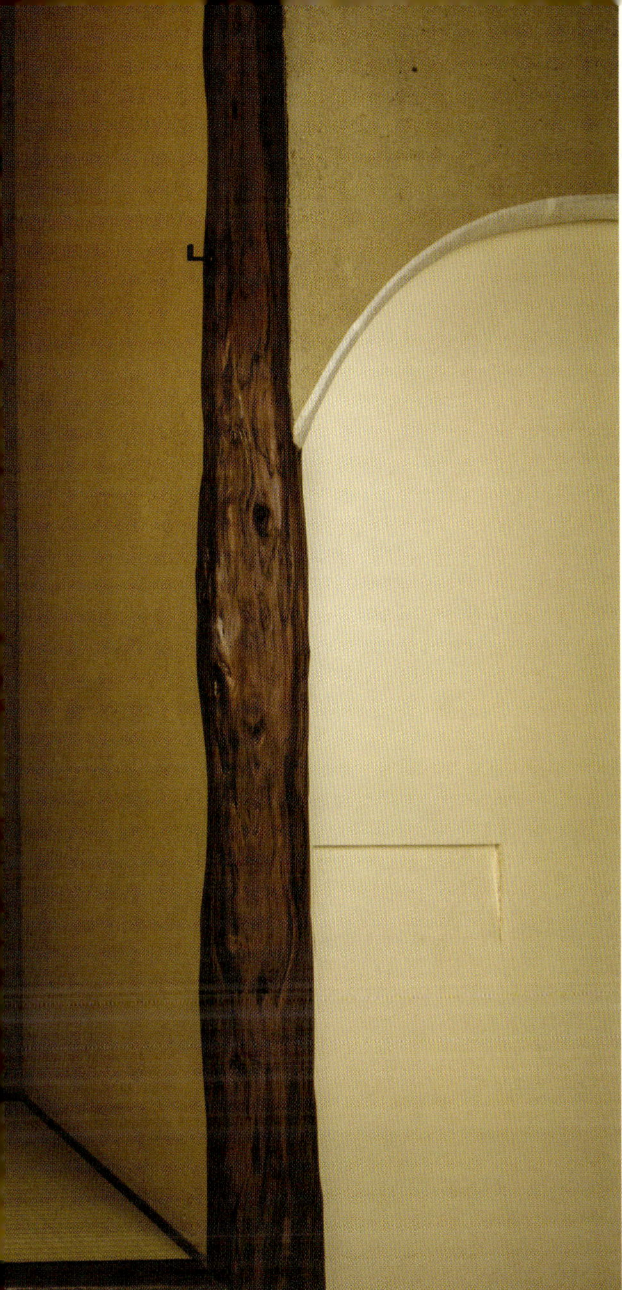

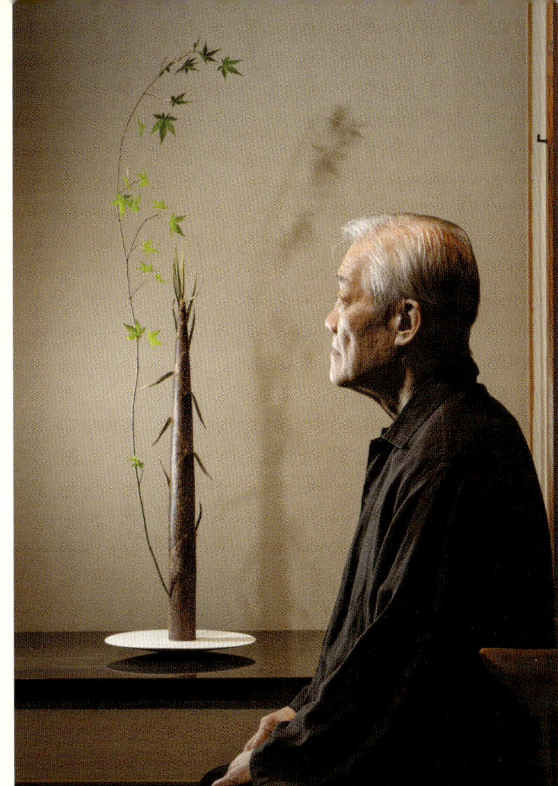

to do with them was truly fascinating. Since they were fresh, they were full of moisture, and if left as is, they would soon rot—so they couldn't be kept. They had to be used, and I felt truly fortunate to be able to use something so luxurious. There were three shoots. I hung one in the alcove of the small tea room, just as I would with a bamboo flower container, and arranged wisteria in it. The remaining two I arranged not in the tea room, but in an earthen-floored space with clay walls (see pages 78–79). There, I used a white porcelain serving dish as a kind of stand or table, creating an arrangement

that has a slightly elevated, buoyant feeling.

The flowers I usually arrange for tea gatherings are mostly white. That's Toda's preference—and mine as well. I think white flowers harmonize most naturally with the other utensils. They assert themselves, but never get in the way. They're clear and composed. It may be a strange way to put it, but I find them masculine. Red and pink feel more feminine. Still, flowers of many other colors arrive during this season. I never expected to see a woodland peony, but Hanacho sent me one, lovingly cultivated, and I used it with care and gratitude.

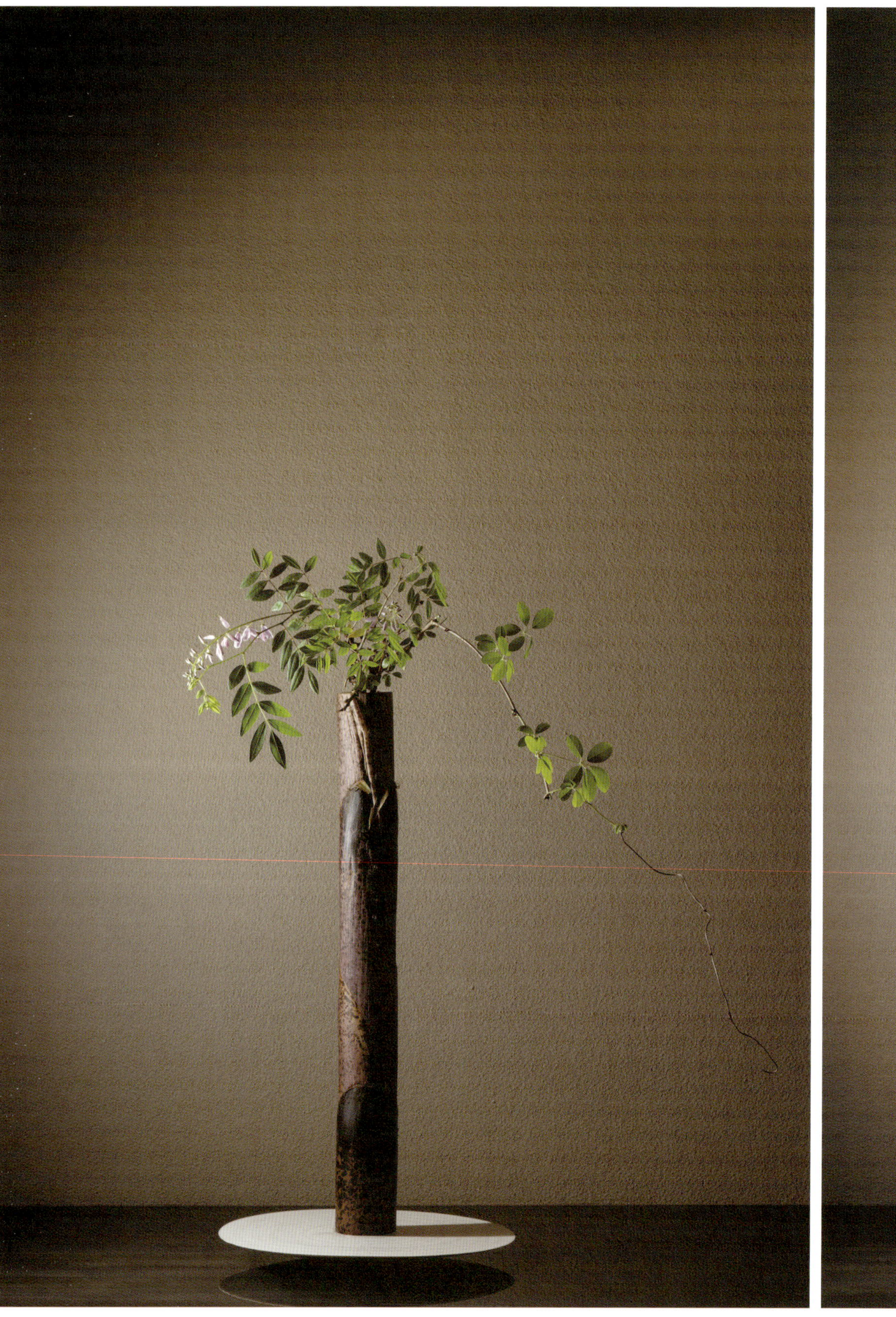

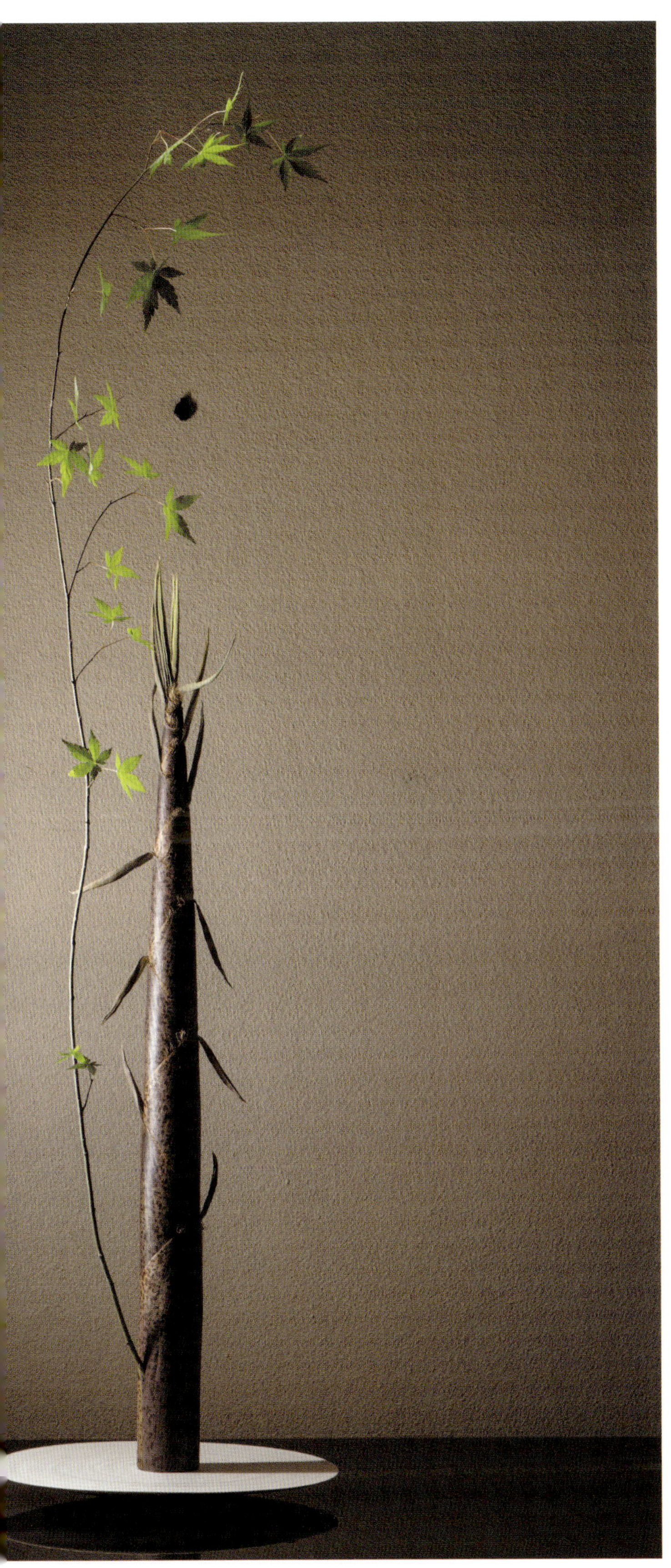

The tip of a bamboo shoot is cut off and used as a flower container, with garden wisteria and chocolate vine leaves arranged inside. This is not a flower for the tea room, but a playful, everyday arrangement. The way the wisteria and chocolate vine gently spill out is like bringing a small slice of the mountains indoors.

The container is placed in the same space with a different composition. Making use of the graceful line of fresh green maple, an opening was cut near the base of the bamboo shoot. Though the bamboo shoot serves as a flower container, it is still alive, standing upright — and together with the maple branches rising even higher above it, the two forms beautifully complement each other.

A Rare Seasonal Encounter — Bamboo Shoots as Containers

Here an upright bamboo shoot is treated as a regular bamboo flower container. In the spirit of *shiseido*, (meaning "cut pure green bamboo, fill it with pure water, arrange pure flowers with a pure heart") both the living vessel and the living flowers express their vitality. On the facing page, the tip of the bamboo shoot is cut off, and garden wisteria and chocolate vine leaves are arranged at the mouth of the container. On this page, a hole is opened near the base of the bamboo shoot, and one slender branch of fresh green maple is inserted. The contemporary white porcelain dish, used as a flower stand, brightens and unifies the overall composition Both arrangements — the flowing line of the chocolate vine leaves extending to the right and the maple rising up from below — convey light, airy movement that expands into the surrounding space.

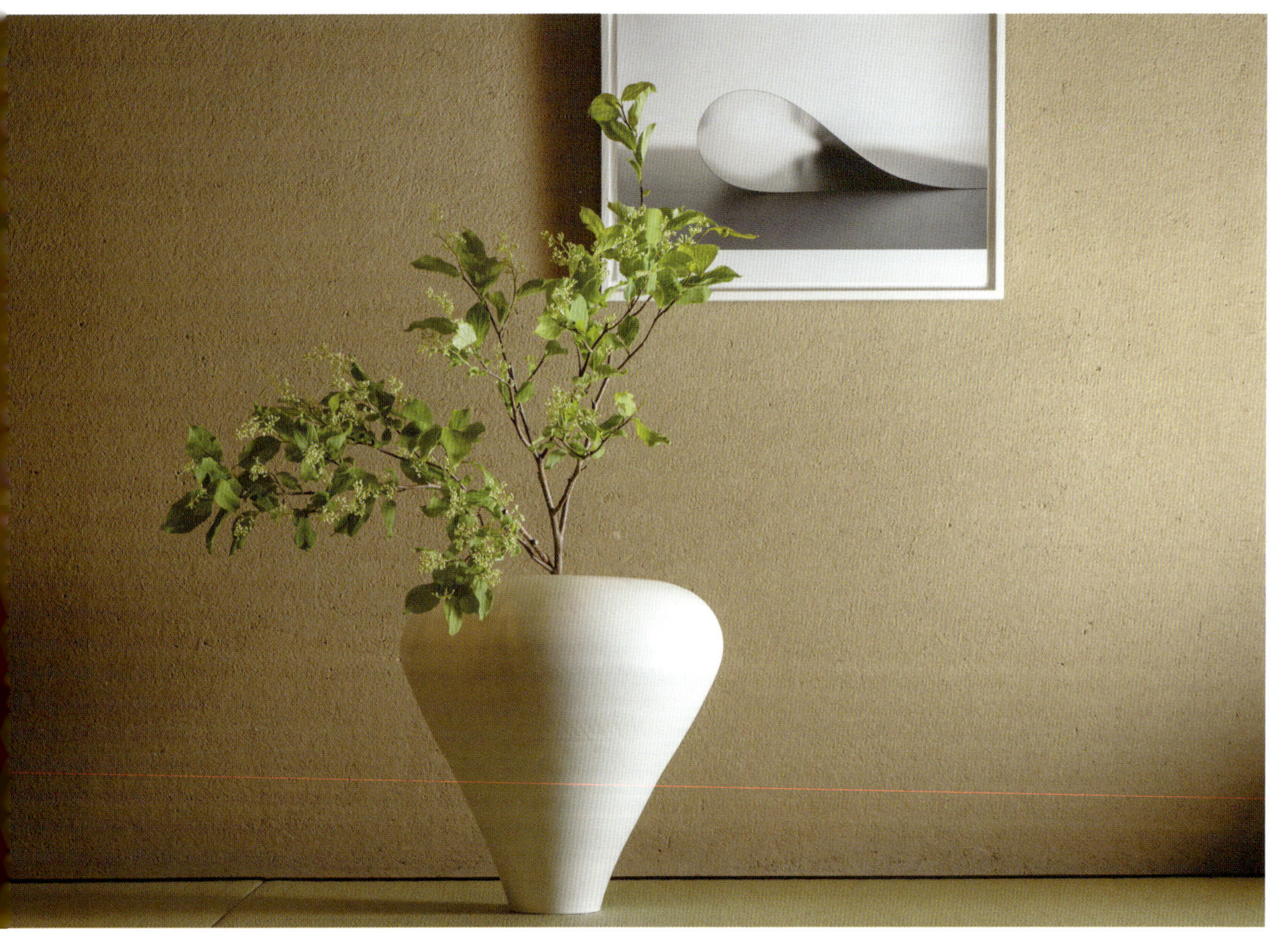

Sapphireberry. White porcelain flower container by Taizo Kuroda (see page 154).

A flower arrangement for everyday living spaces. A monochrome photograph titled *Paper Drop* by German artist Wolfgang Tillmans is hung on the wall, with sapphire-berry arranged in a white porcelain flower container by Taizo Kuroda. The pairing was chosen with the sense that the photo, expressed entirely through gradations of light and shadow, feels like a contemporary ink painting.

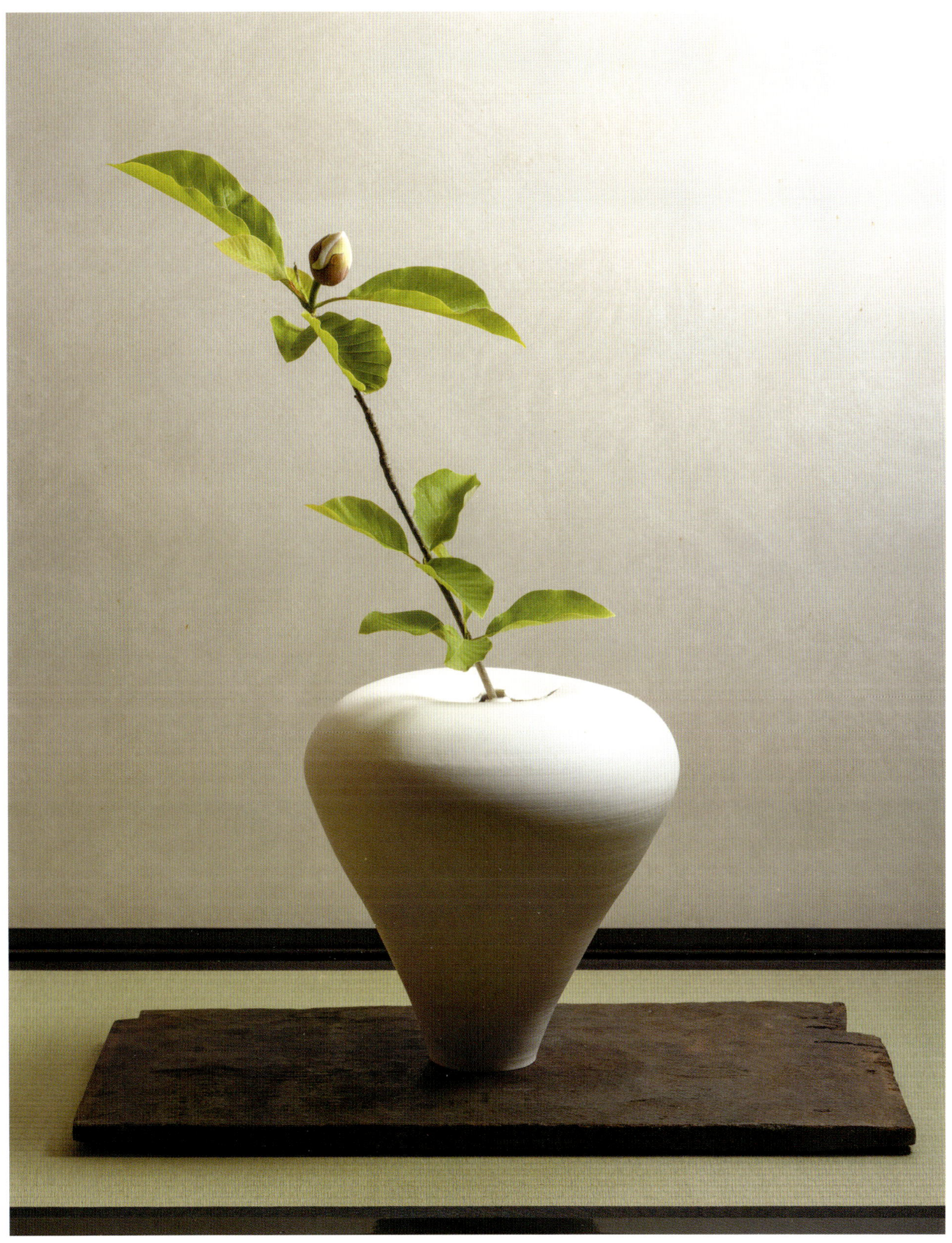

Upward-facing Magnolia sieboldii blossom. White porcelain flower container by Taizo Kuroda (see page 154).

The upward-facing magnolia sieboldii is thought to be a hybrid of the magnolia sieboldii and the Japanese bigleaf magnolia. It has a character closer to the latter — an early- summer flower. "The bloom is so large it's hard to use in a tea room, but it suits this vase, which is 14 inches (35 cm) tall. It's a strong flower, no need to add anything else," says Kobayashi.

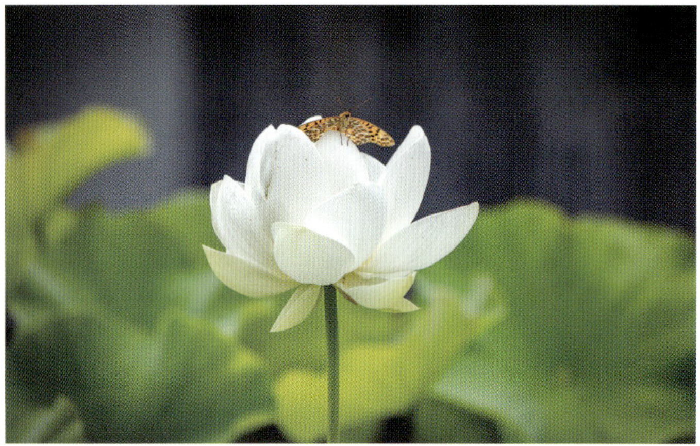

At the mountain retreat lotus pond, blossoms rise straight up from the many overlapping lotus leaves, spreading out like waves. Drawn by the scent of the flowers, bees, dragonflies, butterflies, and various insects gather fluttering around the pond. A butterfly pauses for a moment, resting its wings atop a lotus blossom.

A Mountain Retreat in Izu

White Lotus

I love white flowers, but if I had to choose my favorite flower throughout the entire year, it would be the lotus. And then there's the magnolia sieboldii, which blooms a little earlier. To me, these two flowers are unmatched, and I find that they pair beautifully with any hanging scroll or flower vessel. Especially the lotus—it's beautiful even when depicted in a painting, and when I see the real flower in front of me, I instinctively bring my hands together in reverence.

I felt a strong desire to have them close by, so I built a large lotus pond in the garden of my mountain retreat in Izu, a mountainous peninsula south of Tokyo. Every year, around March, I dig up the roots and, together with my gardener, decide where and how to replant them while eagerly anticipating the season when they will bloom again. The earliest blossoms begin to appear around May, and they can be enjoyed throughout the summer.

In the tea room, lotus flowers are often associated with memorial services, which means that for many people, the lotus has come to be regarded as a "Buddhist" flower. But I think that we should cast aside any preconceptions that we might have and simply say, "It's lotus season, and they're blooming in the garden—so let's use them." That's how tea flowers are meant to be. If certain notions within the world of tea haven't developed into a universally admired aesthetic, then they're nothing more than empty form. It's important not to overthink things, but to approach them straightforwardly. The reason I want to use this flower is because it's the most beautiful one of the season—that's the spirit I want to honor.

At my mountain retreat, a close friend lives on the neighboring property. I've mentioned him briefly before—his name is Takashi Inaba (see page 92). He's a master of flowers and also my teacher. We happen to be the same age, and it's already been over thirty years since we became friends. He's someone who stimulates me on many levels—not just where flowers are concerned, but also when it comes to art, cooking, interior arrangements and spatial awareness. This month, in Inaba's living

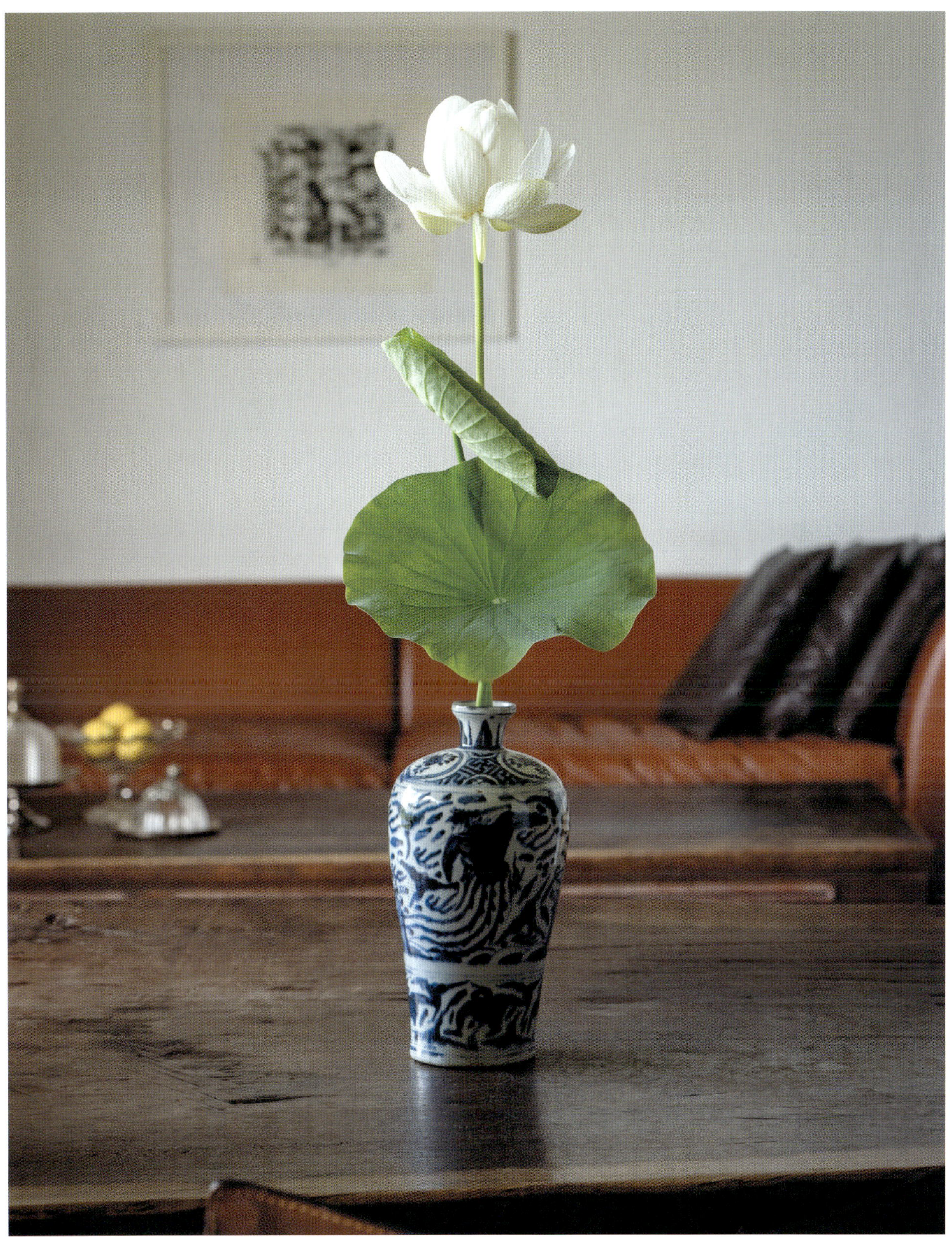

White lotus. Blue-and-white flower container in the classic high-shouldered meiping style, China, Ming dynasty.

A single white lotus is selected from the garden pond and arranged in a Chinese blue-and-white porcelain vessel, which, with its gently rounded shoulders and deep blue glaze, further accentuates the whiteness of the lotus. Using a flower container with a small opening also enhances the upright elegance of the lotus blossom.

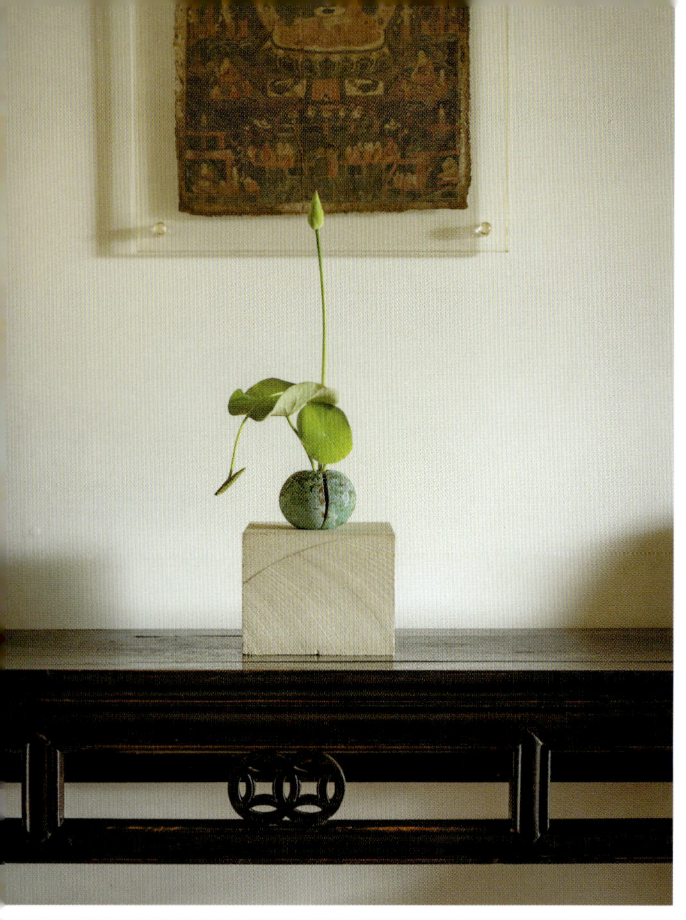

space, Atsushi Kobayashi worked with lotus flowers and brought out their full charm.

Incidentally, my lotus pond is carved into a simple square—this too was Inaba's idea, designed to highlight the beauty of the lotus flowers.

One summer morning, filled with the spirit of the mountains, Inaba and Kobayashi went together to the pond, now blooming with white and pale pink flowers, and picked lotuses. Kobayashi arranged them in a Chinese blue-and-white porcelain flower container (see page 83). While flowers in the tea room are meant for the moment of the tea gathering, flowers that are displayed in a home setting carry a presence that lasts a bit longer. A few days later, Kobayashi revisited the white lotus and, seeing how it had aged, replaced the vessel and rearranged the flower: he selected an Indonesian bronze piece and placed it between a white porcelain jar and stand made by Taizo Kuroda (see page 154). The white lotus, arranged in the bronze vessel, seemed to hover in the space between the soft lines of the porcelain and the blue-green sheen of the bronze—a work that captures a single fleeting life (see facing page).

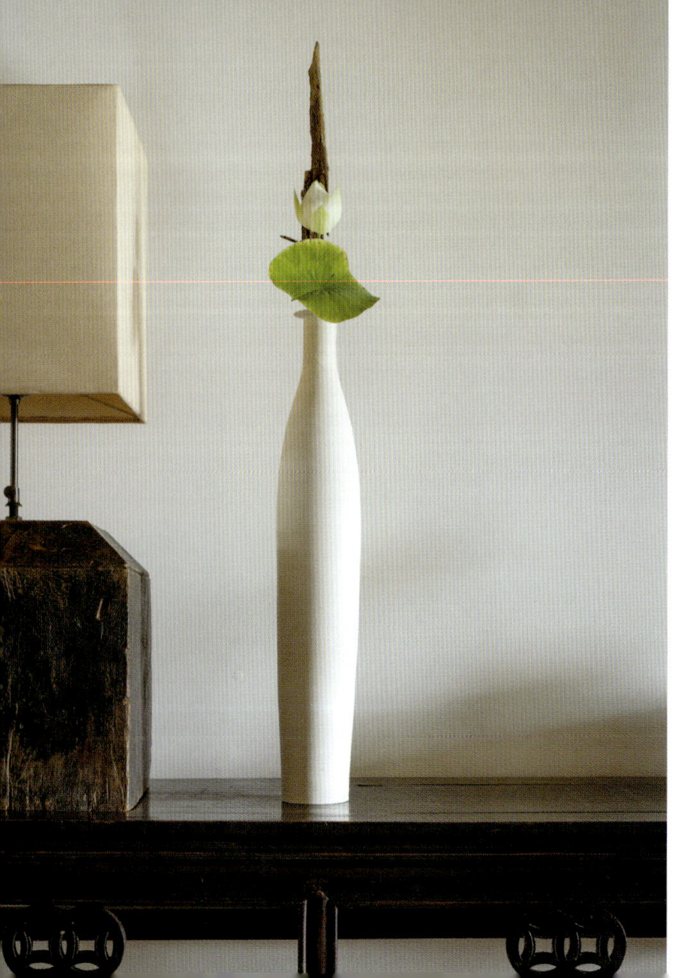

TOP White lotus. Bronze bangle, Java, Indonesia.

A small white lotus is arranged in balance with a vessel made from an old bronze bangle from Indonesia that has an inner holder placed inside. The curve of the leaf is highlighted, while the lotus bud is given height to stand upright.

LEFT White lotus, old branch. White porcelain flower container by Taizo Kuroda (see page 154).

A short-stemmed lotus flower and leaf are placed in a tall white porcelain vessel, and an old branch is added along the extended line formed by the vessel and the flower. By incorporating aged wood in this way, a sense of time is introduced, creating an expression distinct from arrangements using only fresh flowers.

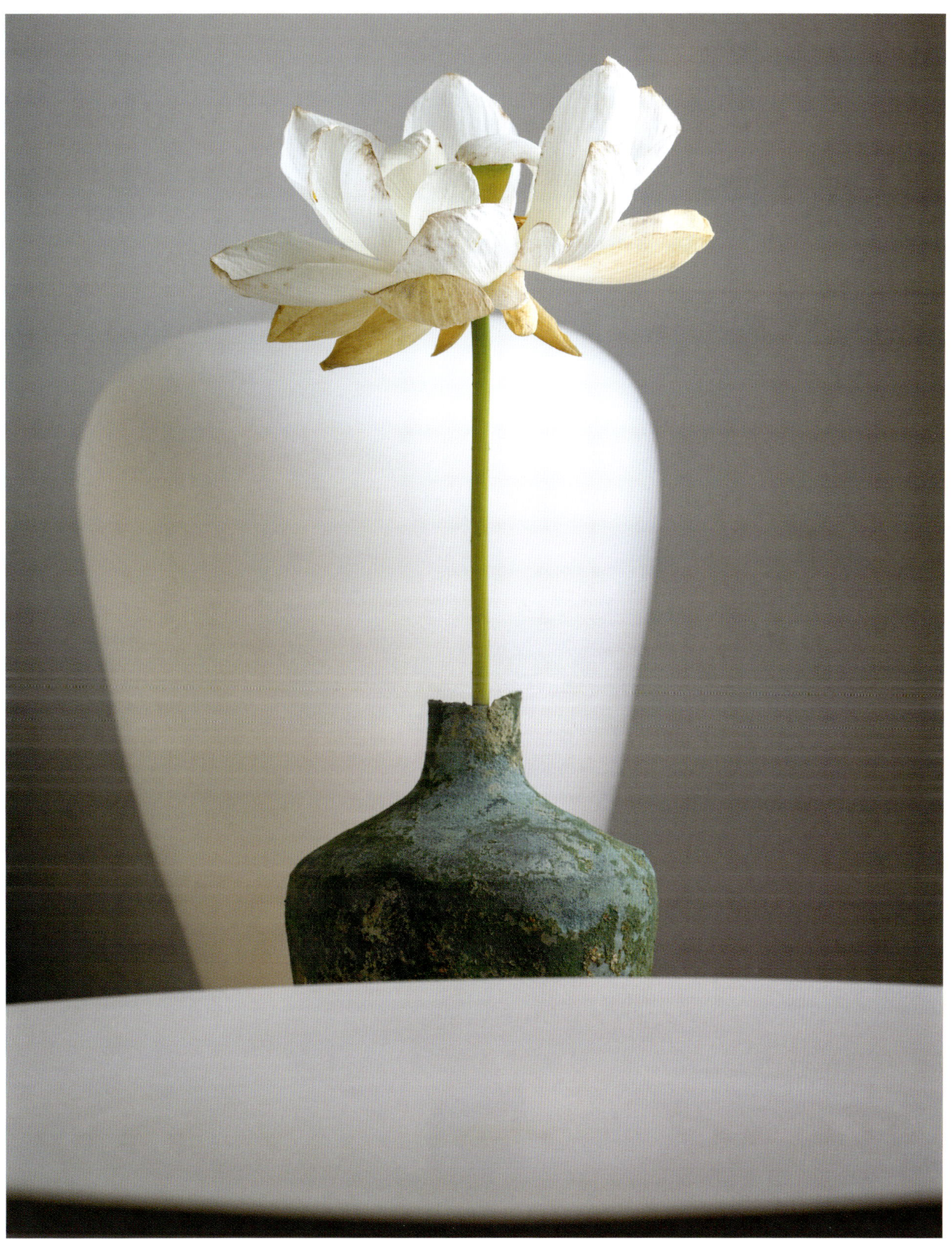

White lotus. Bronze vessel, Java, Indonesia.

The gradual fading of the white petals is appreciated as part of the experience. A single lotus is placed — deliberately without any accompanying leaves — into a bronze vessel, and set between a white porcelain jar in the background and a white porcelain pedestal dish in the foreground. The contrast between the vessels further accentuates the flower.

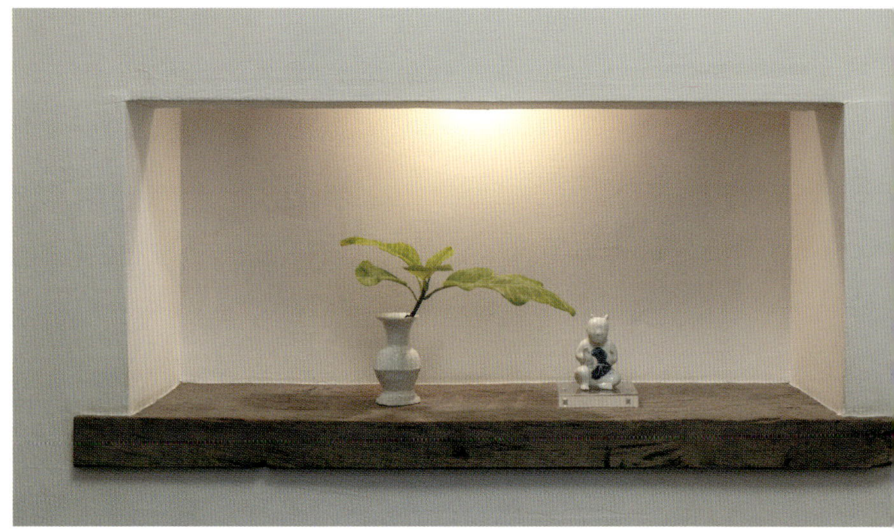

**Japanese bigleaf magnolia.
Small white porcelain flower
container, China, Song dynasty.**

A leaf from the Japanese big-leaf magnolia is placed in the alcove at the entryway to the house. In keeping with the scale of the space, few materials are used, and the height of the arrangement is about half the height of the alcove. The spread of the leaf to the side allows the space to breathe. Alongside is a blue-and-white porcelain *karako* (child figure) from the Yuan dynasty of China.

Flowers and Utensils for July

At the Gyokuhokan Inn

My first encounter with my friend and mentor Takashi Inaba was when, through an acquaintance's introduction, I stayed at his renowned Gyokuhokan Inn on the Izu Peninsula. Inaba has since passed the inn on to someone else and now lives a serene, carefree life surrounded by Izu's natural beauty.

But back then, the atmosphere that filled the Gyokuhokan was extraordinary. I was struck by the interior spaces, the arrangements and the food—all of which were unlike anything I had ever experienced. The furnishings, in particular, were not at all showy, yet there were many stunning floral arrangements. I realized this was no ordinary inn—and it turned out that Inaba was its owner.

I'm by no means well-versed in flowers, but I was deeply moved to see that there was someone who could arrange flowers like that. That was my first encounter with Inaba's floral work—and with *jiyubana*, the art of freestyle flower arranging.

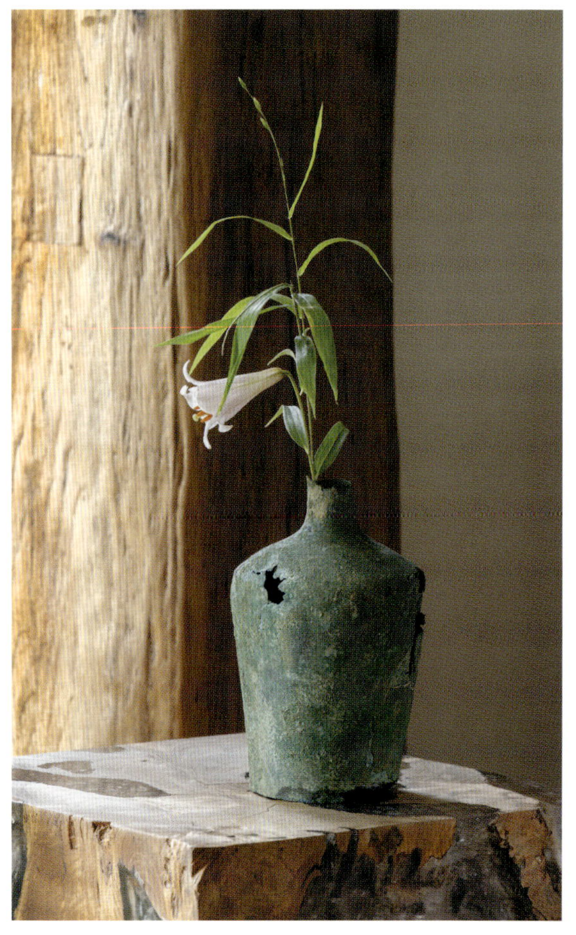

**Bamboo lily and quaking grass.
Bronze vessel, Java, Indonesia**

Even one lily has a strong presence, but the airy lines of the quaking grass add height and balance the composition.

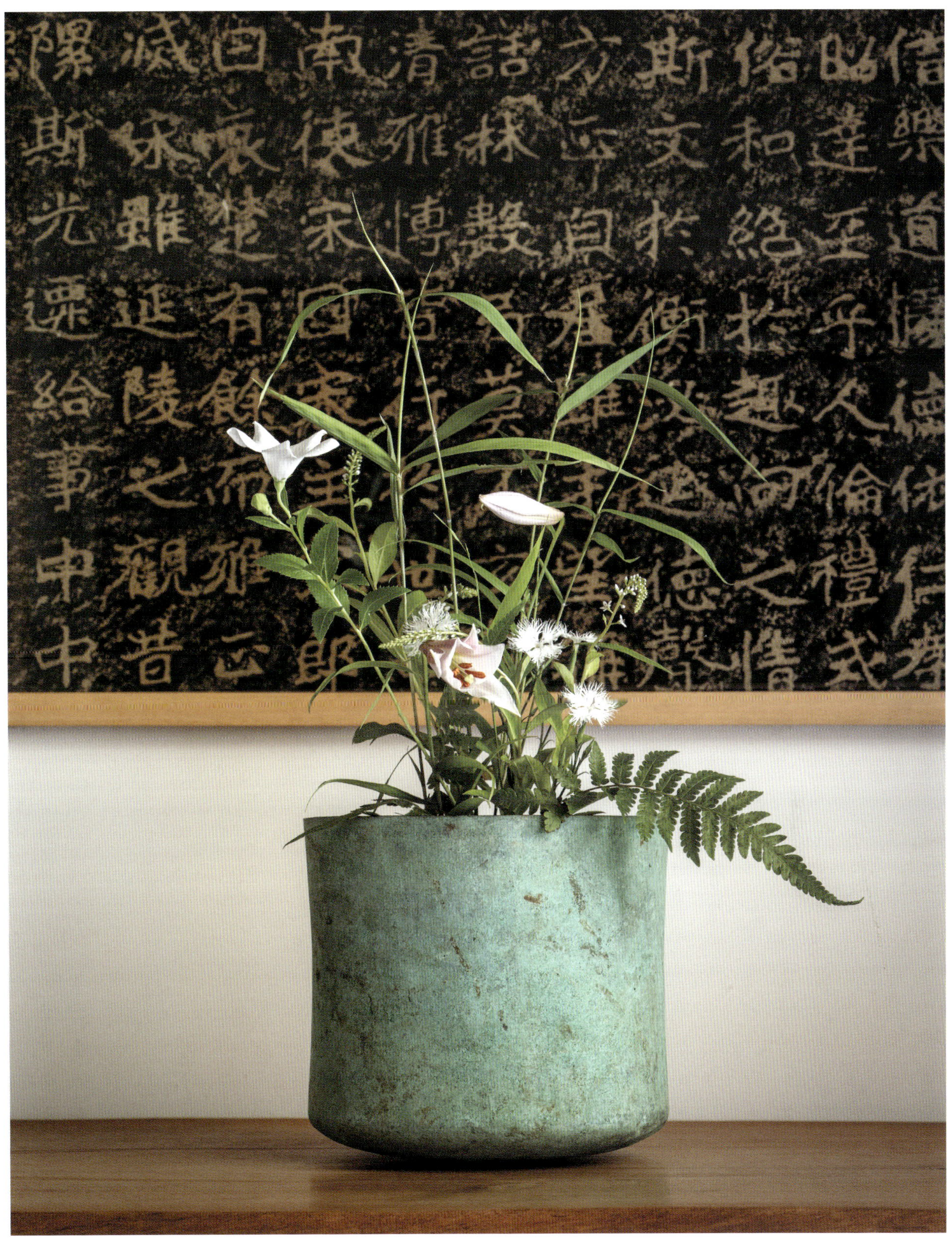

Bamboo lily, fringed pink, balloon flower, lizard's tail, fern, bamboo. Bronze ritual vessel, Java, Indonesia.

Here too, the arrangement centers on the bamboo lily, with six other wildflowers. To create a sense of lightness, all the elements are first placed, then fine adjustments are made — removing or repositioning stems to avoid overlap. On the wall is a rubbing of a calligraphy piece by Zheng Daozhao, of China's Northern Wei dynasty.

After that, I began staying at the inn several times a year, and on those nights, Inaba and I would talk until morning. We'd go back and forth in animated conversation from the night before until eight or nine the next morning. People would say, "How can two men talk that much?" but we never ran out of things to say. We'd talk about art and all sorts of other topics.

Originally, I had operated only within the world of tea ceramics and wasn't used to stepping outside that arena, but when I spent time with him, I would find myself crossing those boundaries without even meaning to. I didn't dislike art—I had dabbled in it a bit when I trained at the Yayoi Gallery in Tokyo after graduating from university—so when I met him, it was as if I suddenly took two or three big steps outside my usual domain.

That said, even when I praised the art he had found, saying, "This is great!" all he would reply was a modest "Yes." Very reserved. But perhaps it was exactly because he was that kind of person that I became so deeply engrossed. As we grew closer, I came to feel that his character combined intuition and intellect. His personality just clicked with mine. Everything he said made sense, and his taste was impeccable—or at least that's how it seemed to us. By "us," I mean that partway through, I began inviting my friend, the ceramic artist Jikinyu Raku, to join me. (Until 2019, he was known as Raku Kichizaemon, the fifteenth-generation head of the Raku lineage.) He too became completely captivated by Inaba's world.

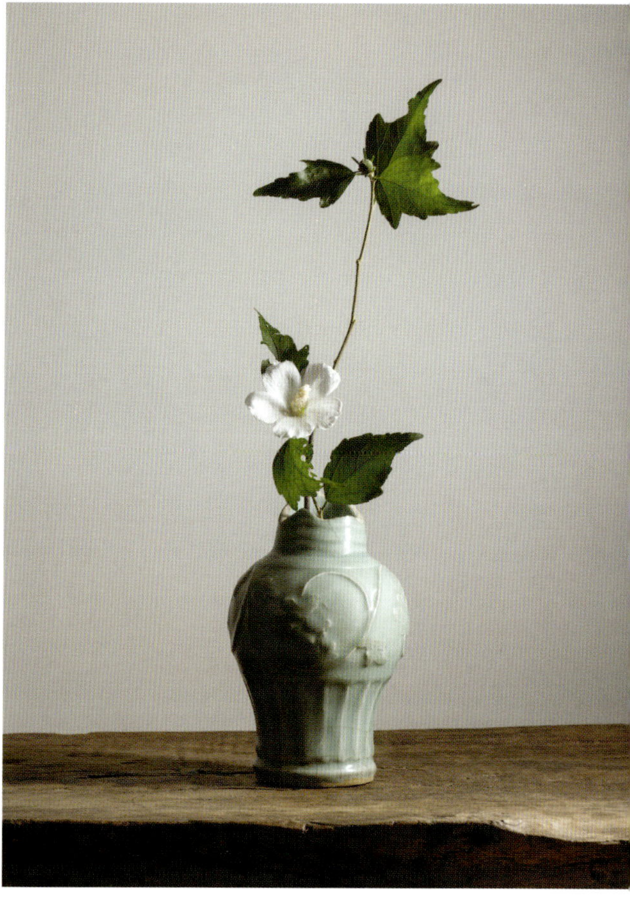

White rose of Sharon. Longquan celadon flower container with floating peony design, China, Ming dynasty.

A white rose of Sharon from Inaba-san's garden is arranged in a small celadon jar. By leaving a branch with small buds extending upward, the composition creates a sense of spatial openness. This piece captures the graceful form of the rose of Sharon, a quintessential summer flower often used in *furo*-season tea gatherings.

Using Flower Stems as a Support Structure

Just as woody branches can be laid across the inside of a container to act as a flower holder, blackberry lily stems are used to secure the arrangement here. When arranging flowers, how you create a support structure is a key consideration, and several methods have been introduced so far. With the container shown on the facing page, the wide mouth and visibility of the flower holder call for a particular support structure. While it's fine to use branches from other plants, using parts of the same flowers in the arrangement helps maintain a natural, cohesive look. Unlike woody branches, the stems of herbaceous plants are less flexible, so it's important to cut them at just the right length and angle so the ends sit neatly against the rim of the stoneware vessel.

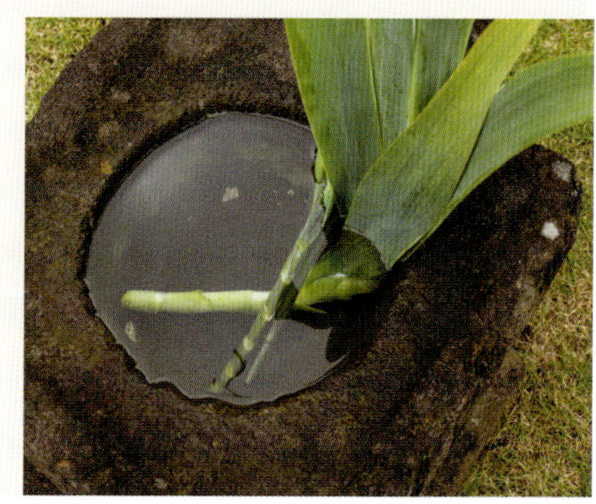

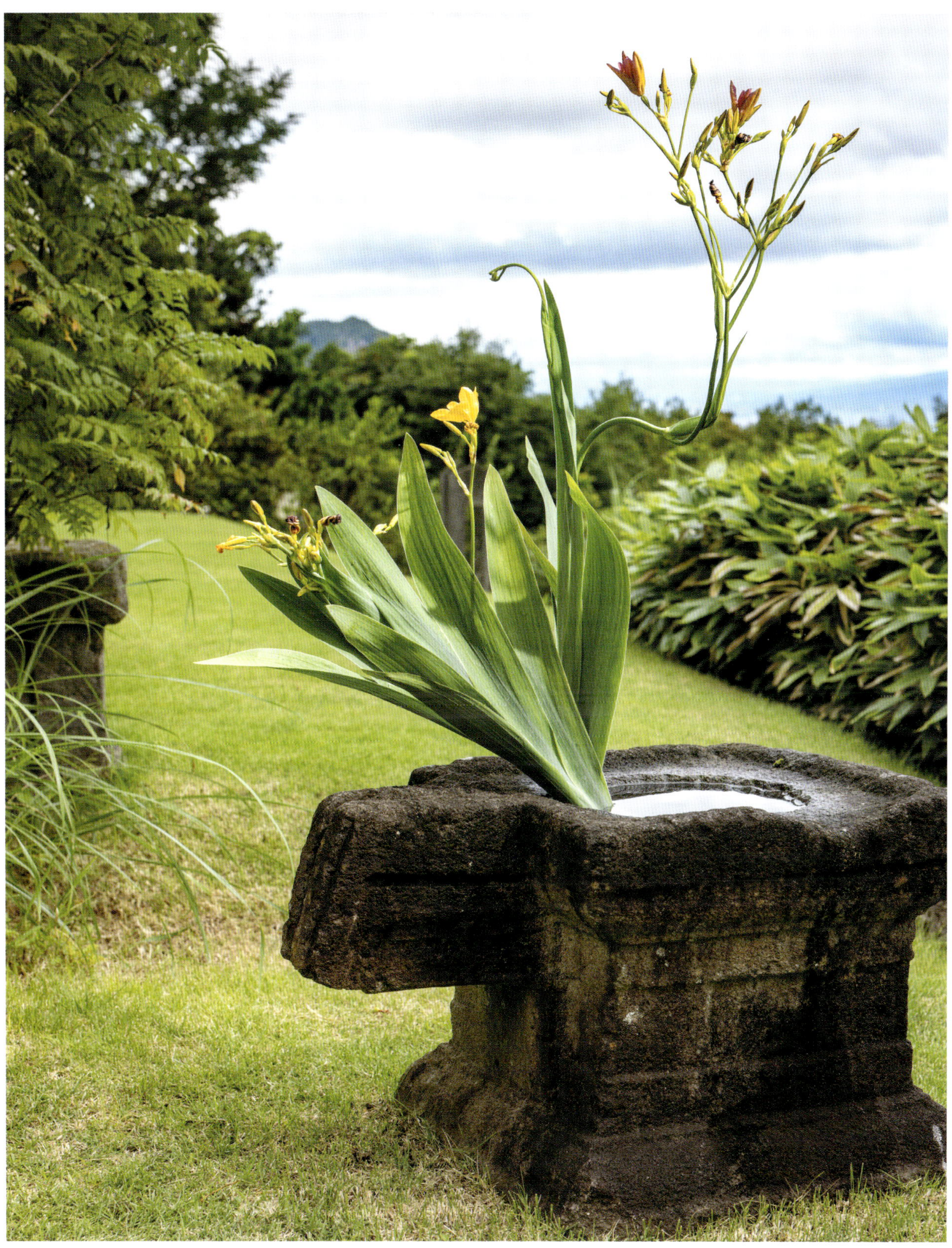

Two varieties of blackberry lily. Stone ritual vessel, Java, Indonesia.

Two varieties of blackberry lily are arranged in a carved stone ritual vessel placed in the garden. The vessel, said to symbolize the feminine in Indonesian ritual culture, is beautifully complemented by the vibrant leaves and blossoms of the blackberry lilies.

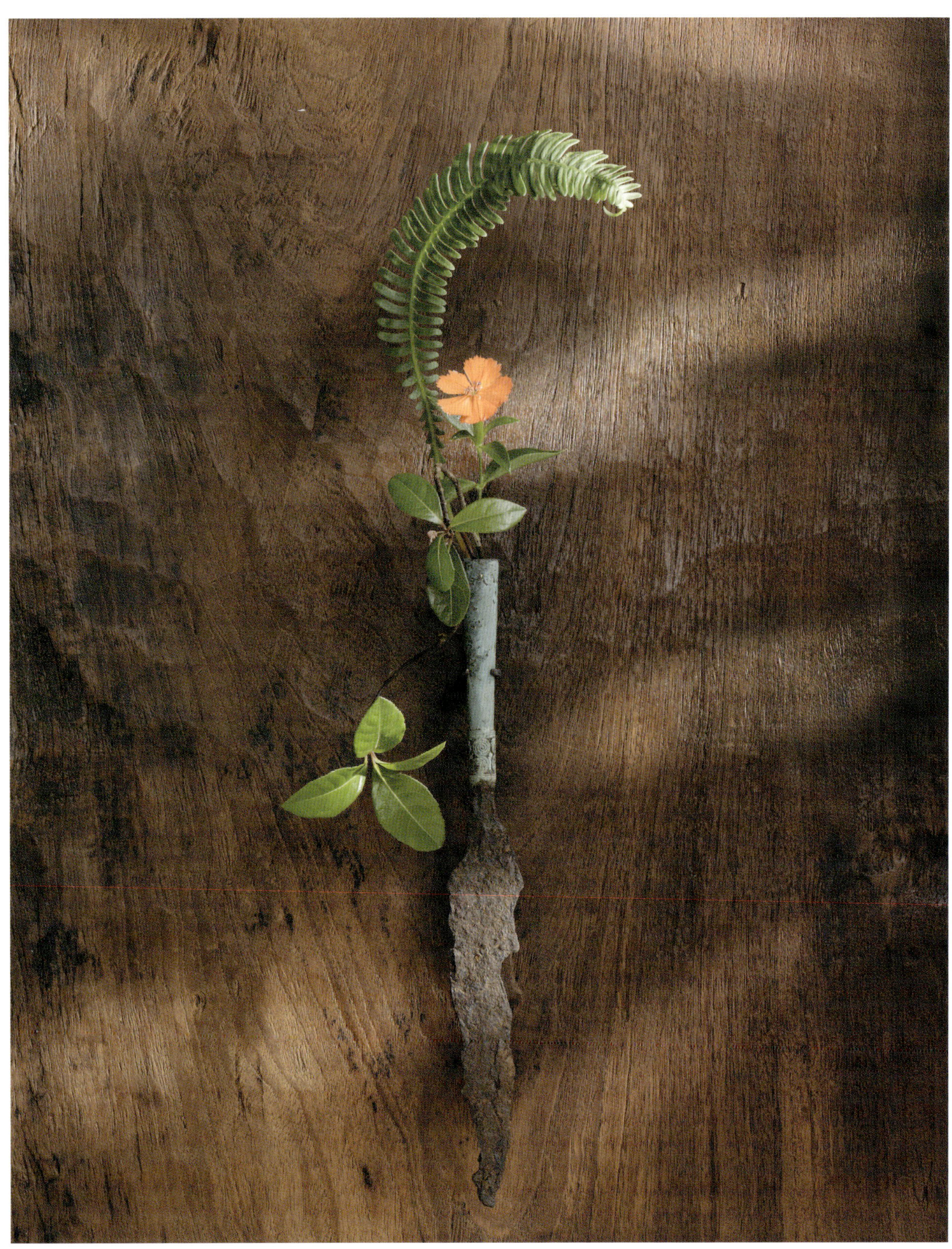

**Japanese campion, Japanese ardisia, fern.
Bronze sword, Java, Indonesia.**

A bronze sword from Indonesia, around two thousand years old, is used here as a hanging flower container, holding three kinds of plants. The vivid-colored Japanese campion, the fern curving gracefully upward, and the ardisia trailing down along the left side of the container — all their lines come together to form a single rhythm.

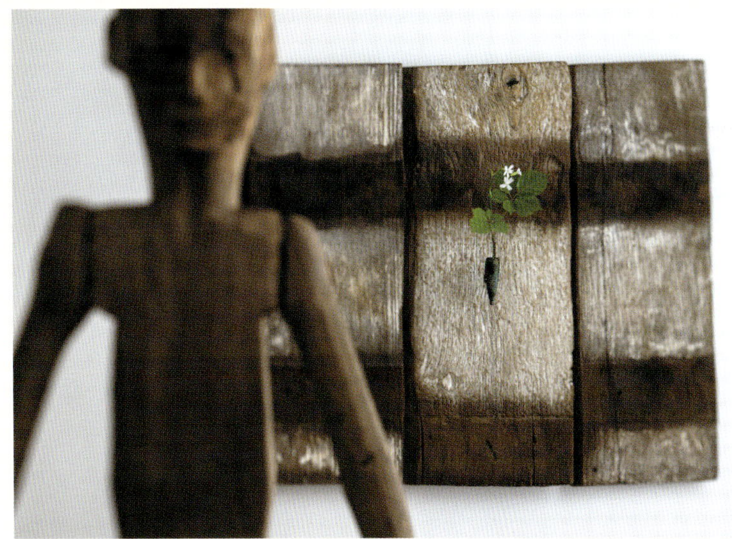

Daphne and koshiabura. Bronze bell, Java, Indonesia.

A bronze bell is used as a hanging flower container, mounted on a panel from an old Javanese house. Rather than appearing to be arranged, the flowers seem to have grown there naturally. In the foreground is a primitive carved wooden figure.

Flowers and the Passage of Time
— Atsushi Kobayashi

Lotus flowers can be surprisingly difficult to arrange. When stems are straight and upright, there's little room for creative variation, so how you incorporate the leaves becomes key. Adding contrast with new shoots or fully opened leaves, and using height differences to shape the space—all of those elements must be carefully considered. Interestingly, lotuses pair well with a wide variety of flower containers. They can suit Chinese ceramics; or jars from the Six Ancient Kilns, such as Tokoname; or even contemporary white porcelain pieces.

At the start of this chapter are several arrangements I made for white lotuses. The most striking reuses a single bloom (page 83) from a lotus pond two days later in a different container (page 85). While tea flowers are usually arranged for short-lived occasions, this time I placed them in an everyday space, which allowed me to enjoy the passing of time a bit more fully. There is beauty in the flower as it blooms, and also in its withering—both are equally captivating.

In my twenties, I lived and worked at the Gyokuhokan Inn, where I learned how to engage with flowers from Takashi Inaba. Later, when I moved to Toda Shoten and began arranging flowers for the tea ceremony, what I learned back then became the philosophical foundation of my approach to flowers.

One example is the balance of time embodied by the flower and the container. A freshly cut flower represents the "now," but when placed in an "old" container, a gap in time emerges between the two. The greater that contrast, the deeper the aesthetic experience. But using a contemporary artist's vessel doesn't mean it lacks appeal. In the white porcelain of Taizo Kuroda, for instance, there is a distinctly modern beauty of form. And when such a vessel is paired with aged materials like old wood, a sense of time again emerges between them.

Whether in tea flowers or everyday arrangements, I've come to realize that the act of arranging is an expression of time itself.

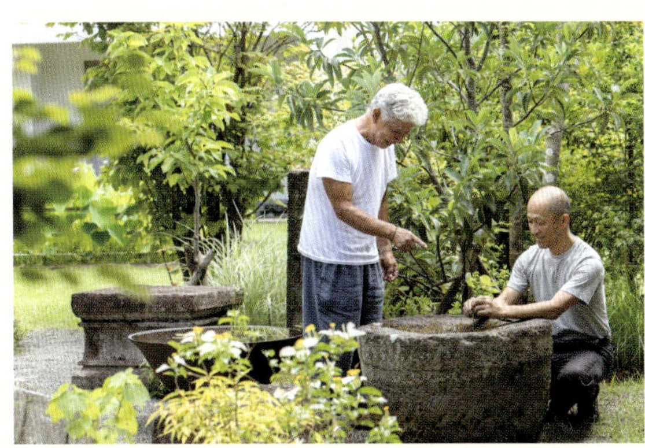

In front of an old Indonesian stone mill filled with water in the garden, Takashi Inaba and Atsushi Kobayashi talk about flowers. Leaves of aquatic plants float on the surface, and Kobayashi is about to add a single flower he picked from the garden (see page 99, bottom photo).

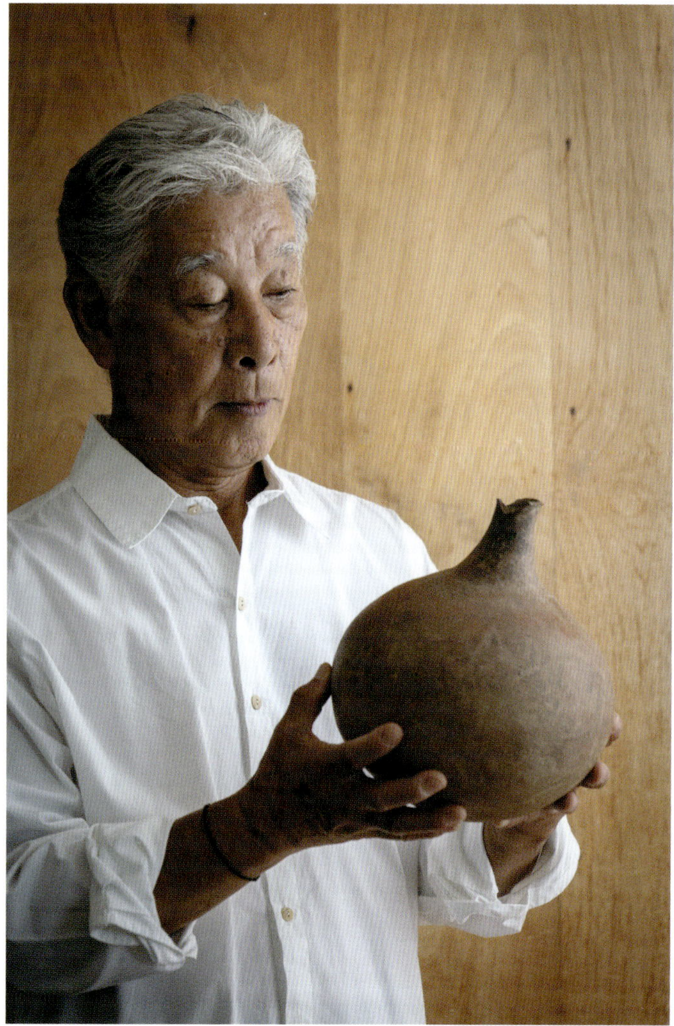

Surrounded by Primitive Art:
Takashi Inaba's Mountain Life

Takashi Inaba is a well-known collector among those familiar with the world of Indonesian primitive art. He is known by the name "Takashi," and the works he has discovered are recognized as the Takashi Collection.

The word "primitive" refers to something primal or original, and in Indonesia, one can find many examples of what might be called primitive or tribal art. Globally, major tribal art collections can be found in places like the Musée du Quai Branly in

Paris, but few collectors focus solely on Indonesian works. Inaba was the foremost figure introducing a calm, peace-oriented art that arose from Indonesia's agrarian cultures. I don't think anyone else in Japan has his level of insight.

From wooden statues of deities and animals to bronze utensils and simple earthenware, I'm deeply drawn to the art he has discovered—not because it can be used in the tea ceremony, but because of the sheer power those objects emit.

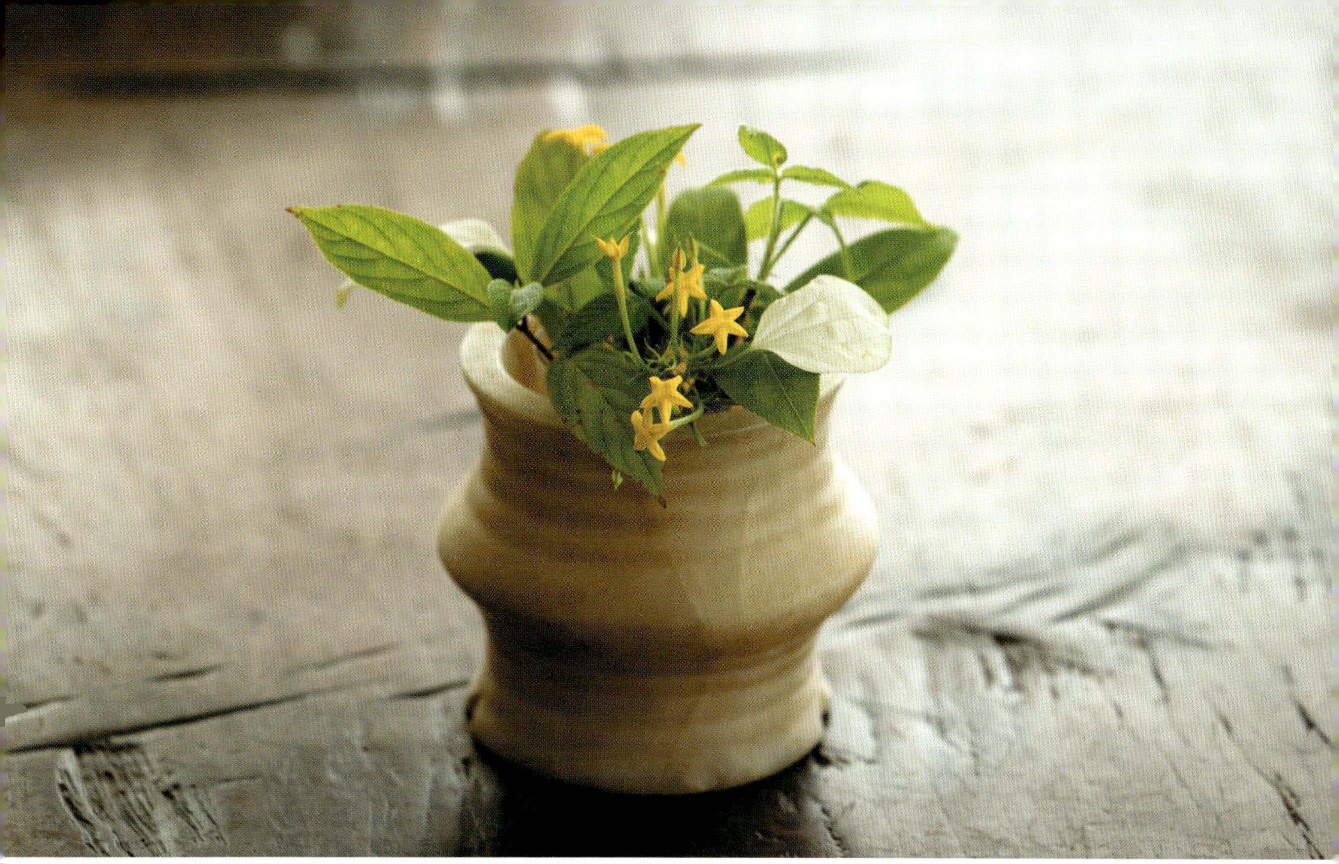

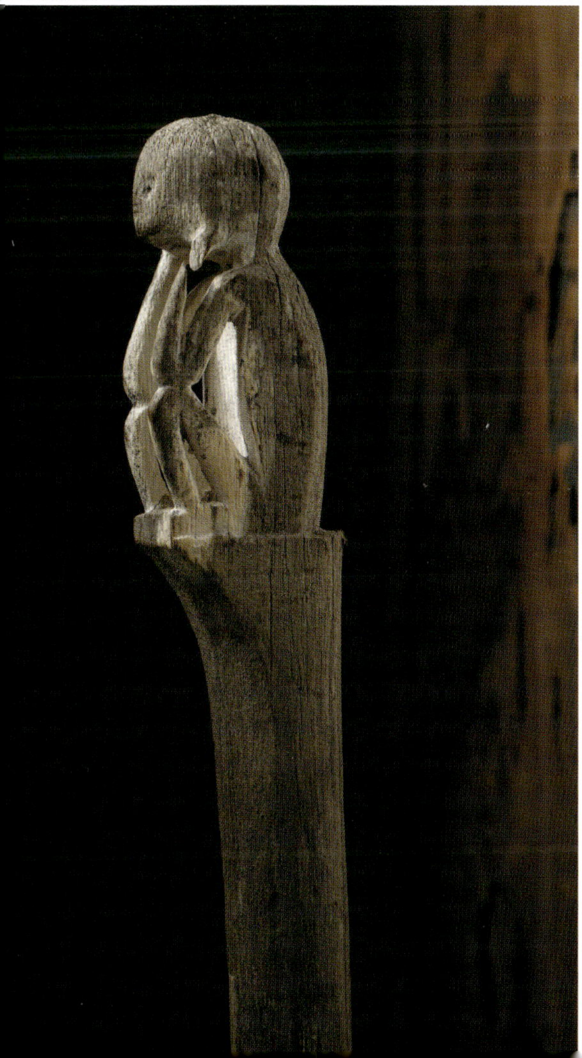

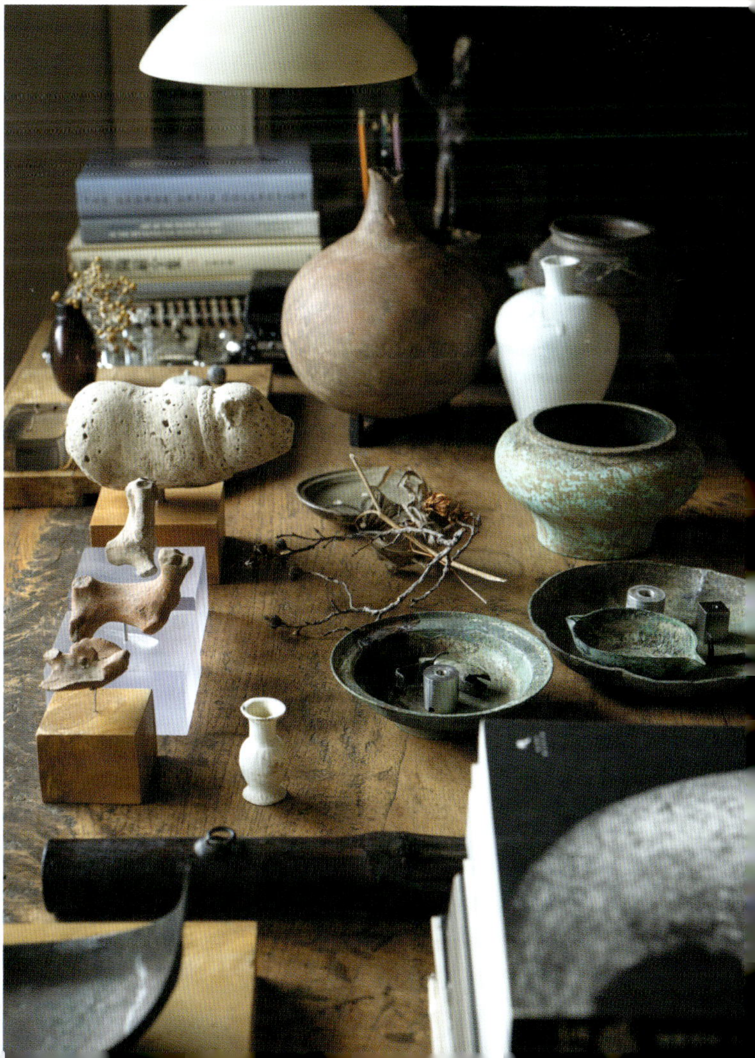

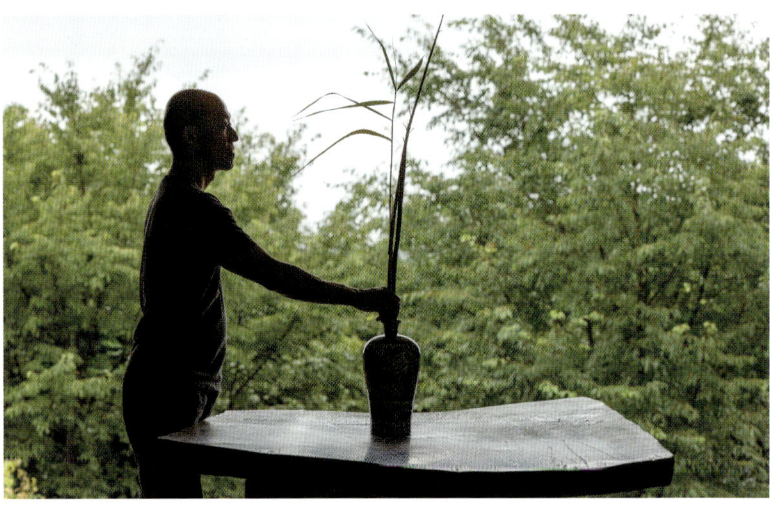

Against a deep green backdrop of flourishing midsummer foliage, the living room window is thrown open and a flower vessel is placed on the table where Atsushi Kobayashi arranges flowers. He adjusts the height and volume of the materials, checking the overall balance as he positions each element in relation to the vessel. A quiet moment in the early morning, when the spirit of the mountains reaches the room.

Arranged with the Heart's Intuition

Midsummer Greenery

In this chapter I visit Takashi Inaba's home in Izu to spend time with flowers. In a space surrounded by the green of the mountains, I arranged flowers in harmony with Indonesian art. Here, I'd also like to share a bit more about the primitive art of Indonesia that continues to draw me in.

Indonesian primitivism is deeply tied to prayers to the divine and is filled with a simple beauty. I believe there is a shared sensibility between the peaceful agrarian people of Indonesia and the Japanese people. On the islands of Indonesia, protected by the sea, there was little fear of invasion by other ethnic groups, and people lived in peace. The one great fear was illness and death which—because they were beyond human control—were regarded as divine, and people offered prayers in hopes of warding off sickness and preserving life. The physical forms of these prayers—such as humble wooden carvings or animal figures etched into the wooden doors of ancestral tombs—are what we now see as Indonesian art. These sincere expressions of prayer touch the heart, not through logic, but through feeling.

Objects from Indonesia were already being incorporated into the tea ceremony in Japan during the time of Sen no Rikyu. For example, the sand-cast bronze hanging boat-shaped flower container was originally an Indonesian ritual vessel that Japanese tea practitioners reimagined as a vase. Other items like old ceramics and lacquerware from Vietnam or China also belong to this category. As I mentioned earlier, I also find a primitive beauty in the bamboo flower containers born from the Japanese tea tradition. The utensils Rikyu selected were the most advanced of his time, yet he had already discovered and incorporated primitive art. When I encounter Rikyu's utensils or look at the art collected by Takashi Inaba, I can't help but feel that the act of using one's own eyes to judge what is beautiful and pursuing that with sincerity, is in fact a truly universal and uncomplicated way of living. And perhaps that is the very essence of tea itself.

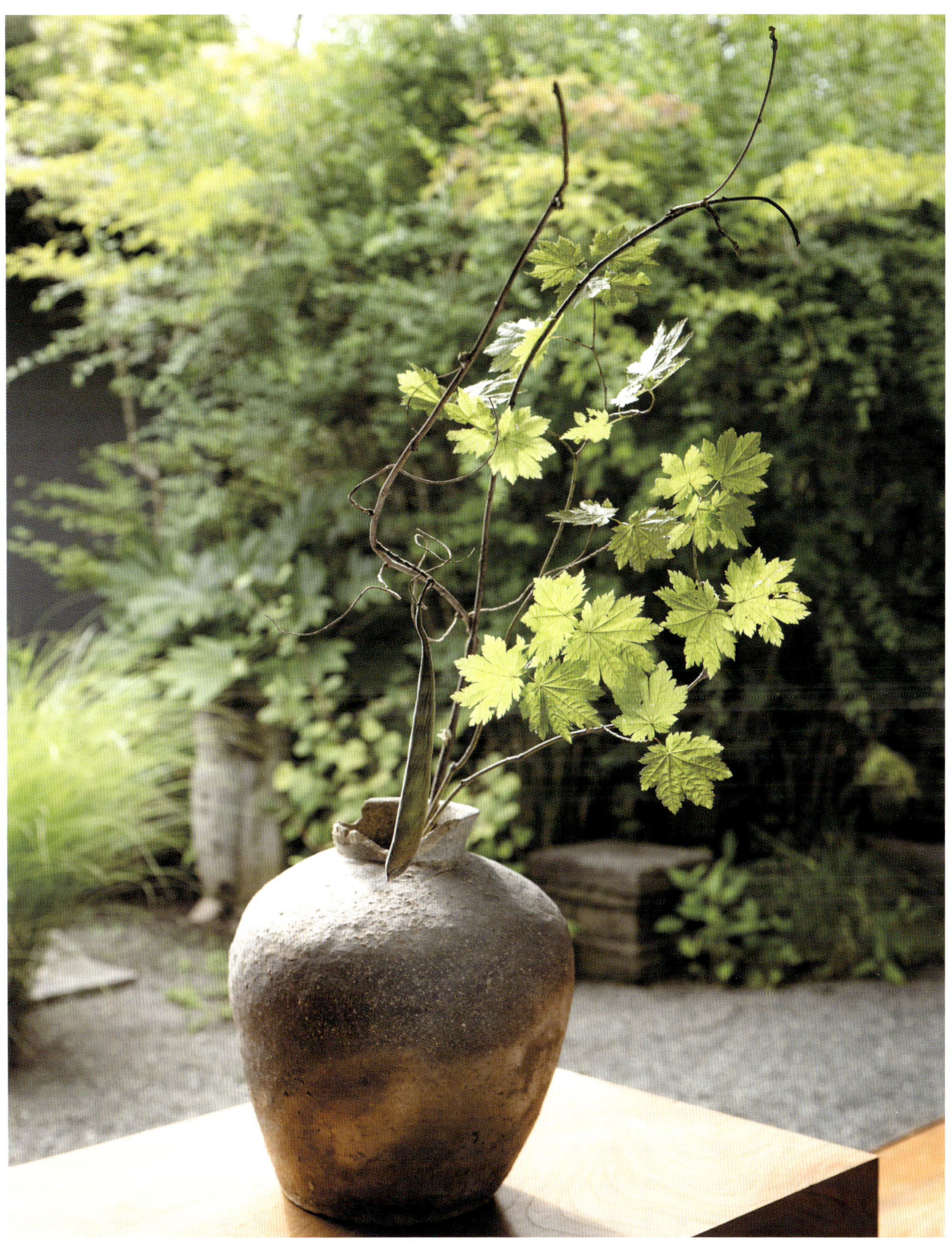

Wisteria pods and green maple. Shigaraki ware flower container, Muromachi period.

Enjoying "flowers" using only green branches. In an old Shigaraki ware flower container with a chipped rim, a twisted branch of wisteria bearing a pod is paired with a maple branch whose leaves spread in orderly fashion. The wisteria enhances the maple, and the maple brings out the beauty of the wisteria — each draws out the other's charm.

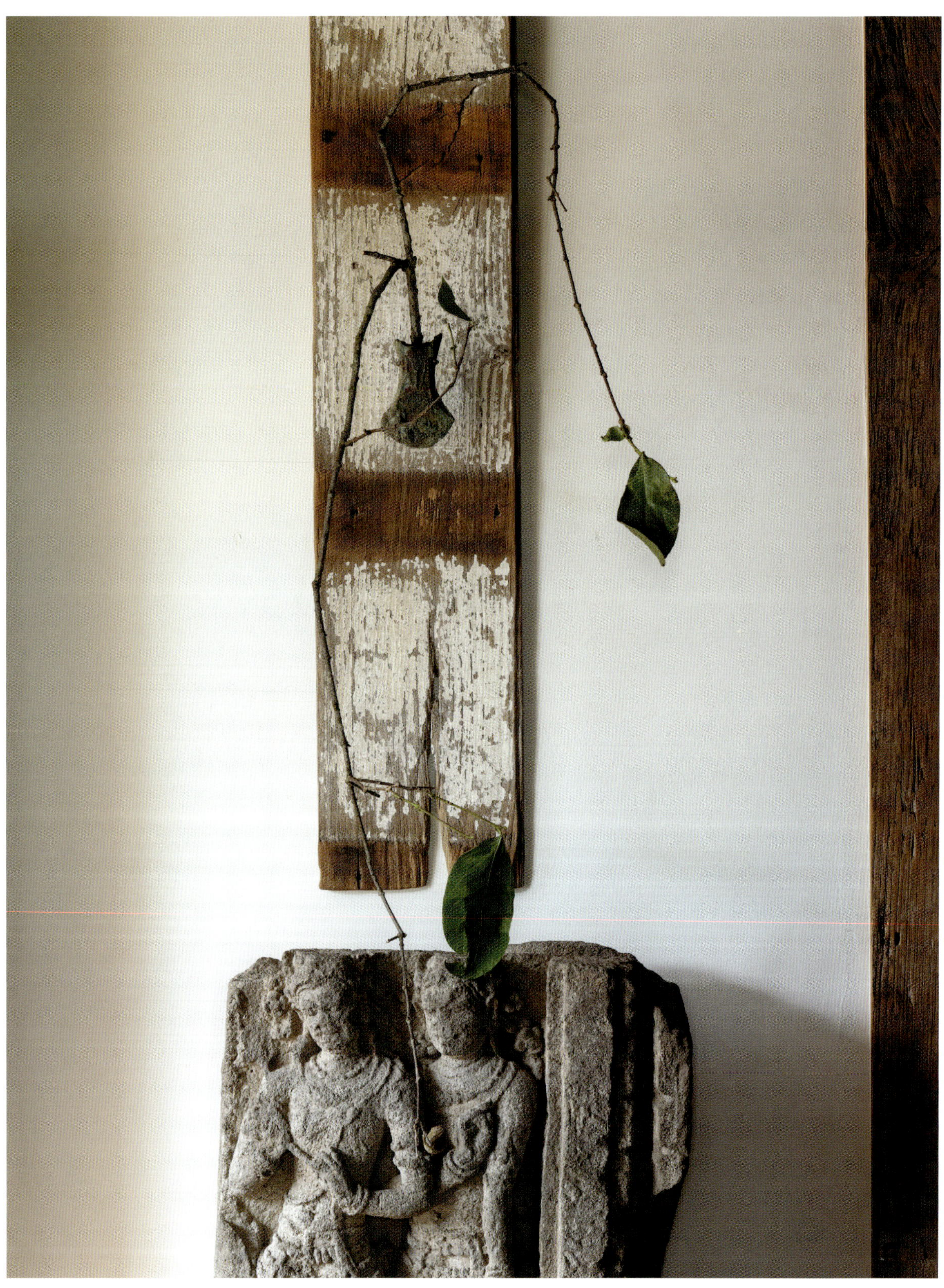

Wintersweet. Bronze arrowhead, Java, Indonesia.

A branch of wintersweet, with several leaves removed, is placed in a bronze arrowhead from Java and hung on a panel from an old Javanese house. Beneath it rests a carved stone featuring deities.

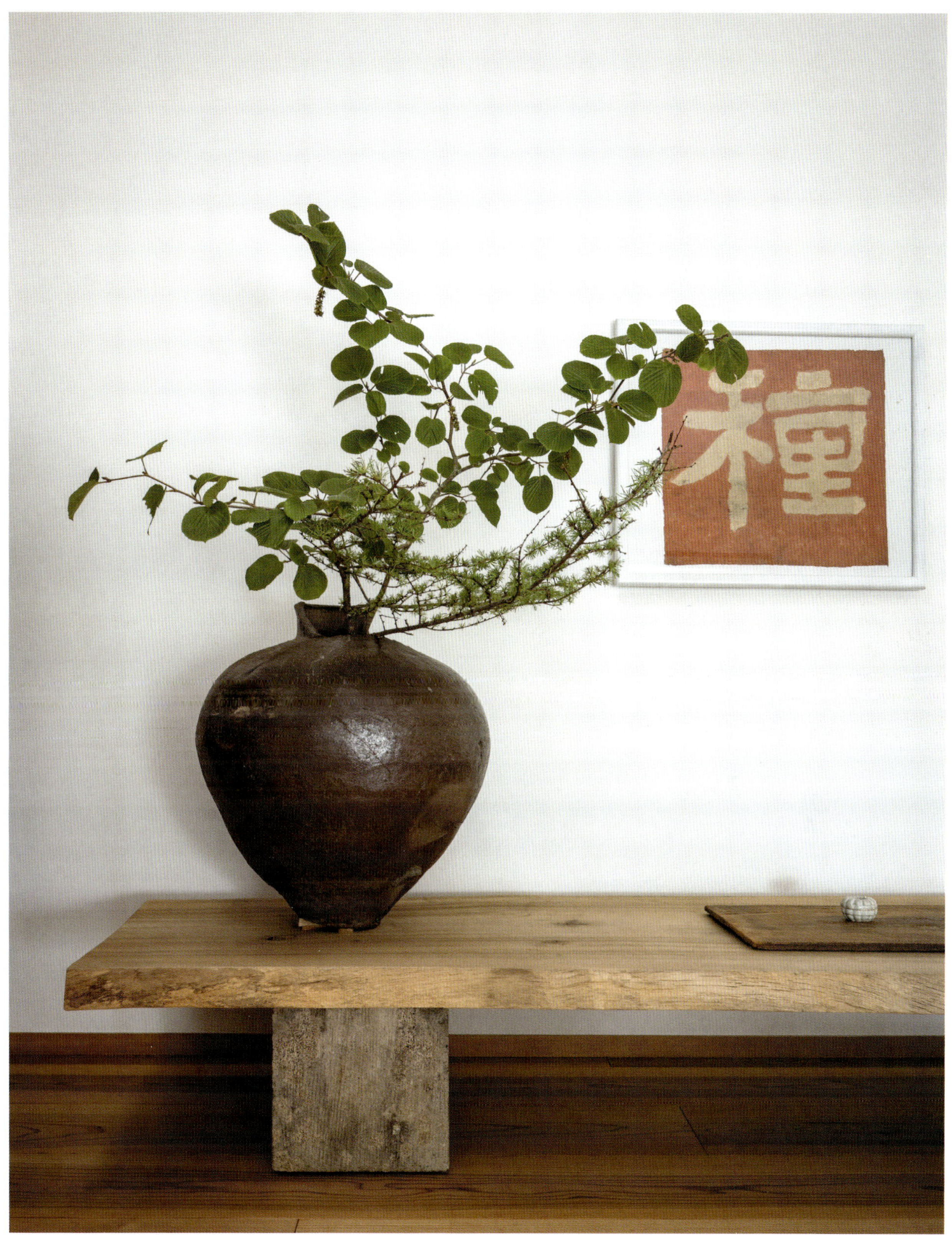

Spike winter hazel and larch. Large Toko-name ware flower container, Momoyama period.

The bold form of the large flower container has such presence that no flowers are used, only two types of green branches. The unique shapes of each branch and their leaves are meant to be appreciated. Hanging on the wall is a rubbing of the character "seed" from the *Diamond Sutra* carved on Mount Tai, from China's Six Dynasties period.

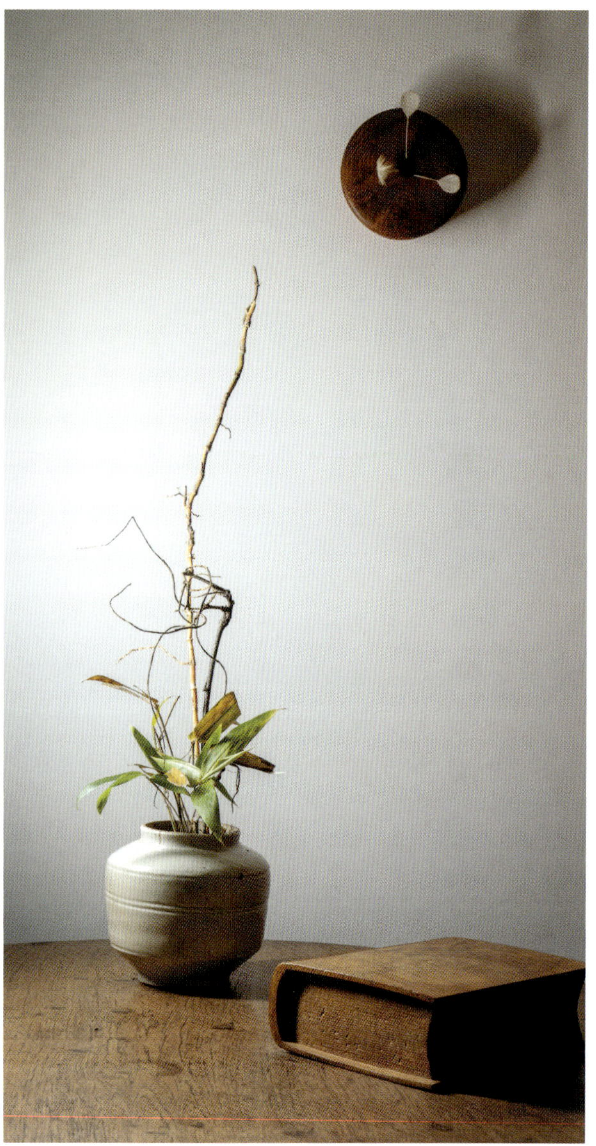 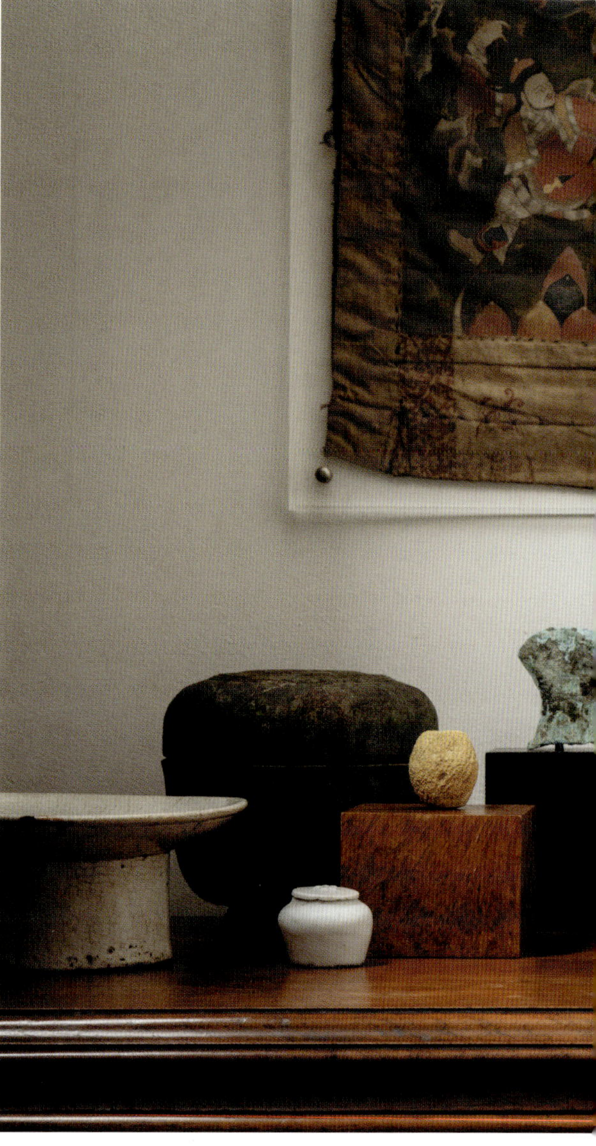

Dialogue: Awakened by Flowers—A Life Transformed

Toda: So it was Takashi Inaba who taught you about flowers. I guess you mostly learned by watching. Inaba was a type of man I hadn't encountered before. He was masculine—and yet, flowers?

Kobayashi: I heard he had been arranging flowers since he was a child.

Toda: Even in kindergarten or elementary school, he'd spend the whole day at the beach collecting seashells, then line them up at home. He'd also pick flowers and just casually arrange them at home. By the way, when I first went to Gyokuhokan, were you already there?

Kobayashi: Yes, I was.

Toda: That must've been when I was in my late thirties or had just turned forty. And you were . . . ?

Kobayashi: Around twenty-five, I think.

Toda: You were there for surfing, right?

Kobayashi: Yes, I originally went to Izu just to surf, visiting with a friend. At the time, I had no interest in flowers or art.

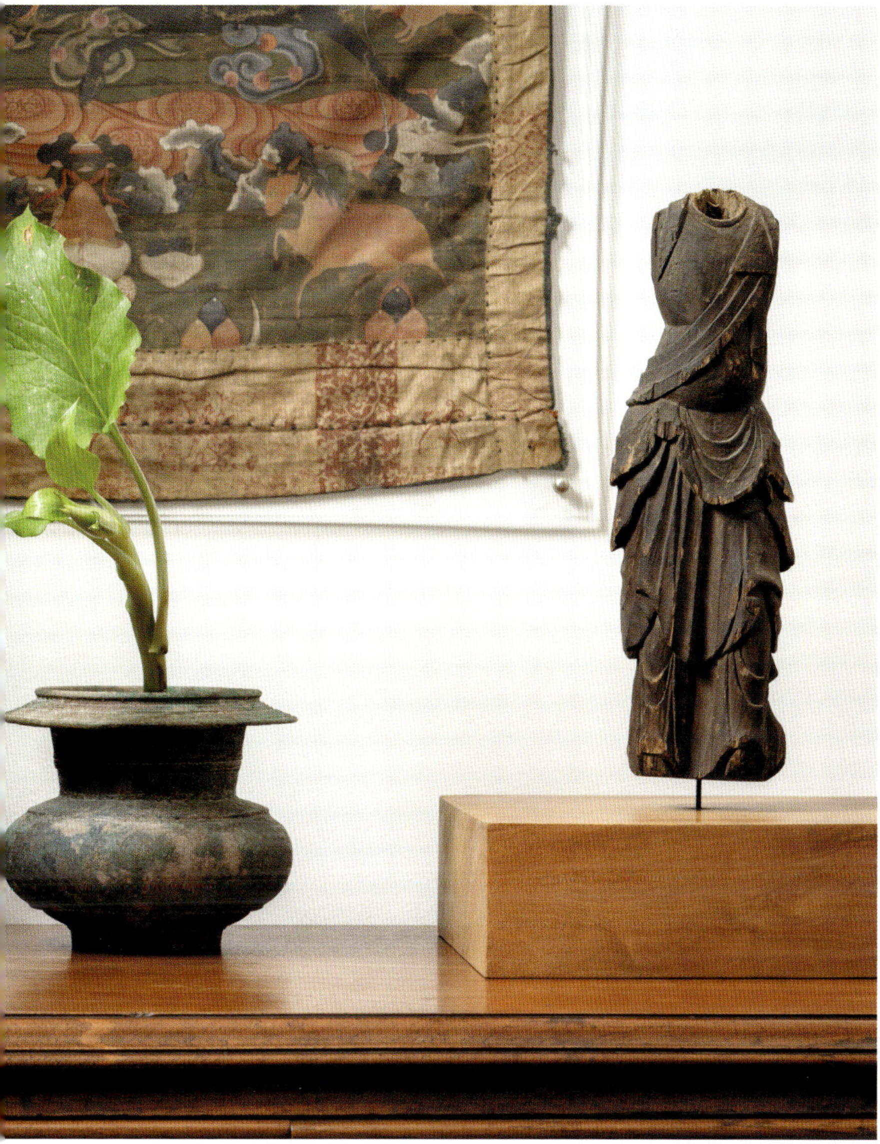

A single yellow ixora flower is gently added to a Javanese stone mortar with yellow floating heart leaves. In everyday flower arrangement, there is charm in adding something new to what already exists and enjoying the subtle change that results.

An arrangement of bamboo grass and Japanese cowpea placed in a white porcelain container from Korea, valued for its distinctive texture and subtle color. The composition has a refined, scholarly air. It is displayed on an Indonesian table alongside a wooden book-shaped object, custom-made by a Balinese craftsman.

A tenth-century Javanese bronze vessel for holy water, used here to hold a giant lily. Surrounding it are artworks from across Asia: a wooden Buddhist torso from Japan's Edo period, Indonesian bronze pieces, a small white porcelain jar from the Chinese Qing dynasty, a white porcelain pedestal dish from the Korean Joseon dynasty, and a Tibetan *thangka* painting on cloth.

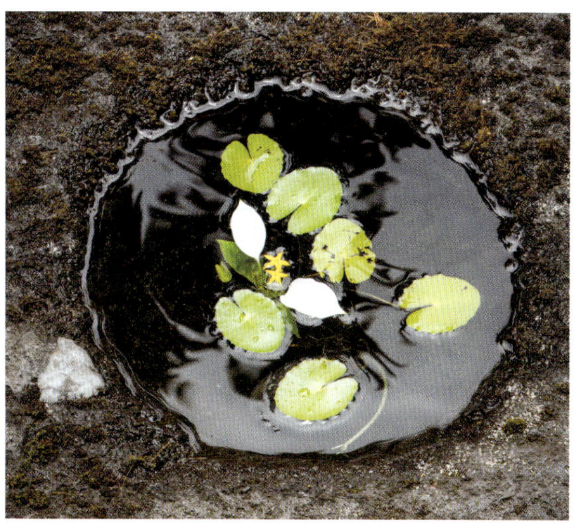

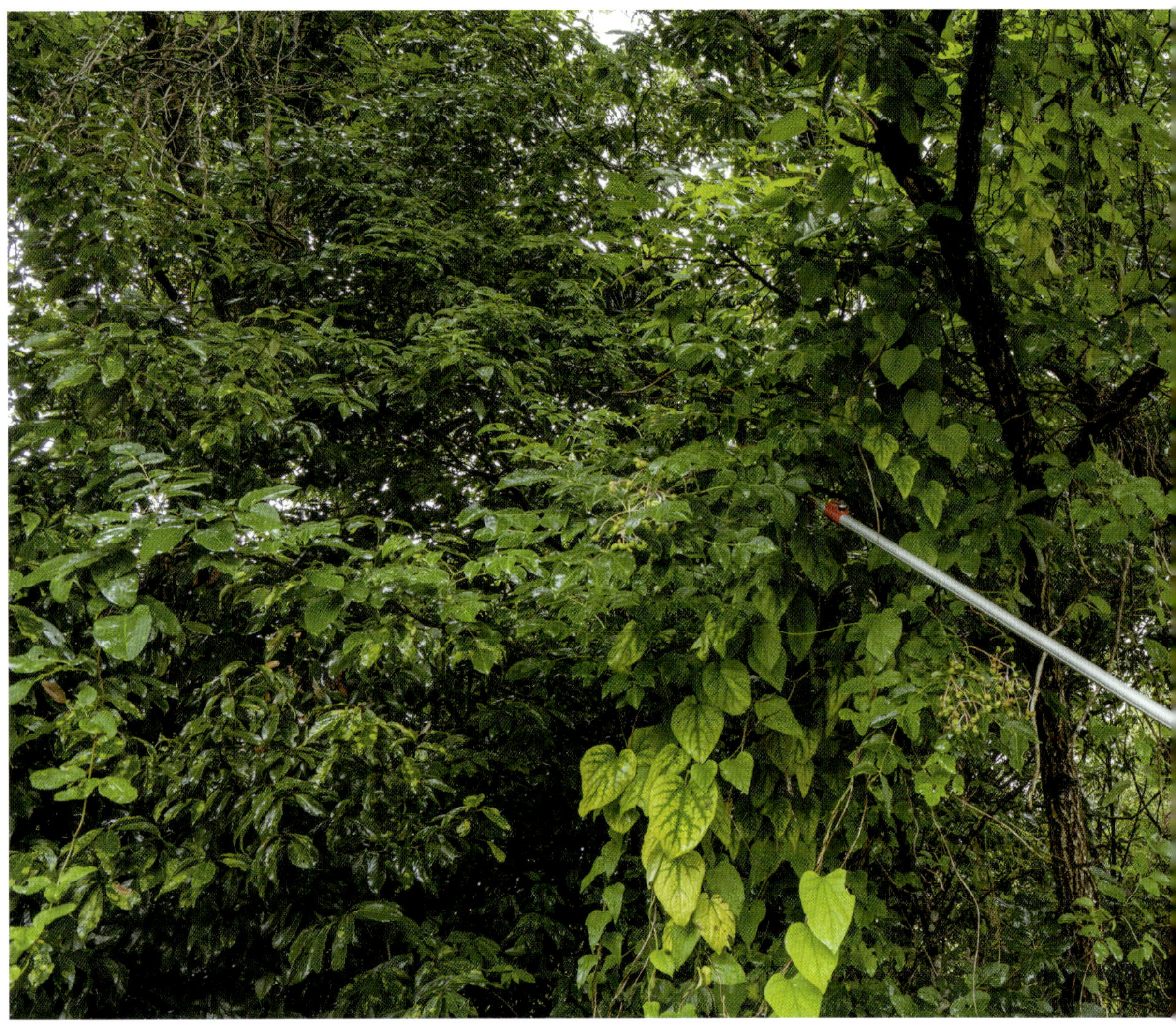

Toda: You were staying at Gyokuhokan, working in exchange for meals and lodging. Since I heard you were from Osaka, I felt a sense of connection. I'm a bit of a rough type myself and had never arranged flowers, but when I visited Gyokuhokan, I was captivated by Inaba's flowers—the way they were freely arranged, following the heart. Back then, you were probably just looking at Inaba's arrangements and slowly got drawn in, right?

Kobayashi: At first, I thought, "Isn't flower arranging something the hostess of a ryokan does?" The idea of a man arranging flowers didn't sit right with me. But after seeing it for about a year, I started thinking, "Wow, this is nice." I wanted to try it myself.

Toda: At first, you couldn't really tell that what he was doing was amazing, right?

Kobayashi: Exactly. I had no knowledge or information about flower arranging. I just liked nature and had gone to that place to surf. I wasn't interested in flowers or art—and honestly didn't even want to work. So I was constantly being scolded. But Inaba-san would use his senses to arrange flowers in an empty space, and suddenly the space would come alive. Seeing that transformation firsthand really struck me.

Toda: You had talent, though you didn't know it. But your encounter with Inaba brought it out all at once. Life is like that sometimes. Sometimes the people watching from the outside can see it more clearly than the person themself.

Kobayashi: At the time, Inaba-san often traveled to Bali. I asked if I could arrange the flowers in his

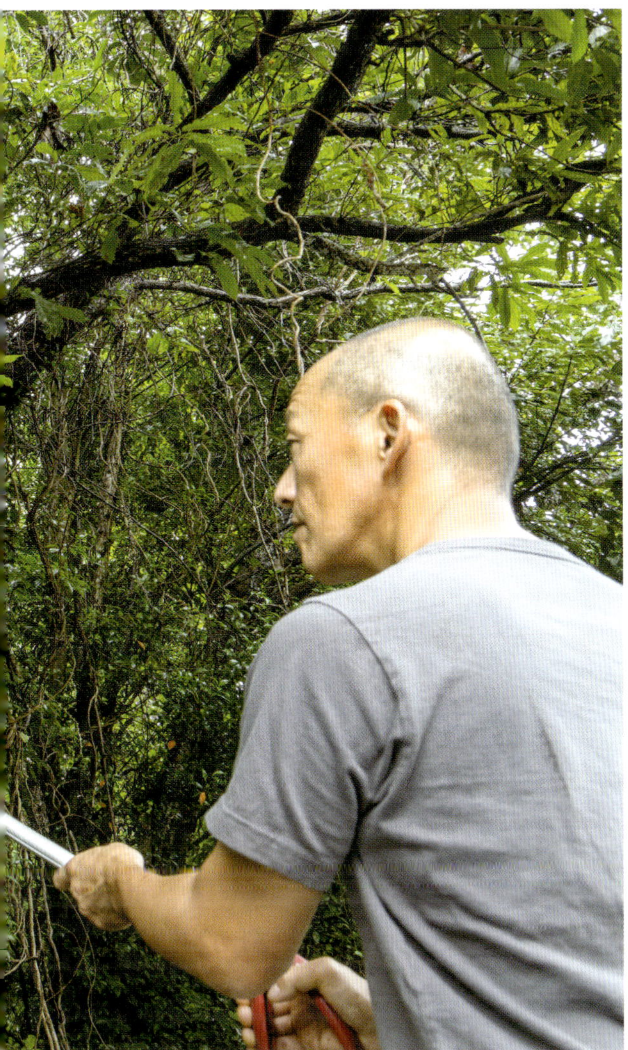

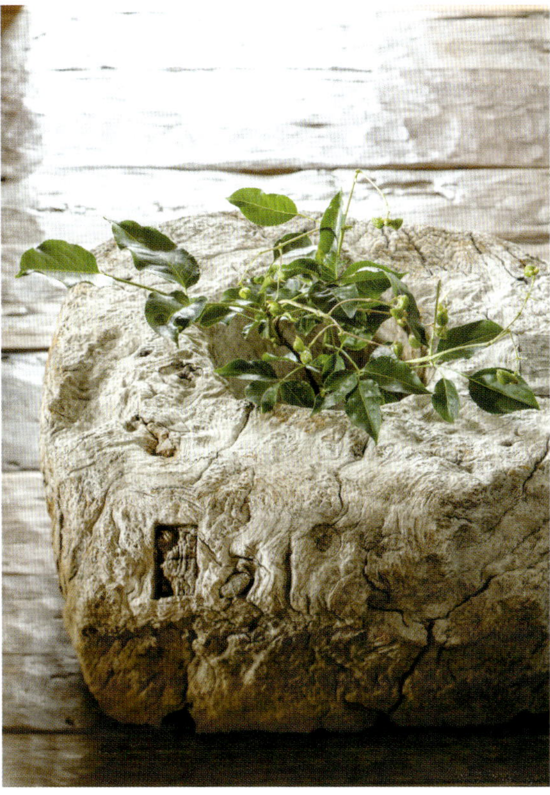

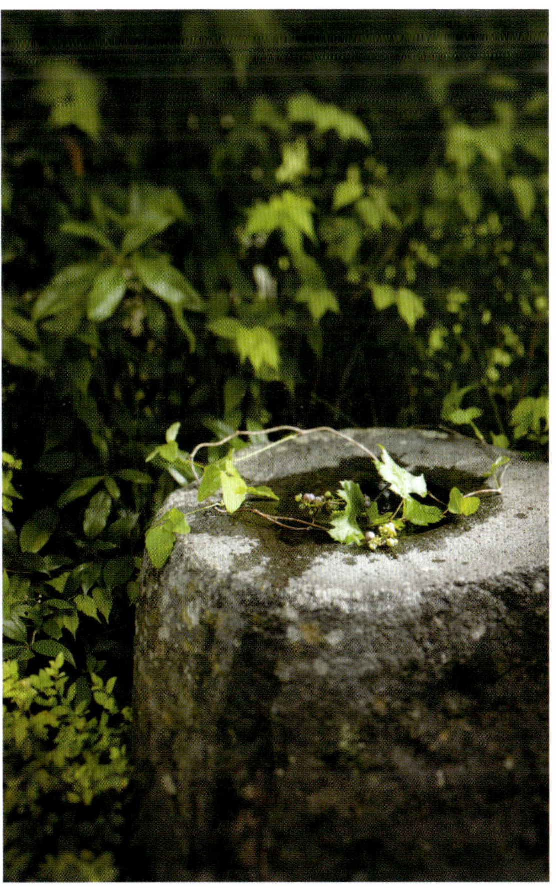

 In the cool of the morning, Atsushi Kobayashi uses shears to cut a branch of gonzui from the thicket around Inaba-san's home. "It's not about cutting indiscriminately, but choosing the right branch," he says. "When I was at Gyokuhokan, I would gather various flowers and trees from the surrounding hills and fields."

 Gonzui. Wooden mortar, Java, Indonesia.

A branch of gonzui bearing green fruit is arranged in an old wooden mortar. The contrast between the aged, grain-rich texture of the mortar and the fresh green branch Kobayashi gathered from the mountain that morning is strikingly beautiful. Gonzui fruit turns red in autumn.

 Grapevine (Western variety) and chocolate vine. Stone mill, Java, Indonesia.

Water is poured into a tall stone mill, and wild grape and chocolate vine are arranged just as they are, in their natural form. The twining vines create gentle lines across the top of the mill, blending seamlessly into the surrounding greenery with a natural, unforced presence.

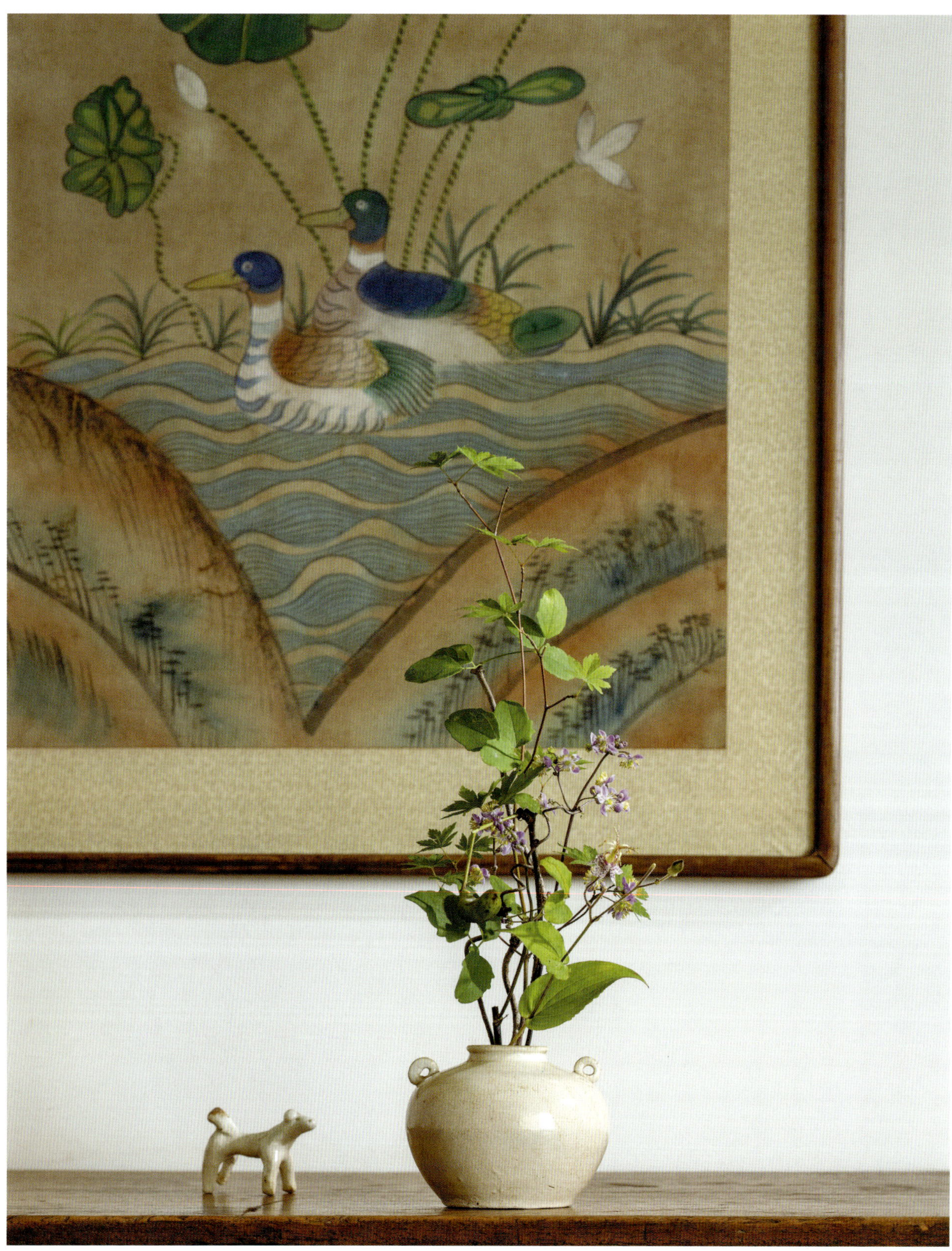

Toad lily, purple houseleek, chocolate vine, green maple. Small white porcelain flower container, China, Tang dynasty.

Against the backdrop of a Korean folk painting, four types of wild plant are arranged in a small flower container. When using many varieties, the composition tends to spread outward, but by emphasizing vertical lines and letting the branches extend upward, it keeps a clean, balanced form. Beside it is a Song dynasty porcelain dog from China.

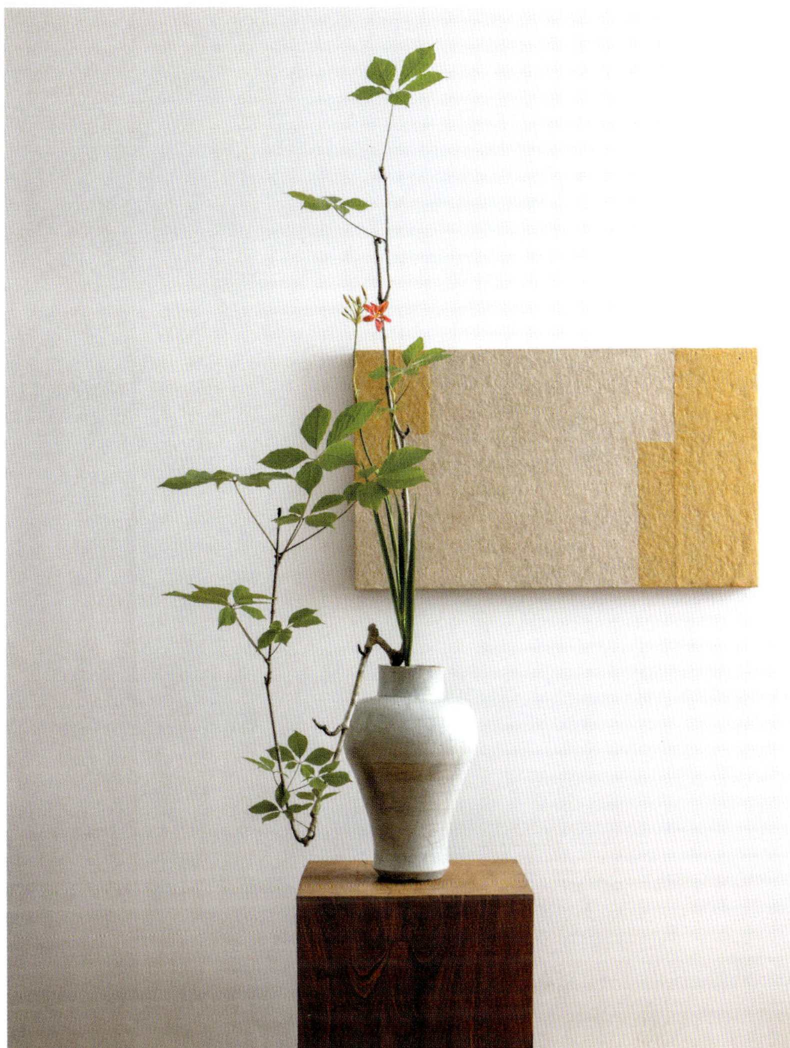

**Blackberry lily and koshiabura.
White porcelain flower container,
Korea, late Joseon dynasty.**

The natural lines of the honey
tree branch take center stage,
with a blackberry lily flower added as an accent. The contemporary artwork in the background is
Inaba-san's own creation — a
panel covered with banana fiber.
Simply hanging this panel on the
white wall brings depth and expression to the space.

place while he was away. But when he came back
from Bali, he pulled out every single flower I had
arranged. Like, "What is this?!" (laughs)

Toda: All of them?

Kobayashi: Yes, and he was furious.

Toda: Really that angry?

Kobayashi: Extremely. He threw everything out. I
was arranging those flowers for the guests, but right
before he returned, it became about arranging them
for him. So having everything discarded—it was
really tough.

Toda: It's almost like having your very self rejected.
But it's not something one masters overnight. Still,
at some point, when you began arranging flowers
yourself, you must have come to realize, "Wow, Inaba-san is really something."

Kobayashi: I would put flowers all around the inn,
and he'd remove them all. I didn't understand what
was wrong or what to do differently. Then someone
told me, "Try focusing on just one flower and really
engage with it." So I did. I spent a whole night facing a single flower, knowing that Inaba was returning from a trip the next day. The whole night. And
in doing so, I felt something click.

Toda: You felt it.

Kobayashi: Yes. When Inaba-san came back from
Bali and saw that flower, he didn't remove it.

Toda: And from that night, everything changed?

Kobayashi: After that, he never removed my flowers again.

Toda: So the talent had always been there in you
as a latent ability. You'd probably never even really

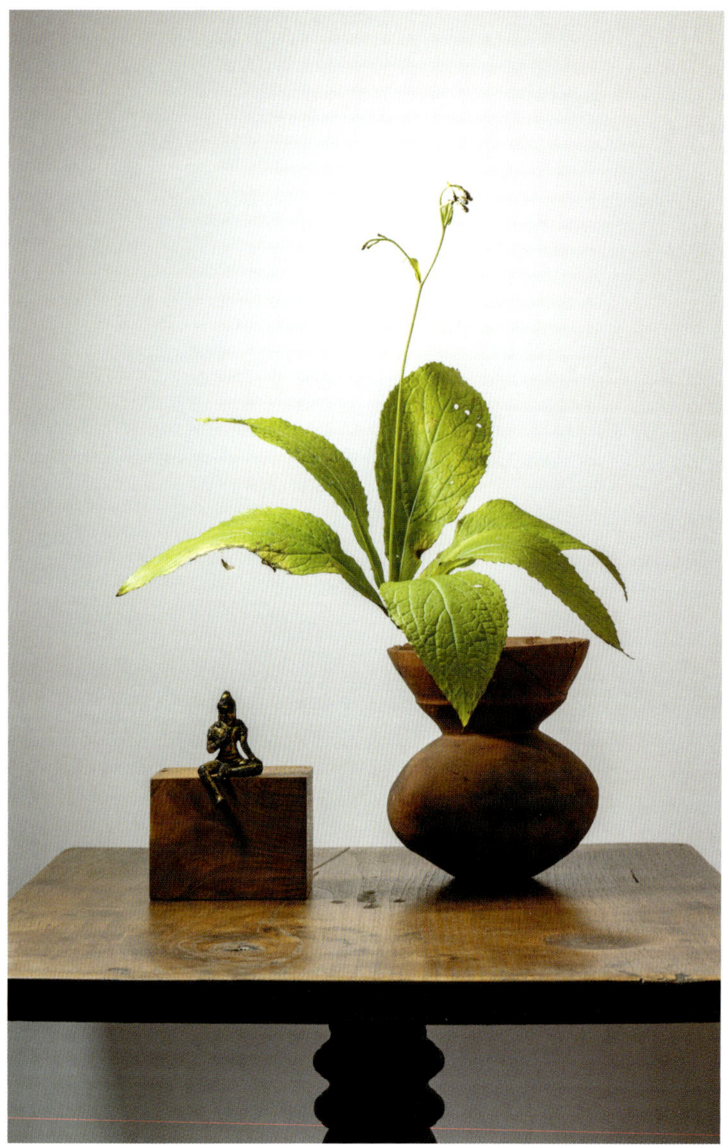

Pertya rigidula. Yayoi-period earthenware.

An arrangement on a table pairs a Yayoi-period flower container with an old Vajra Buddha statue from eighth or ninth century Java. The distinct shape of the leaves and the upright line of the stems are used simply and effectively. The statue, the container, and the flower together form a harmonious space.

paused to admire flowers before, let alone considered making a career of art or flower arranging.
Kobayashi: That's true.
Toda: How many years were you with Inaba?
Kobayashi: Seven or eight. I spent nearly all of my twenties there. I was at a point in life where I wanted to find something I could be passionate about and turn it into a job. Meeting Inaba-san made me think the world of art was incredibly interesting. That's when I started studying both flowers and tea.
Toda: And that eventually led you to join Toda Shoten. Of course, after leaving Gyokuhokan, you also spent time working at a flower shop to deepen your knowledge.

Kobayashi: By then, I'd decided to make a living through flowers. I was studying tea as well, but I didn't really know what kind of shop Toda Shoten was. I vaguely understood it dealt in tea utensils.
Toda: Even after you returned to Osaka, I kept an eye on you and eventually recruited you to join us. At Toda Shoten, most of our trainees come from families in the art-dealing world, so your case is quite rare.
Kobayashi: Right. So after I joined the company, people would always ask me, "Whose son are you?" It was constant. But I'd have to say, "I'm not really anybody's son" (laughs).
Toda: Well, I had already seen your potential. I was sure you'd be an asset to us.

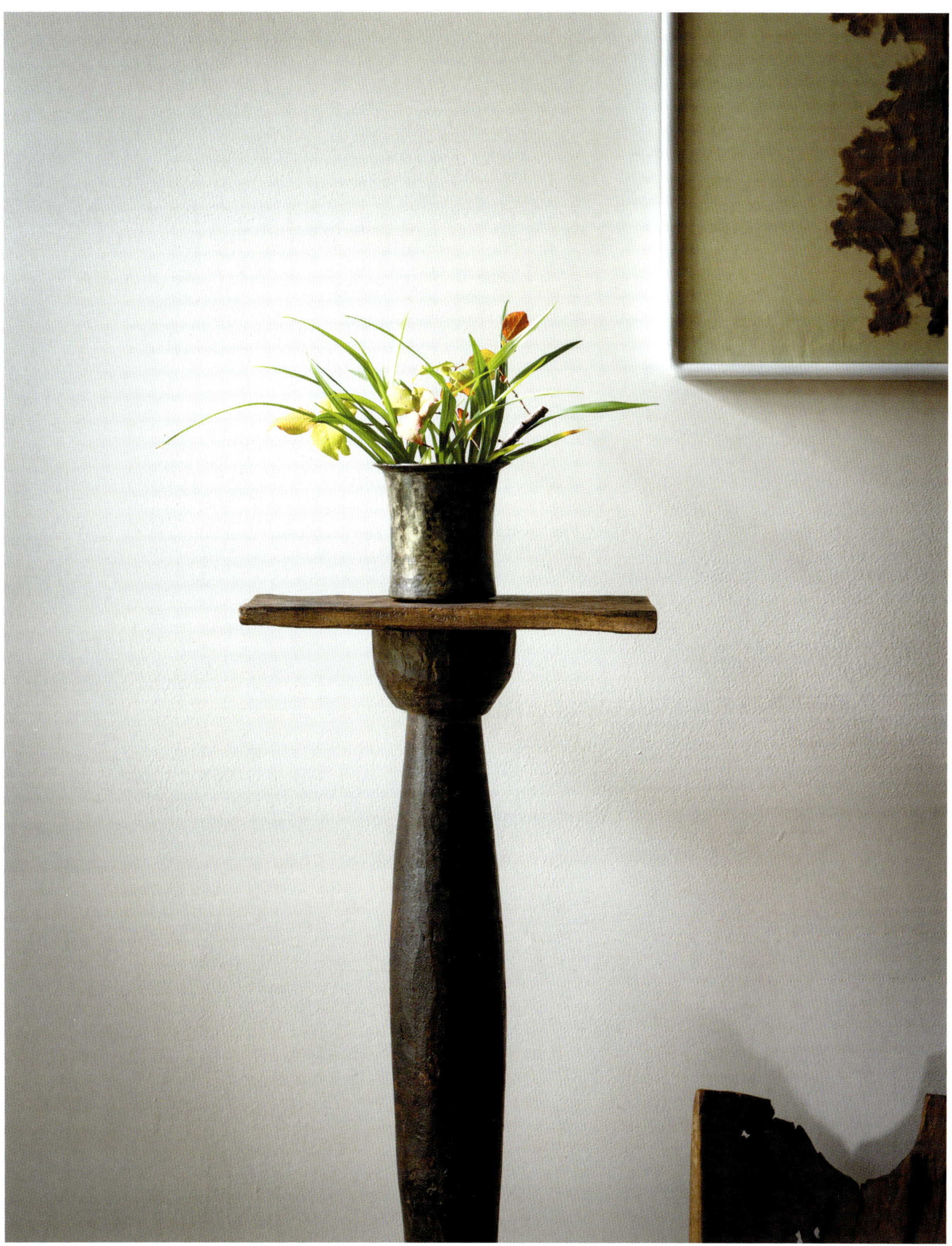

**Leaves of black huckleberry and orchid.
Bronze vessel, Indonesia.**

On an old wooden stand from Indonesia rests a cylindrical bronze vessel, holding branches of black huckleberry and orchid leaves. The two kinds of foliage — different in both shape and color — bring out each other's beauty, expressing the vitality of plants without the need for flowers.

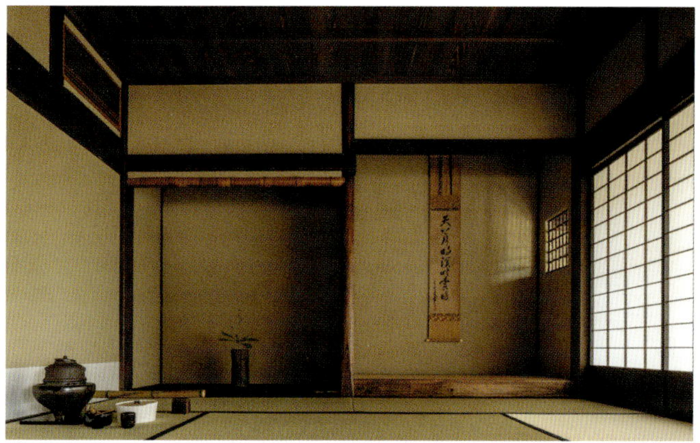

A tea setting to appreciate the autumn moon. The alcove calligraphy scroll is by Shun'oku Soen, a monk from Daitokuji Temple, active from the late sixteenth to early seventeenth centuries. The old scroll is combined with utensils by contemporary artists. In response to the commanding presence of the calligraphy, a flower arrangement is placed on the wooden floor to the left of the alcove.

A Tea Gathering with Wildflowers under the Autumn Moon

Pertya Rigidula

This September tea gathering was in an old farmhouse on the shores of Lake Biwa in Shiga Prefecture. The space was an eight-mat tatami room with a *tokonoma* alcove about six feet (two meters) wide. Next to the alcove was a recess of the same width, often used for displaying utensils or flower containers. The earthen walls and shoji paper screens surrounding the space were simple and typical of traditional Japanese homes. Built entirely from natural materials and without affectation, such a space is truly beautiful. Light from the lakeside filters in through the shoji and the floor-level windows, softly illuminating the dim interior of the farmhouse.

With the theme of appreciating the autumn moon, I hung a calligraphy scroll by Haruya Soen in the alcove. The verse, which pairs the brightness of the moon in the heavens with the darkness of the clouds at a mountain stream, expresses the natural law that opposing forces exist in harmony in this world. More than anything, the scene evoked by the phrase "The moon above shines bright; clouds darken the streamside below" and the beauty of its brushwork are deeply moving. With this hanging scroll as the focal point, I then considered what utensils would harmonize with it.

On the wooden flooring beside the alcove, I placed a flower vessel made by potter Jikinyu Raku (see page 34), the fifteenth-generation head of the Raku family, and arranged in it a plant called Pertya rigidula (*kurumaba haguma* in Japanese). Most autumn wildflowers are rather small and delicate, but these broad leaves have a strong presence that harmonizes beautifully with the solid form of Raku's vessel.

I've been close friends with Jikinyu Raku for many years, and about twenty years ago, we traveled together to France to meet ceramic artist Andoche Praudel. The meeting came about when Andoche contacted us, saying he wished to meet through a mutual acquaintance. That trip to France remains a special memory for me. It also marked the beginning of an artistic exchange in which Raku-san and Andoche would travel between each other's studios, creating works together across borders.

This flower vessel is one of those collaborative pieces. When Andoche visited Japan, he would stay at my home in Osaka and work at Raku-san's studio in Kyoto. Later, Raku-san would travel to Andoche's studio in Loubignac in the south of France, where he'd stay for two or three months, a collaboration that

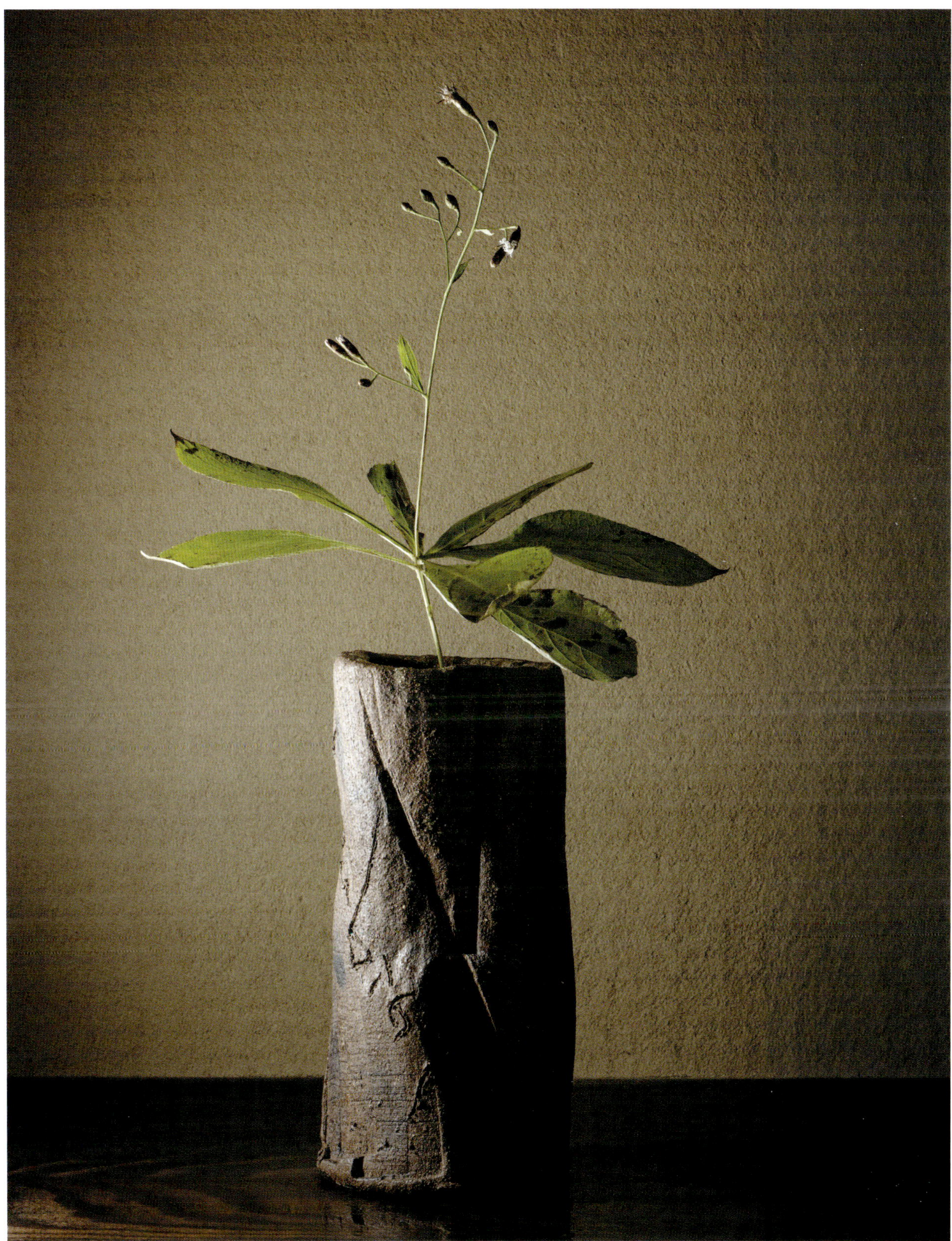

Pertya rigidula. Flower vessel by Jikinyu Raku (see page 34), made of clay from Loubignac, France.

This is a plant in the aster family that grows in mountainous areas, with whorled leaves and small white flowers. In this arrangement, the emphasis is placed on the leaves. The vessel was made by Jikinyu Raku in 2004, in Loubignac, France, using local clay. The surface has a richly textured pattern, as if struck with a wooden spatula, adding to its charm.

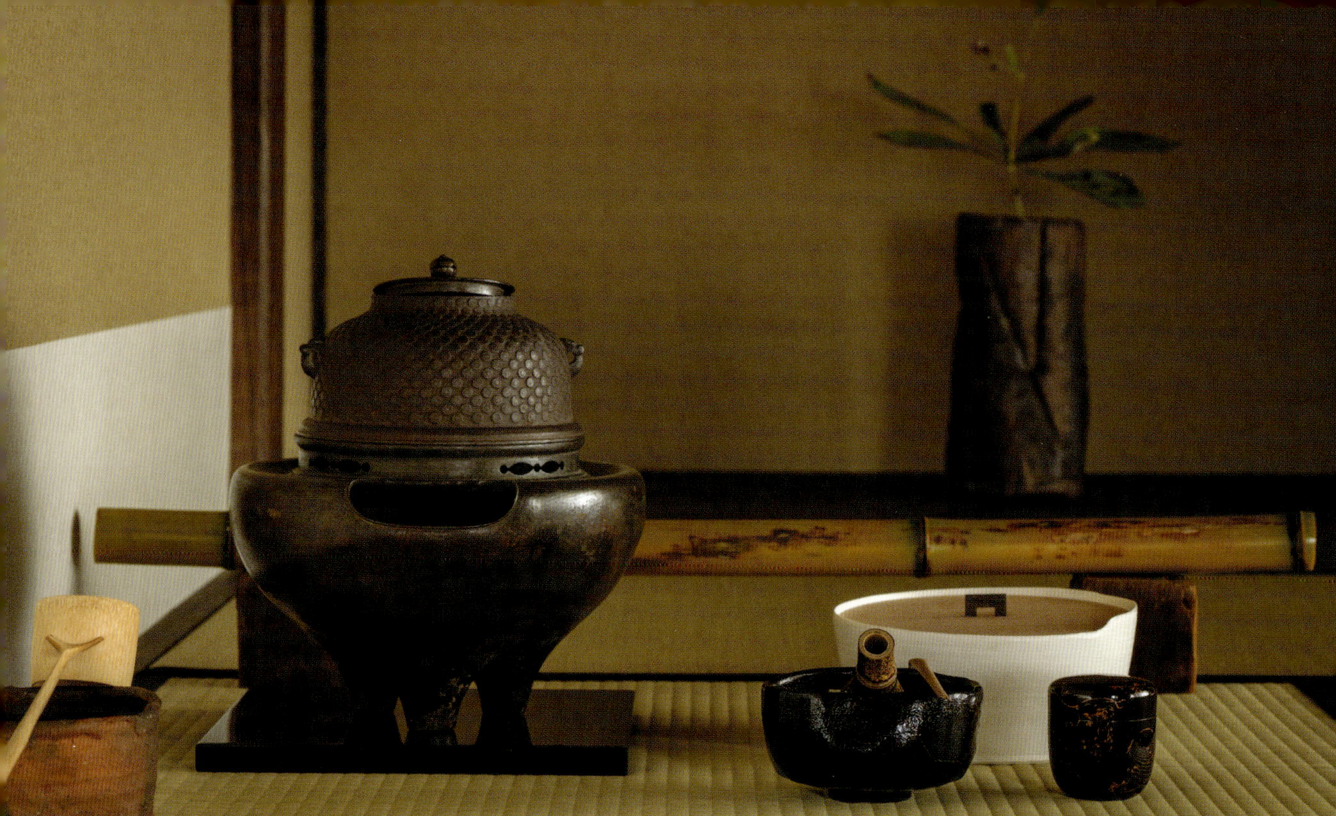

lasted about four years. Having long worked with traditional tea ceremony ceramics, Raku-san went to France alone and created pieces using local clay. As a result, the sensibility of these pieces is distinctly different from those made in Kyoto.

For the preparation area, I paired a black Raku tea bowl attributed to Koetsu, with visible repairs, with a tea caddy featuring worn patterns. To this, I added a contemporary white porcelain fresh-water container by Taizo Kuroda (see page 154), and a tea scoop by Kaida Kyokko. I acquired the tea scoop over twenty years ago. It is a *shingata* type without a visible node and bears the name "Soshin" (simple heart). It possesses both a modern sensibility and a classical tone, yet it is unforced and unaffected   truly the one tea scoop by Kaida-san that I feel captures his essence.

ABOVE The tea setting as a whole was composed to express a soft, faint radiance, like the delicate glow of a hazy moon, with pieces such as the tea caddy that seem to catch that subtle light. "This time, I entrusted most of the utensil selection to Kobayashi," says Hiroshi. "We paired the calligraphy of Shun'oku, a tea bowl attributed to Koetsu, works by contemporary artists, and even a collaborative piece between Japan and France. The composition intuitively weaves together both time and space."

FACING PAGE The calligraphy by Shun'oku Soen reads "The moon above shines bright; clouds darken the streamside below." Evoking the vast space between the moon in the heavens and the clouds in the valley below, the phrase subtly alludes to a Zen worldview. The deep black ink and characters — quiet yet powerful — convey stillness and strength.

RECORD OF THE GATHERING

Alcove: Calligraphy by Shun'oku Soen
Flower container: Made by Jikinyu Raku in Loubignac, France
Flower: Pertya rigidula
Furo brazier: Bronze, Korean style
Kettle: Ashiya-style with chrysanthemum design

Kekkai boundary marker: Bamboo
Fresh-water container: White porcelain by Taizo Kuroda
Tea caddy: *Saga-natsume* black lacquer
Tea bowl: Black Raku, attributed to Koetsu
Tea scoop: Made by Kaida Kyokko, named "Soshin"
Waste water bowl: Namban (Southern barbarian ware)

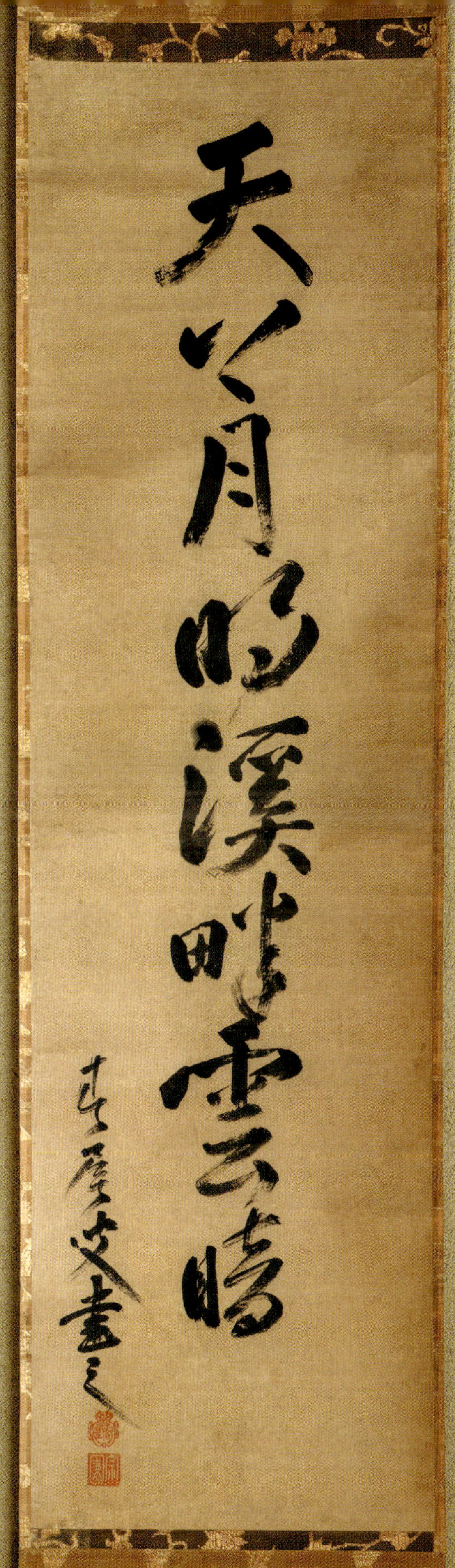
天以月明溪畔雲晴

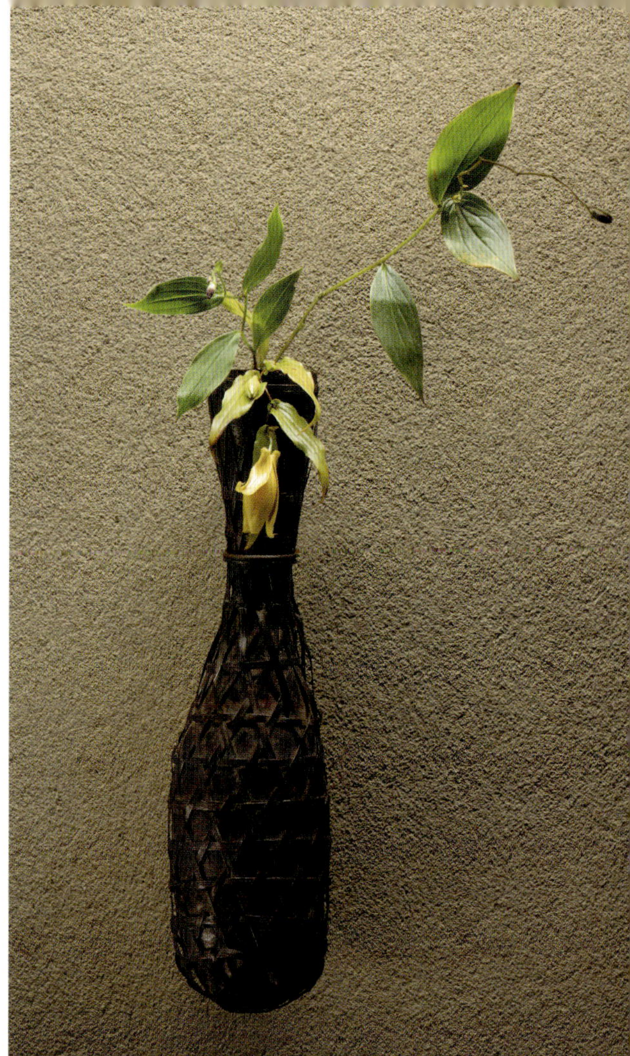

**Kii toad lily and Taiwan toad lily.
Gourd-shaped basket flower vessel with
Sen no Rikyu seal.**

Though both are delicate varieties of toad
lily, the arrangement weaves together a rich
array of expression: the yellow blossoms of
the Kii toad lily, leaves shifting from green to
yellow; the tiny buds of the Taiwan toad lily,
and, reaching upward to the right, a withered
bud at the tip of a branch. These elements are
skillfully combined to highlight subtle varia-
tions on a single theme.

Flowers and Utensils for September

Baskets for Autumn

As summer moves toward autumn, basket flower
containers come into their own in the tea room.
Many are used in the spirit of *mitate*—reinterpretation—and among the most famous is the Katsura
basket, originally a fishing basket used by fisher-
men on the Katsura River, which Sen no Rikyu reimagined as a flower container. In the photographs
above, I'm using a gourd-shaped basket flower vessel bearing Rikyu's seal. The gourd is wrapped in
woven bamboo, and over time, both the bamboo
and the gourd have taken on a rich, aged patina.
Though weathered and subdued, the vessel has a
strong presence. As with bamboo flower containers,

it's best to keep the arrangement minimal—one or
two carefully chosen flowers. Not only blossoms,
but withered leaves or fruit nearing decay can also
make interesting seasonal materials. I feel basket
flower vessels have a kind of generosity—they can
embrace the slightly faded, subdued look of plants
in this season. Like bamboo containers, baskets
make use of natural materials in their raw form,
maybe why they blend so harmoniously into the
setting. Many reinterpreted basket vessels come
from China or are Chinese-style objects. For the
tea room alcove, I brought out a large "shin-guard"
basket (page 115). Its name comes from its resemblance to protective shin guards used in armor.

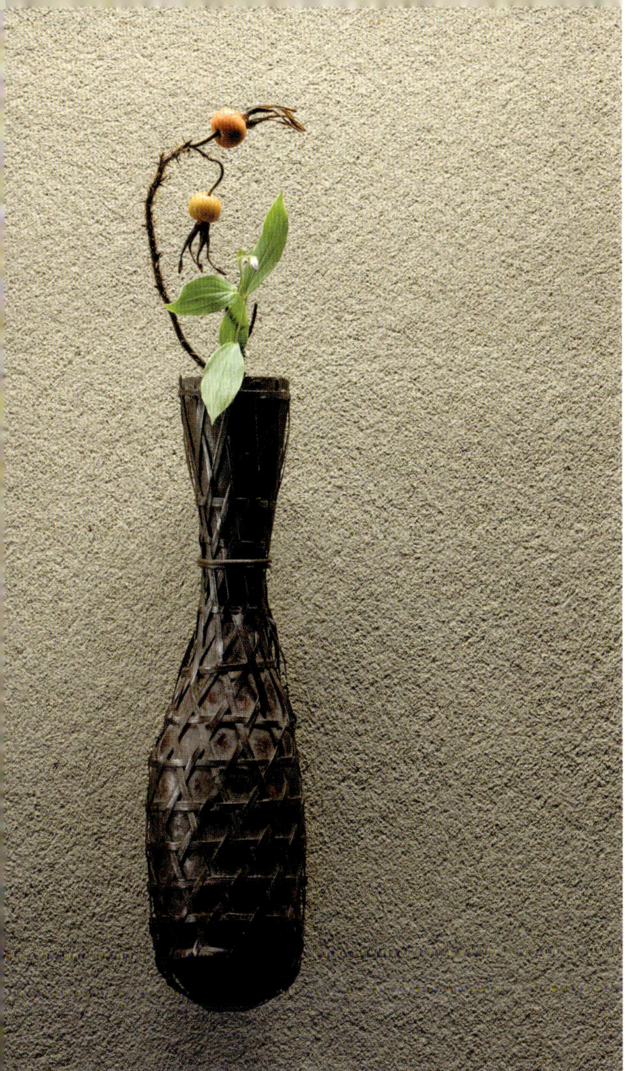

A compact arrangement of tiny toad lily buds and
rugosa rose fruit. The addition of the ripened rose
fruit evokes the deepening of autumn. The classic
form of the gourd-shaped basket highlights the
natural beauty of the plants.

Autumn Grasses in Rikyu's Gourd Basket

Two arrangements in the same container: on the
far right, a pairing of two varieties of toad lily; on
the near right, a combination of toad lily and small
rugosa rose fruit. In both arrangements, the toad
lily, a quintessential autumn flower, takes center
stage, while the accompanying materials evoke
different seasonal nuances. The arrangement
with only toad lilies conveys a lingering sense of
late autumn through the way the flowers bloom
and the changing colors of the leaves. The other,
with less toad lily and the addition of berries, suggests the deepening of the season. The flower
container, a rare form made by weaving bamboo
around a gourd, bears Sen no Rikyu's ink-brushed
seal on the back (see below). By carefully selecting autumn grasses that harmonize with the vessel's deep, aged patina, the arrangement brings
forth a subdued and wistful sense of autumn.

Similar weaving techniques can also be seen in char-
coal containers. The one on page 115 is likely from
southern China or somewhere else in East Asia. I'm
deeply drawn to its strong, primitive form.

Since ancient times, the Japanese have been emo-
tionally attuned to the plants of autumn. Wildflowers
beaded with dew, pampas grass, and the moon depicted alongside them have long been beloved motifs
on folding screens, sliding door paintings, textiles,
lacquerware and more. I believe the attraction to autumn plants and the moon is a sensibility we all share.
Designs featuring autumn themes appear frequently
on tea utensils as well. After all, the essence of tea lies
in collaboration with the natural world.

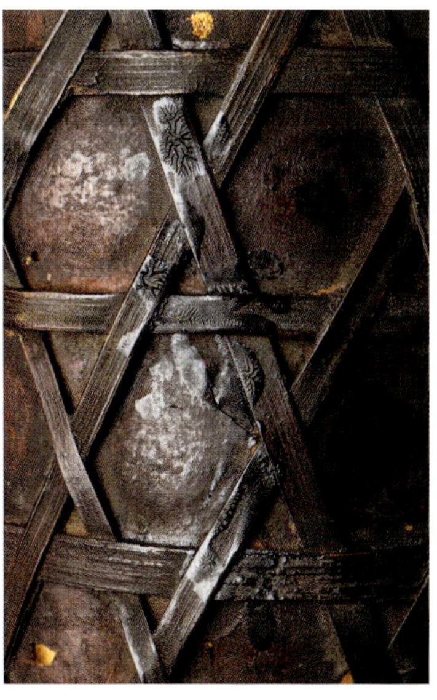

On the back of the gourd-shaped basket flower vessel
is Sen no Rikyu's seal. This was one of the flower seals
he used throughout his life, named *kera* ("cricket")
because of its resemblance to the insect's shape.

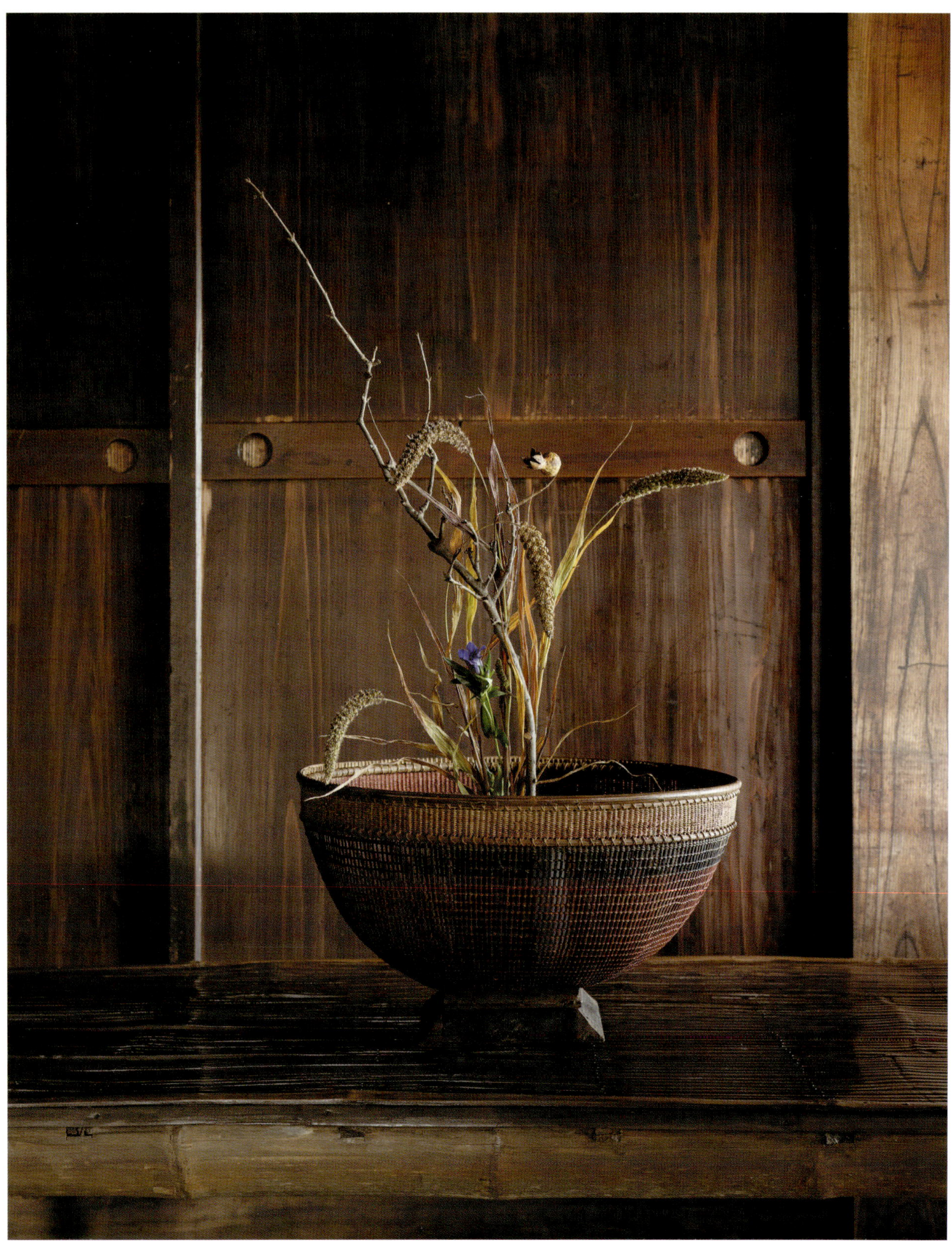

Gentian, foxtail millet and dwarf pomegranate. Rattan basket, Java, Indonesia.

An Indonesian rattan basket on a table is the setting for a floral arrangement for a living space. The muted tones of the old farmhouse door, the timeworn colors of the basket, and the withered branches and leaves overlap harmoniously, allowing the fresh purple of the gentian to stand out — a combination that perfectly captures the feeling of the season.

Playing with Flowers in a Thatched-Roof Farmhouse

— Atsushi Kobayashi

I believe autumn is the season when basket flower vessels feel most at home. For September, in the setting of a traditional farmhouse, I tried using several basket-style containers. It's the time of year when summer is drawing to a close, and plants begin to wither—something I try to express through the arrangements. In tea flowers, there's the term *zanka*—"lingering flowers"—which reflects an aesthetic that cherishes blossoms past their peak: smaller flowers, or leaves that are just beginning to change color. In the arrangement on the facing page, I paired a pomegranate branch, its leaves fallen and only the fruit remaining; millet with golden, ripened seed heads hanging low; and wild gentian, still holding on to a few buds. The pomegranate and millet are already dried and won't change much, but the delicate gentian at the heart of the arrangement fades little by little each day. Through changes like these, we become more aware of the passage of time. Tea flowers are fleeting by nature, but this kind of ongoing enjoyment is possible with flowers arranged for daily life. When the gentian wilts, I leave the pomegranate and millet as they are and simply replace the gentian with another flower. In this way, I can enjoy the arrangement for quite a long time. Even if it's just a dried branch, I find it hard to throw it away—it feels wasteful somehow. These are the kinds of things I do as part of my everyday practice.

What led me to engage with flowers so deeply was my encounter with Takashi Inaba, as mentioned earlier. Inaba-san has made arranging flowers every day part of his life. That hasn't changed in the thirty years since we met, and I've learned so much from watching him. One important insight I gained from him is that flowers have yin and yang. This concept is embedded in many aspects of Japanese culture, and the tea ceremony is no exception. The same applies to flowers. When arranging them, you bring together elements of both yin and yang. Neither yin alone nor yang alone is truly beautiful. People often ask, "Which part is yin and which is yang?"—but there are no fixed answers. What matters is being constantly aware of yin and yang through your own intuition. For instance, in the arrangement on the facing page, the pomegranate and millet are yin, while the gentian is yang. They enhance each other. I also often use a plant called Japanese sweet flag, which tends to feel more yin, so

A Holder for Spreading Grasses

When arranging flowers, branches tend to come together at a single point near the base, so once that point is secured, the whole arrangement remains stable. On the other hand, with softer grasses and wildflowers, the stems and leaves tend to spread out, which makes it difficult to achieve a stable and natural shape. In such cases, gather and gently twist the base of the grass stems into a bundle, securing it within the inner container. You can also use the gaps between other materials as part of the holding structure, which makes arranging easier. In the example shown on the facing page, the base of the millet stems is rounded into a bundle and used as a flower holder.

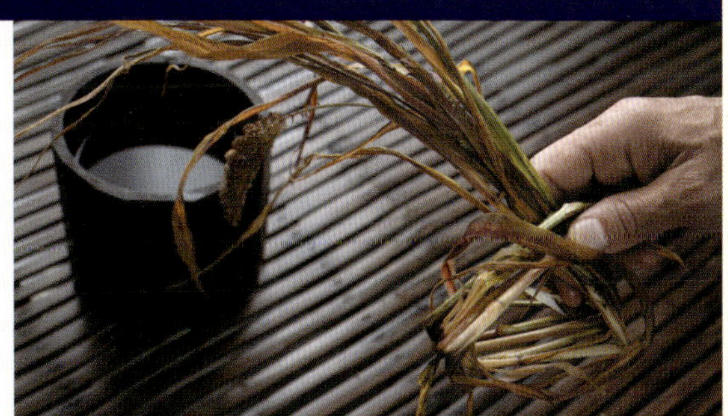

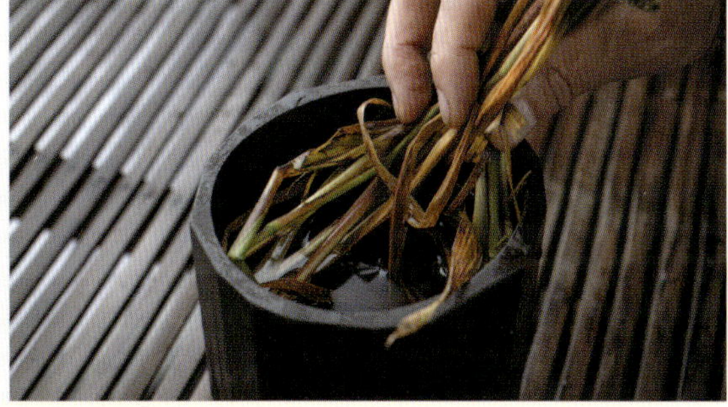

I pair it with a brighter material (see page 17). Adding a dead branch in that case doesn't feel right. When you introduce a yang element into something yin, it brings a sense of light, or life. That light, in turn, strengthens the presence of the yin. Both elements are brought to life. This concept also applies to the relationship between flowers and the vessels that hold them. If the flowers feel strongly yang, then I choose a vessel that carries a sense of yin. When you approach arranging flowers with an awareness of yin and yang, the act of arranging begins to change and deepen.

While some arrangements, like the one on page 112, can be enjoyed over a long period of time, the flowers arranged on pages 110–111 are meant to be appreciated in the moment. In this case, I hung the flower container on an old, weathered earthen wall near the entrance of the farmhouse, where it acts almost like a welcoming flower. Yet there's something about it that connects to the flowers of a tea room. The Kii toad lily is a rare variety with yellow blossoms. The leaves around it gradually take on yellow tones as well, blending with the flower—a transformation that's quite interesting. At the tip of a branch extending to the right, there's a tiny, withered bud of another species—a true lingering flower. This is a September arrangement that carries the feeling of late summer. The other arrangement, created with October in mind, features short-cut Taiwan toad lily paired with small fruits of rugosa rose. The flower vessel, bearing the seal of Sen no Rikyu, is the sort you'd typically use in a small tea room, but here I'm using it in a more

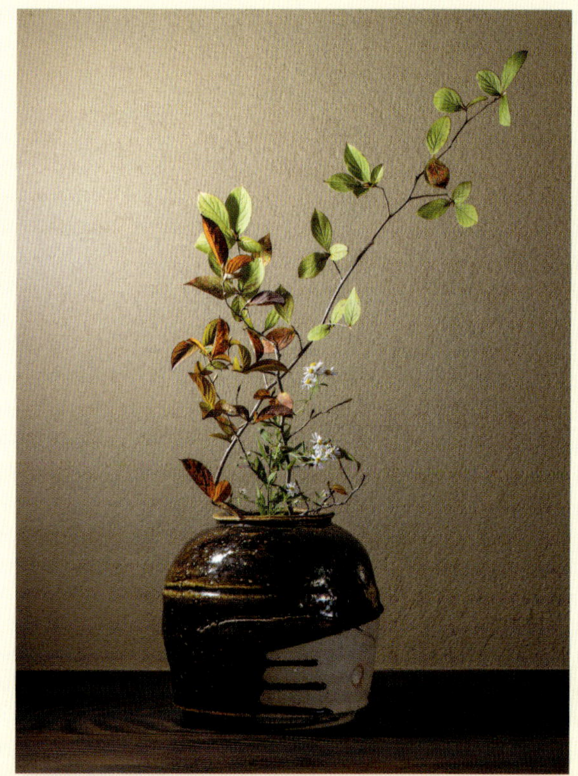

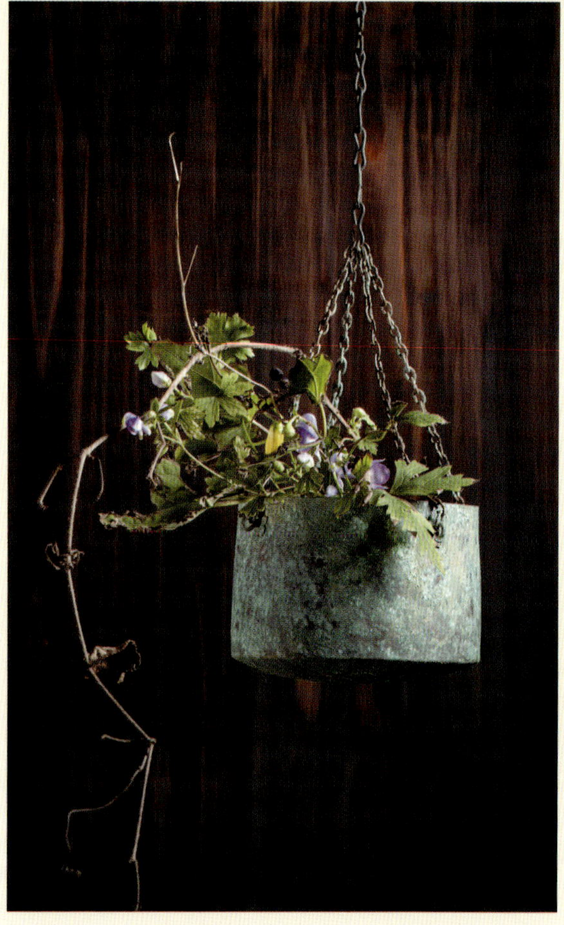

 Wild chrysanthemum and Japanese stewartia leaves. Oribe-style flower container by Ryoji Koie.

In a solid, weighty Oribe ware flower container, a tall branch of stewartia is arranged, with wild chrysanthemum placed near the mouth. On a single stewartia branch, green leaves intermingle with glossy, colored leaves, evoking the changing of the seasons. The overall effect is a natural, uncontrived presence — like wildflowers growing in the field.

 Monkshood, globeflower, bugbane, and crimson glory vine. Bronze hanging vessel, Java, Indonesia.

In this everyday setting, four types of autumn plants are arranged in a hanging bronze vessel from Indonesia. "Autumn flowers tend to be modest, so even when you include several types, they harmonize well," says Kobayashi. A key feature of the arrangement is the trailing branch of wild grape.

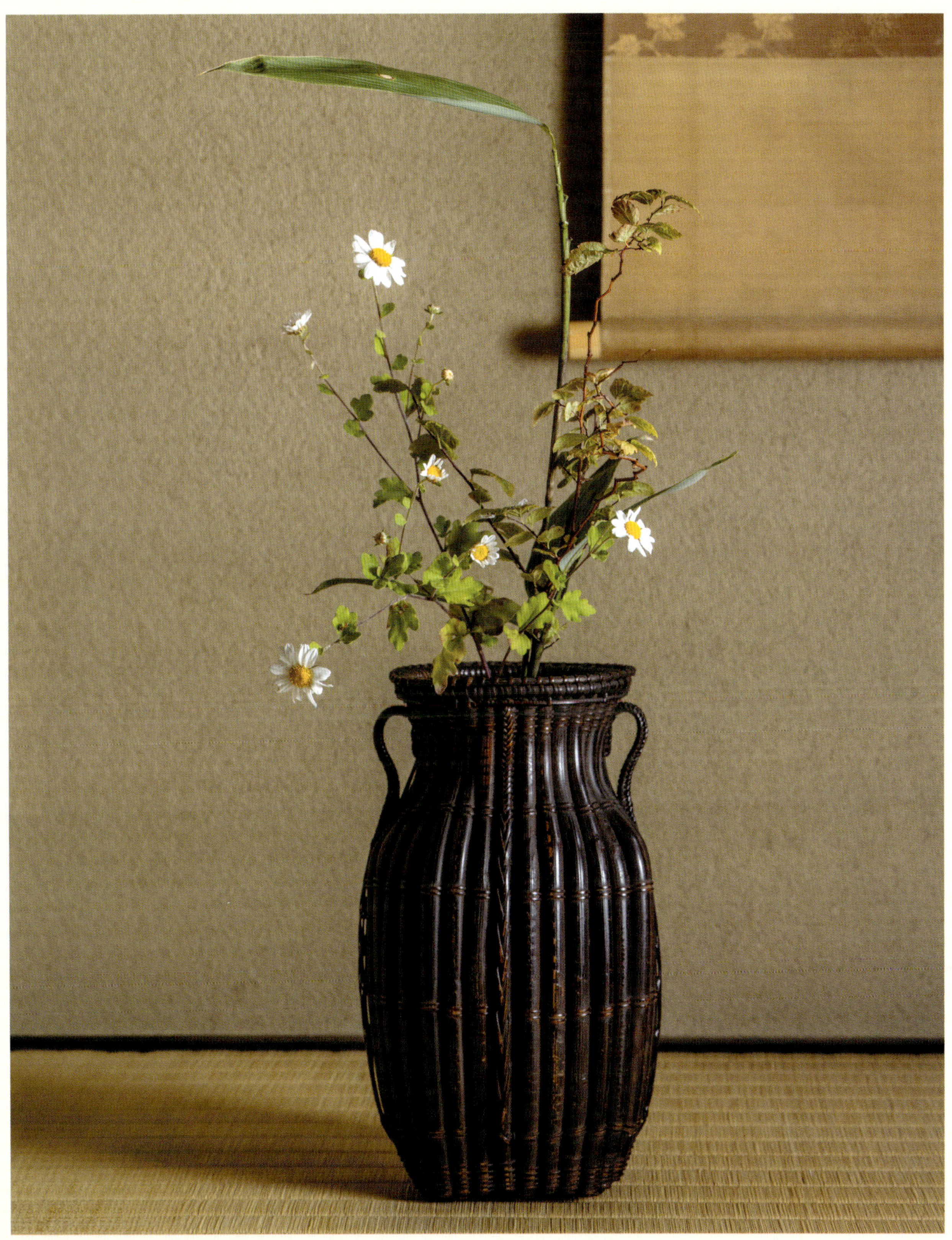

Wild chrysanthemum, bamboo grass, spiraea. Chinese "shin-guard" basket.

In the tea room alcove, delicate chrysanthemum serves as the main flower in the arrangement. Because the Chinese "shin-guard" basket (see page 110) has a strong presence, the chrysanthemum alone would feel unbalanced — so branches and bamboo grass are added as a highlight. The upward-reaching bamboo leaves are particularly effective.

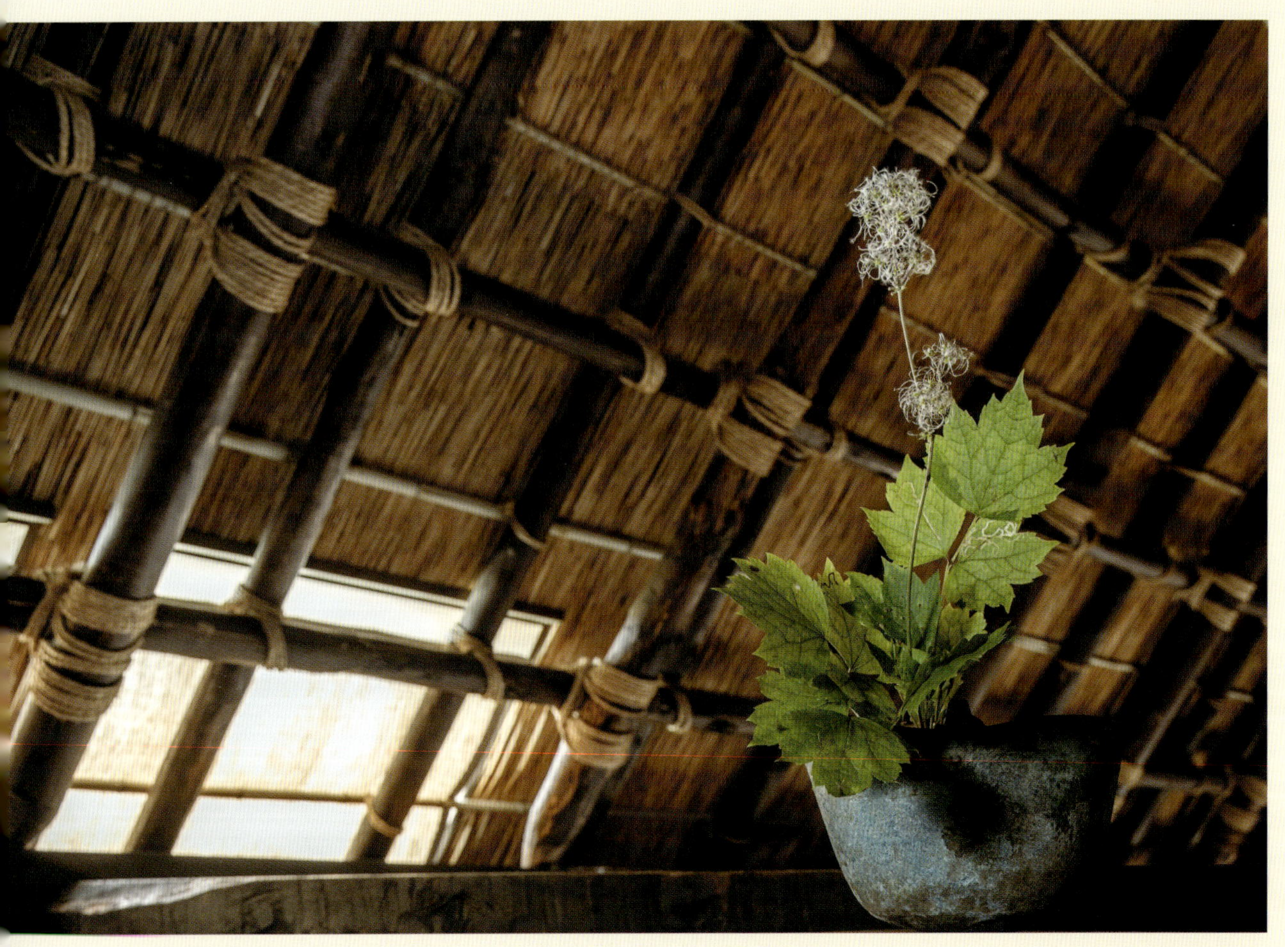

Kusabotan ("grass peony"). Bronze bucket-shaped vessel, Java, Indonesia.

Kusabotan is a wild Japanese mountain plant with large leaves and clusters of small flowers blooming at the tops of upright stems. Here, its striking foliage is featured in a simple, single-variety arrangement placed in a bronze vessel. A quiet, everyday display making use of the intimate atmosphere of a small upstairs room of this old farmhouse.

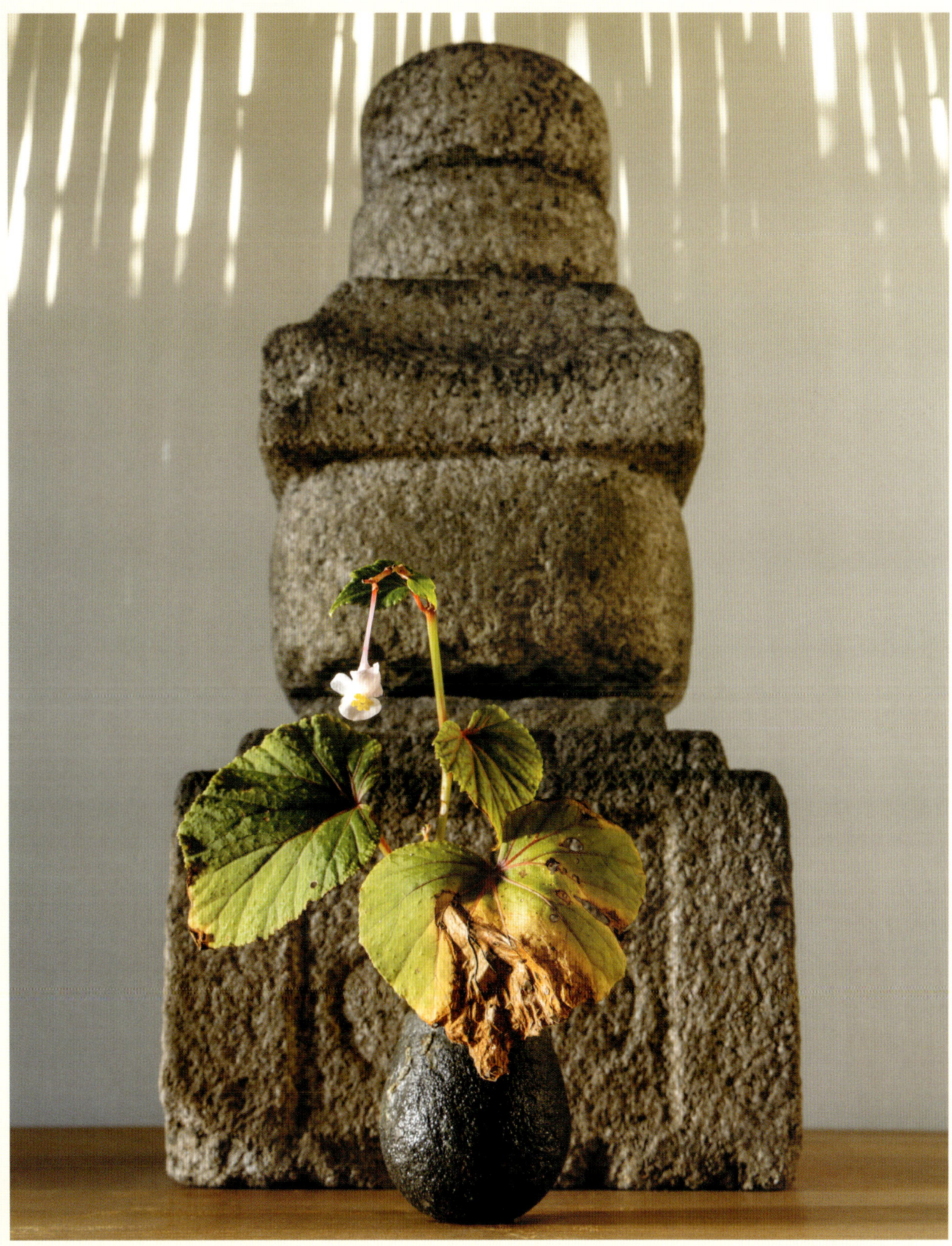

Hardy begonia. Small bronze flower container, Java, Indonesia.

A lingering blossom of hardy begonia, picked from the garden of the old farmhouse. A small bronze jar is the flower vessel, placed near a modest five-tiered pagoda sculpture in the room. The large withered leaf is left intact, preserving the plant's natural form as it was in the garden.

everyday space. This, too, reflects a yin–yang balance: because the flowers carry a more subdued (yin) tone, I intentionally chose a small yet strong (yang) flower container.

Something else I learned from Inaba-san is that traditional rules can be reinterpreted—if you understand the meaning behind them. For example, it's long been said that one should not place branches in basket flower containers; that baskets should be used only for grasses and wildflowers. But why? If you understand the reasoning, then even branches can be acceptable. Flowers are soft and airy—not rough or rigid, like branches. So, if a branch carries that soft, airy quality, it can work. That's absolutely true. If you understand why something is considered "wrong," if you grasp the original intent, you can go beyond it. Tea ceremony is about enjoying beauty within certain constraints. If anything goes, then tea loses its form. But even when something breaks a rule, if you find it beautiful, isn't that reason enough to use it? After all, tea is about expressing beauty. It's not about rejecting something because it has thorns or a scent. The important thing is to ask *why* it's said to be unsuitable. If you understand why it doesn't fit, you can move beyond that rule. Longstanding traditions exist for good reason—but the real question is whether you can reinterpret that meaning in your own words. What I came to understand through my time with Inaba-san is that a true master can articulate the reasoning behind their actions. Transcendence doesn't mean ignoring the rules and doing whatever you please. It means internalizing their meaning—and then going one step beyond. That's what I've come to know through Inaba-san's approach to flowers.

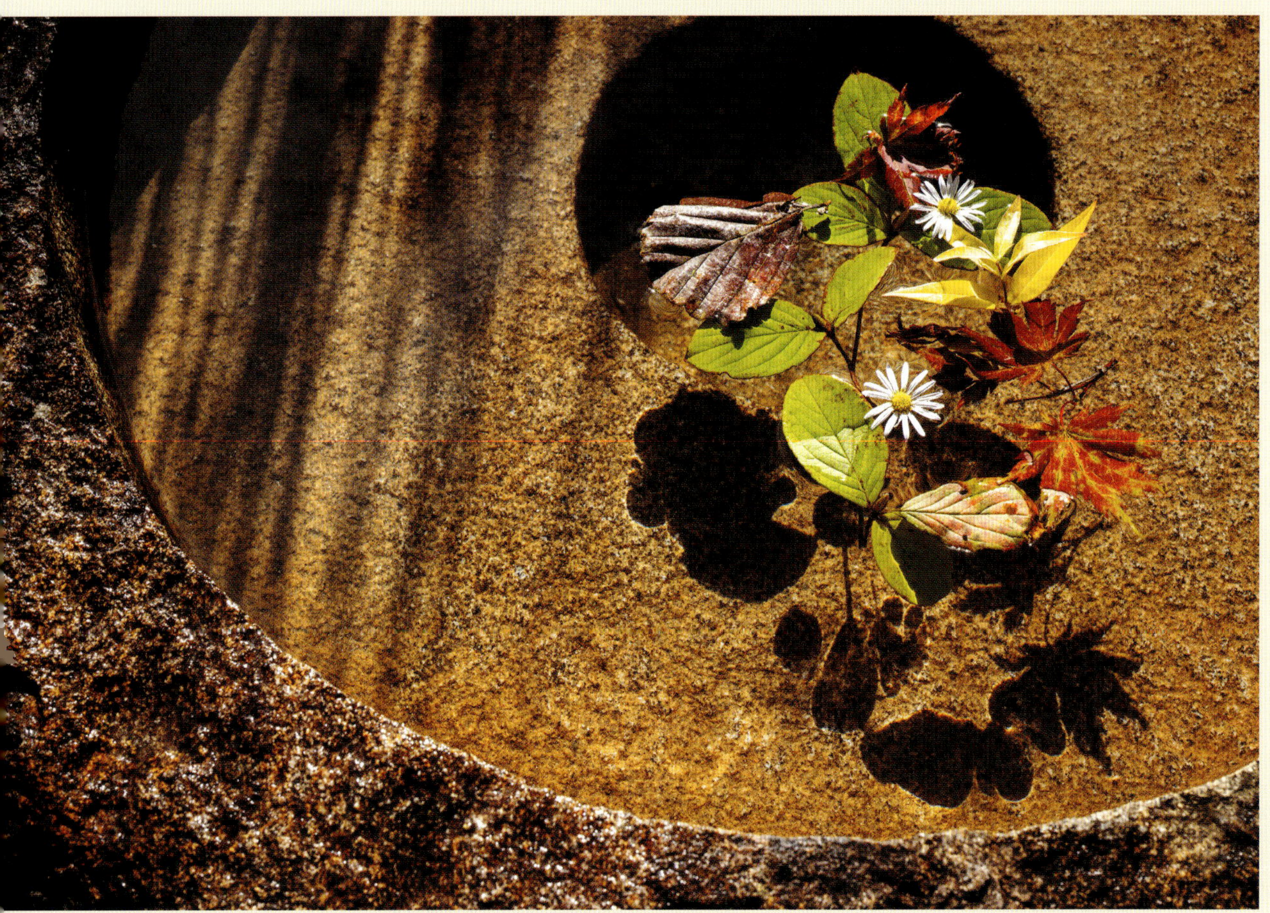

Wild chrysanthemum, Japanese stewartia, mountain maple leaves, witch hazel, and blue star. Stone water basin.

Several types of autumn plants are floated in a *tsukubai* stone water basin in the garden of the old farmhouse. Arranging floating flowers in a fixed basin or in a water bowl, and changing them daily is one way of engaging with flowers. It's also fascinating to see how changes in light cast shifting blossom shadows.

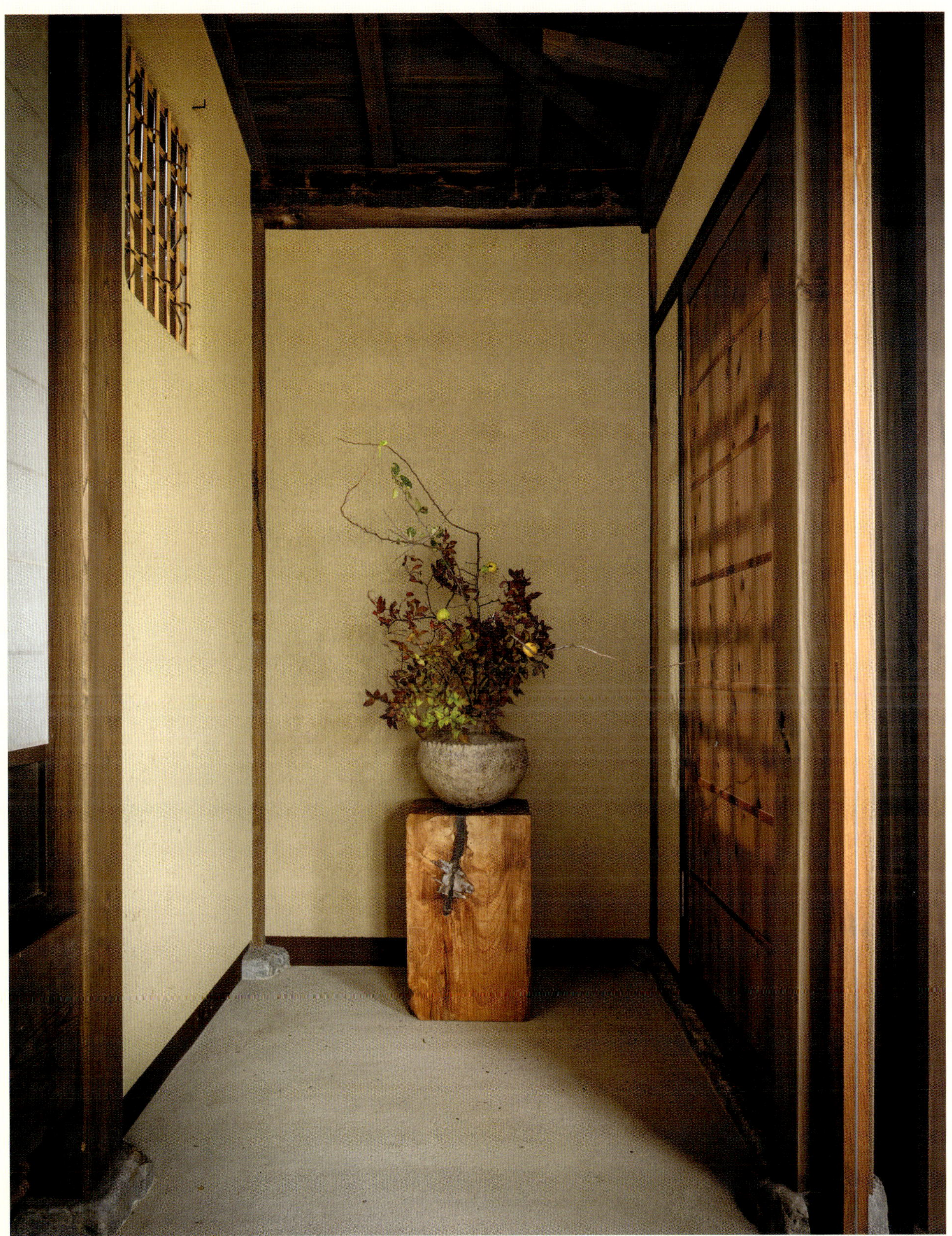

Quince fruit and blueberry. Earthenware vessel, Java, Indonesia.

In the earthen-floored entryway, an earthenware vessel is filled generously with blueberry branches whose leaves are turning red. A branch of flowering quince with fruit extends upward, adding a sense of openness to the space. The display is part of an everyday living area, but care is taken to preserve a feeling of empty space — nothing is placed around it.

The Final Glow of the Season

Japanese Anemone

In the world of tea, October marks the final month of using the *furo* portable brazier, a time known as *nagori*—the lingering end of a season. After enjoying half a year of tea with the furo since May, the conclusion of this season is met not with sadness, but with a sense of quiet appreciation. Utensils that have been used repeatedly—cracked, chipped, worn with age—are embraced as they are. Continuing to use them in their weathered state is a uniquely tea-centric way of finding beauty. This season offers abundant opportunities for expression, making it a particularly engaging time for those who host tea gatherings. Flowers that have passed their summer peak, with smaller blooms or leaves tinged with signs of decay—called *zanka*, or "lingering flowers"—are often chosen. And for these fading autumn grasses and blooms, bamboo baskets are especially well suited.

Among the baskets used for tea, some—like the ones we used in September—are repurposed everyday objects. Others, like the Sozen-style basket on the facing page, were developed specifically for tea. This basket is associated with Hisada Sozen, an early Edo-period tea master of the Senke school, and is considered a classic example of the Senke-style basket flower container. The design Sozen created was later formalized and widely adopted: a trapezoidal shape with a handle, offering good stability and ease of use for arranging flowers. Though it's common to use multiple blooms in this basket, here only a single type—Japanese anemone, with its slightly singed leaves—is arranged. While the change in a flower's form is often appreciated, here the subtle transformation in the leaves alone evokes the passage of time.

This month's photographs were also taken in the farmhouse featured in the September chapter. Built in northern Shiga Prefecture about 160 years ago, the home has a steep thatched roof—characteristic of snow-heavy regions. In the simple tea room of such a traditional farmhouse, a solitary lingering flower seems just right. Ornate surroundings would not suit the quiet style of tea practiced in the lingering season. As the hot summer ends, one feels both reluctance and gratitude for the close of the furo season, and turns toward the coming one. It is a deeply poignant moment—looking back on what has passed, and quietly anticipating what lies ahead.

Japanese anemone. Sozen-style basket container.

The Japanese anemone is one of the flowers favored for tea arrangements in this season. It bears white or pale pink blossoms, but here I've used only the buds, highlighting the expressive beauty of the leaves instead. A key consideration is how to balance the handle characteristic of the Sozen basket with the placement of the plant material.

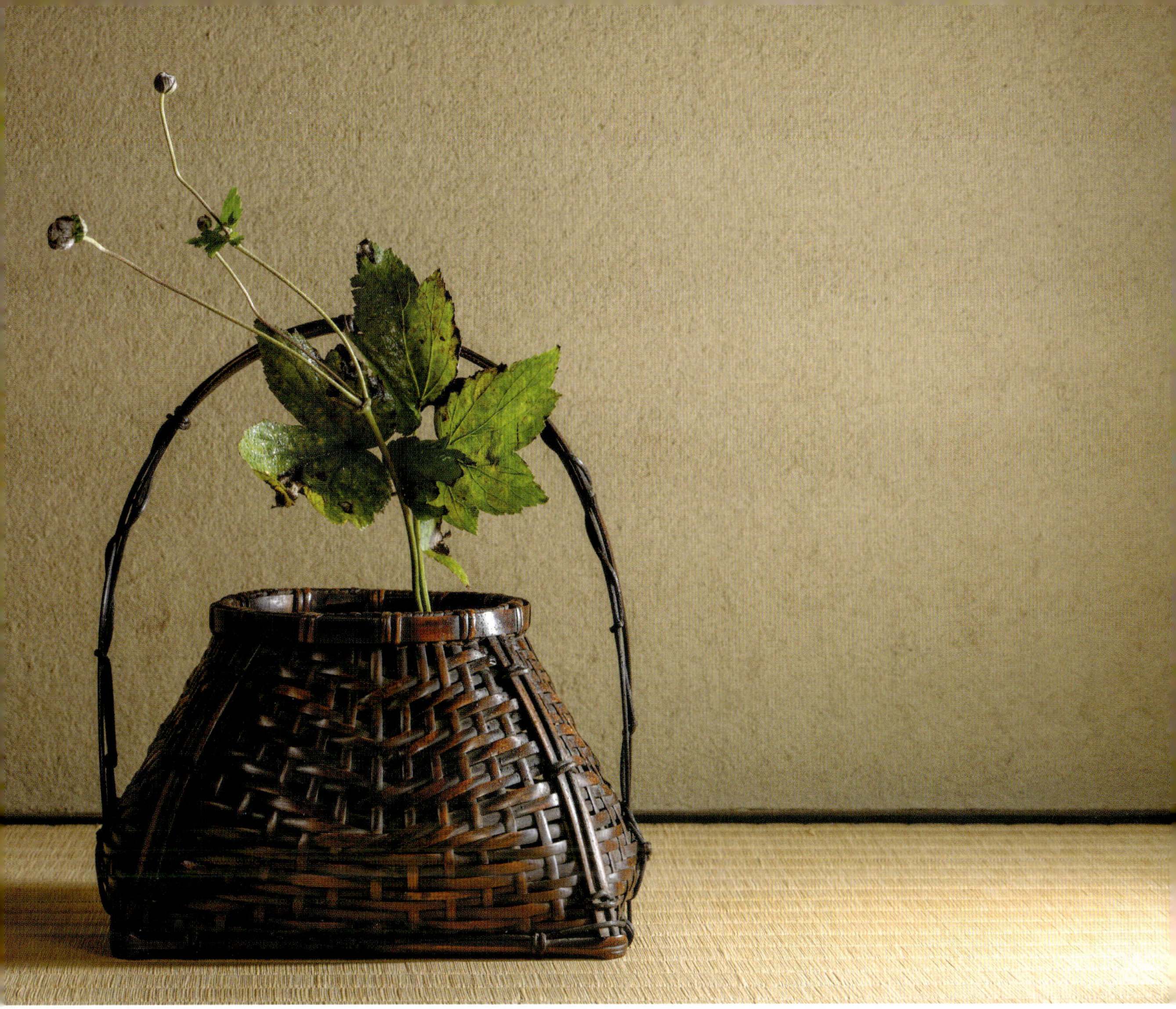

Bending Slender Branches to Create a Natural Flower Holder

It's common to cross two branches inside the inner cylinder of a basket vase to hold the flowers in place. In this case, however, a single branch is laid horizontally across, and its naturally flexible twigs are skillfully bent upward to form a vertical support. Unlike crossed branches, which must be trimmed to fit the cylinder exactly, these curled twigs are easier to adjust and offer a more stable hold. Whether it is visible or hidden, a flower holder should appear as natural as possible. It's important to always consider how the materials at hand — both flowers and other plant elements — can be used creatively to form a suitable support.

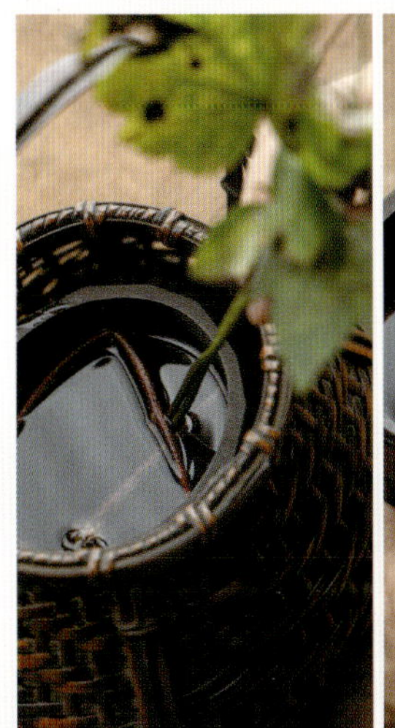
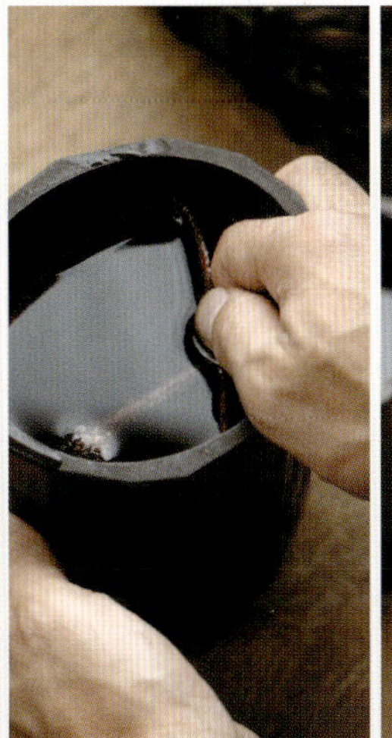
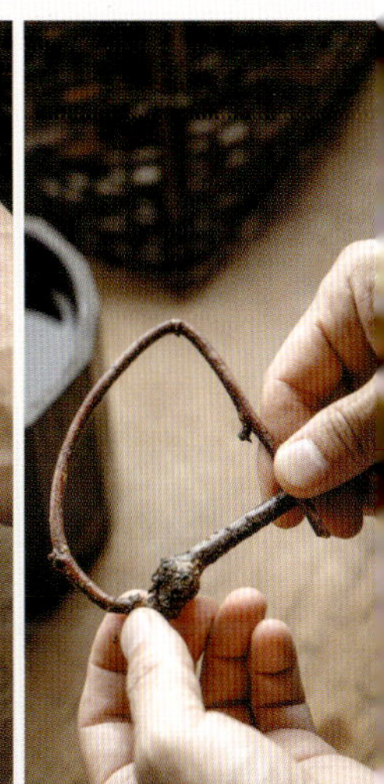

Flowers and Utensils for October

The Omotesenke Lineage

This season, in addition to the remaining late-blooming flowers, the floral materials become richly varied, with glossy autumn leaves and berries. In response to that, not only baskets but also other interesting flower containers start to appear. Whether in a tea room or in everyday spaces, this is a season that invites us to enjoy experimenting with different combinations of flowers and vessels.

That said, I have very definite preferences, and among the arrangements this time, the bamboo flower container by Kanamori Sowa on the facing page left a strong impression on me. Bamboo flower containers have appeared in many forms, but I'm drawn to the intense presence of this particular one. The strong hatchet marks on the lower section are its most distinctive feature. I believe these marks weren't made by a bamboo artisan, but rather by Sowa himself as he cut the bamboo. Even after hundreds of years, the force of that original cut remains vividly intact. The way the piece has naturally aged and worn over time has a beauty beyond words.

The box inscription for the bamboo shakuhachi flower container by Kanamori Sowa on the facing page reads "Flower Container by Lord Sowa," written by Kuwayama Kasai, a warrior of the early Edo period as well as a tea practitioner, and he studied tea under Katagiri Sekishu.

Japanese spindle and crimson glory vine. Bamboo basket.

These two fruiting branches — Japanese spindle, with its small, bright fruits and autumn leaves, and crimson glory vine, with its trailing stems — are classic materials for this season. The natural droop of the grapevine is used to full effect, with the other branches and foliage thoughtfully arranged to complement it.

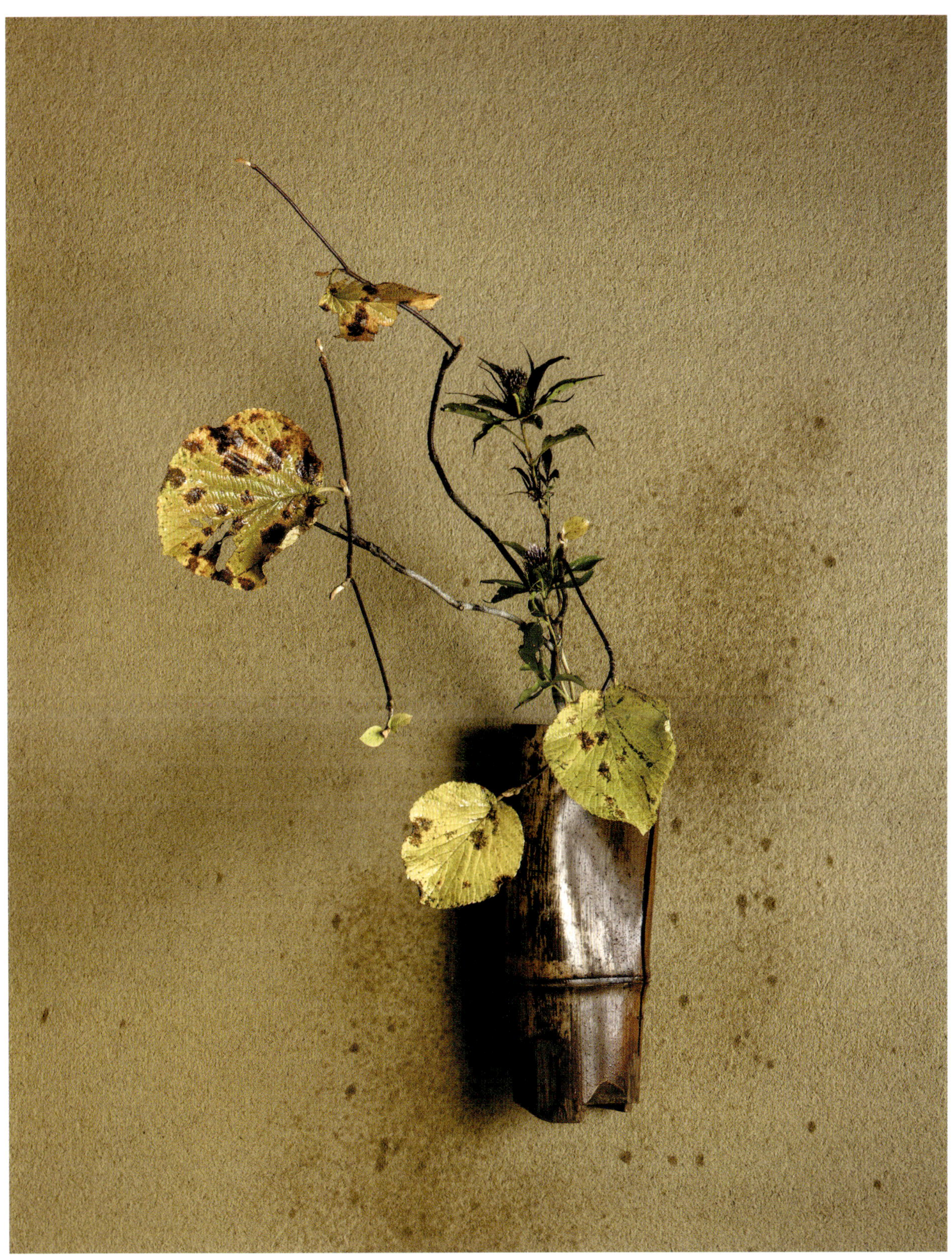

Atractylodes and daylily. Bamboo shakuha-chi flower container by Kanamori Sowa.

A late-blooming stalk of atractylodes is paired with daylily leaves, now yellowed and beginning to decay. Though modest in size, Kanamori Sowa's shakuhachi-style bamboo container has a powerful presence. Hiroshi remarks that the way it hangs on the tea room wall is "beyond words." "It's magnificent with flowers — and just as magnificent without them."

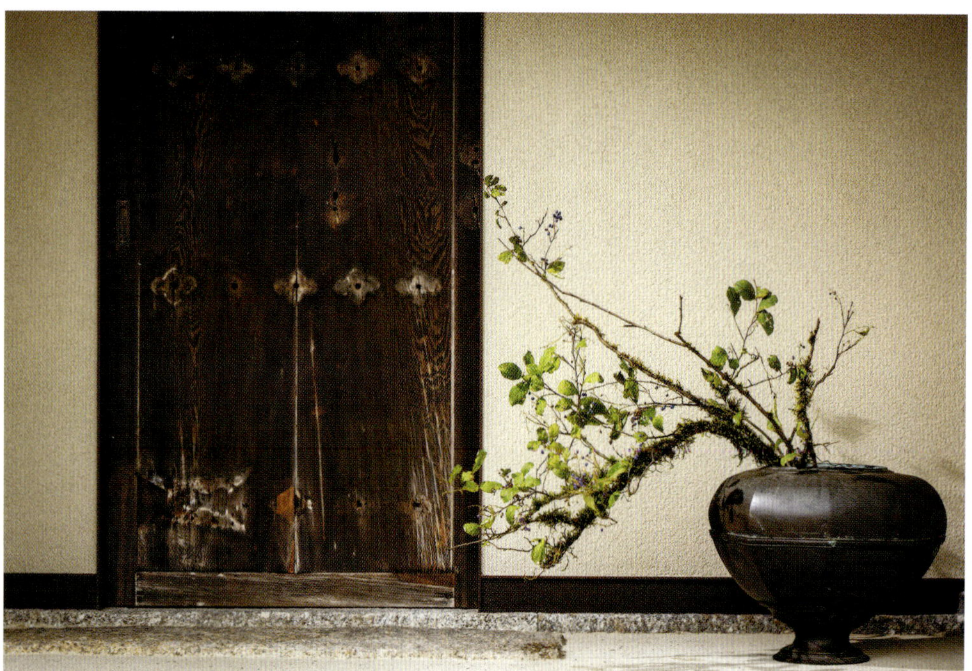

**Sapphireberry, moss-covered branch.
Large bronze flower container, Java,
Indonesia.**

At the entrance to the old farmhouse is a large bronze flower
container from Indonesia. A thick, moss-covered tree branch
(species unidentified) is arranged inside, accompanied by
a branch of Japanese sapphireberry bearing fruit. The solid
weight of the bronze vessel anchors the arrangement, harmo-
nizing beautifully with the earthen walls and wooden doors.

Early twentieth-century bamboo craftsman
Takahara Shakuan wrote a commentary for the
Chado Bijutsu Zenshu (Complete Works of Tea Ceremony Art) saying that this kind of hatchet-marked
bamboo container is characteristic of either Katagiri Sekishu or Kanamori Sowa. In fact, when I first
saw this flower container, I thought it might be by
Sekishu. Shakuan, too, admired it, saying, "I didn't
know Sowa had such powerful work." He also wrote
that both Sekishu and Sowa were influenced by
Sen Doan, oldest son of Rikyu. That makes sense—
Sekishu was a warrior, so the boldness seen in the
hatchet marks on the bamboo is easy to understand. But Kanamori Sowa was called *Hime-Sowa*
("Princess Sowa") and was known more for his refined, elegant *kirei-sabi* style. That he had this kind
of inner intensity is quite striking.

If we trace the lineage back, both Sekishu and
Sowa inherited the tea aesthetics of Sen Doan. So
the boldness seen in their bamboo flower containers may also be seen as an expression of Doan's
spirit. I find myself deeply drawn to Sen Doan as a
historical figure, and I think his utensils are truly
remarkable.

Even though Doan was the son of Sen no Rikyu,
he was disowned and left the family. As a result,
he fell outside the lineage of the Senke schools that
have continued for over four centuries. And yet, I
wonder if his tea may not have carried the inner
spirit of Rikyu more than anyone else's. Perhaps
it was precisely because they were so similar that
father and son clashed. Through the beauty and
energy embodied in Doan's utensils, I find myself
reflecting on these things.

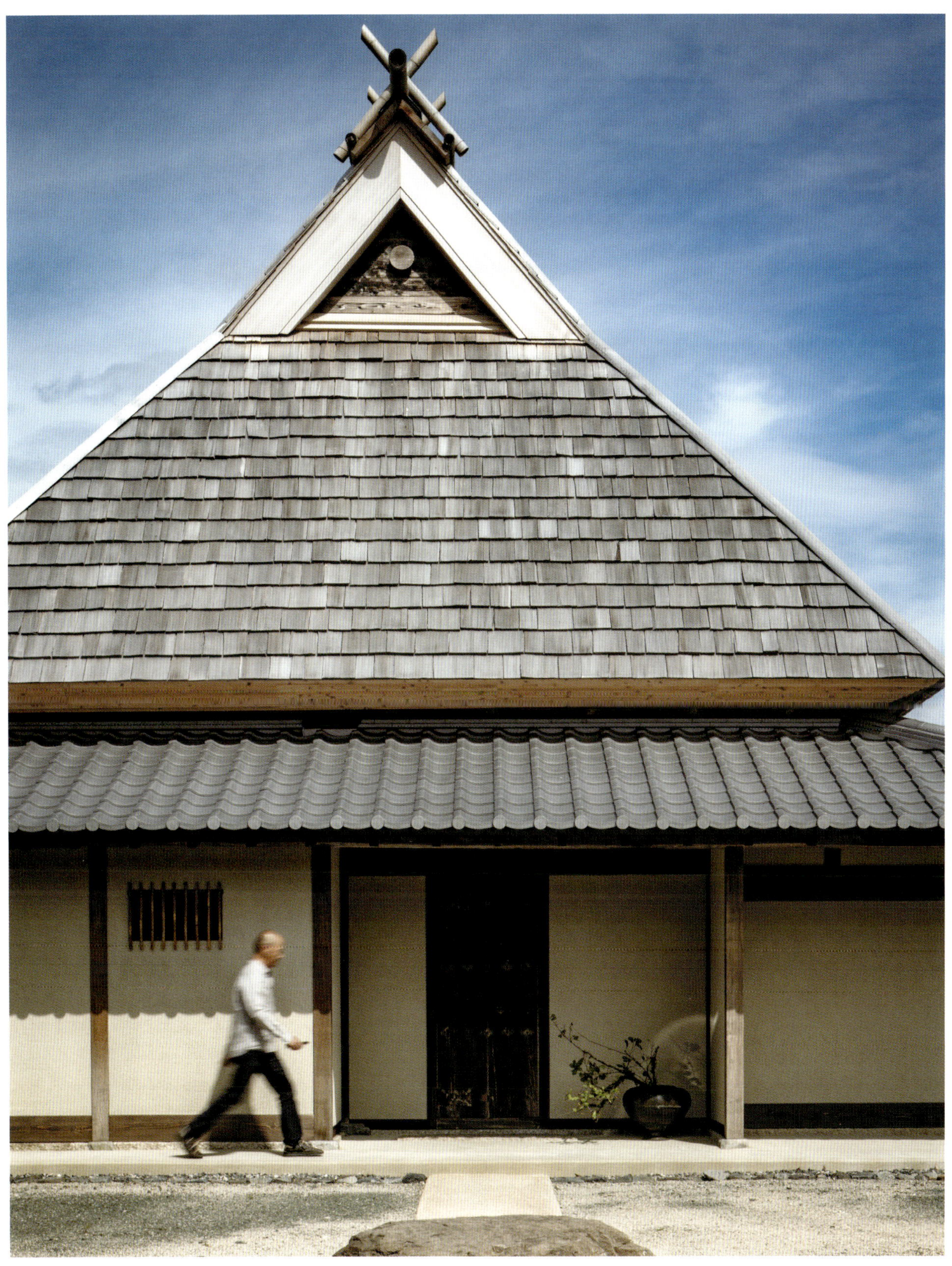

The old farmhouse in the town of Yogo, northern Shiga Prefecture. The area has heavy snowfall, so the roof is built at a steep pitch. The roof is covered with wooden shingles, but underneath, it is thatched with straw (see page 127).

All of Life Is Reflected in Tea

— Atsushi Kobayashi

Arranging flowers in daily life is a real joy. As I've mentioned before, flowers in the tea room are reduced to the barest essence—but flowers in everyday life show a different side altogether. While flowers in a tea gathering exist for only a fleeting moment, everyday flowers stay with us much longer. That's why, if we approach them with too much precision or intensity, it can become exhausting.

One way to deepen your relationship with flowers, I think, is to designate a specific spot in your home—a place where nothing unnecessary is placed—just for flowers. Then, try to make it a habit to always decorate that space with something you love, or to arrange flowers there. Each time, look at the flower and ask yourself a question, such as, "Would it look better on a stand?" or "Would it be more natural without one?" That process, over time, helps to refine your sensibility. People often talk about "cultivating sensibility," but I don't think it's something that can be taught by someone else. You have to discover your own answers through experience. You recognize what you personally like. In order to sharpen your own sensibility, you need to consciously make time to engage with flowers, or create a space for that engagement. Without bringing those actions into your daily life, it's hard to develop anything lasting. It's no different from what you choose to eat. When you pick up a readymade convenience-store meal in a plastic pack, you have no idea what ingredients went into it or how it was prepared. That kind of lifestyle doesn't nourish the senses. You come to understand which ingredients taste good, how to prepare them to bring out their flavor—and by repeating those actions every day, you gradually refine your sensibility.

To arrange tea flowers well, ultimately it comes down to how you engage with flowers on a regular basis—and beyond that, how you live your life as a whole. You need to carve out creative time in your daily life and pour your energy into it. It takes a great deal of energy, but in doing so, you're also building up your own inner strength. It's the same when it comes to a tea gathering. Guests who are attuned to these things can sense the thought and care the host has put into preparing the occasion—especially if they live that way themselves. But you won't understand that unless you've tried it yourself. Once you have, you start to understand what others are doing too.

What tea teaches us, in the end, is how we live our daily lives. That connects directly to the spirit of Zen, which forms the philosophical foundation of the tea ceremony. It's not enough for the tea setting alone to be beautiful. How you live day to day—and even more broadly, how you live your life—ultimately finds expression in the tea. Your everyday life becomes part of your tea. I think the same is true when it comes to flowers.

In the attic space typical of old Japanese farmhouses — wooden beams supporting a thatched roof — the natural beauty of traditional Japanese architecture using entirely organic materials is paired with a bronze water bucket once used in daily life in Indonesia. In the spacious interior, the white blossoms of the rose of Sharon stand out vividly.

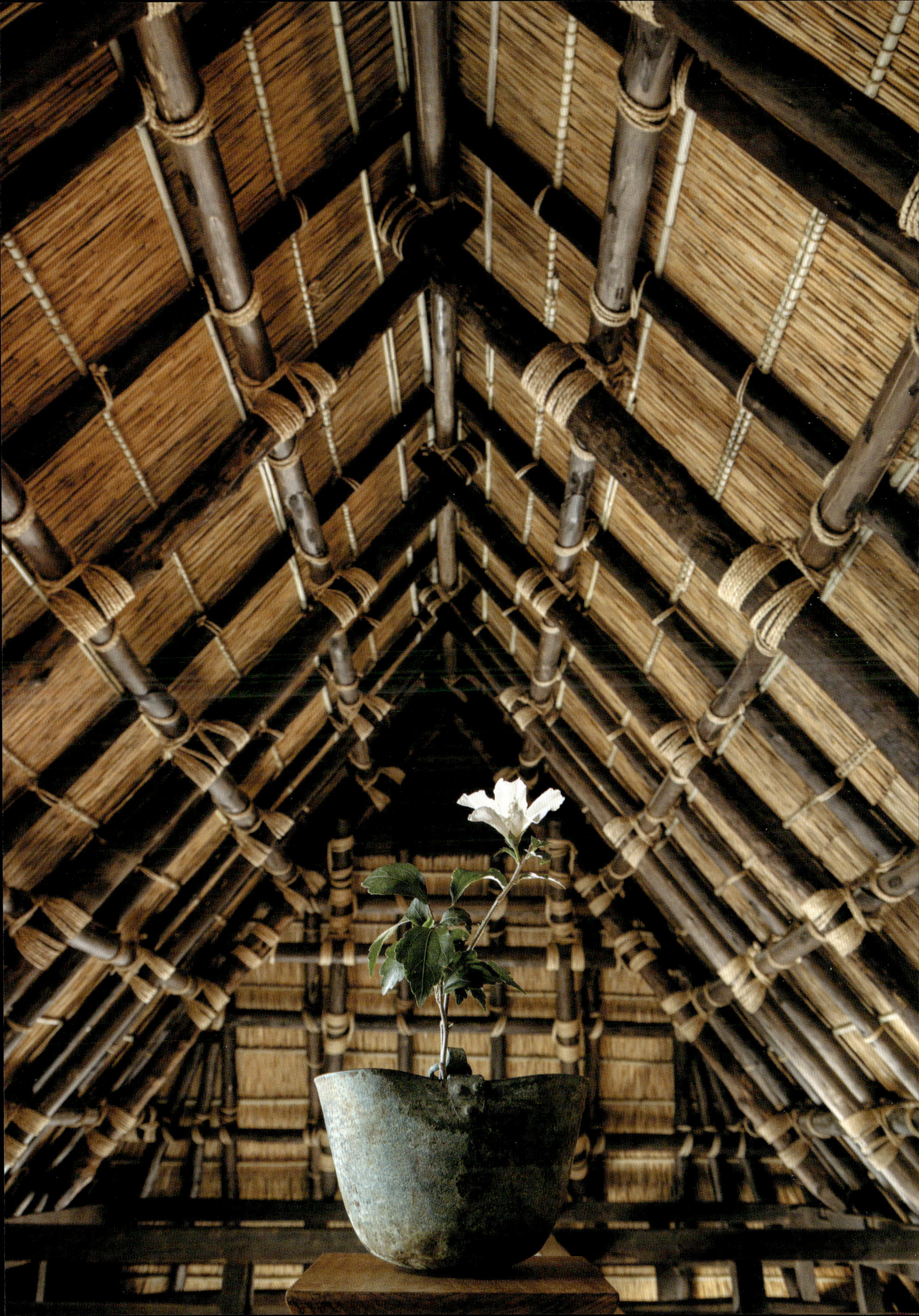

Unobtrusive Seasonal Flowers in Everyday Spaces

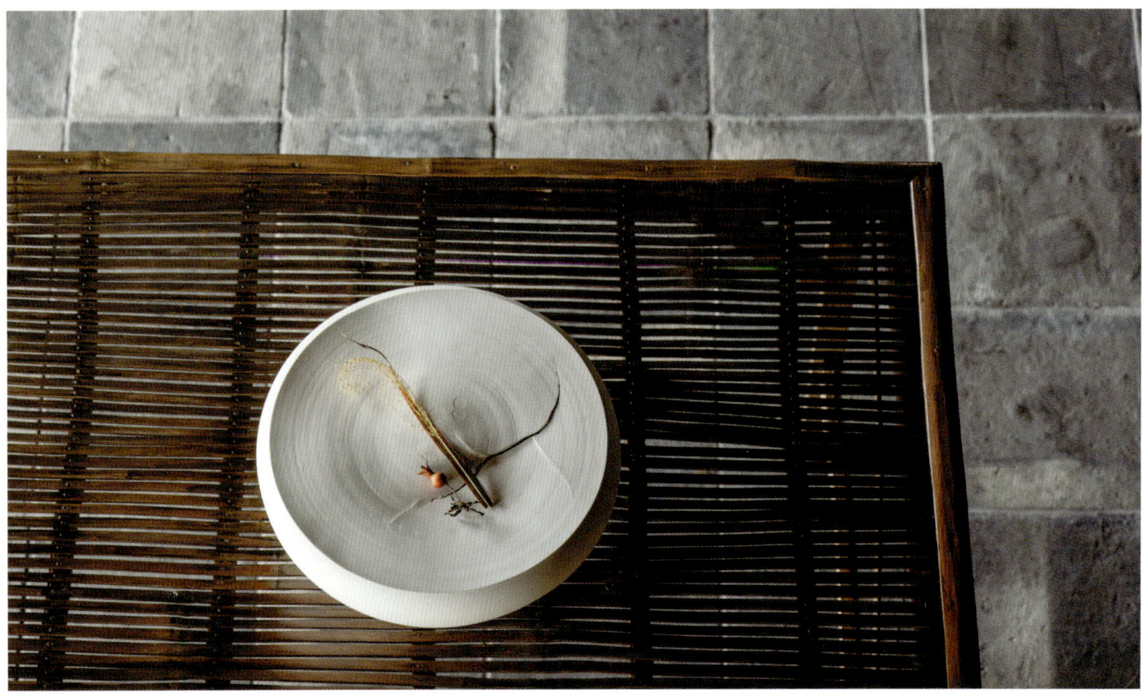

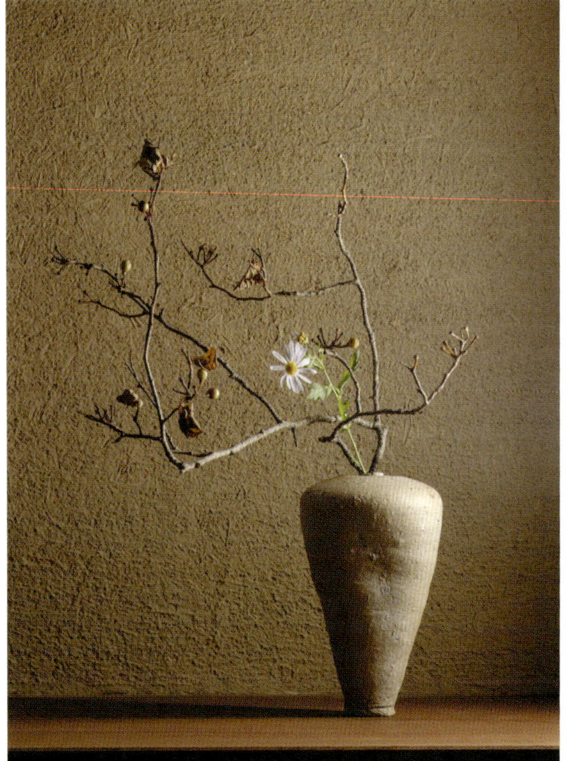

ABOVE Dwarf pomegranate and pampas grass. White porcelain pedestal dish by Taizo Kuroda (see page 154).

Flowers that blend naturally into the everyday living space of an old farmhouse. On a bamboo table sits a white porcelain display plate, holding a withered dwarf pomegranate and pampas grass. Because the display plate cannot hold water the question becomes how to best draw out the beauty of the vessel itself. The dried materials are placed directly on the plate to create the effect of floating flowers (see page 118).

LEFT Wild chrysanthemum and edgeworthia. Sea-recovered flower container, China.

Ceramics that have been submerged in the sea are referred to as *umi-agari* ("sea-recovered") and this flower container is believed to be of Chinese origin. Its narrow mouth holds flowers securely, making it a convenient vessel for arranging. Here, a rhythmically shaped branch of edgeworthia is paired with a single delicate wild chrysanthemum.

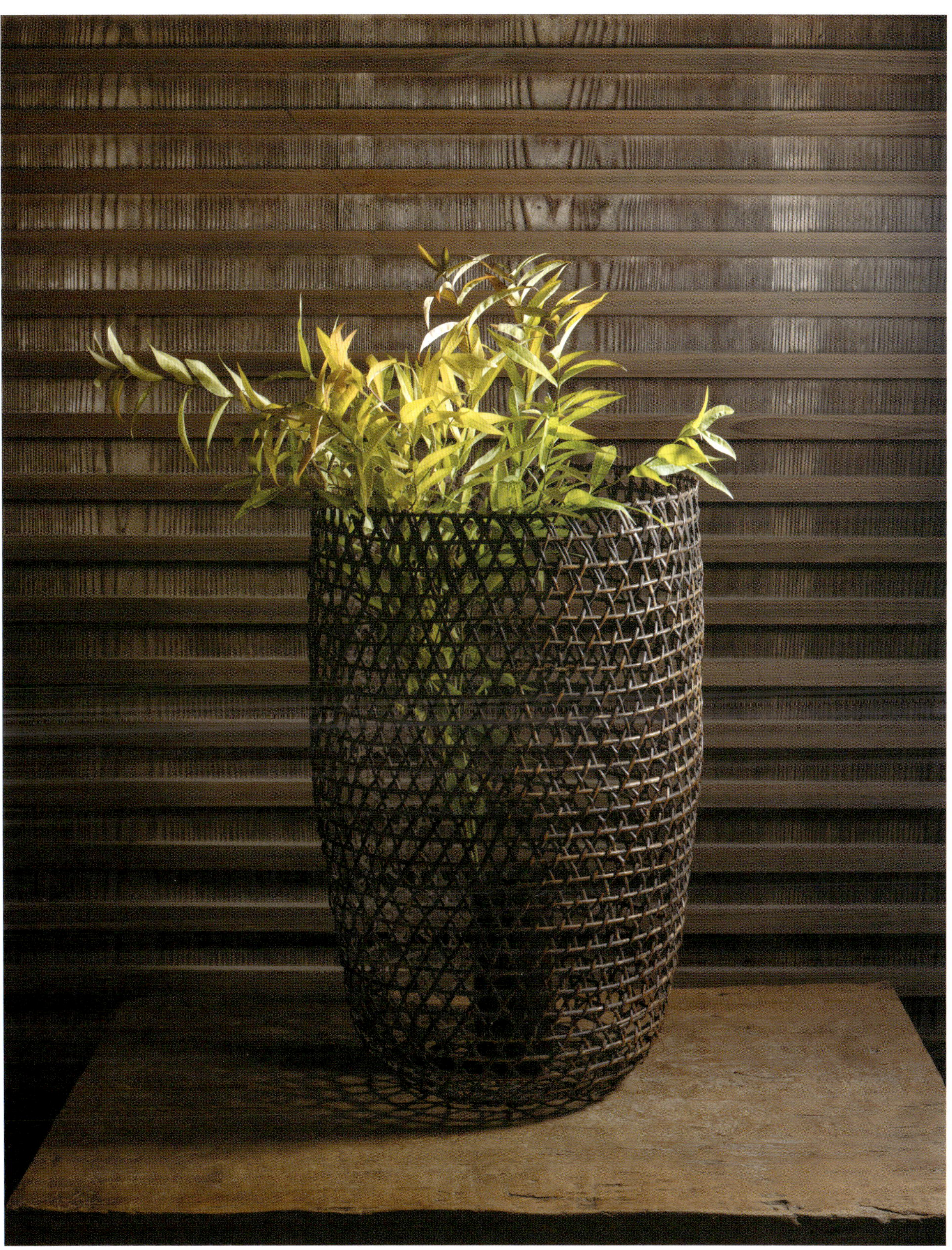

Blue star. Bamboo basket. Mentawai Islands, Indonesia.

A bamboo tube is placed inside a basket 31 inches (80 cm) tall, and blue star leaves are arranged in it. Only a small portion of the foliage rises above the rim of the basket. But as the leaves can be seen through the basket's open weave, that visibility is also taken into account when considering the overall balance and height of the arrangement.

Everyday Vessels as Flower Containers

RIGHT Dewberry and crimson glory vine. Bamboo blowpipe holder, Borneo, Indonesia.

A bamboo vessel that is beautiful even when simply placed on its own. Kobayashi says: "Unlike the bamboo flower container by Sowa (page 123), which was made by a tea practitioner specifically for arranging flowers, this piece was not originally intended for that use. But it has a natural beauty as a crafted bamboo utensil. You can imagine it was once used with great care."

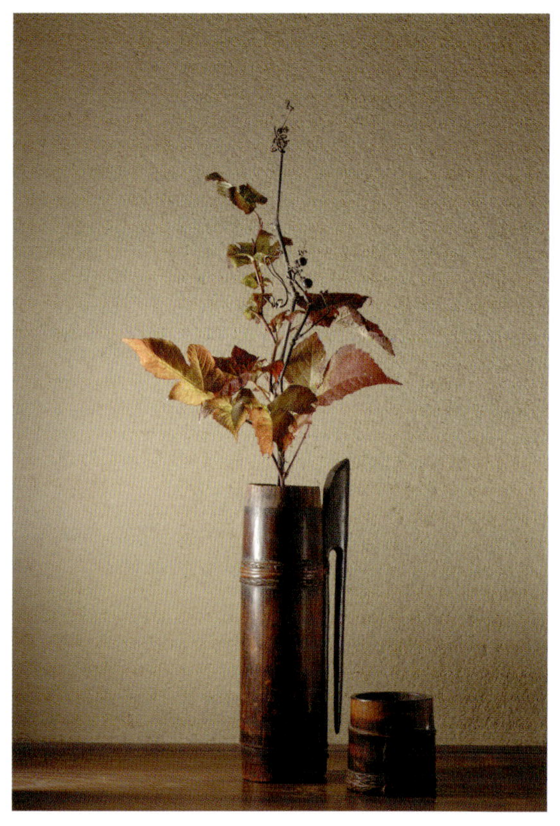

BELOW Japanese bittersweet. Bronze vessel, Java, Indonesia.

A large natural branch of Japanese bittersweet is arranged almost as is on a shelf by the entrance. To show its trailing form, the branch is displayed resting on the shelf. Because the material is both heavy and wide-spreading, a weighty bronze vessel has been repurposed as a flower container to provide stability and balance.

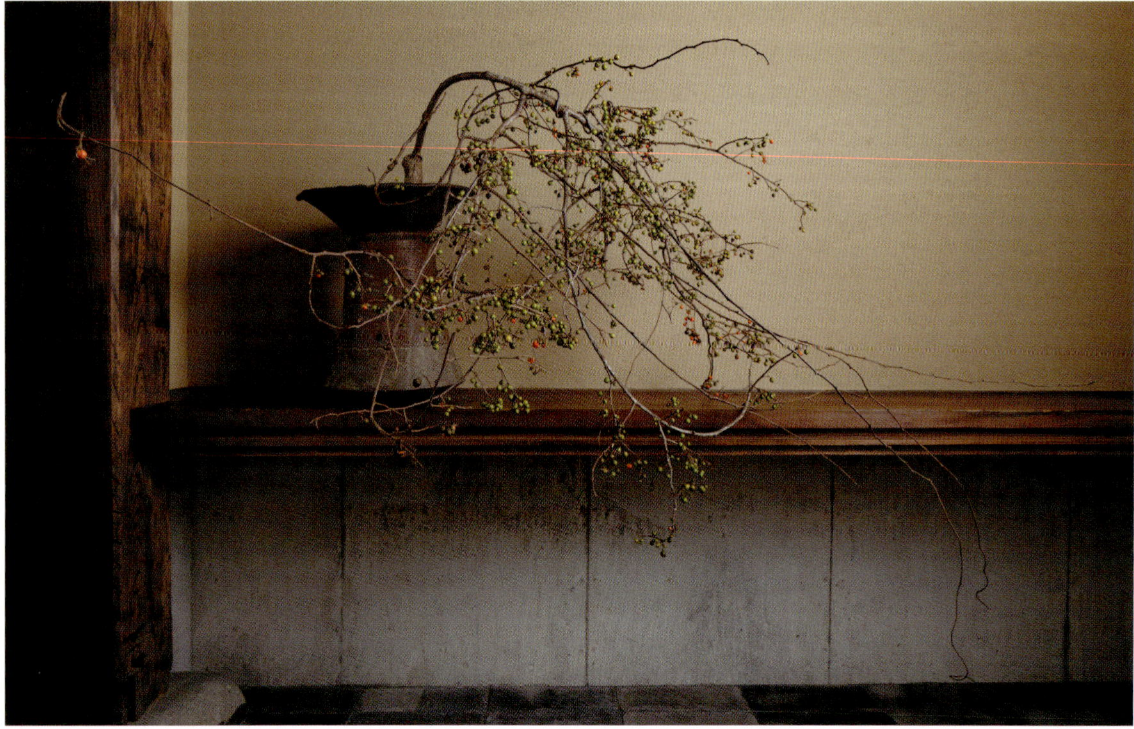

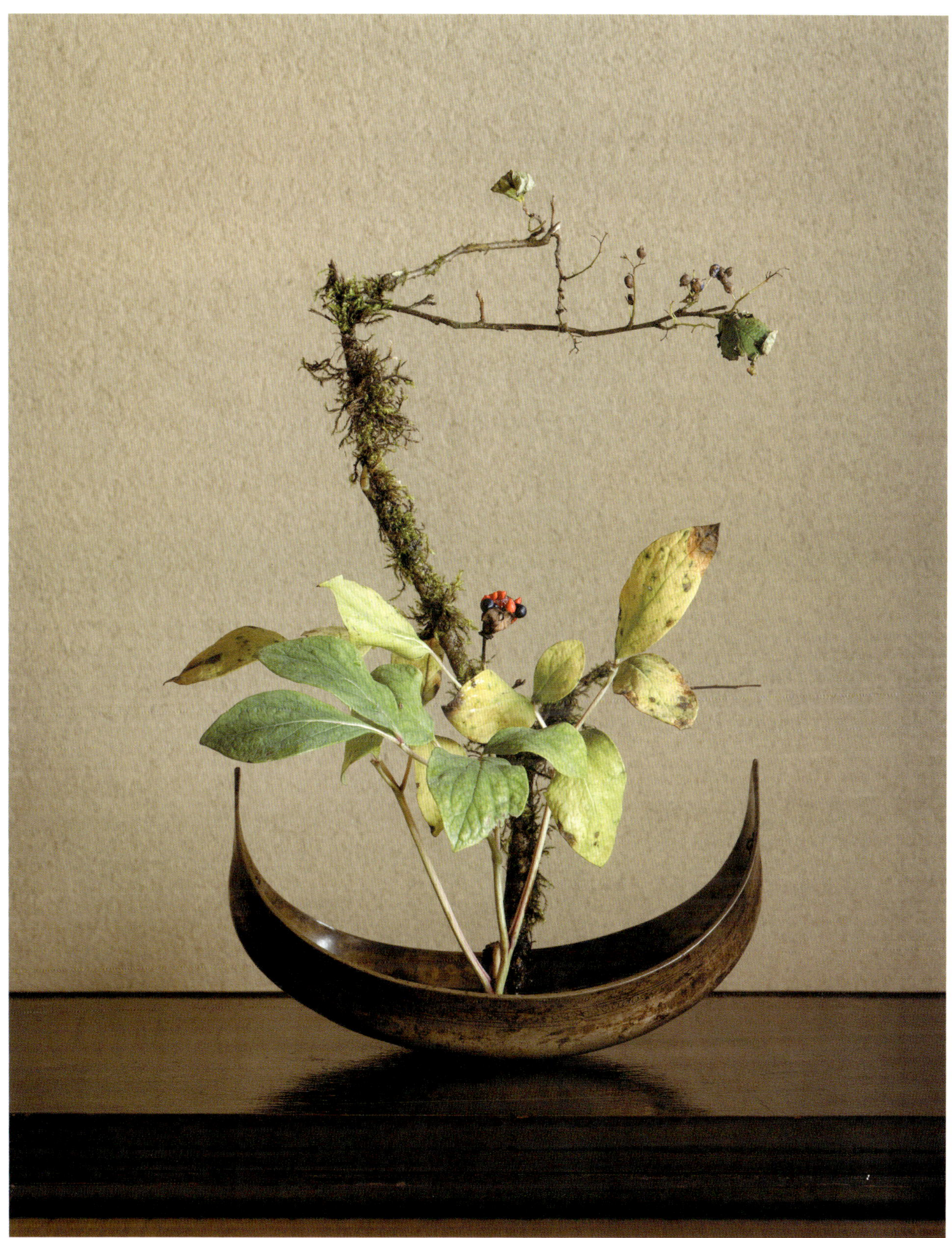

**Woodland peony fruit and sapphireberry.
Sand-cast bronze hanging-boat flower container, Sumatra, Indonesia.**

In the tea room alcove. A well-shaped branch of sapphireberry is paired with the brightly colored fruit of woodland peony. Although the vessel is a hanging-boat style container, the arrangement looks more striking when placed on a surface. It is therefore set on a low black-lacquered display table.

A Memorial Tea Gathering

Narcissus

November marks the beginning of the *ro* sunken-hearth season and is a time of renewal in the world of tea. This month, I prepared a tea gathering in memory of the twelfth-generation head of the Toda family, Shonosuke, my father, who passed away in 2012. He was the one who rebuilt the Toda shop during the chaotic years after the war. Now, as I pass the baton from myself to my son, I once again reflect on my father, and in the alcove I hung a calligraphy scroll by Seisetsu Shocho titled *Senbetsu-ge* (Farewell verse).

Seisetsu, who came from China to Japan in the Kamakura period (1185–1333) and deepened the practice of Zen in our country, had presented this verse to one of his disciples. In the middle of the verse is the line: "I fear that, being led astray by some other false teacher, you may fall into the demon's cave beneath the Black Mountain." In other words, it expresses the master's concern that his student might be led astray by impostors and lose his true path—a message of deep concern for a beloved disciple as he sets out on his own.

The flower container is a sixteenth century Iga ware piece named "Iwakado." It was a favorite of my father's. At one time, he presented it to a certain distinguished family, but later had it returned to my hands. Fine utensils like this often travel back and forth between hosts and guests over the course of many years. Yet such relationships are only possible with mutual trust and a shared understanding of the true nature of tea implements.

My father cultivated many friendships through the medium of tea utensils. Seisetsu Shocho's words feel as though they echo my father's feelings toward me. As I remember the man who rebuilt the shop and passed the baton to me, I take a moment— through a single bowl of tea—to reflect on the path we've walked.

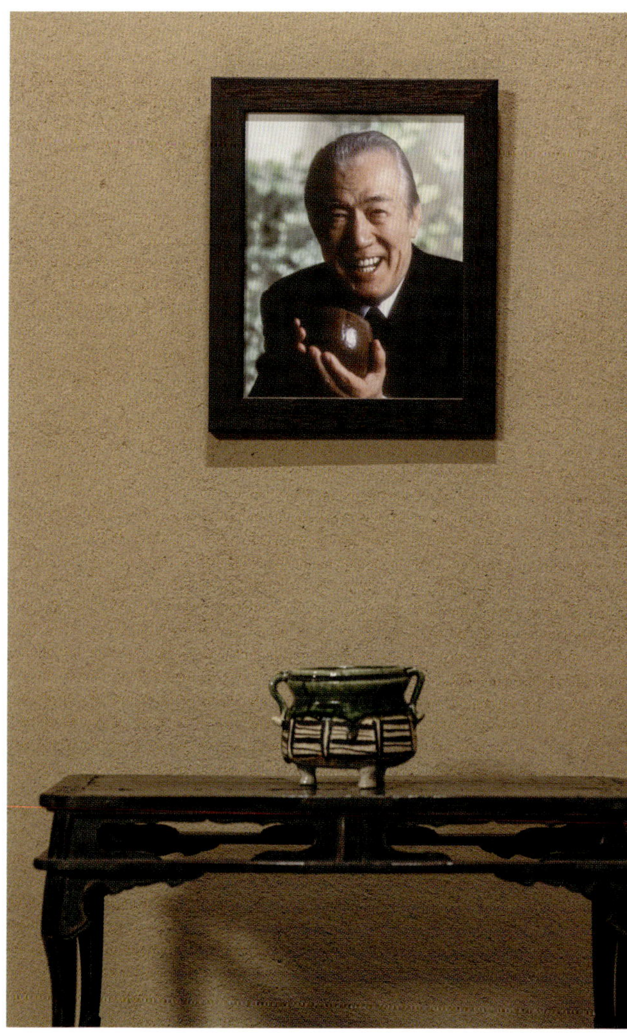

The late Shonosuke Toda, smiling broadly as he holds the famed tea bowl "Otogomae" by Hon'ami Koetsu. Shonosuke was known as one of the most distinguished connoisseurs in the world of classical art, and his sensibility, eye for quality, and words of wisdom were passed down among fellow dealers almost like scripture. Sociable and cheerful, he had a wide circle of acquaintances beyond the art world, which in turn helped expand his business. "He was a handsome man from a young age, and in his twenties he was apparently scouted several times to become a movie actor. He had a reputation as a charismatic man-about-town — good-looking, outgoing and often at the center of attention.

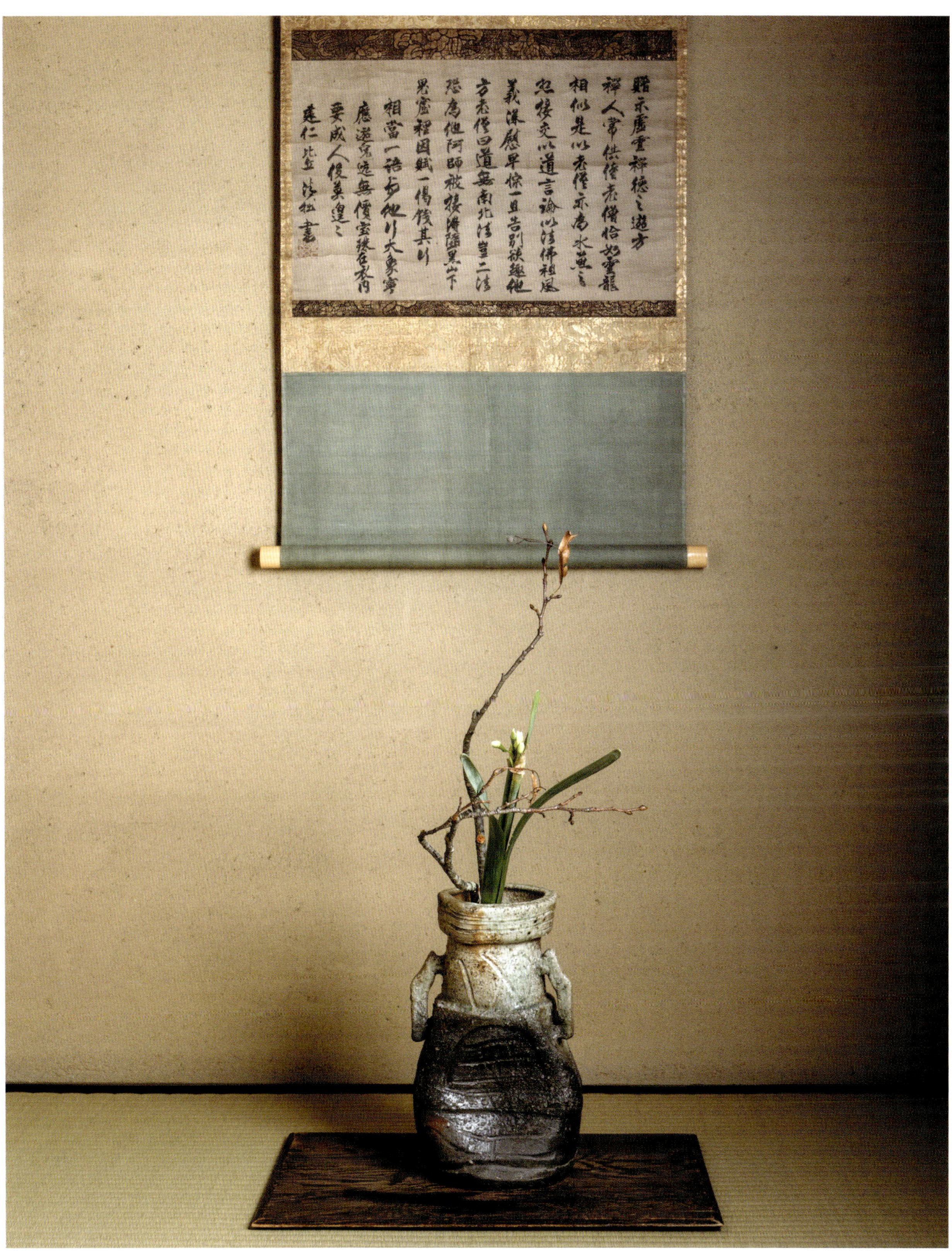

Narcissus, linden. Iga ware flower container "Iwakado," early Momoyama period.

The calligraphy is *Senbetsu-ge* (Farewell verse) by Seisetsu Shocho. "Usually Zen calligraphy would be paired with an old bronze vessel, but as this is a memorial for former president Shonosuke, I chose a regional pottery flower container he liked. The choice of container also depends on whom the tea gathering is meant to honor," says Atsushi Kobayashi.

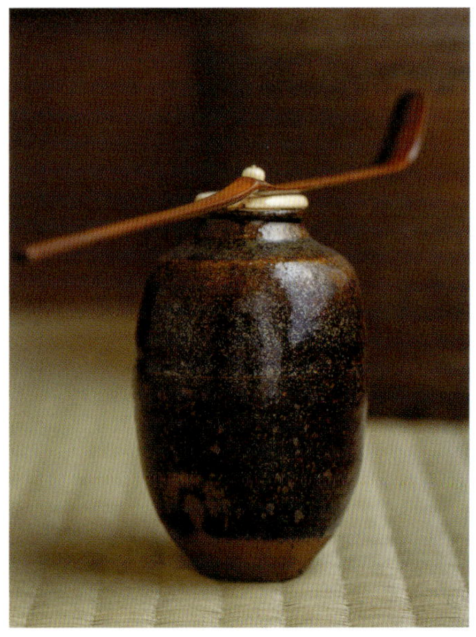

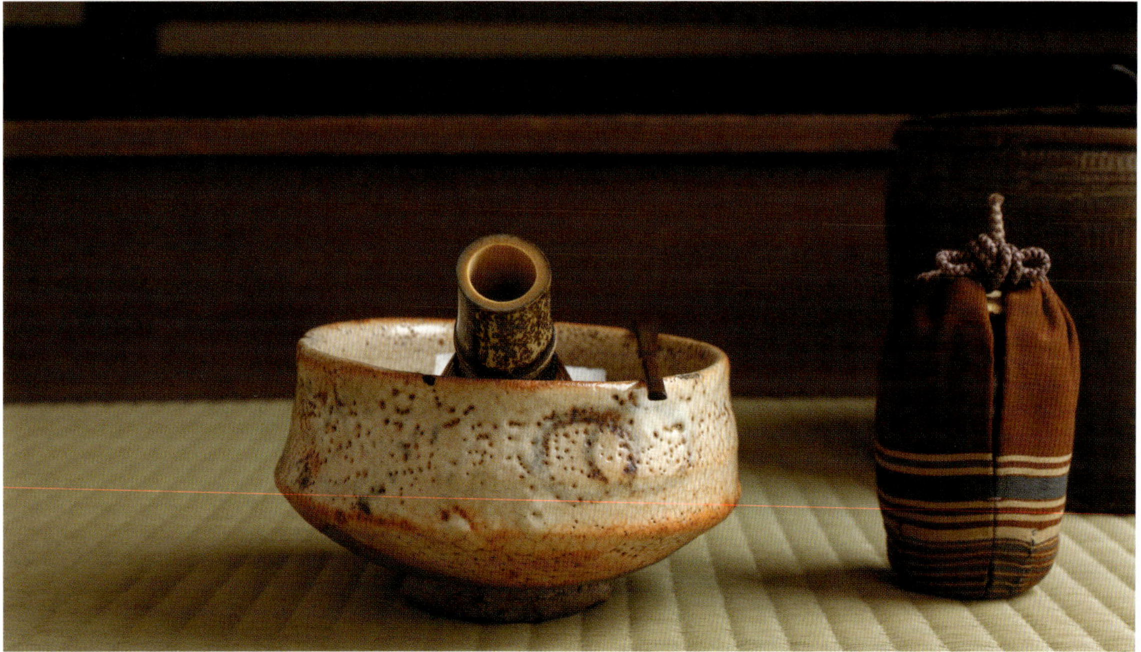

RECORD OF THE GATHERING

Alcove: Calligraphy *Senbetsu-ge* (Farewell verse) by Seisetsu Shocho
Flower container: Iga ware, "Iwakado"
Flowers: Narcissus and linden
Flower stand: Charred cedarwood
Kettle: Ashiya kettle, Onjoji Temple–style
Hearth frame: Unfinished wood, made by Hisayoshi
Fresh-water container: Namban–style woven bamboo
Tea caddy: Old Seto ware, *Sendai katatsuki* shape

Tea caddy pouch: *Mochizuki kando* fabric (striped silk pattern)
Tea bowl: Shino ware, named "Tsuten." Heirloom of the Hirase family, with storage box inscription by Shonosuke Toda
Tea scoop: Made by Sen Doan (the eldest son of Sen no Rikyu), with inscriptions by Sottakusai and Roko Hirase
Lid rest: Old bamboo, made by Yoken Fujimura

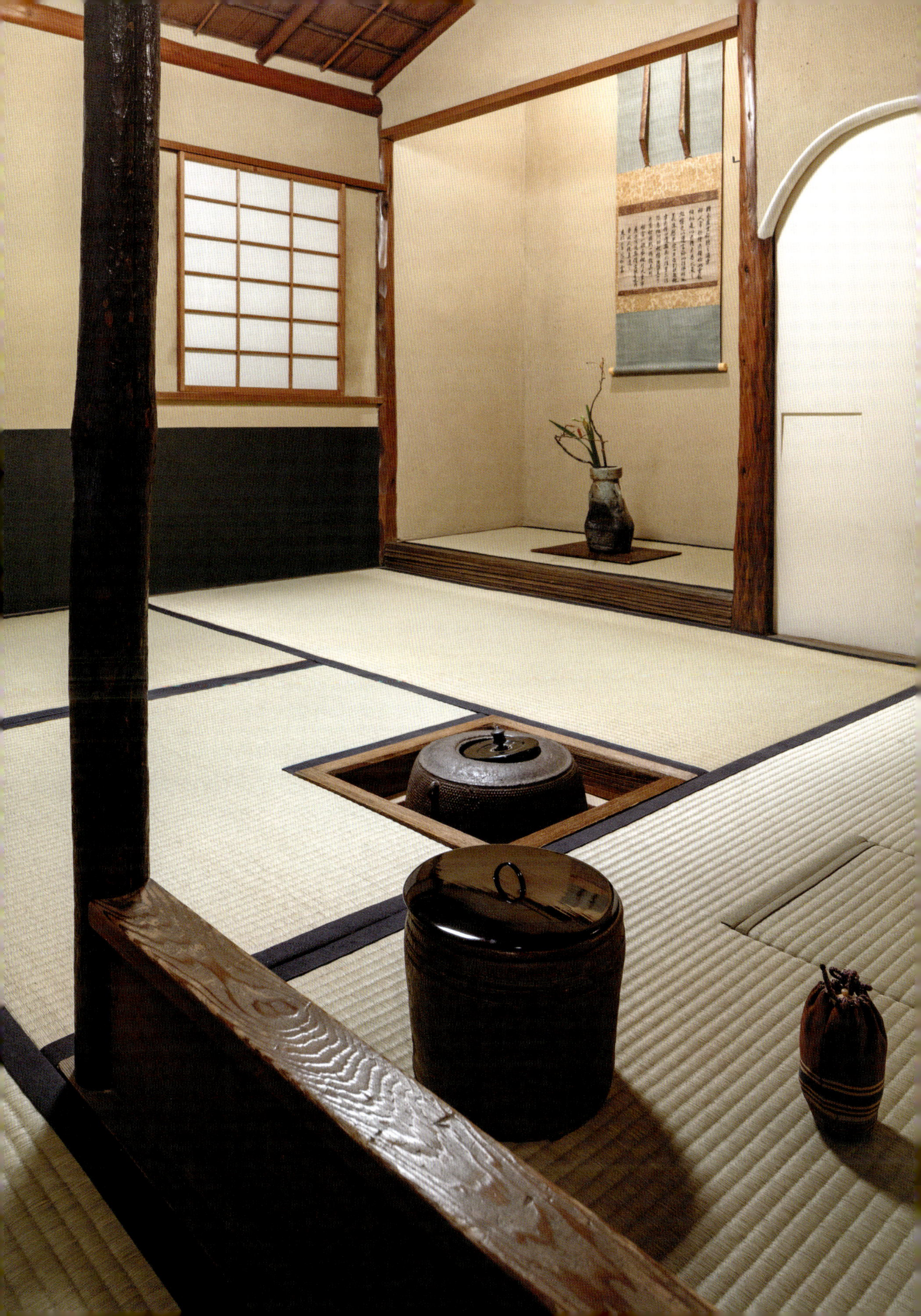

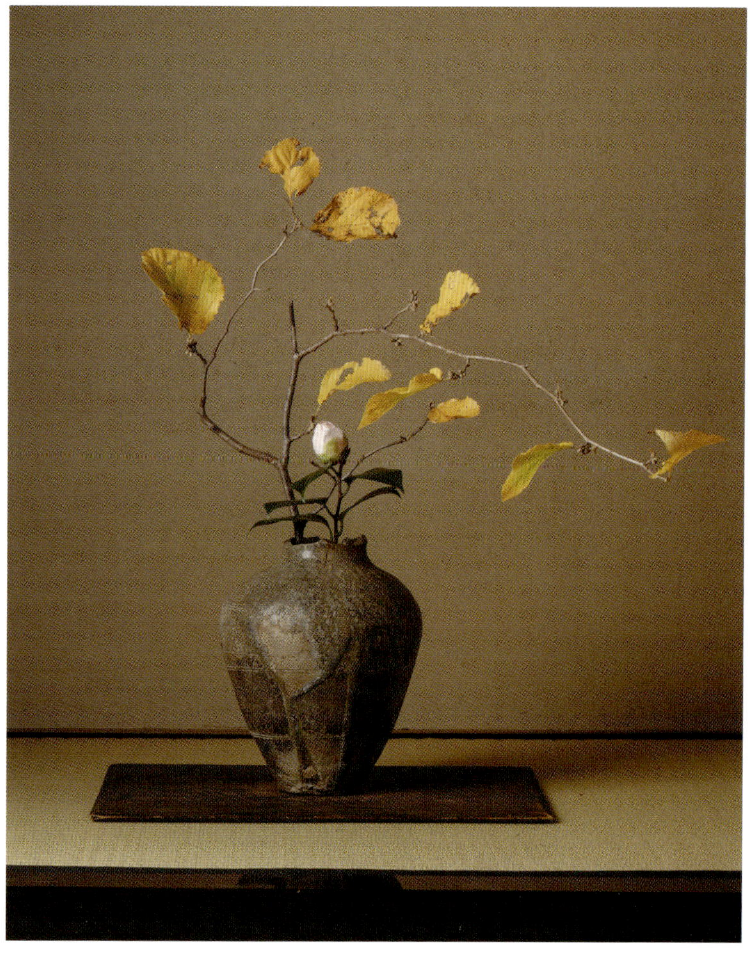

Flowers and Utensils for November

Shonosuke Toda

Iga ware flower containers are the kings of ceramic vases. They're fired at very high temperatures in climbing kilns, giving them an underlying strength. The same can be said of Shigaraki ware and Bizen ware. These three are often compared as kindred traditions. But Iga ware has relatively more flower containers, while Bizen is known for its fresh-water containers. Iga also tends to feature more imaginative and free-form shapes. Bizen is more standardized—its fresh-water containers, for instance, generally follow a consistent form.

The flower container named "Iwakado" (page 133) has distinctive "ears" and a deep indentation pressed strongly into the lower part of the body. If not handled carefully, that kind of design can end up looking disjointed or awkward, but in this case it all comes together in a beautifully unified form. It was made in the sixteenth century, and it has long been recognized as one of the masterpieces of Japanese ceramics. Its form doesn't feel old—it embodies the modernism of that era. It emerged at a time when there was no such thing as "ceramic appreciation," which makes it fundamentally different from Chinese ceramics. Japanese culture embraces distortion and asymmetry. But even when something is warped or off-center, a true masterpiece never feels disordered. That's what sets it apart.

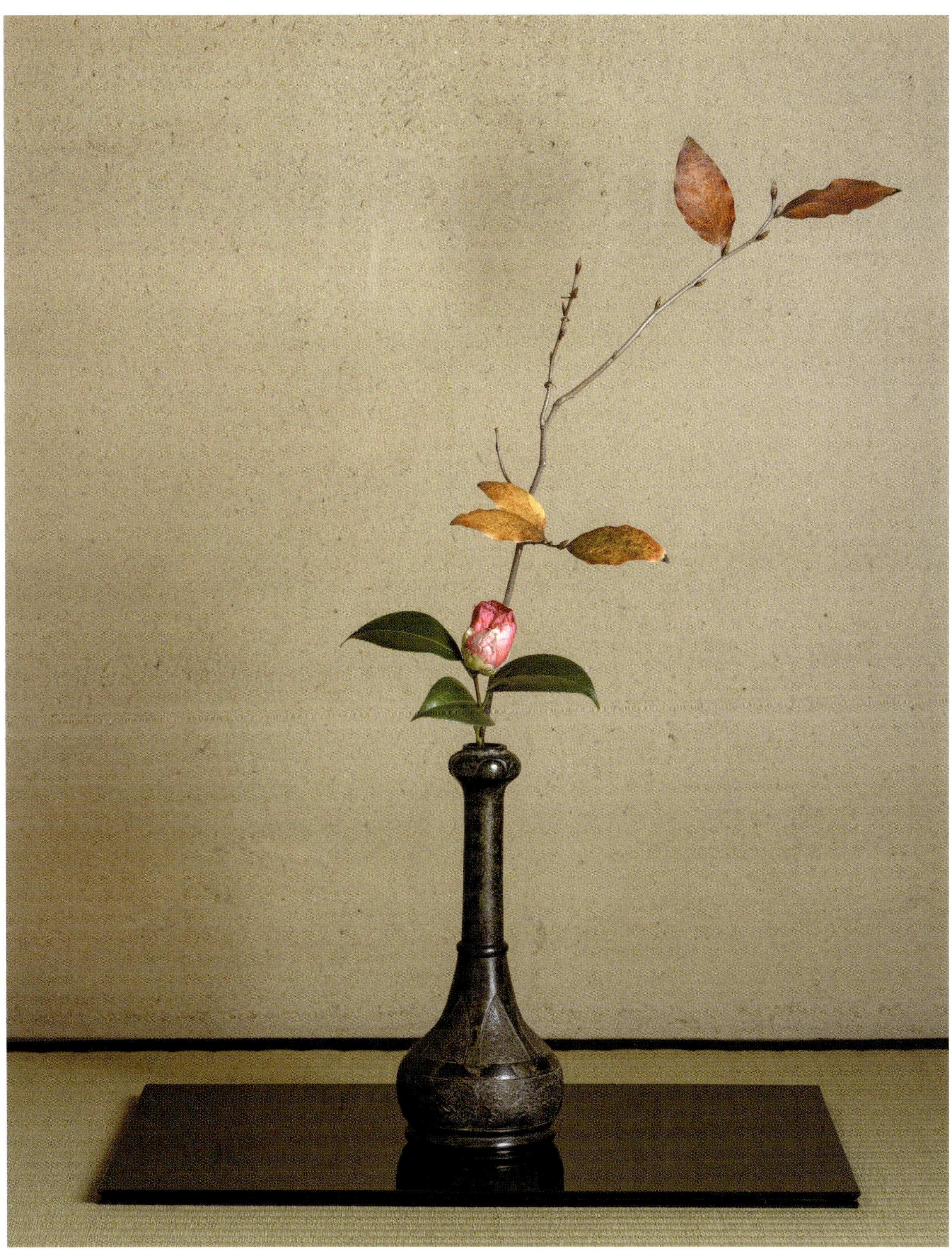

Benimyorenji camellia, Japanese spice-bush. Chinese narrow-necked bronze flower container, Ming dynasty.

A narrow-necked flower container is easy to work with and often gives a well-balanced look, but the key lies in deciding the right height for the floral material. The pairing of glossy camellia leaves with a camellia blossom, as seen here, is a seasonal classic — and because of that, finding subtle ways to add variation is essential.

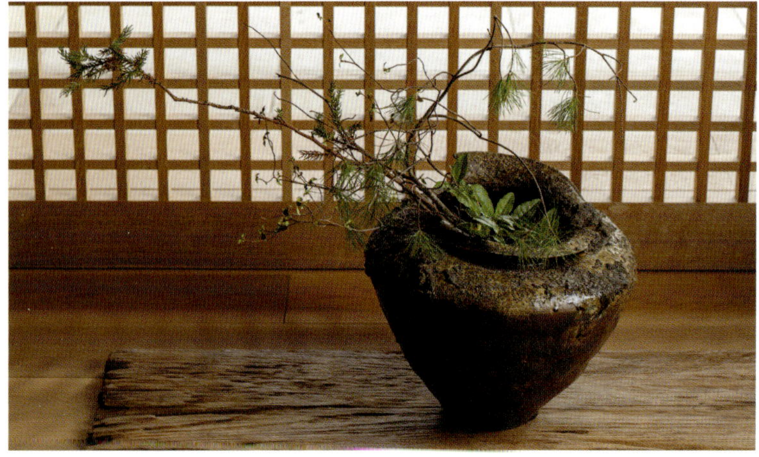

Tea plant, wild azalea, pine, cedar. Large Tokoname ware flower container, Heian period.

Four types of branches — tea plant, wild azalea, pine and cedar — are arranged in a large flower container with a strong sense of age and grounding. Embracing the flower container's presence, which evokes the spirit of the earth itself, the branches are placed without contrivance or overworking, each retaining its natural form. Though situated in a living space, the arrangement feels deeply connected to mountains and forests.

My father came from the Nozaki family, antique dealers in Nagoya with a very close relationship to the Toda family. After the war, he was adopted into the Toda family. He had been drafted during the war, and having once prepared himself to die, he had little attachment to things. He was independent and had a good head for business. Right after returning from the war, the idea came up that he might marry into the Toda family, which had no heir at the time.

As a side note, my father and mother happened to be born on the exact same day: December 14, 1925—the traditional date commemorating the Forty-seven Ronin's vendetta. My father apparently thought that by marrying into the Toda family, life would be easier—but when he looked into the storehouse and found it empty, he was quite disappointed. Still, in those days—whether by good luck or bad—there were plenty of items on the market. In the confusion of the postwar years, few people were buying tea utensils, so when he did make purchases, he could do so quite advantageously. The fact that the Toda shop managed to survive at all is thanks to his business sense.

My father always felt a deep connection to Mino, his home region and instinctively felt that Mino ware would be more highly valued in the future. Guided by that instinct, he began collecting great pieces. Even today, Toda Shoten is known for its expertise in Mino ware—that's the result of my

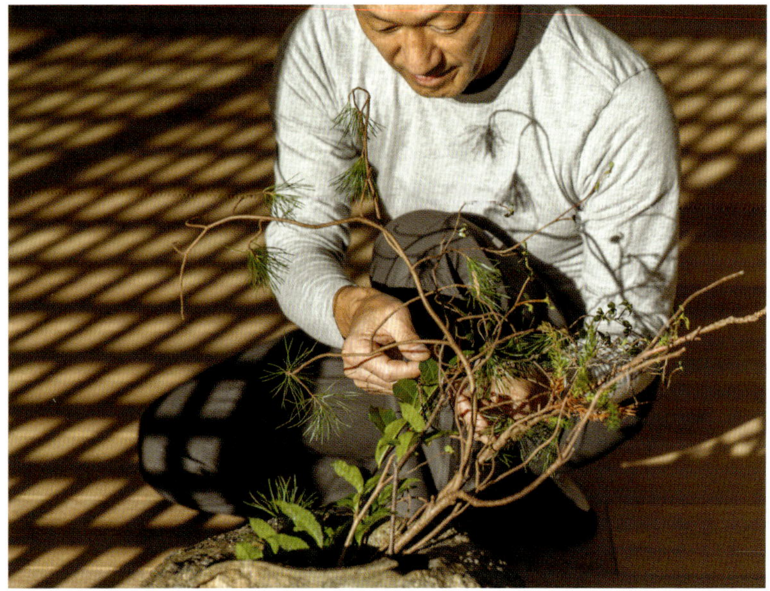

Atsushi Kobayashi arranges flowers in a large Tokoname ware flower container. "The way the rim is chipped is just perfect, and the distortion is really beautiful. Vessels like this seem to accept anything you put in them, as if they're telling you, 'Go ahead, do whatever you like,' which makes it truly enjoyable."

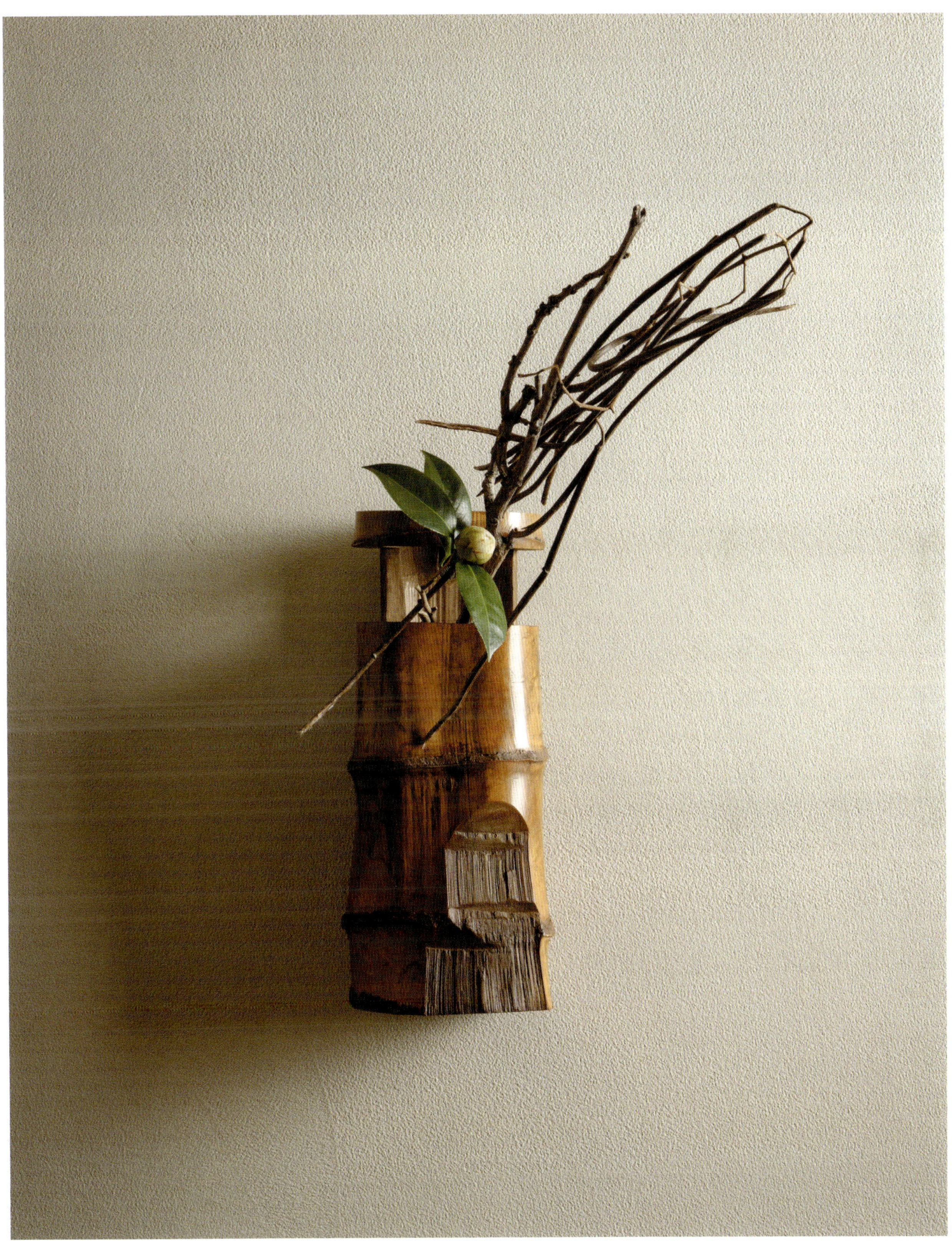

Shiratama camellia, catalpa. Single-node bamboo flower container by Katagiri Sekishu.

A striking bamboo flower container with bold hatchet marks near the base holds catalpa and camellia. "Catalpa is a strong material, so it suits a container with this kind of presence," says Kobayashi. "The branch rises diagonally upward before bending — those lines contrast beautifully with the straight cylindrical form of the container, the kind of movement I love."

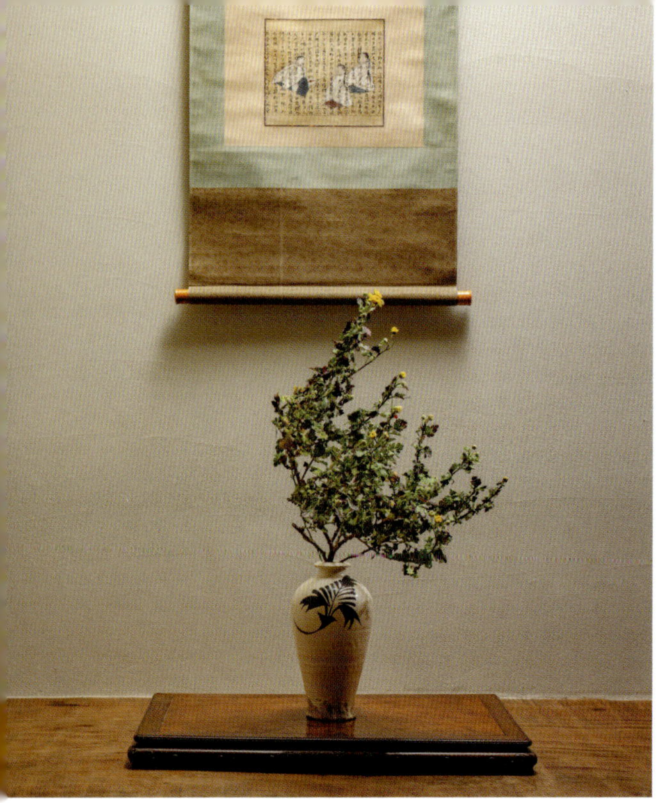

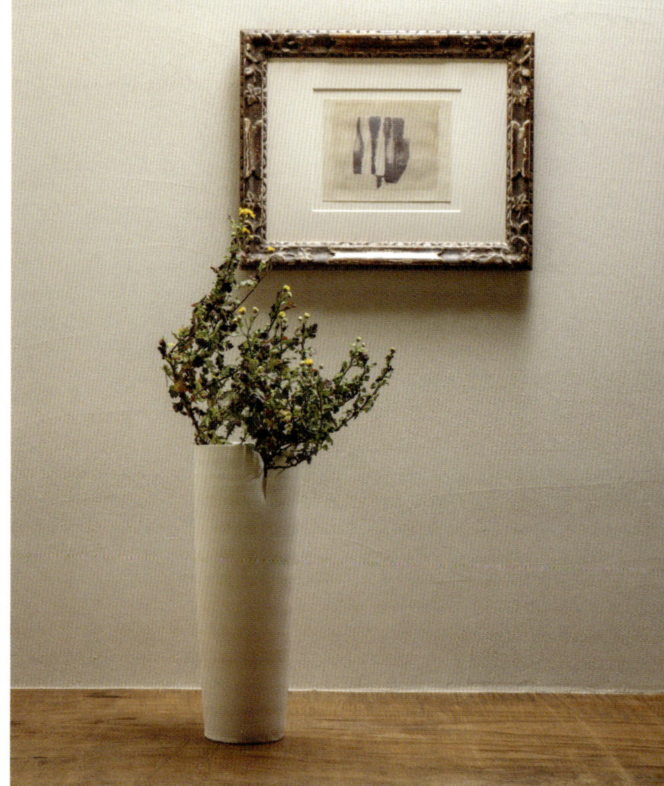

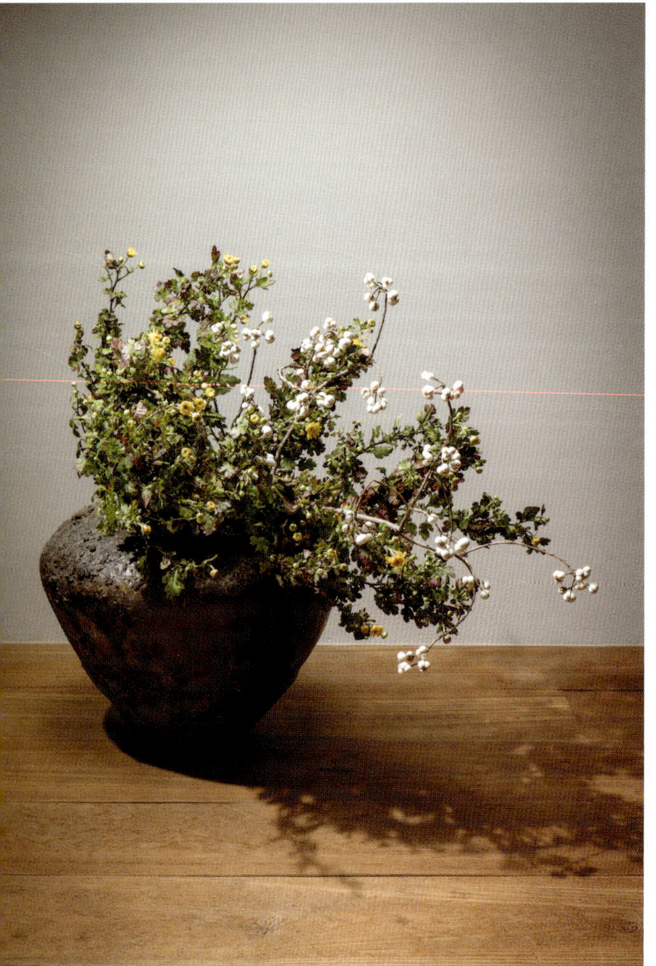

 Winter-blooming chrysanthemum. Iron-painted flower container, Cizhou ware, China, Ming dynasty.

This alcove display is on a Chinese-style stand, and paired with a Kamakura-era copy of the *Lotus Sutra*. "Let winter chrysanthemums absorb plenty of water so they look soft and moist" says Kobayashi.

 Winter-blooming chrysanthemum. White porcelain flower container by Taizo Kuroda (see page 154).

The same arrangement with a modern painting by Italian artist Morandi, and a contemporary white porcelain container.

 Winter-blooming chrysanthemum, Japanese wax tree berries. Tokoname ware flower container, Heian period.

This home display builds volume on the left and lets the right-hand branches flow outward,, for movement and balance. The yellow flowers and white berries enhance each other's presence.

Winter-blooming Chrysanthemums

Winter-blooming chrysanthemums are prized for their full leaves and blossoms. The red-tinted foliage touched by frost, the small yellow flowers, and the stems that branch out in many directions all contribute to their charm. Try to avoid trimming too many leaves or branches. As seen in the photographs above, attention to the balance between the height of the container and the shape of the floral material is important. Or, as in the photo on the right, you can explore creative pairings with other materials to bring out their best qualities.

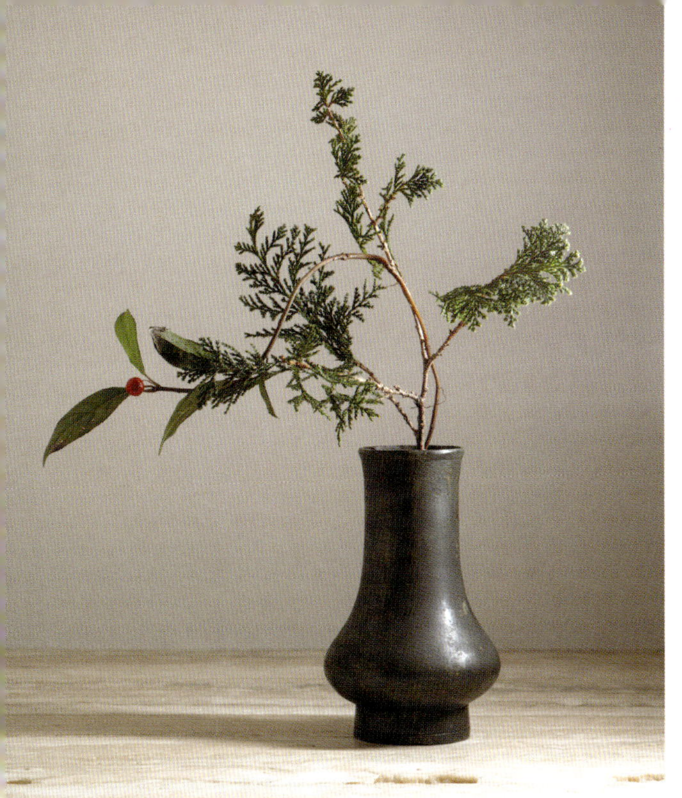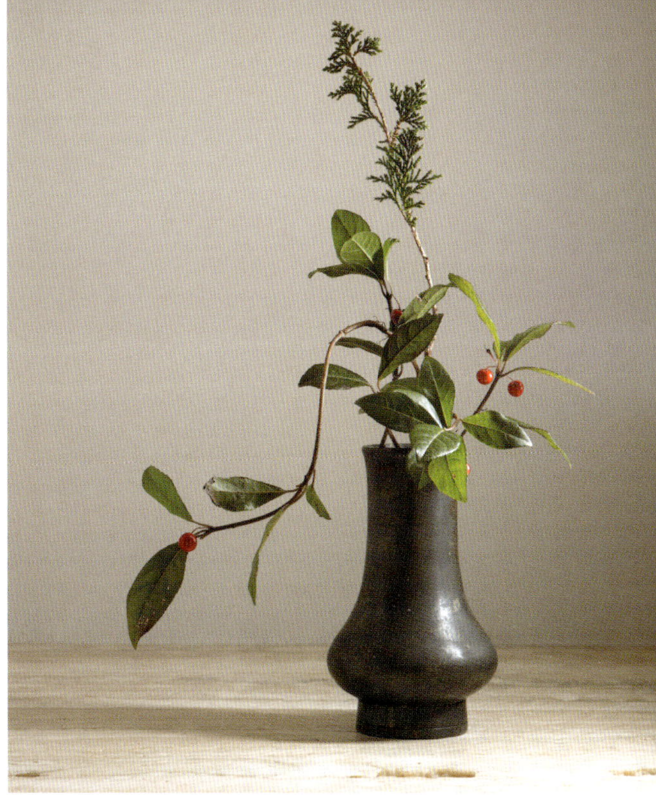

Japanese ardisia and hinoki cypress. Bronze *shimo kabura* (turnip-shaped) flower container, China, Ming dynasty.

Two arrangements using the same combination of ardisia and hinoki cypres, with different emphasis. On the left, the flowing line of the hinoki branch is highlighted, with the ardisia used as an accent. In contrast, the one on the right plays down the hinoki and makes the ardisia the main element. Even with the same materials, the expression can change significantly depending on which element is emphasized. That's part of why working with floral materials so enjoyable — the endless possibilities as you consider how *you* would arrange them.

Arranging Two Types of Branches in a Small Vase

An example of enjoying the same flower container and the same materials repeatedly in daily life. At times, no flowers are used — just branches. In this case, red-berried ardisia is paired with a small hinoki cypress twig. The soft, curving lines and almond-shaped leaves of the ardisia contrast beautifully with the straight, upright branch and fine foliage of the hinoki. The pairing of these distinctly different forms creates a variety of intersecting lines, resulting in a small but expansive floral composition.

father's foresight. His approach was to choose pieces he had a personal connection with, then build a set around them. I work in the same way.

I was raised without hardship, and I respect my father so deeply that I end up talking about him all the time. Once, the late ceramic scholar Seizo Hayashiya said to me, "Hiroshi, you're always going on about your father. But somehow, it doesn't come off as obnoxious." I took that as a compliment—not to me, but to my father.

A Father-and-Son Bond

The tea scoop I used for my father's memorial tea gathering this time was made by Sen Doan. It's one

I'm particularly fond of. Doan defied Rikyu and was disowned, yet I feel he understood Rikyu better than anyone—he *was* Rikyu. Even when he rejected his father, he still resembled him. And when he embraced him, he grew even closer. Though it was Rikyu's son-in-law, Shoan, who carried on the Senke lineage, I feel that Doan had a stronger blood tie to Rikyu.

I may be speaking too boldly, maybe even exaggerating, but I feel something similar when I think about my own father, Shonosuke, who I regard as a great man. I sense that the tea scoop by Doan (page 134) used in this month's tea ceremony was created in a spirit of closeness to Rikyu—not as an imitation of form, but in a deeper, more inward sense. To me, it truly embodies Rikyu. The confident shaping of the scoop's tip, for example, isn't something you see in Rikyu's scoops. Just by looking at the form, you can tell it's Doan's work. Compared to Rikyu's delicate scoops with narrow "ant waist" curves, Doan's are generally broader and more assertive, as can be seen in this scoop.

Rikyu's utensils contain his aesthetic sensibility within them; Doan expresses that sensibility outward. Shoan, on the other hand, seems to have carried on more of Rikyu's external forms than his inner spirit. His scoops are slender, refined, and feature that signature ant waist. He interpreted Rikyu through form and sought to pass that form down to the next generation—and the one after that. As for Rikyu himself, I believe he saw too much of himself in Doan's inner nature, and that's why he couldn't bring himself to acknowledge him.

Of course, my own father accepted someone like me—clearly lacking in many ways—as his successor, so the relationship between Rikyu and Doan isn't quite the same. I inherited the family line with a completely different sensibility than my father, and even after taking over, I didn't really do much—but my father silently let me go my own way. I didn't train with tea utensil dealers; instead, I apprenticed at Yayoi Gallery in Tokyo. That gave me a different outlook, and when I brought that sensibility into the Toda shop, my father didn't object. He may have smiled wryly, but he never complained, and let me try things freely. Of course, when I really overstepped the mark, he would speak up—but that kind of quiet support stayed with me. It's something I hope that I can offer to my own son as well.

This work is deeply rooted in relationships—between people and objects, and between people and people. And that's what makes it meaningful. It's about cultivating those connections over time. You can't think only in the short term; you have to take a long view. So I intend to watch my son's path with that same long perspective. I may not have the presence my father had, but strangely enough, the things I wish to pass down do seem to be received in some way—by both me and my son. Rikyu and Doan. My father and me. These aren't things that can be directly compared, but as I reflect on the nature of parent-child relationships, I've chosen this set of utensils for the occasion.

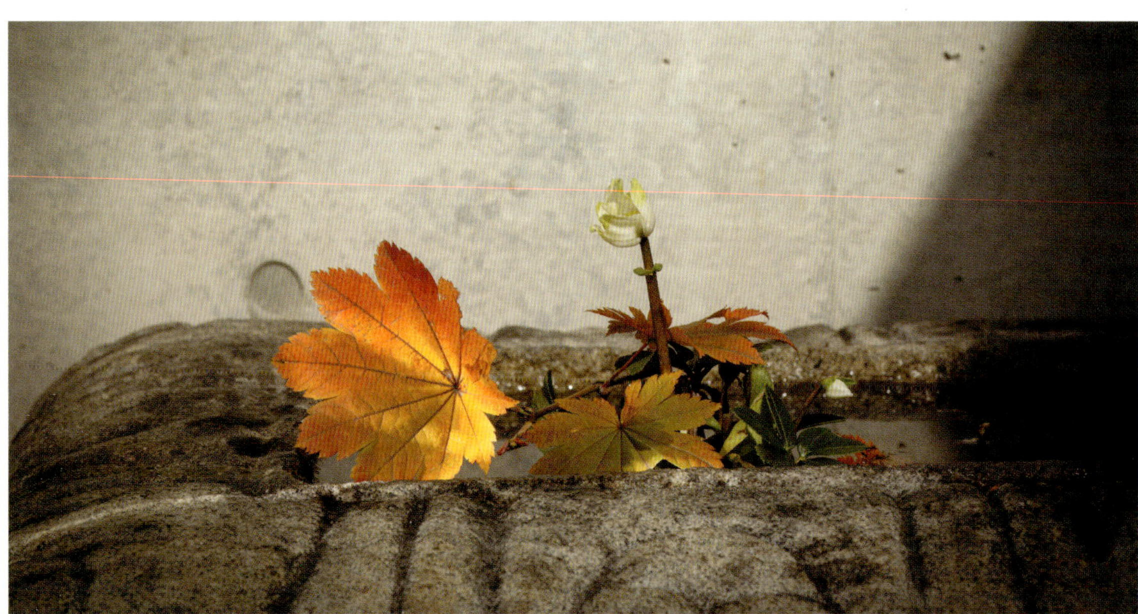

Hellebore, fan maple. Four-sided stone basin.

This tightly composed arrangement in the *tsukubai* stone basin at the tea room entrance emphasizes the glossy beauty of the leaves. A potted hellebore is placed at the back, creating a natural and relaxed presence. As a welcoming display, this arrangement captures a fleeting moment of outdoor light and quietly conveys the changing of the seasons to the arriving guests.

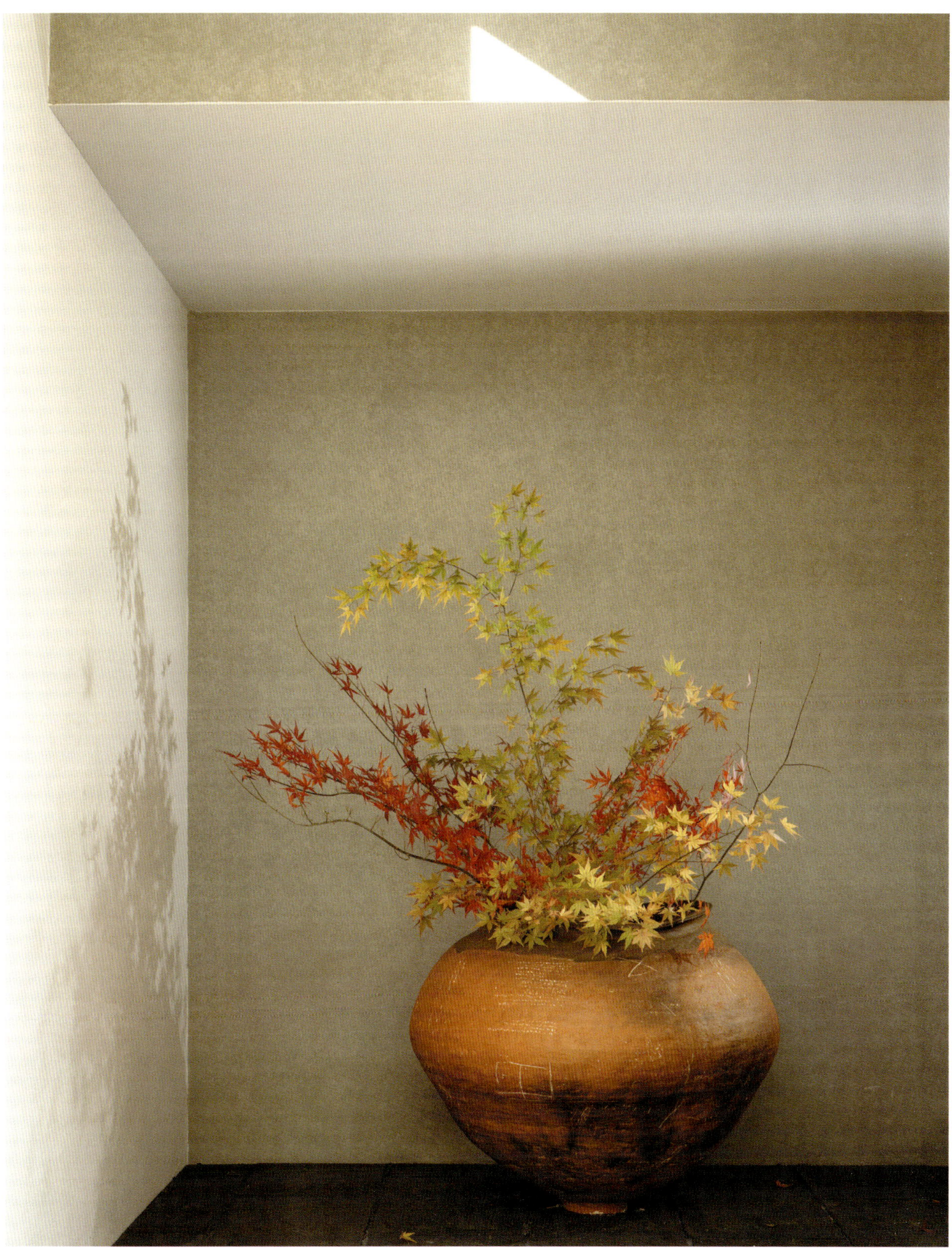

Japanese maple Leaves. Large engraved vessel by Koichi Uchida.

Branches of different glossy autumn leaves are arranged in a large jar. The stark, unadorned concrete space is suddenly filled with the vivid colors of fall. Normally, only the jar is displayed in this entryway, but with this arrangement, it feels as if the autumn mountains themselves have arrived — an expressive everyday flower display that brings the season indoors.

With Prayers for the Year to Come

Buddha's Hand

These days, more and more Japanese homes are built without tatami mat rooms or even a *tokonoma* alcove. It's only natural—living spaces reflect changes in lifestyle. Rather than lament that fact and try too hard to reintroduce traditional Japanese elements in an awkward way, it's better to embrace the space as it is. As dealers of tea utensils, we see *shitsurai*—the art of arranging a space—as fundamentally a collaboration with nature, so we try to avoid anything that feels forced or unnatural.

For example, the Toda shop building was constructed in 1962, which means it has now stood for more than half a century. There is a tea room in the back, but the office space is Western-style. About ten or fifteen years after the building was completed, I seriously considered remodeling it. I even consulted with an architect. The original design was good, but I was still young and wanted to alter it somehow. No matter how much I thought about it, though, I kept coming back to the feeling that the design was already right the way it was. I'd stare at the exterior, thinking maybe just a few changes would help—but in the end, I always returned to the original.

That experience with architecture made me think that tradition works in the same way. Whether in architecture or tea, there's a long line of practices that have been handed down, and even if something feels slightly outdated, it often carries a kind of universality that shouldn't be lightly discarded. It's not that tradition should be clung to out of sentimentality—but rather that we return to it because it has genuine value. You often hear about blending Japanese and Western styles, or incorporating Japanese elements into Western rooms, but

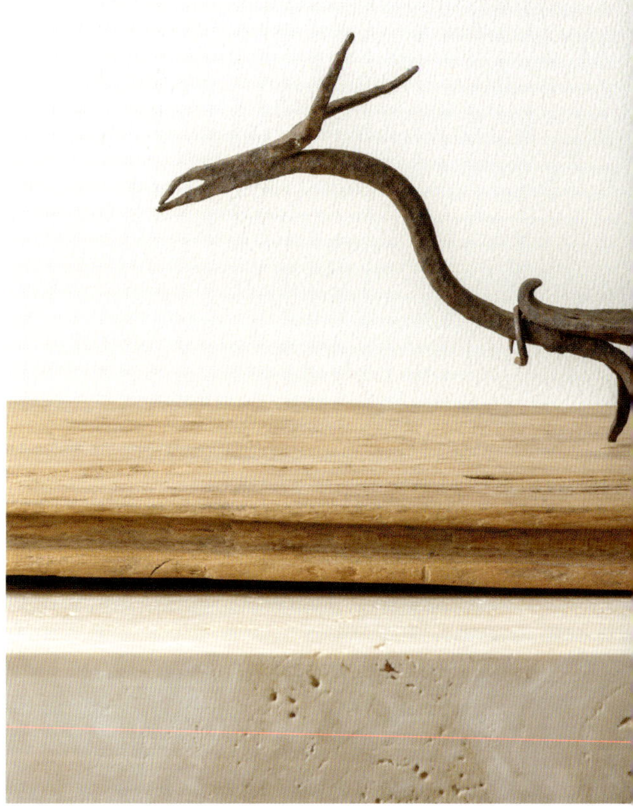

those things often end up feeling half-hearted and unconvincing. If a space is Western, why not embrace that and make the most of it?

This month, for example, I've displayed a Buddha's hand citron in the living room. It's a fruit considered auspicious at this time of year, and some people might place it in the *tokonoma* alcove. Here, I've placed it on top of an iron ritual vessel from Indonesia. What matters is thinking about the balance between objects and space, and arranging things in a way that fits the home they're in.

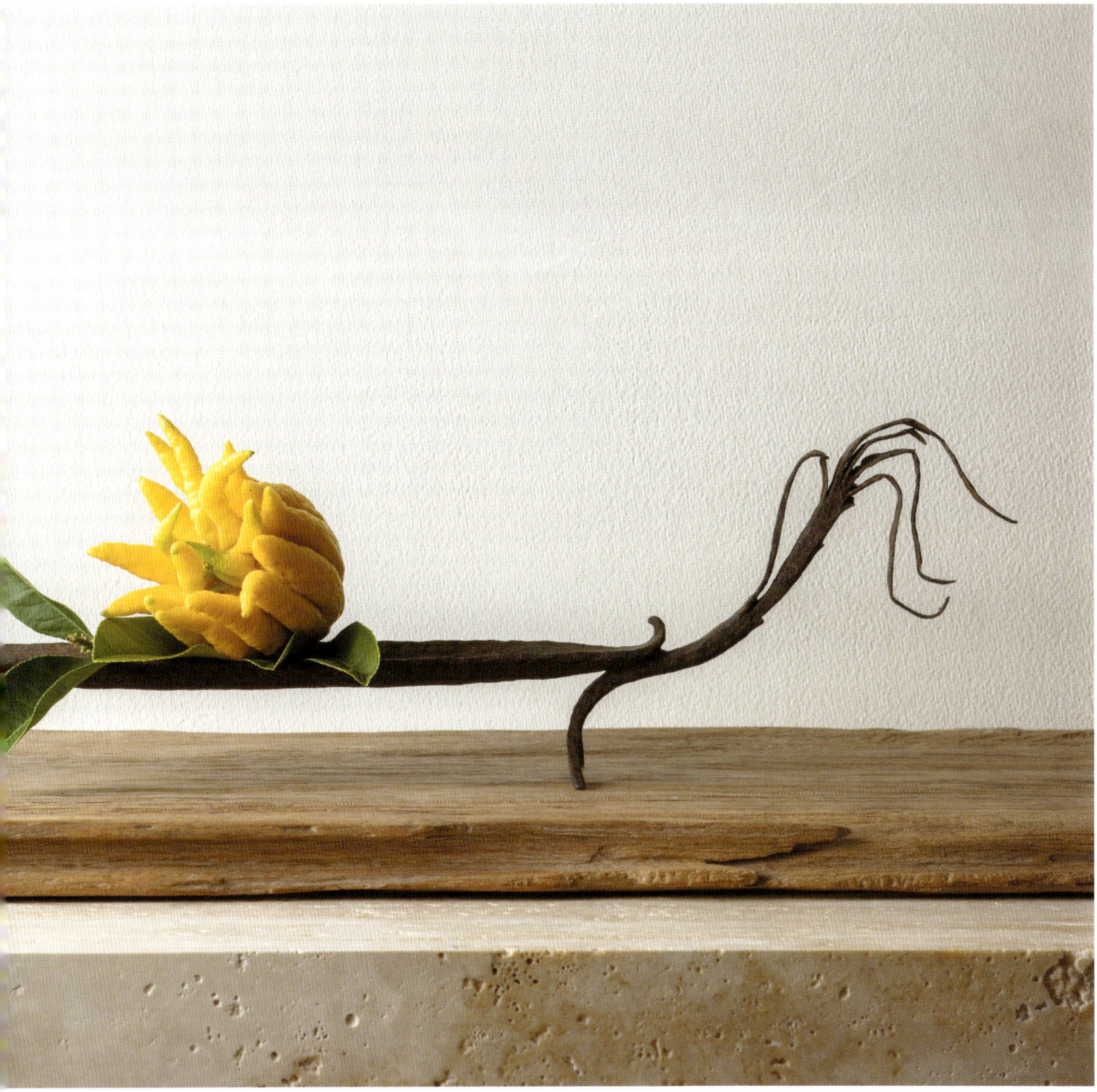

The Buddha's hand citron is a fruit named for its shape, which resembles the hand of the Buddha. It is often used in New Year's decorations as a symbol of good fortune. Here, the fruit is displayed with green leaves atop a primitive-looking ceremonial vessel shaped like an imaginary beast. "It's less about arranging flowers," says Atsushi Kobayashi, "and more about finding the right way to present the Buddha's hand."

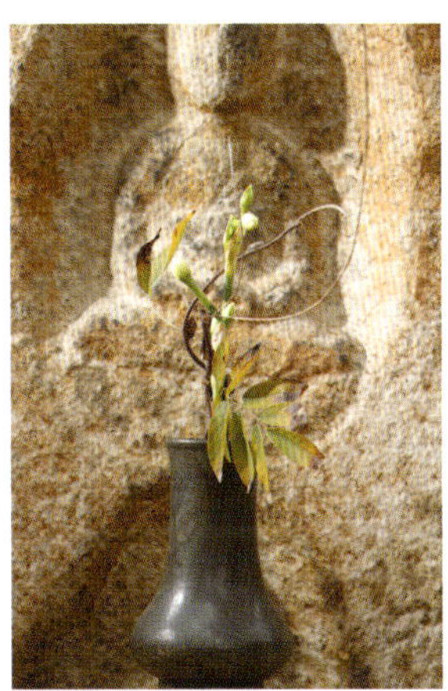

In this arrangement, wisteria leaves — beginning to wither in the season — are paired with budding narcissus and placed in an antique bronze flower container. The combination of something fading with something about to bloom is offered before a large stone Buddha.

Flowers and Utensils
for December

Trust Your Instincts

I think tea is all about the moment. When you're practicing tea, there are these fleeting moments where something suddenly strikes you as beautiful. Like the soft, rustling sound of the tea whisk as you prepare thick tea—*sara sara sara*. That sound alone can move you. It's in these glimpses, in these short moments that flash before you, that you find the fascination. And it's those moments that make you want to do tea again. You think, *I want to share this with someone*. Whether they know tea or not doesn't matter—as long as they're someone who can feel it too.

For instance, when you enter the tea room and see a single flower placed in a side alcove, a hanging scroll displayed, and then the sound of the kettle rising—each of those engages your senses. The tea room naturally encourages you to sharpen all five senses: sight, sound, smell, taste and touch. And when that happens, things begin to reveal themselves through intuition. I've always felt that. It's not about theory—you just feel, *Wow, this is something special.* That kind of experience never betrays you.

This isn't unique to tea. For some people it might happen in sports—the kind of moment where you say, *This is incredible!* Whatever the context, when someone experiences one of those moments, they get hooked. And once you're hooked, you stop worrying so much about others—you begin to engage with it through your own senses, in your own way. You don't need to show anyone. And yet, paradoxically, because you've created something so complete, you may start to feel like sharing it. You go deep into your own world without thinking about others—but eventually, you want to communicate that world to someone else. I think that's how it works with tea.

And this kind of sensitivity isn't something you can force to grow, even if you try. It develops naturally, over time. If you spend time with it patiently, and you love it, your sensitivity will deepen.

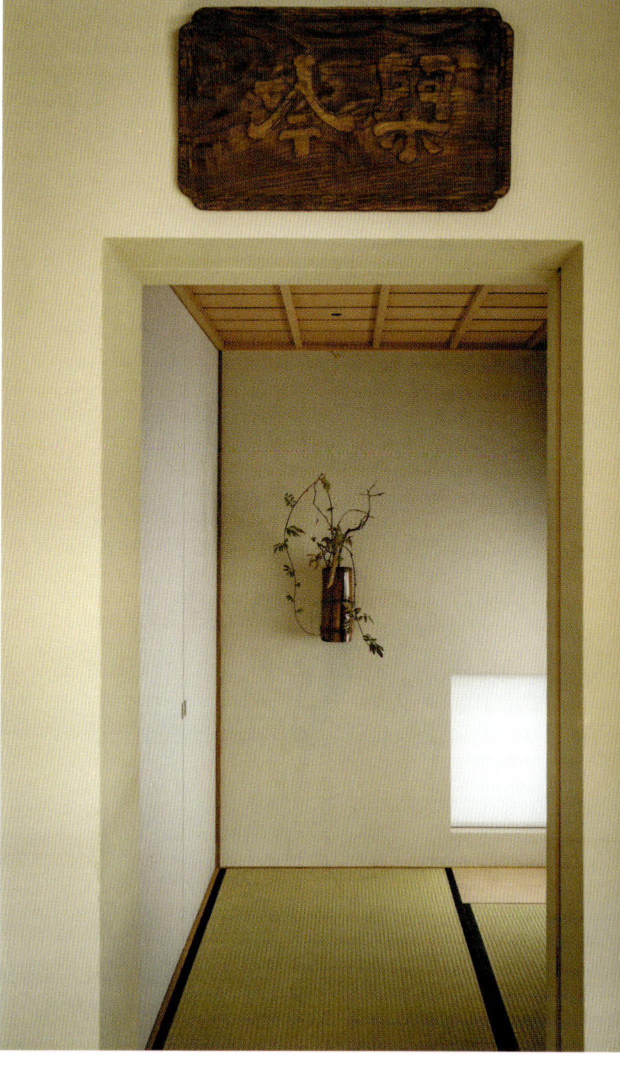

A bamboo flower container is hung on the simple, gray-toned wall of a modern building. "In the end, doing something like this actually makes the true tradition stand out more," says Hiroshi. "You could even call this 'play.' It's an art display — flowers arranged not with tea in mind, but simply in response to the space."

When you love something, you'll naturally seek it out—you'll see more, experience more. Just walking down the street, you might start to notice flowers and think, *How beautiful*, and stop to look. In doing so, you gradually absorb things—internalize them. You grow through your senses. And to cultivate intuition, you first have to refine your senses.

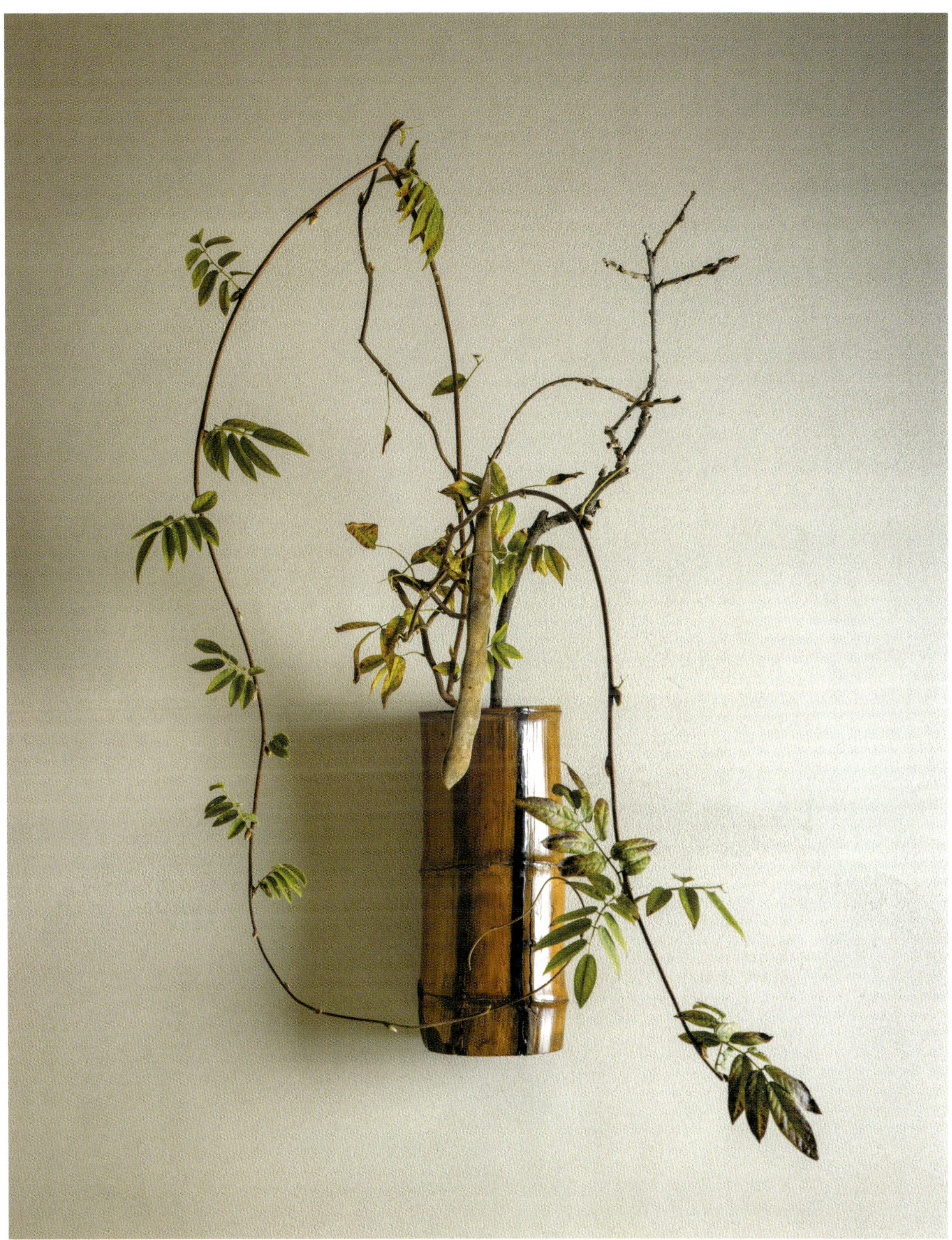

Wisteria seed pods. Bamboo shakuhachi-style flower container by Katagiri Sekishu.

Aged utensils are carefully restored and passed on when the time comes. "You repair them, apply lacquer — this kind of thinking doesn't really exist elsewhere," says Hiroshi. "Usually when something breaks, that's the end of it. But in tea, we take the time to mend things properly and continue to cherish them. That's something unique to the tea tradition."

Sensing Power Through Objects

— Atsushi Kobayashi

When I was training under Takashi Inaba (see page 92), what I realized was how much effort the work required. Without that kind of effort, you don't gain anything. Of course, having a genuine love for the work is the starting point—but unless you actively seek, you won't find. If you keep seeking, though, there are moments when things suddenly click into place, almost unexpectedly.

At Toda Shoten, we handle many antique utensils. The people who made them are no longer alive. And yet, from the art objects themselves, or from the history that surrounds them, I feel a kind of power. A power from those who were striving toward something. That's what draws me in. That's why looking at many different works of art is the best kind of study. It's not just about arranging flowers. Whether it's an art object or a painting—anything really—there's something you can feel from looking at it. The same is true of nature. These impressions accumulate inside me and often spark the desire to create a certain kind of flower arrangement. Sometimes I'll see a painting and think, "Next time, I want to try placing flowers like that."

Normally, looking at something is a passive act. But creating something is the opposite—it's active. So the question becomes: when I see something, how would I express it? I think that mindset is what refines your sensibility. Imagining something becomes nourishment for your intuition.

And this isn't anything special, really. You could even say that coordinating tea utensils is like coordinating an outfit—just the tea version. Everyone does it differently. Sometimes you'll see someone's style and think it's wonderful. Other times, you'll feel that their taste doesn't quite match yours. Then you start asking: what about *my* style? You try things out, think through different ideas, and gradually your own sense becomes more concrete. It may not be 100 percent "correct," but you arrive at a version of the answer that's right for you. And I think that's true not just for tea flowers, but for tea as a whole.

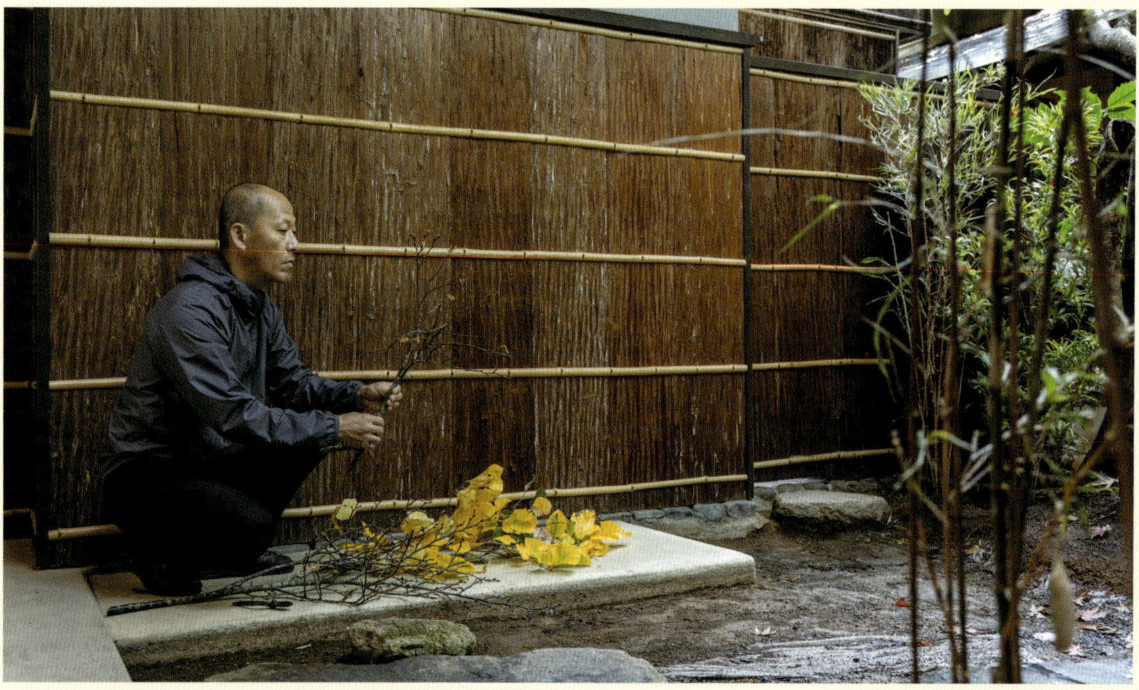

Atsushi Kobayashi sorts freshly gathered branches in the garden. As he gently trims and adjusts each branch and leaf, he carefully considers which parts he will actually use. At this stage, he's already envisioning the space the arrangement will occupy, the utensils he'll use, and how the final composition will come together.

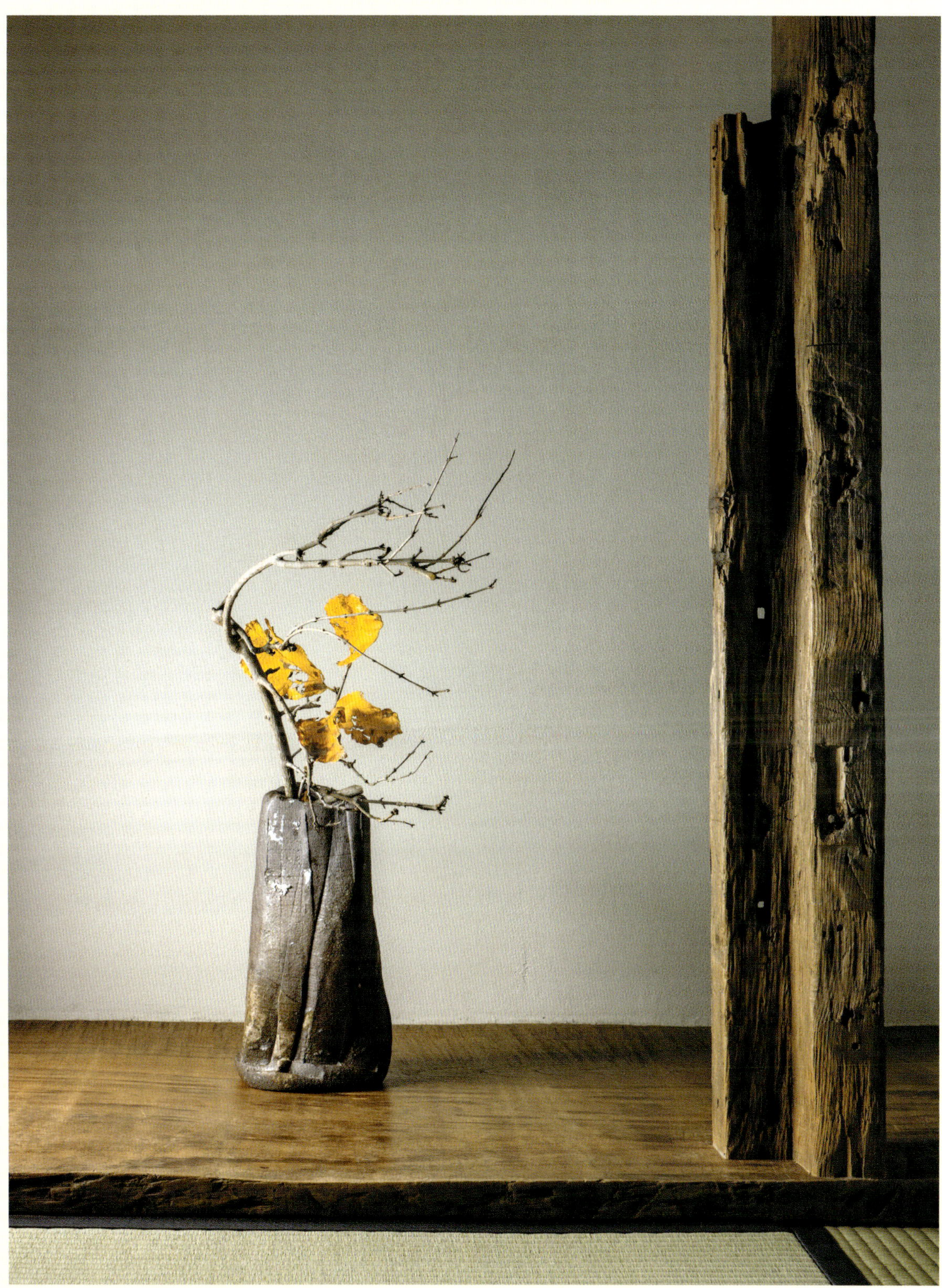

Pomegranate and witch hazel. Flower container made by Jikinyu Raku (see page 34) using clay from Loubignac, France.

A flower container by Jikinyu Raku is placed in the alcove, holding a withered pomegranate branch and glossy witch hazel leaves nibbled by insects. "When the flower vessel has a strong presence," says Kobayashi, "it can embrace anything — the withered, the weathered, even the insect-bitten."

Bringing Out the Most Beautiful Line in the Flower

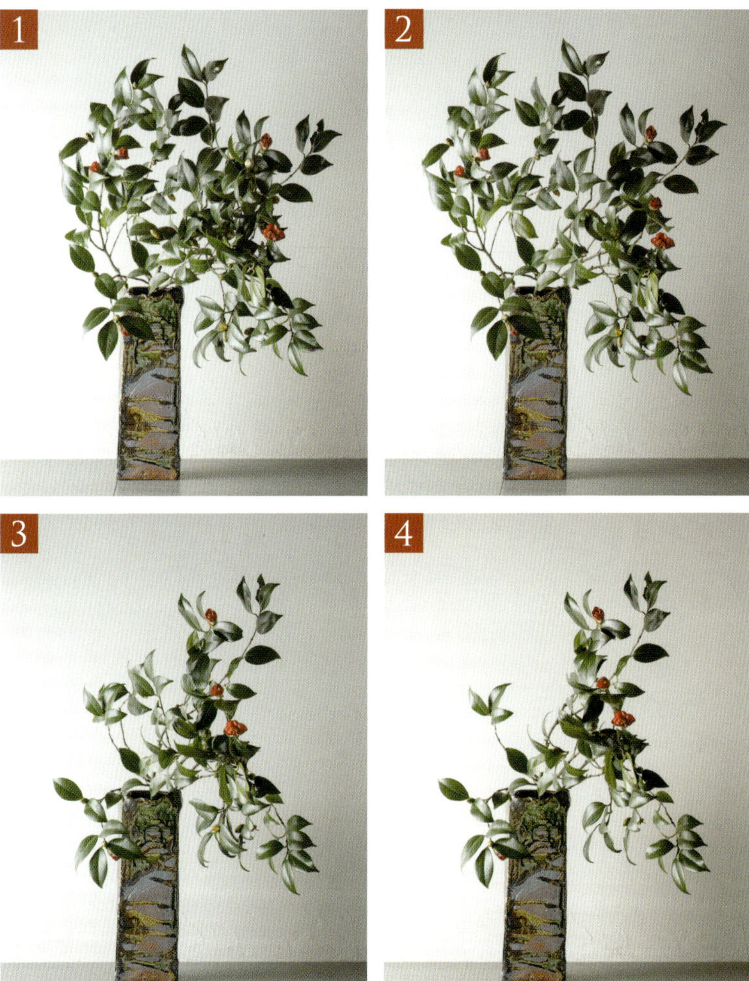

Let the Flowers Be as They Are in the Field

One of the essential principles for arranging flowers in the tearoom is the phrase: *"Let the flowers be as they are in the field."* But does that mean simply placing natural flowers and branches just as they are? "Trees growing outdoors exist in a vast open space," says Atsushi. Kobayashi. "If you bring them indoors as is, the scale is often too dense for the room. So to make them feel 'as they are in the field' in an interior space, you have to prune some of the branches." The key when trimming branches is to consider which lines or forms will look most beautiful in relation to the space. On these pages, the process of shaping the arrangement is illustrated: **1** Original state. **2** Thin out the right-hand branches and leaves. **3** Think about the overall flow of the composition and remove two unnecessary branches from the top. **4** Trim the left-hand branches further. This careful editing brings out a natural, spacious feeling — true to the spirit of the field, but in harmony with the room.

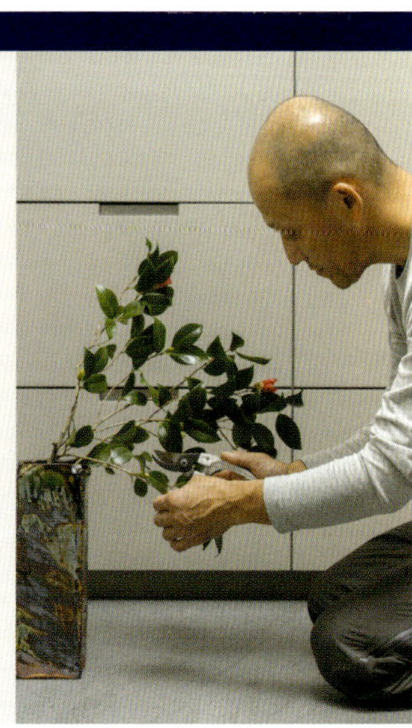

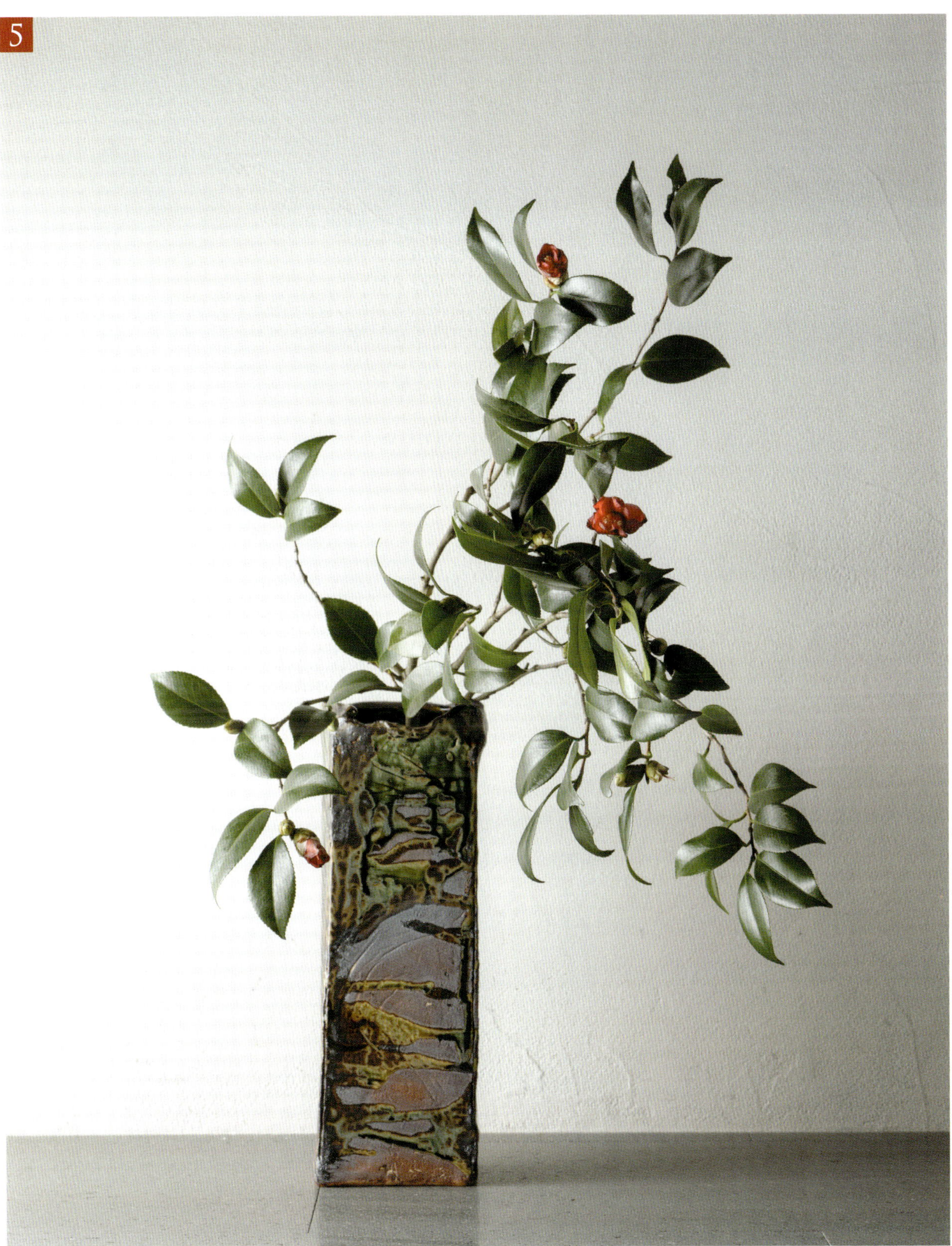

Ichiko Wabisuke camellia. Oribe-style flower container by Ryoji Koie.

The finished arrangement. One more blossom has been removed since photo 4. By thinning out the branches and leaves, the composition now blends gently and naturally into the space, as if it were growing in the field. From step 1, each branch was carefully considered and trimmed, guided by a clear image of which lines to keep.

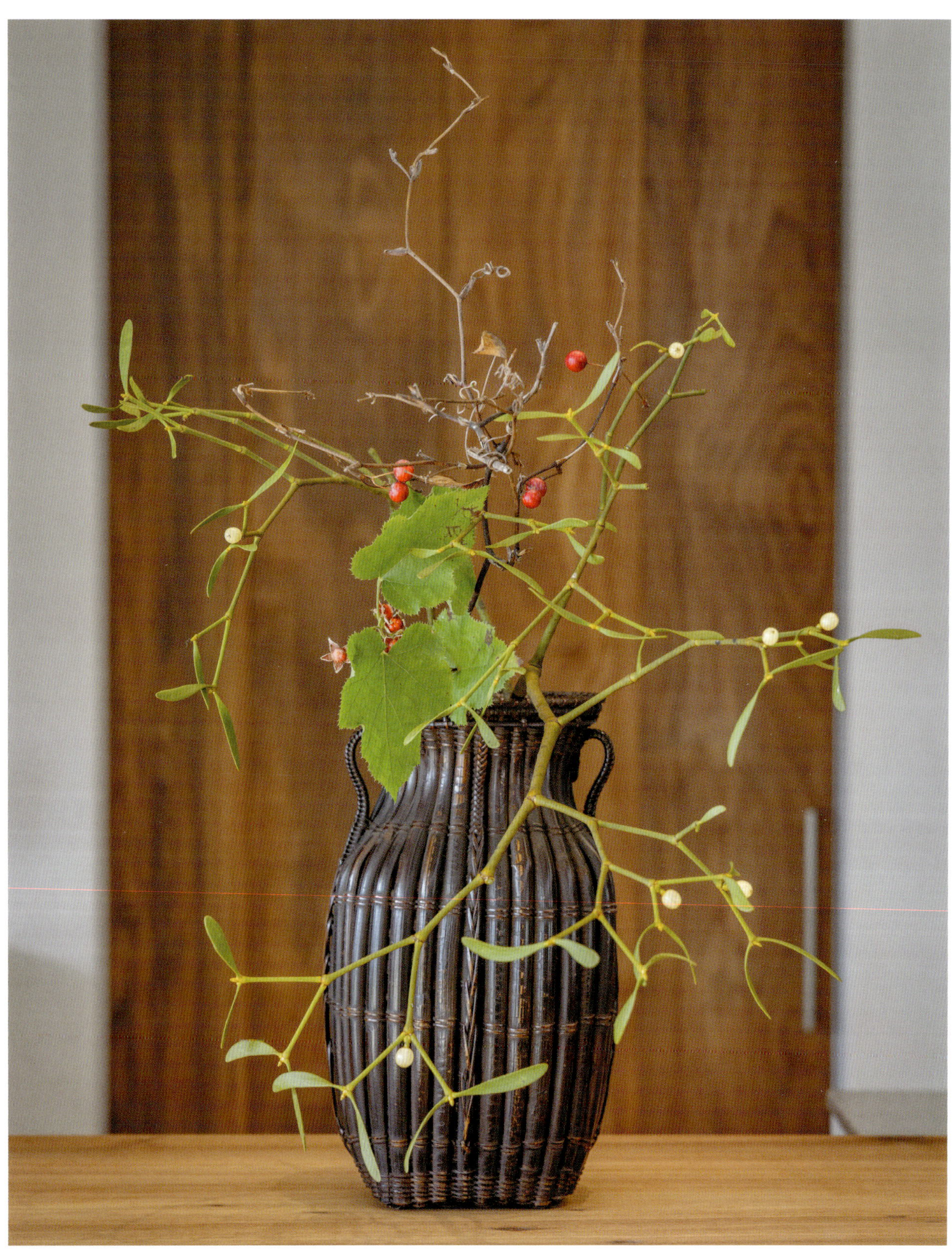

Winter strawberry, mistletoe, Japanese greenbrier. Chinese "shin-guard" basket.

Three types of soft, flowing fruiting branches in a robust Chinese-style basket. Centered around the winter strawberry leaves, the branches extend lightly upward, to the sides, and forward. The scattered, star-like berries add visual accents throughout the composition. The strength of the container is balanced by the gentleness of the foliage.

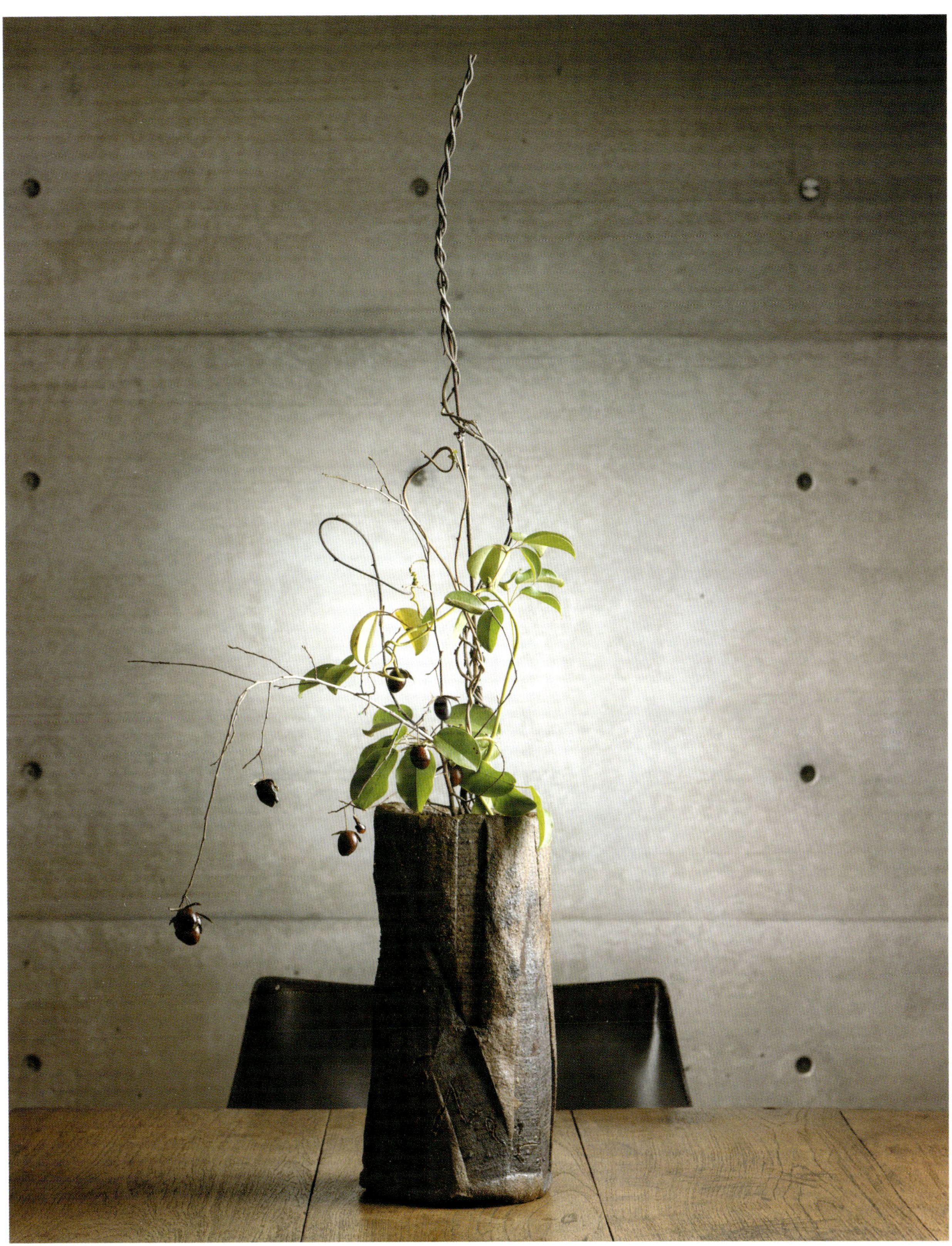

Dwarf persimmon, akebia vine. Flower container by Jikinyu Raku (see page 34), made with clay from Loubignac, France.

A dining table display. In a stark, exposed-concrete interior, the organically shaped clay vessel and flowers bring warmth and life. Within the subdued and unified tones of the space — the colors of the walls, the container, the table and the chairs — the soft green of the akebia leaves stands out beautifully.

About Taizo Kuroda

Taizo Kuroda (1946–2021) is a well-known ceramic artist, but when I first met him, he had not yet focused exclusively on white porcelain and was still experimenting with various materials. In the world of Japanese ceramics, there's a saying that "if you work with white porcelain for three days, you'll end up poor," and white porcelain was something people avoided. It was time-consuming to produce and didn't sell. So everyone steered clear of it. But it was art collector Takashi Inaba (see page 92) who said, "No, on the contrary, we should be doing white porcelain"—the remark of someone who has a truly discerning eye—and, after giving this pronouncement serious thought in his own way, Kuroda agreed. There were no guarantees that this direction would work, so it must have taken courage. But in the end, he became completely captivated by white porcelain. He discovered the fulfillment of working with it for himself and that was the path he followed until his passing.

It was around the time that Kuroda decided to devote himself to white porcelain that I too had a sense that perhaps it was time to turn the established thinking around tea-related crafts on its head—that it might be interesting to do so. Recently, when I look at the flowers arranged in Kuroda's pieces, I find myself thinking that maybe it's time to rethink what "tea flowers" conventionally mean within the tearoom. Of course, I understand that the fundamentals are important, but even so, when I look at the rigid state of today's tea world, there are few instances where I find myself admiring something and saying, "That arrangement was beautifully done." In that sense, I feel all the more deeply the significance of what the works of Taizo Kuroda express. Through the flowers and vessels in this book, I hope to convey at least a small part of that message.

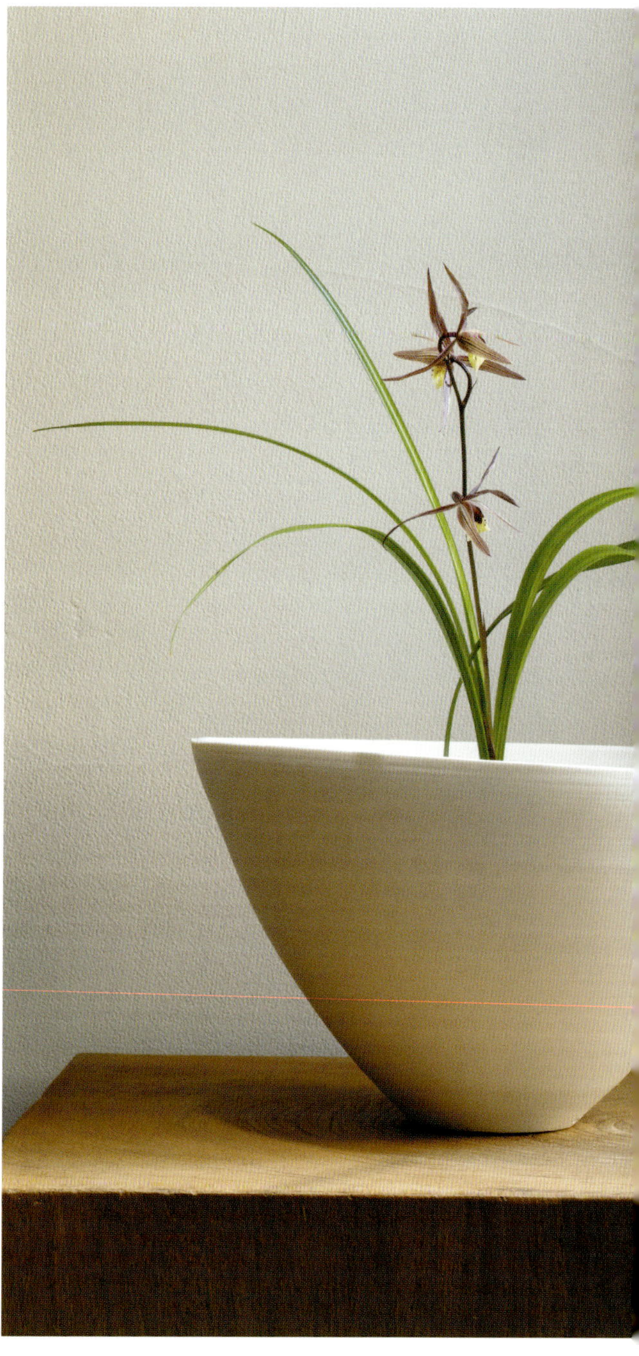

Kanran orchid. White porcelain bowl by Taizo Kuroda.

"Taizo Kuroda was making pottery in Izu and was an acquaintance of Takashi Inaba," Hiroshi says. "I first met him when Inaba took me along to visit." From then on, for over thirty years until Kuroda's death — and even after his passing — Hiroshi's connection with Kuroda has continued through his works.

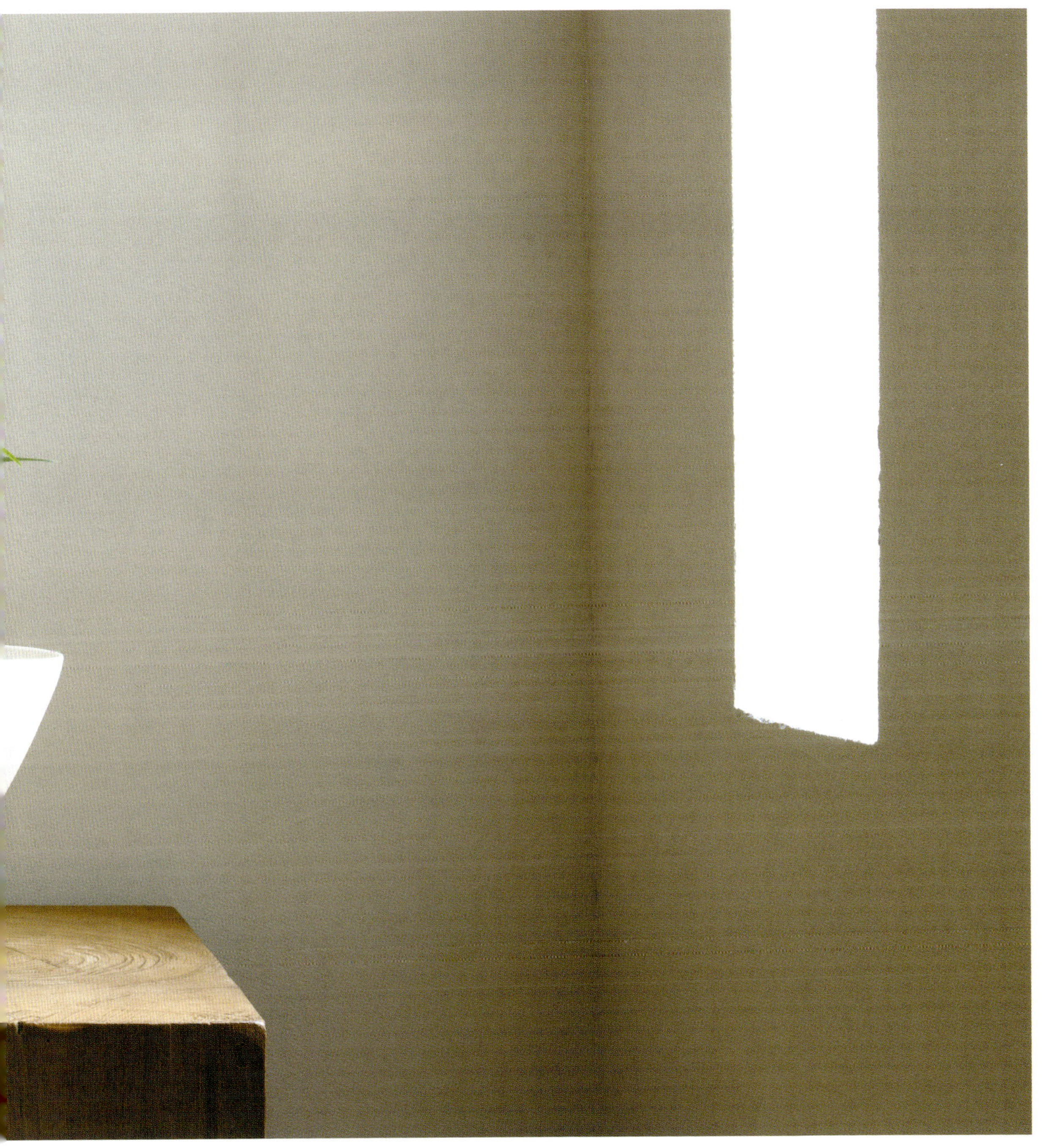

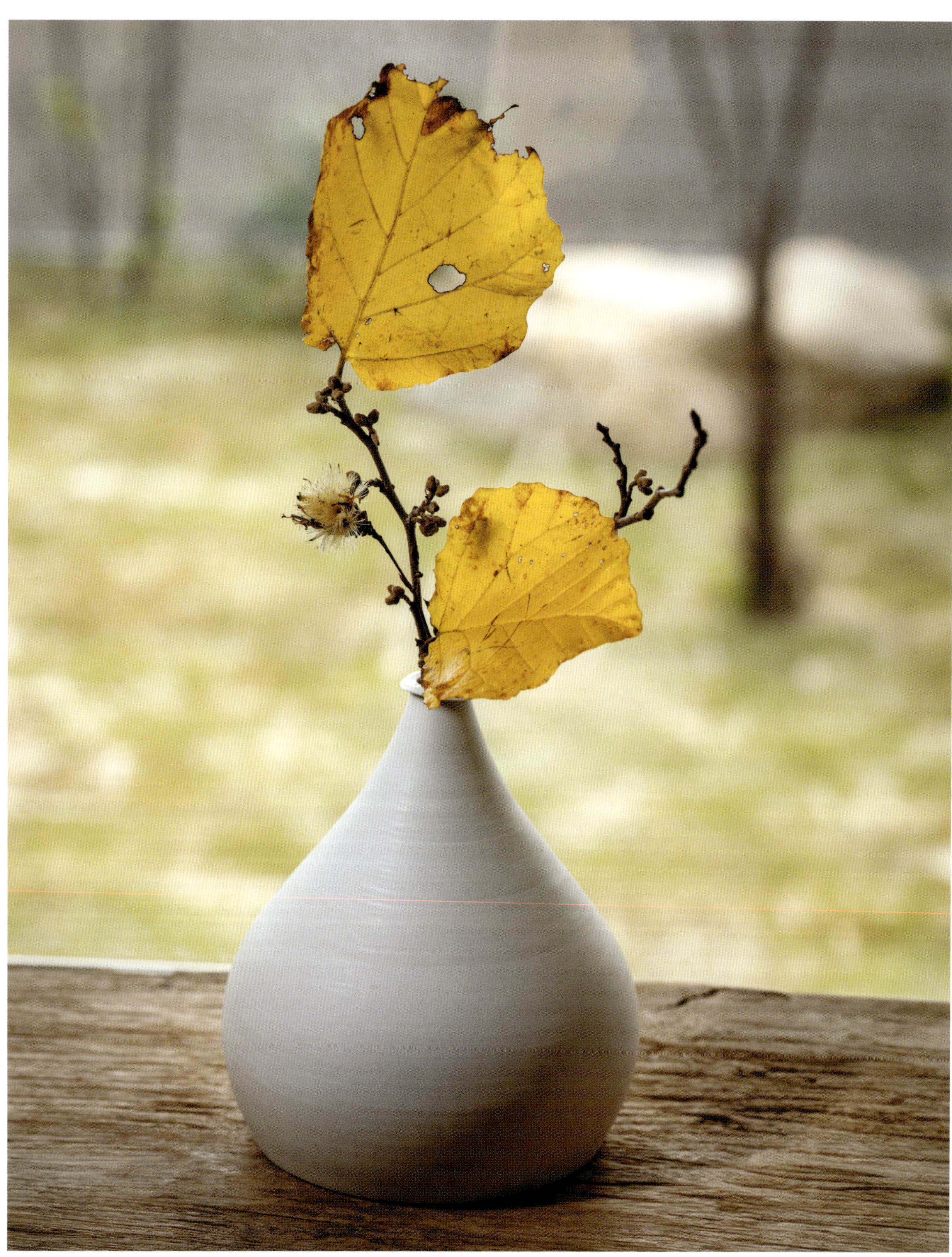

Koya broom, witch hazel leaves. Small white porcelain flower container by Taizo Kuroda (see page 154).

A small white porcelain flower container that looks complete with just a single small branch. Having one such flower container in your daily life invites you to think each day about what to place in it. A vessel meant for conversing with flowers.

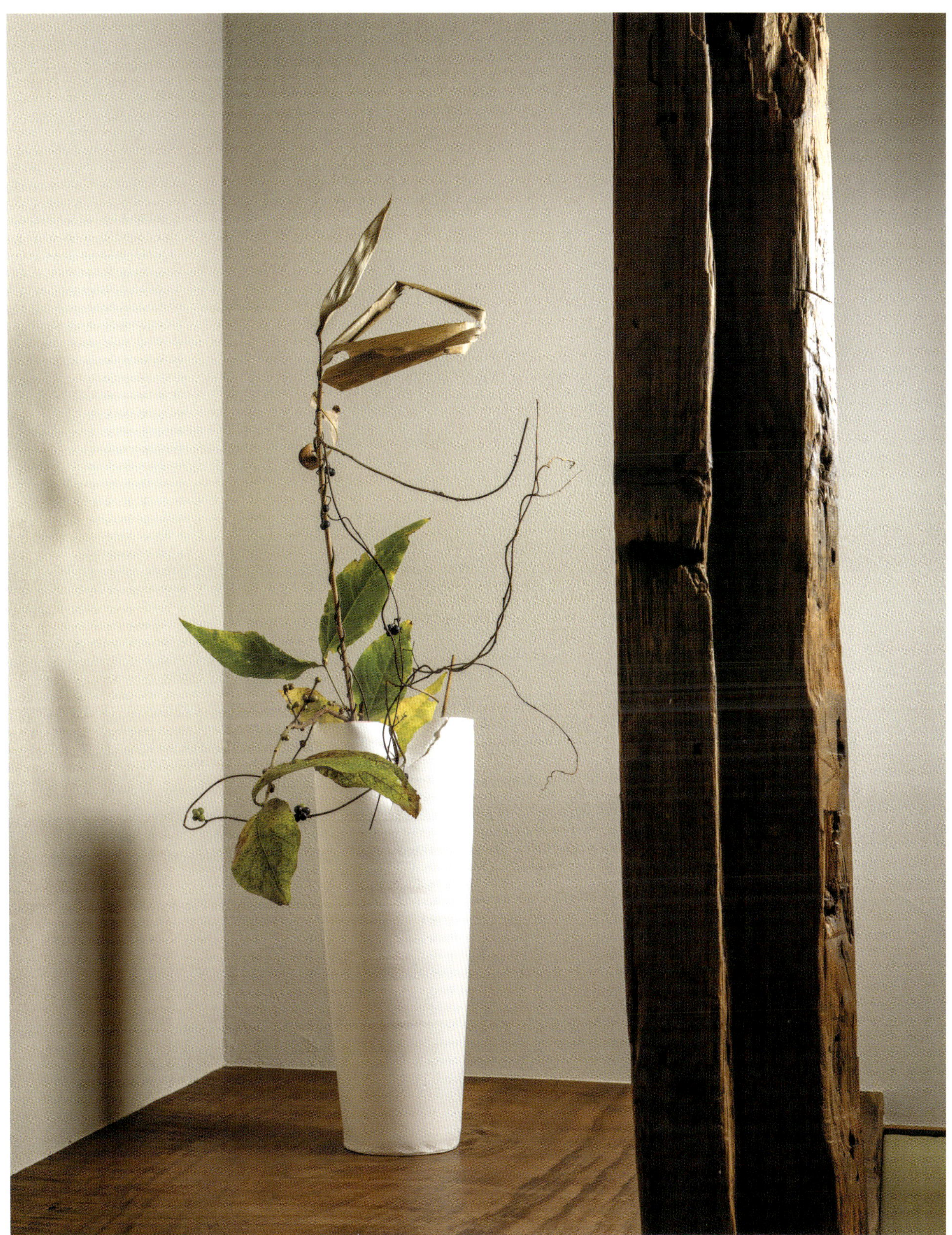

Snake vine, wintersweet, bamboo grass. White porcelain cylindrical flower container by Taizo Kuroda (see page 154).

"Kuroda's white porcelain works give the impression of 'stripping away and stripping away, until only what truly matters remains,'" says Hiroshi.

Afterword

by Atsushi Kobayashi

From my flower master, Takashi Inaba, I learned that while there is art in painting and creating objects, there is also an art that lies in *not* creating things. Arranging flowers is one such art. What to place in a given space? What flower container to use? The choices are infinite, and they serve as a means of expressing the space you envision.

Whether for a photo shoot or for a tea gathering, the choice of flowers must often be made instantly, within a limited time. Unlike private, everyday arrangements, there is a sense of tension involved. Later, I often reflect that perhaps I could have done this instead, or I'll try that next time. But I believe all those experiences become nourishment for the self.

There is always someone who offers a comment at tea gatherings: "One leaf too many," or "Just a little bit too tall." Sometimes I already feel the same way myself, and when that happens, it can be quite frustrating.

But to make a decision in the moment, one must not hesitate.

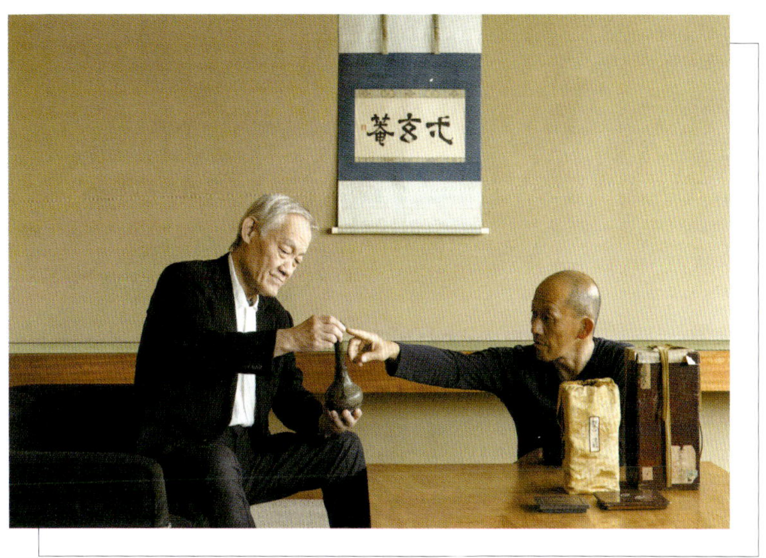

Seeing various works of art and experiencing the beauty of nature builds something within you—and arranging flowers is also the joy of creation. Creating starts with imitation of what one has been taught, but going beyond that—thinking for oneself, creating, and expressing something original—is what makes it art. I hope that many who arrange flowers will find joy in doing so through this book, and that it will serve as a source of inspiration.

In the course of making this book, I am deeply grateful to Kikuto Nomura of Hanacho for his generous support. I would also like to thank Takashi Inaba, who provided locations, and Takeshi Surukawa of Takayamaso Hanano. My sincere thanks go to Shunichi Nakano of Sekai Bunka Publishing, who has known me since my apprentice days and made this project possible. Photographer Masayuki Sakamoto, writer Hiroko Fukui, and Saika Inubushi from the *Kateigaho* editorial team—thank you all for a truly enjoyable year of work together.

"Books to Span the East and West"

Tuttle Publishing was founded in 1832 in the small New England town of Rutland, Vermont [USA]. Our core values remain as strong today as they were then—to publish best-in-class books which bring people together one page at a time. In 1948, we established a publishing outpost in Japan—and Tuttle is now a leader in publishing English-language books about the arts, languages and cultures of Asia. The world has become a much smaller place today and Asia's economic and cultural influence has grown. Yet the need for meaningful dialogue and information about this diverse region has never been greater. Over the past seven decades, Tuttle has published thousands of books on subjects ranging from martial arts and paper crafts to language learning and literature—and our talented authors, illustrators, designers and photographers have won many prestigious awards. We welcome you to explore the wealth of information available on Asia at **www.tuttlepublishing.com**.

Published by Tuttle Publishing, an imprint of Periplus Editions (HK) Ltd.

www.tuttlepublishing.com

Tanimatsuya Toda Shoten Oriori no Chabana
Copyright © Toda Shoten Co. Ltd., 2023
Originally published in Japan by Sekaibunkasha Inc.
English translation rights arranged with Sekaibunka Holdings Inc. through Japan UNI Agency, Inc., Tokyo

English translation copyright © 2026 Periplus Editions (HK) Ltd.

ISBN 978-4-8053-2036-5

GPSR Representative
Matt Parsons
matt.parsons@upi2mbooks.hr
UPI-2M PLUS d.o.o. Medulićeva 20
10000 Zagreb, Croatia

Distributed by

North America, Latin America & Europe
Tuttle Publishing
364 Innovation Drive
North Clarendon, VT 05759-9436 U.S.A.
Tel: 1 (802) 773-8930
Fax: 1 (802) 773-6993
info@tuttlepublishing.com
www.tuttlepublishing.com

Japan
Tuttle Publishing
Yaekari Building 3rd Floor, 5-4-12 Osaki
Shinagawa-ku, Tokyo 141-0032
Tel: (81) 3 5437-0171
Fax: (81) 3 5437-0755
sales@tuttle.co.jp
www.tuttle.co.jp

Asia Pacific
Berkeley Books Pte. Ltd.
3 Kallang Sector #04-01, Singapore 349278
Tel: (65) 6741 2178
Fax: (65) 6741 2179
inquiries@periplus.com.sg
www.tuttlepublishing.com

29 28 27 26   4 3 2 1

Printed in China   2602EP

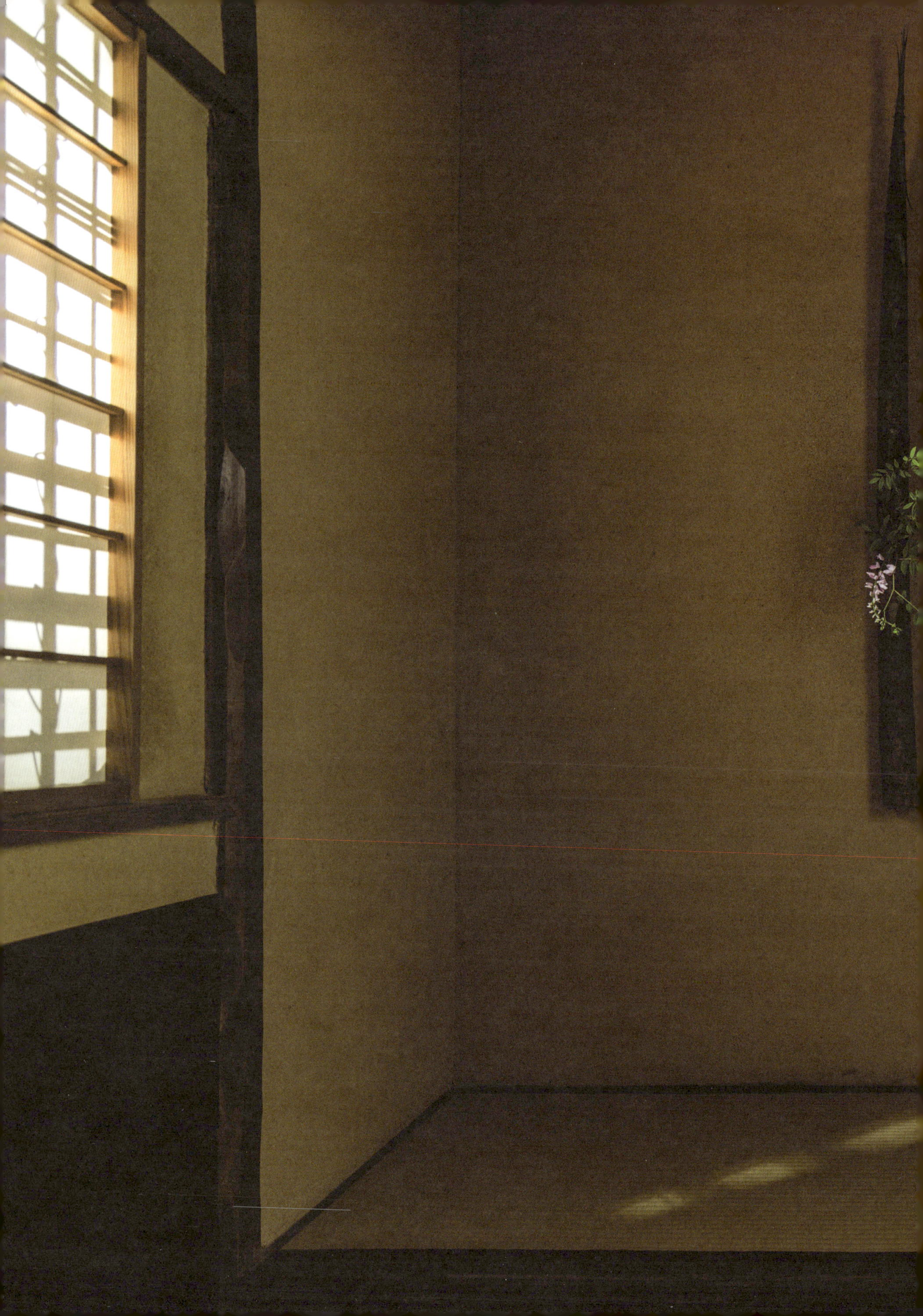